٥٦٦

CATHERINE HAYES
1818–1861

Frontispiece: The 27 year old, Catherine Hayes at the time of her La Scala debut, November 1845 in *Linda di Chamounix* by Donizetti (Courtesy of the Theatre Museum, Teatro alla Scala, Milan).

Catherine Hayes
1818–1861

THE HIBERNIAN PRIMA DONNA

BASIL WALSH

With a Foreword by
Richard Bonynge

IRISH ACADEMIC PRESS
DUBLIN • PORTLAND, OR

First published in 2000 by
IRISH ACADEMIC PRESS
44, Northumberland Road, Dublin 4, Ireland
and in the United States of America by
IRISH ACADEMIC PRESS
c/o ISBS, 5804 NE Hassalo Street,
Portland, OR 97213–3644.

website: www.iap.ie

British Library Cataloguing in Publication Data
Walsh, Basil F.
  Catherine Hayes, 1818–1861 : the Hibernian prima donna
  1. Hayes, Catherine   2. Women singers – Ireland – Biography   3. Singers – Ireland –
  Biography   4. Opera
  I. Title
  782.1'092
  ISBN 0–7165–2662–X

Library of Congress Cataloging-in-Publication Data
Walsh, Basil, 1934–
  Catherine Hayes, 1816–1861 : the Hibernian prima donna / Basil Walsh ; with a
  foreword by Richard Bonynge.
      p. m.
  Includes bibliographical references and index.
  ISBN 0–7165–2662–X (hb)
    1. Hayes, Catherine 1818–1861. 2. Sopranos (Singers)—Biography.   I. Title.

  ML420.H247 W35 2000
  782.1'092—dc21
  [B]   00–040959

Typeset in 11.5 pt on 13.5 pt Dante by
Carrigboy Typesetting Services, County Cork
Printed by Creative Print and Design (Wales), Ebbw Vale

Contents

List of Illustrations

Foreword

RICHARD BONYNGE

'BOY, WHO'S the greatest tenor in the world?' asked my great grandfather in the early 1940s. 'Sims Reeves', I immediately replied. I knew the answer as my grandfather in his 90's had become not a little repetitive with his questions. Note that he said 'who is?' and not 'who was?'

Being curious by nature I looked up Sims Reeves and found that he was indeed the greatest English tenor of the second part of the nineteenth-century. In the year of my great grandfather's birth, 1849, he sang in Dublin with a beautiful red-headed Irish soprano called Catherine Hayes. He later called her the ideal Lucia and the greatest interpreter of the role he had ever sung with, notwithstanding that Persiani, the first Lucia, was another of his partners.

And so began my fascination with Catherine Hayes, 'the Swan of Erin', which increased when I learnt that she visited Australia in the early 1850s. I'm more than grateful to Basil Walsh for filling in all the missing details of the 25 year career of this woman who took hold of my imagination.

It was a busy and honourable career – La Scala, Covent Garden, La Fenice as well as theatres in Florence, Rome, Genoa, Vienna, and world-wide tours of North and South America, Hawaii, Australia, India, Batavia and Singapore. She sang an interesting repertoire which included several Donizetti operas – Linda, Maria di Rohan, c120 Lucias, Verdi's I Masnadieri, Gluck's Iphigenie en Tauride, Bellini's I Puritani, Meyerbeer's Le Prophéte. In this latter she sang the role of Berte in the London premiere to Viardot-Garcia's Fides and Mario's Jean.

A fascinating life of which no biography has heretofore existed.

Thank you, Mr. Walsh, for extending our horizons with this delightful story of an entrancing heroine.

Richard Bonynge
Les Avants, March 1998

Preface

A NUMBER OF years ago I was engaged in research into the nineteenth-century opera seasons that took place in Dublin, Ireland. During my work, I was amazed to find how significant an impact a young Irish soprano called Catherine Hayes had had in Dublin and other cities in Europe, America, Australia and around the world.

My curiosity was sufficiently aroused to pursue a more single-minded approach to her life and career. This in turn led to a broadening of my focus to include not only Catherine Hayes' activities in opera and concert, but also to touch-on people she came in contact with as she pursued her career, as much of her life was intertwined with leading operatic composers, great singers and events of the period.

Despite her prominence at that time, it is tragic that she has virtually disappeared from the record books without a trace, except for a few limited references in some very specialised publications. I didn't start out with the intention of writing a book about her, it more or less became the obvious direction for me to take as I researched the period. As a result this book evolved into a biography of Catherine Hayes and also a time-capsule of the early days of opera and concert life in Europe, America, Australia and some of the more remote parts of the world which she visited in the 1840s and 1850s. However, Catherine Hayes is the central figure throughout the book.

Like many prominent personalities of the nineteenth-century, there are 'facts' about her that have appeared in print but cannot always be verified. Unfortunately, no diaries are known to exist, although there is a high probability that she kept them. In any event, whenever facts come from credible sources such as the *Illustrated London News* or other quality publications of the periods, then it has been assumed that they must be reasonably accurate. And as a result I have, in selected instances, included them in the book. Virtually all of the facts included about her travels and her performances have been verified by newspaper reviews or articles in local musical journals that covered her presence in a particular city or location.

In referring to her contemporaries I have, whenever possible, included the date of birth and demise. Additionally, for convenience, opera titles and arias are given in today's spelling even though many were spelled differently during the nineteenth century. For example the opera *Linda di Chamounix*, which was prominent in Catherine Hayes's career was generally spelled *Linda di Chamouni* during her lifetime.

The book covers a great deal of territory, following her on her travels. but it is not meant to be a travelogue of a prominent nineteenth-century singer. It is more a record of how Catherine Hayes emerged as part of the musical structure in the nineteenth-century and how and why travel played an important part in her career. It also focuses on the cultural scene in Europe, America and Australia and the key participants, and the forces which influenced her direction both professionally and personally.

One of her accomplishments, which had a strong influence on those who came after her, was that she set patterns for extended concert tours and the format of concert programmes, many of which have lasted into this century. There is also a good probability that, in the process of pursuing her singing career, she may have been the first prima donna to circumnavigate the globe.

Strangely, no book has ever been written about Catherine Hayes, despite her many achievements. She shared the stage in leading roles with many of the greatest operatic singers of her century. From humble beginnings in rural Ireland, her talent, spirit and courage enabled her to experience a lot in her short life, at virtually the dawn of opera and concert life as we know it today. She and the sensational Jenny Lind were contemporaries and knew each other well. They had the same singing teacher in Paris around the same period. Their paths crossed many times over twenty years, sometimes staying in the same hotel and even singing the same prima donna roles on the same night in different theatres in the same town.

Catherine Hayes' time occurred during a period of great change around the world, variously caused by social reforms, disease, famine, revolution and a massive expansion in transportation with the advent of steam and the railways. The time period covered coincides roughly with the first half of the nineteenth century. Because of this expanded scope of interest, my research ended up as a six year project, including contact with over eighty libraries, numerous archival sources, many private collectors and museums in about eighteen different countries involving several different languages.

Catherine Hayes and her achievements are basically forgotten even in her native Ireland, a country where heroes and myths tend to live side by side forever. Except for in her home city of Limerick, she is virtually unknown today. Her era was long before the advent of phonograph recordings, so her vocal legacy has been lost, except for the reviews of her performances which appeared in local newspapers and periodicals of the time. Hence, these are quoted extensively throughout the book, as they provide a valid 'on the spot' record of how she was perceived both as a singer and a person. They also give us some very specific information about her personal appearance and overall demeanour, important when trying to understand her motives and actions.

Catherine Hayes was unique in her time, and even more so in terms of Ireland's contribution to the operatic world in the nineteenth century. She was the first major female operatic star to come out of Ireland. She was a woman with vision and a great sense of her time and of the opportunities open to her. When she died prematurely from a stroke at the age of 42 in London in 1861, while still a prominent concert artist, her obituary appeared in all of the major papers. The Times considered her death important enough to give her virtually a full column as an obituary, something that was almost unheard of then for a singer. Around the globe, in Italy, America and Australia, other major publications wrote about her death with sadness and a deep sense of loss to the musical world. This sadness was felt, most of all in Ireland. With this definitive account of her life, perhaps Catherine Hayes can take her rightful place as an important contributor to nineteenth-century musical history.

The subtitle to this book, 'The Hibernian Prima Donna', is derived from a name given to her by the London music critics in the late 1850s. It was their way of recognising her unique style and personality as an ambassador of her birthplace. Despite her Italian training, fluency in several languages and extraordinary international experience, she was always fiercely proud of the fact that she was born in Ireland. As a result, it seems appropriate to reflect this in the subtitle for the book.

BASIL WALSH
Boynton Beach, Florida, 1999

Acknowledgements

When starting a book of this type there is no way of knowing the amount of help that will be needed to get it into print. While technology has made great strides in the last decade or two, much research material, so important to produce a work of substance, remains in hard-copy format in libraries around the world with little or no opportunity to gain access to it. Unfortunately, most libraries worldwide are under funded and do not have the people or time available to help with research, short of suggesting the names of local people who will do the work for a fee. Yet, with all these drawbacks, it was amazing how many librarians and individuals who are collectors or connoisseurs were prepared to go the extra measure to help with my research. Their efforts made it possible to obtain copies of newspaper reviews, concert advertisements, letters or programmes relating to performances of Catherine Hayes in some of the more remote parts of the globe.

In particular I want to acknowledge with special appreciation and thanks the following people: first and foremost, my wife Eileen and my son Jay for their continued support over a period of six years during which much of my focus was on researching the career of 'my other woman', as my wife called Catherine Hayes.

And our many friends in Miami, for their patience in putting up with me talking about my favourite subject.

My brother Derek Walsh, who sowed the seeds of the idea of doing something on Catherine Hayes one day several years ago while we were in San Francisco. In his inimitable style, he happened to come across a pamphlet on Catherine Hayes, in a used bookstore. Without his untiring efforts to check out elusive dates and information relating to her early student concerts and activities in Limerick and Dublin, the early section of the book would have been incomplete. Much of his efforts necessitated poring through years of dust-ridden bound hard-copy newspaper files in libraries, because the particular materials were not available in microfilm format.

Anne Makower for her help in reading the raw unedited first draft of the manuscript and providing comments on the substance and quality of the work for the publisher. Managing Editor Linda Longmore of Irish Academic Press in Dublin for her interest in the subject matter and her help in making publication of the book possible.

Richard Bonynge – one of today's foremost musicians with an incredible understanding and knowledge of nineteenth-century operatic performance and musical history. He was kind enough to express his interest and provide comments on Catherine Hayes' career. He also provided the initial reference to the Staffordshire figures of Catherine Hayes and Sims Reeves. He was kind enough to commit to writing the Foreword to the book and to take time out of a very active conducting schedule in Europe, America and Australia to deliver on his commitment.

Clarissa Lablache-Cheer who, incidentally, is working on a biography of her illustrious family of singers that started with the great Luigi Lablache; for her kindness and gracious gift of one of Catherine Hayes' original letters, and for her help with research on selected dates and performances. Tom Kaufman, the foremost opera chronologist of today, is to be thanked for his help with providing operatic data for France. He also provided data for Italy and Peru and copies of newspaper reviews of Catherine Hayes' first professional operatic performances in Marseilles in 1845. His important book, on Verdi and his contemporaries, was also very helpful with its references to performance dates. Mary Jane Phillips-Matz for her wonderful biography of Giuseppe Verdi, in which there is a brief mention of Verdi's interest in Catherine Hayes for his opera *I Masnadieri,* and also for her help in tracking down information relating to this reference.

The late Kevin Hannan, who was one of the most ardent admirers of Catherine Hayes and her achievements, for his help in providing information on her early years in Limerick. Sadly, Kevin did not survive to see the book published.

Ileana Adam for her help in translating reviews from South American Spanish-language publications. Jane Nagy for her unrelenting research efforts in the Public Records Offices in London relating to information on the more obscure part of Catherine Hayes' friends. Girvice Archer, Jr., Harwinton, Connecticut, for providing performance material. R.H. Cane for making available copies of Catherine Hayes' letters from his collection and information on Manuel Garcia, her great vocal teacher. Julian Peck, Oliver Knox of England and Roger Gross for his help in procuring Hayes' opera programmes and other important material.

Special appreciation is also expressed for the gracious permission of Her Majesty, Queen Elizabeth II, to use extracts and comments from Queen Victoria's diaries relating to Catherine Hayes' performance at Buckingham Palace in June 1849.

I also want to thank Gregg Sapp and the staff of the University of Miami, Richter Library, Miami, Florida, and in particular the people in the microfilm department who were always so pleasant and helpful over a four year period of studying their wonderful collections, without which this book could never have been written. In addition my gratitude and appreciation are also expressed for the assistance rendered by the following: Colette O'Daly, The National Library, Dublin; Noel Kissane, The National Library, Dublin; Mary Clarke, Irish Theatre Archives, Dublin; Larry Walsh, Limerick Museum; Noreen Ellerker, St. Mary's Cathedral, Limerick; Mary Pyne, Limerick Regional Archives; George Spillane, photographer, Corbally, Limerick; Samantha Melia, Cork Public Museum; Eddie Geoghegan; James Gawley, Irish Embassy, Rome; Caroline Gray, Trinity College Library, Dublin; Norma Jessop, Main Library, University College Dublin; Roger Duce, National Library of Scotland, Edinburgh; Mark Jones, National Museum of Scotland, Edinburgh; Pamela Clark, The Royal Archives, Windsor Castle; Katherine Hogg, Royal Academy of Music, London; C.M. Hall, The British Library, Manuscripts Collection; Stewart Gillies, The British Library, Newspaper Divison; City of Liverpool Libraries; Paul Moorhouse, Central Library, Manchester; Richard Martin and John Coulter, Lewisham Library; Glen F. Jones, The Royal College of Surgeons Library, London; P.M. Coleman, Birmingham Library Services; Barry Norman, Theatre Museum and National Museum of the Performing Arts, London; Dr. Stephen Roe, Sotheby's; Jonathan Stone, Christie's; D.J. Burkett, Kensal Green Cemetery, London; C.A. Williams, Public Records Office, Kew; Roger Flury, National Library, Wellington, NZ; Tony Marshall, State Library of Tasmania; Rhonda Hamilton, Community History Museum, Launceston, Tasmania; Elizabeth Bernard, Victorian Arts Center Trust, Melbourne; Alannah Kelly, La Trobe Collection, State Library of Victoria; Janine Barrand, Victorian Arts Center, Melbourne; Sarah Platts, National Library of Australia, Canberra; Jo Peoples, South Australia Theatre Museum, Adelaide; Viv Szekeres, Migration Museum, Adelaide; Frances Love, Sydney Opera House Trust, Sydney; Linda Brainwood, State Library of New South Wales, Sydney; Professor Agostino Zecca Laterrza, Biblioteca del Conservatorio di Musica Giuseppe Verdi, Milan; The Director, Museo

Teatrale alla Scala, Milan; Maria Pia Ferraris, BMG/Ricordi Archives, Milan; Laura Ciancio, Accademia Nationale di Santa Cecilia, Rome; Dr. Carla Guiducci Bonanni of the Biblioteca Nationale di Firenze; Dr. Angela Miciluzzo, Archives of State, Verona; Dr. Ennio Sandal, Biblioteca Civica, Verona; Sig. Gherardo Lazzeri, Bivigliano Campagna, Florence; Dr. Gino Badini, State Archives, Reggio Emilia; Dr. Curzio Bastianoni, Biblioteca Comunale Degli Intronati, Siena; The Director, Biblioteca Civica Angeleo Mai, Bergamo; Marco Capra of CIRPeM, Parma; Italy, Dr. Barbara Lesak, Osterreichisches Theater Museum, Vienna; Dr. Robert Kittler, Nationalbibliothek, Vienna; Tere Schwarz-Blokhuis, National Library of the Netherlands, The Hague; Justo Alarcon, Bibloteca Nacionale, Santiago; Ang Seon Leng, National Library Board, Singapore; Patricia Lai, State of Hawaii Archives Division, Honolulu; Joan Hori, University of Hawaii Library, Honolulu; Barbara Dunn, Hawaiian Historical Society, Honolulu; Dr. Dale Hall, University of Hawaii, Honolulu; James W. Campbell, The Whitney Library, New Haven Connecticut Robert Pelton, The Barnum Museum, Bridgeport, Connecticut; Mel E. Smith, Connecticut State Library, Hartford; Megan Hahn, The New York Historical Society; Bernard R. Crystal, Columbia University; Barbara Tringali, Tufts University Special Collections, Medford; The staff of the Massachuse Chicago Historical Society; Carrie Marsh, The Libraries of Claremont Colleges, Claremont; Mimi Tashiro, The Stanford University Libraries, Stanford; California, Shyamala Balgopal, University of Illinois Library, Urbana; Barbara Bezat, University of Minnesota Libraries, St. Paul; J. Rigbie Turner, The Pierpoint Morgan Library, New York; Michael T. Dumas, Harvard Theater Collection, Cambridge, Massachusetts; Martha Clevenger, Missouri Historical Society, St. Louis; Matthew W. Buff, San Francisco Performing Arts Library and Museum.

The staff of the following public libraries: Coral Gables, Florida, Main Library, Inter-Library Loan Dept, Miami, Main Library, New York city, Charleston, South Carolina, Savannah, Georgia, and Providence, Rhode Island.

CHAPTER ONE

The Early Days

LIMERICK 1818–1839

O N 9 FEBRUARY, 1995, an auction was held at Sotheby's in London.[1] Among the items for sale was a pair of Staffordshire figures of the nineteenth century Irish born soprano Catherine Hayes and English tenor Sims Reeves as Lucia and Edgardo in Donizetti's immortal opera. The pair was featured in the exclusive auction catalogue of operatic costumes, photographs and memorabilia belonging to Dame Joan Sutherland and her long-time conductor husband Richard Bonynge.[2]

Catherine Hayes sang her first London *Lucia di Lammermoor* at the Royal Italian Opera, Covent Garden, on 26 April 1849. She was at the summit of her career, with Giovanni Mario, the greatest Italian tenor of the time singing opposite her in the role of Edgardo for the first time in England. Interestingly, Joan Sutherland's brilliant international career was launched in the same role at the same place one hundred and ten years later, almost to the month.

The great bel canto tradition of the coloratura soprano, which has been so wonderfully upheld in our time by Dame Joan Sutherland, began in the first half of the nineteenth century. During that period, a unique group of talented young women from various European countries emerged to become the pioneers of a long line of great operatic stars. Composers wrote operas especially for some of them. They earned fabulous amounts of money and achieved international recognition. The public adored them. Their status allowed them to mix with royalty, heads of state, presidents, business and military leaders in the principal cities of Europe, Russia, the Americas and Australia. Catherine Hayes was one of them.

Catherine's success during her short life – she was 42 when she died in 1861 – was due to a mixture of luck, raw talent, strong character, timing and an innate business sense. Overshadowing all of this, however, was an incredible desire to sing.

1

Catherine Hayes was born on 25 October 1818 at 4 Patrick Street in the city of Limerick in Ireland into abject poverty. The house where she was born still stands in Limerick today, but is somewhat derelict.

Catherine Hayes's name only appears in a few selected biographical dictionaries, and, where it does, her birth year is usually given as either 1821 or 1825, neither of which is correct.[3] This inaccuracy tends to have been perpetuated by Catherine herself. Several times during the course of her career she indicated her year of birth to be 1825. This seems to have been a conscious decision on her part. Perhaps she recognized she was a late starter in a profession where youth dominated. In any event, her mother lived and travelled with her everywhere and her mother would have known when she was born. Her mother was also literate and articulate. Birth registrations did not occur in Ireland until later in the century. However, Catherine's baptism is recorded in the books of St. Mary's (Protestant parish) in Limerick as 8 November 1818.[4] It is reasonable to assume that baptisms in a town such as Limerick probably took place about a week or two after birth, which would make the date of 25 October correct for her birth date.

Limerick at the time of Catherine's birth was the fourth largest town in Ireland with a population of around 40,000 people. Its location at the mouth of Ireland's largest river, the Shannon, which emptied into the Atlantic, gave it strategic importance for the military and for trade and commerce that continues to this day.

Catherine's father was Arthur William Hayes, a bandmaster attached to the local militia. Later in life Catherine, elected to refer to him as a professor of music, not a bandmaster. Mary Carroll, her mother was a servant working in the household of the Earl of Limerick. As far as is known, both of the parents were born in Ireland. Hayes and Carroll are common Irish surnames. Arthur and Mary were married on 18 January 1815 at St. Michael's in Limerick, which at that time was a Church of Ireland (Protestant) parish.[5] Catherine Hayes was baptized in the Protestant religion.

There were four children from the marriage. Henrietta the eldest was baptized in January 1816, Charles in October 1817, Catherine in November 1818 and William in September 1820.[6] All of the children were baptized at St. Mary's church in Limerick. Charles and William apparently died in infancy. Later records at St. John's in Limerick indicate that two infants with no first names but with the last name of Hayes were buried there one in May of 1818 and the other in May of 1823.[7] Arthur was

1. Baptismal registry of St. Mary's, Limerick showing that Catherine Hayes was baptised in the Anglican Church on 8 November 1818. (Courtesy of the Dean of Limerick and Ardfert, Limerick City Parish).

indicated as the father. There is no record of any other children from the marriage that might have been born after the year 1820.

From about 1816, after the battle of Waterloo and the end of the Napoleonic era, England and its sovereign territories started suffering from a post-war depression.[8] There was even talk of national bankruptcy, given England's enormous public debt, which was almost £1 billion pounds. There was also grave concern that uprising and revolution might occur. During this period, Ireland was particularly hard hit, with its rural economy and the return of many soldiers who had served in the Peninsula wars and elsewhere. There were also the ever present pressures and unrest over English rule and its policies towards its sister island.

Perhaps military cutbacks and recession in the post war years found Arthur William Hayes, Catherine's father, without a job. We don't know. However, it is believed that sometime around 1823 Arthur William Hayes abandoned his family. He is not mentioned during her early years and he never appeared on the scene during Catherine's days in Limerick when she started to gain local prominence. No records can be found to indicate that he had died in Ireland. Since he was not an army officer, only a bandmaster, there are no military records available in the British Public Records archives that might have told us where he went or when he might have died. He was probably in his mid to late thirties by 1823, so perhaps he went to America or Canada, which were attracting many young people of his age. If so, assuming he was still alive in the 1850s, it is surprising that he never did not come forward when Catherine achieved celebrity status and sang extensively on the east coast of both of those countries with considerable publicity.

However, there are very two interesting situations that are probably more fiction than fact, which might have some dubious linkage. In this century, two very famous American women of the theatre, Helen Hayes and Metropolitan Opera star Dorothy Kirsten, independently claimed direct relationship to Catherine Hayes.[9] Both of them mention her as a 'great aunt' in their respective biographies.[10] However, there is no evidence that Catherine or her one and only surviving sister Henrietta left any descendants. Henrietta did spend some time in New York but, as far as we know, she never married. We do not know if Catherine's father had any brothers who may have emigrated to America who could possibly have had descendants.

During her lifetime Catherine only referred to her father a couple of times and this was for legal reasons. As far as she was concerned he was dead. Catherine's mother continued to work for the Earl of Limerick during those early years and raise her family on her meagre earnings. She also did various odd jobs to earn additional money. What little we know about Catherine in those days shows her to have been a devoted daughter, helpful to her mother, but shy and reserved with outsiders. She was considered to have a happy disposition. In adulthood her personality never really changed; she was always considered a slightly withdrawn and shy person, and always lady-like.

While national schools were introduced into Ireland in the 1830s, females in Ireland, particularly of Catherine's social class, generally did not participate. Whatever education girls received usually came from the home or the church. This probable lack of any early formal education makes Catherine's lifetime achievement even more remarkable.

It was in this environment that Catherine grew up with her sister Henrietta. Those years of poverty with her mother struggling to survive and make life tolerable for her two young daughters made a deep impression on Catherine. She never forgot the hardship experienced by her family at that time without a father.

As she achieved success, she had no hesitation in providing for both her mother and her sister, even to the point where she insisted on having their needs included in her first major operatic contract. She never wavered on this subject during her lifetime. When she died, her mother and sister were beneficiaries of her will. Both of them survived her by several years.

In the 1830s Limerick had an arts and cultural lifestyle that was typical of the age. This consisted of theatres or concert rooms where visiting artists performed in musical comedies or farces. A theatre had been built in 1770, but was destroyed by fire in 1818.[11] Another theatre was also built in 1810. This was later acquired by the clergy. It was several years after that before a permanent theatre, to be named the Theatre Royal, was established. Interestingly, the town also had been able to support several newspapers that had been published since the previous century, which said something for the literacy of the town's inhabitants.

Because of the town's size and population, its sophistication and commercial base, Limerick was usually on the circuit for visiting musical personalities and troupes. Paganini played there in 1831. Balfe conducted one of his early operas slightly later. It became a regular site for visiting operatic companies from the about the late 1830s. In addition, many of the wives of the landed gentry, the upper class military and the Protestant clergy gave functions and parties at which musical compositions of the day were performed. The Osborne family was among those active in musical circles. The elder Osborne was the organist and choral master at Limerick Cathedral. One of his sons, George Alexander Osborne (1806–93), who would have a strong influence on Catherine's career, was born in Limerick on 24 September, 1806.[12] Initially, George Osborne studied music with his father and subsequently had a very prominent career as a teacher in Paris and London. Osborne's mother was a MacMahon and a cousin of the famous Marshal MacMahon who was a hero in France.

When he was about 18 years old, George Alexander visited an aunt in Brussels, Belgium, with the idea of possibly studying theology there. He later decided to take up music after meeting various musical personalities including the Belgian violinist, Charles De Beriot (1802–70), and his wife to be, Maria Garcia Malibran (1808–36), the renowned prima donna. At De Beriot's suggestion, around 1830 Osborne moved to Paris, where he spent fourteen years, first as a student and then as a professional musician.

Initially, in Paris, Osborne studied the piano with Friedrich Kalkbrenner (1785–1849) and composition with Francois Fetis (1784–1871). Then as a music teacher and a composer he became a close friend of the ageing Luigi Cherubini (1760–1842), Frédéric Chopin (1810–1849), Hector Berlioz (1803–69), Daniel Auber (1782–1871) and Gioachino Rossini (1792–1868), all of whom resided in Paris during this period.[13] He also knew Franz Liszt and considered him to be the greatest pianist of the time. Osborne performed publicly with Chopin in 1832.[14] Later he also accompanied Chopin and Berlioz on a visit to London. Berlioz mentioned him in his memoirs. Berlioz considered him to be tasteful and refined as a composer and pianist[15] Osborne was also a good friend of Berlioz's Irish born wife Henriette Smithson (1809–1854), whom he had met when she visited Paris with a Shakespearean group performing Hamlet.[16] The relationship with Berlioz extended to Osborne's sister Bessie of whom Berlioz thought very highly, as a non-professional singer, and who had studied with Giulio Bordogni (1798–1856), a famous singing teacher in Paris.

Osborne was the teacher of Charles Hallé (1819–95), then a student in Paris, who could not afford Liszt's fees, and who afterwards would become world renowned through the Halle orchestra in Manchester, England, which he founded.[17] Osborne's friendship also extended to fellow Irishman, composer and singer Michael W. Balfe (1808–70), who was active in Paris during these years. He worked with the Irish composer while Balfe was still an operatic performer, and as a result told some amusing stories about Balfe's career as an operatic baritone. In Paris,

2. The property at 4 Patrick Street, Limerick where Catherine Hayes was born in October 1818. The building is now (1998) more or less derelict. (Author's collection).

under Rossini's direction, Balfe was studying the part of Figaro in *Il Barbiere di Siviglia*. One day Balfe asked Osborne to stand in as the buffo-bass Dr. Bartolo during rehearsals. Osborne said Balfe (as Figaro) scared him to death when he started to throw plates, napkins, cushions and anything he could find at him for effect. Balfe seemed oblivious to what he was doing. Osborne as a result opted to act only as Balfe's accompanist from that point forward.[18]

During this period other Osborne friends included great opera stars such as Luigi Lablache (1794–1858), Adolphe Nourrit (1802–39), Pauline Viardot-Garcia (1821–1910) and Maria Malibran. The last two were members of the famous Garcia family of opera singers. Their brother Manuel Patricio Garcia (1805–1906), who was born in Spain on St. Patrick's day (hence the name Patricio), was the pre-eminent nineteenth century singing teacher, who also lived and taught in Paris at this time.

There was an interesting incident involving Osborne and the famous tenor Nourrit, who was having vocal problems but who was highly popular at the Paris Opera, having performed Rossini and Meyerbeer operatic roles there.[19] In April 1837 Berlioz and Osborne accompanied Nourrit, who was still in his prime at 34, to the opera to see the new 31-year-old tenor sensation, Gilbert Duprez (1806–96). Nourrit was so upset with the enthusiastic reception given to Duprez that it took Osborne and Berlioz several hours of walking the boulevards with him in order to dissuade the tenor from suicide. Some years later, sadly, the despondent Nourrit did in fact take his own life in Naples, where he had been studying to try to change his vocal style and technique without much success.[20]

George Osborne knew all of these great musical personalities intimately, and his friendship with several of these people would have a profound influence on the personal life and the musical career of Catherine Hayes.

In the spring of 1844 George Osborne moved with his wife from Paris to London to take up a teaching position at the Royal Academy of Music. He spent the rest of his long life as a professional musician in London, where he died in 1893.

In Limerick, sometime during the autumn of 1838, the local Anglican bishop, the Reverend Edmund Knox (1772–1849), apparently heard Catherine sing. There are many different versions of when and how this event occurred; however, the most credible seems to indicate that Catherine was casually singing in the garden of the Earl of Limerick's home, where she had gone with her mother. Bishop Knox, who happened to be nearby – the Bishop's Palace was located next to the Earl's estate – heard her singing. Reverend Knox was greatly impressed and proceeded to find out who it was that had the beautiful voice. In later years Bishop Knox would look back with pride on the fact that he was the first to recognize Catherine's vocal talent.

The Reverend Edmund Knox was an interesting man. He was a member of the Knox family of 'Northlands', Dungannon, in County Tyrone. He was the third and youngest son of the Earl of Ranfurly, and a highly cultured man, who was deeply interested in music and the arts. He spent time with royalty in London, and had many friends in high places, both in London and Dublin. The family had a townhouse also called 'Northlands', in Dublin's fashionable Dawson Street which they used for concerts and social gatherings.

The Bishop had been appointed the Anglican (Church of Ireland) Bishop in Limerick in 1834, which was also a cathedral city. He remained Bishop of Limerick until his sudden death in Birmingham, England, in

1849. There was an extraordinary and highly controversial article written about him in the London Times shortly after his death.[21] The article was highly critical of his behaviour and absenteeism from Limerick during the Great Famine years in Ireland.

The Reverend Knox's diocese included Limerick, Kerry and parts of Clare and Cork. He received an annual sum of £5,000 for his services to the church, which was a significant amount of money in those days. However, much of his time was spent in continental Europe, not Limerick. Italy seemed to be his primary place of interest in Europe; where, no doubt, he had the opportunity to see and hear some of the greatest singers of the day. After meeting Catherine, he was sufficiently impressed to gather together a number of the leading citizens of Limerick to hear her sing. What she sang at these auditions is not known.

The reaction of the audience to these sessions, in addition to the Bishop's influence was sufficient to get a consensus to set up a fund for Catherine to receive musical and vocal training. The Bishop's wife Agnes was the fundraiser. This occurred towards the end of 1838, just as Catherine turned 20.

At this time it was considered too early to decide who would be Catherine's vocal coach. However, it's possible that a female member of the Osborne family may have given Catherine her first music and vocal lessons during this period. It was reported that the Bishop had persuaded a well-known lady in the community who was an amateur musician, to provide training for Catherine.

Catherine's progress was excellent. She was a willing and intelligent student of music, and she was also quick to learn. This learning capacity was very important to her in later life. After a few months she gave a private performance for her mentor and his friends. It was then decided to seek the advice of a prominent musical family in Dublin by the name of Pigott. The Pigott name is still associated with the retail music business in Suffolk Street, Dublin, today.[22]

Catherine at 20 years old was at an age when singers in Italy, France or Germany would be full-scale professional performers. In 1838, Jenny Lind (1820–1887), two years younger than Catherine and soon to become the premier prima donna of the age, was already performing extensively in opera and operetta in her native Sweden. Erminia Frezzolini (1818–1884), another important contemporary soprano, born in Italy the same year as Catherine, had already made her debut in 1837 in Florence in a new Donizetti opera. Catherine was starting late by any standards. However, her focus was on becoming a concert singer not an opera singer. Age was less significant for the concert platform. She had never been to the opera and didn't understand it. In a few years all of that would change dramatically.

Bishop Knox had made the right choice in asking the advice of the Pigott family. They were well connected in social and musical circles and had a retail music store at 112 Grafton Street, in central Dublin. One member of the family, Samuel J. Pigott (1800–53), was a leading musician in Dublin and much in demand as a performer on the violoncello. His instrument was a rare 1720 Stradivarius, later known as the 'Piatti cello' – the very best of its kind.[23]

The Pigott family recommended a singing teacher called Antonio Sapio (1799–1851) who gave lessons at his residence at 1 Percy Place, Dublin, not far from the city centre.[24] Pigott and Sapio were both respected members of the Anacreontic Society in Dublin, an important group in the city. And so Catherine prepared herself for a meeting with Sapio, who was to become her new vocal teacher.

CHAPTER TWO

Student Years

IRELAND 1839–1842

SINCE the middle of the eighteenth century, Dublin had been a prominent musical centre. It had a population of over 200,000 by the early 1800s. George Frideric Handel's (1685–1759) *Messiah* was first performed there in April 1742 at Neal's music hall in Fishamble Street, directed by Handel himself. The first volume of Thomas Moore's (1799–1852) *Irish Melodies* appeared in 1808 and the Philharmonic Society commenced activities in 1826. The city had several music halls, theatres and concert halls.

The newest and largest was the Theatre Royal in Hawkins Street, which was opened in January 1821. It was built under Royal Charter in the classical style by a London theatre architect, Samuel Beazely, Jr. (1786–1851), who was also a composer. It was leased to a Mr. Harris, the manager at the Covent Garden theatre in London. Reportedly, it was able to accommodate an audience of almost 3,000,[1] which made it one of the largest theatres in Britain. King George IV attended a performance of Richard Brinsley Sheridan's (1751–1816) *Duenna* there in August 1821. English ballad operas, plays and musical farces were performed regularly during the 1820s. In 1823, gas lighting was introduced into the theatre's chandeliers through mock candles.[2]

Another important theatre was the Rotunda Concert Rooms on the north side of the River Liffey, a place where many leading performers of the day had held the audience captive since its opening in 1757. The Rotunda building exists today in Dublin.

Dublin had a number of musical societies that were chartered for educational purposes and to provide musical events. The Dublin Academy of Music was founded in 1728,[3] and the Royal Irish Academy of Music opened its doors in 1856.[4] Generally Dublin was considered second only to London in terms of musical appreciation and activity by the middle of the nineteenth century.

The first major international vocal star to appear at the Theatre Royal was the erudite and highly paid Italian mezzo-soprano, Angelica Catalani (1780–1849). In 1823 she gave a programme called 'A Musical Intermezzo', which consisted of English airs mixed with 'God save the King', 'Nel core piu non si mento', followed by Rhode's air and variations and Mozart's 'Non piu andrai' from the opera *Le Nozze di Figaro*.[5] This Mozart aria for baritone was one of her famous concert pieces! Many years later Catherine had the pleasure of meeting Catalani at her villa in Florence, Italy. Another soprano, Madame Maria Caradori Allan (1800–65), followed Catalani's Dublin visit. At a future date, Catherine was destined to participate in a benefit concert for this lady.

By the end of the 1820s, opera had emerged as an important social and entertainment factor in Dublin. In 1827 an English version of Weber's *Der Freischutz* was performed with Mary Ann Paton (1802–64), who was 25 at the time.[6] Paton was the creator of the role of Agathe in English in London in 1824.[7] Later she was mostly to be known as Mrs. Wood, after she divorced her husband Lord William Lennox and married Joseph Wood (1801–90), a tenor in 1831. She was a friend of the celebrated mezzo-soprano Maria Malibran, having been introduced to her by Lord Lennox. She also participated in Malibran's London concert debut.

In 1827 *Oberon* was first staged in Dublin. The soprano music in this opera had been composed by Weber in 1826 in London, especially for Mary Ann Paton, who sang it in Dublin on this occasion. Several years later Catherine Hayes, as a youthful and inexperienced performer, would join Mrs. Wood on the concert platform in Dublin.

Other operas continued to be performed in Dublin, including works by Auber, Mozart, Weber and Meyerbeer. In October 1829 the renowned Italian buffo-baritone, Giuseppe De Begnis (1793–1849), brought an Italian opera company to Dublin.[8] He mostly performed Rossini operas. De Begnis was probably the most famous Figaro in Rossini's *Il Barbiere di Siviglia* in Europe. His first endeavour in Dublin was so successful that he returned with another troupe in December 1831. Antonio Sapio was a performing member of the company.[9] He was about 32 years old at the time.

Antonio Sapio was born in London of Italian French parents. In 1839, he was to become Catherine's first professional singing teacher. Sapio's father was a celebrated Italian singing teacher from Sicily who had settled in France, married a French woman and become singing teacher to Marie Antoinette.[10] When the French revolution shattered the social order in

France, Sapio senior and his family immediately moved to London. Antonio was born there around 1799.

Antonio Sapio had a classical education with music as a secondary subject. After completing his military service he decided to take up singing.[11] He attended the Royal Academy of Music and in 1823 he gave a concert in London where he was warmly received. He was perceived to be an emerging singer of importance. This was quickly followed by his operatic debut in 1824 at the Drury Lane theatre in Stephen Storace's (1762–96) comic opera the *Siege of Belgrade*. The critics praised him as an accomplished singer, musician and actor. His style was compared to John Braham (1774–1856), the leading English tenor at the time.

In 1825, Sapio first appeared briefly in Dublin in a popular musical farce called *The Cabinet*.[12] This was followed by various other performances in and around London where he was again compared to Braham in vocal quality and style. At Covent Garden in 1827 he sang Belmonte in a pasticcio of Mozart's *The Seraglio* in English, which ran for ten performances. Madame Lucia Elizabeth Vestris (1787–1856) was the only distinguished member of the cast.[13] Also at Covent Garden he sang the role of Sir Huon in Weber's *Oberon* which had been created by John Braham a year earlier. Shortly after, he sang at the Argyle Concert Rooms in London. The great dramatic soprano Giuditta Pasta (1797–1865) also performed at this concert.

He continued in this way for the next few years and in May 1829 he made a series of appearances at the Royal Academy of Music in the company of students.[14] Pasta and the lesser known but important Italian born Maria Caradori Allan also performed at these concerts. Sapio primarily sang Mozart arias.

His voice appeared to be on the decline by early 1830, when critics were citing a loss of power and top notes. Over the next year, he made the transition to buffo-baritone roles and it was in Rossini's *Il Barbiere di Siviglia* in the role of Dr. Bartolo that he next appeared in Dublin in 1831, with De Begnis as Figaro.[15] His last appearance in opera in Dublin was also with the Giuseppe De Begnis Italian company in October 1834 when he sang bass-baritone roles in Rossini's *Il Turco in Italia* and in *Semiramide*.[16] In March 1835, he sang at a Philharmonic concert in London. In Dublin later that year, he again appeared with De Begnis in a concert at the Rotunda Rooms. Samuel J. Pigott, a local violoncellist, also performed at this concert.[17] Mr. Pigott was ranked as one of the premier 'cellists in the British Isles.

When De Begnis next brought his Italian Company to Dublin in October 1837, Sapio was not a member of the group, as he had now settled in Dublin as a singing teacher. Giuseppe De Begnis went on to be a successful operatic manager in New York in the 1840s. He died there in August 1849, having had a distinguished career on two continents.

In preparation for Catherine's move from Limerick to Dublin the Reverend Knox wrote to the Pigott family. He laid out the terms of the agreement he was proposing for Sapio's fee and the expected period of study. Sapio was considered well qualified as a teacher. In addition, since Sapio was married it seemed appropriate to suggest that the arrangements include board and lodgings for Catherine and her mother, both of whom would be going to Dublin. Sapio agreed to the terms. Mary Hayes and her daughter would be able to stay at the Sapios' residence, at 1 Percy Place in Dublin. The Bishop sent the Pigotts an advance on Sapio's fees, advising them that he would shortly be coming through Dublin on his way to London, when he would provide additional funding if needed.

Dublin was growing rapidly. It got its first railway in 1834,[18] a short stretch of track running from Westland Row station on the south side of the city to what was then called Kingstown, now Dun Laoghaire. Limerick did not become connected to Dublin by rail until after 1844 when the Great Southern Railway was created. Transportation options between Limerick and Dublin in 1839 were coach or boat. Catherine and her mother, who was then about 45 years old, made arrangements for their move to Dublin. The trip of about 120 miles to Dublin by coach would take almost two days, allowing for stops along the way and given the condition of the roads in early spring. Two years later in January 1841, however, the great Franz Liszt was able to complete the same journey in a blinding snowstorm in sixteen and a half hours, travelling virtually non-stop, with Liszt at the reins some of the time![19]

The less expensive mode was by waterway via the river Shannon and a series of canals that eventually ended up in Dublin at Portobello Harbour. There were two levels of boat service, departing from Limerick at six in the morning. The slower service cost ten shillings and sixpence for a one-way ticket and required an overnight journey. The 'swift boat' arrived in Dublin at four thirty the same day; however, it cost slightly more – eleven shillings and sixpence.

During the month of March 1839, Catherine prepared herself for what was to be her first trip away from her home town of Limerick. There was a lot of excitement, mixed with anxiety, at the modest home in Patrick

Street, in anticipation of the move to the big city. For a 20-year old Irish country girl it must have felt like a step into the unknown. She had the confidence to know that she could sing well. If she was able to perform in concerts in Dublin, where there were many theatres she felt she would be able to achieve most of her ambitions. However, her mother was about to give up her work and their residence. Her sister Henrietta would have to move in with their aunt, Mrs. Daly, in Limerick. Catherine must have been experiencing considerable doubts and concern for her family and herself. If she didn't make it, there was no going back. Her early months in Dublin would be critical. She had to prove herself to Sapio, to Pigott and to the Reverend Knox back in Limerick who had shown such confidence in her. Above all, she had to sing in public in Dublin and be accepted. This more than anything else would justify everything.

Early on Monday morning, 1 April 1839, Catherine and her mother set off for Dublin, having said their farewells over the weekend. The contrast between Limerick and Dublin must have been awesome for young Catherine. By this time, Dublin had a population of around 250,000, which was about six times greater than Limerick. However exhilarating all the sights of the new city may have been to this young woman, it was probable that when she arrived at Percy Place that Catherine must have felt truly breathless. She was about to meet Antonio Sapio, the singing teacher who would make her into a concert singer.

In time, Catherine would get to know Dublin and many of its residents very well. She was destined to have great success there both in concert and opera. There would be many opportunities to meet important people who could help her. Just a few months before her arrival, two of Europe's leading opera singers, Fanny Tacchinardi-Persiani (1812–67) and Giovanni Battista Rubini (1794–1854), had closed the Dublin opera season with an abbreviated version of Donizetti's *Lucia di Lammermoor*.[20] Persiani had created the part of Lucia in Naples four years earlier and Rubini was known everywhere in Europe and Russia for his performances of Edgardo in Donizetti's opera and for other romantic operatic roles. Catherine would meet both of these personalities in the not too distant future. She didn't even dream of it then, but in a few years she would actually sing the love duet from Lucia with the renowned Rubini at a special celebration in his home town of Bergamo in Italy. At a slightly later date, she would share the same concert platform as Persiani at one of London's premier theatres.

As time would prove, this initial step of moving to Dublin really represented the beginning of a long journey across many countries, continents and oceans. Catherine would meet kings, queens, princes, great showmen and world leaders, and would fall in love. She would experience incredible success in some of the world's greatest opera houses and concert halls, earning enormous amounts of money, always accompanied by her mother. One day she would return to Ireland and Limerick triumphant. However, she had countless hours of study with Antonio Sapio ahead before she would emerge as a professional concert singer and move into the next phase of her career.

Catherine's studies with Sapio started immediately. There is no record of Sapio's comments during these early years of learning. Sapio had several other pupils, some of who were already performing professionally. In addition to singing, he also offered students lessons in Italian, French and English.

Catherine was impatient to get started and wanted to sing at a concert. Sapio apparently felt confident enough in her abilities to arrange for her to appear at the Rotunda rooms on Friday 3 May 1839,[21] just one month after her arrival in Dublin. We are fortunate to have reviews of this and other concerts that took place during those early months.

Sapio knew the routine. He had performed at the Rotunda several times and during the previous March he had participated in two concerts with Nicholas Bochsa (1789–1856), the great French harpist. An advertisement appeared the day before Catherine's first Rotunda concert announcing 'A Young Lady' (Pupil of Signor Sapio makes her first appearance in public). Her name was never mentioned. Her opening number was a duet with Sapio, 'O'er shepherd pipe' from Balfe's opera *Joan of Arc*, which had premiered at the Drury Lane Theatre, London in November 1837. This was followed by a Saverio Mercadante (1795–1870) duet, also with Sapio, 'Se un istante'. The press review for the concert stated:

> the debutante made her first appearance as a vocalist of promise and before long she would stand high in the profession …, she sang most effectively with a voice of considerable volume and compass.[22]

While this experience may have proved exhilarating for Catherine, it must have been obvious to Sapio that she was not yet really ready. She had only been under his tutelage a few weeks and had little or no experience of singing publicly. However the press had in some small way recognised her talents, which must have been rewarding for her. Afterwards, vocal lessons with Sapio continued almost daily.

While Catherine was quite literate and generally a good letter writer, no correspondence that we know of survives from this time Therefore we do not have any indication of her thoughts and feelings during these early days. There were few distractions around Dublin during time that were affordable. Catherine had no interest in opera and in any event, there was no Italian opera season in Dublin in 1839.

By the end of the year Sapio had taught her numerous songs and selections from operas. Her favourites included arias from Bellini's *I Puritani* and *La Sonnambula*. On Tuesday 7 December 1839, a notice appeared in the Dublin *Evening Packet* stating that:

> It is the intention of the conductors of the Anacreontic Society to introduce to their friends at the forthcoming concert a young lady of great promise who has the advantage of instruction from Signor Sapio. The musical world are tiptoe of expectation of the treat provided for them for this antient [sic] and highly distinguished Society.

On 9 December, 1839 she made her appearance at the Anacreontic Society in the Rotunda. This time she sang Bellini arias, such as 'Qui la voce' from I *Puritani* and 'Come per sereno' from *La Sonnambula*, which was loudly encored. Reviews referred to her as a 'highly promising young vocalist, despite her timidity.' It was recorded that she sang very sweetly and expressively and that with more experience and public practice she would be a decided acquisition to the concert rooms of Dublin. This concert was such a success that Sapio set up another performance for the following week on 16 December 1839. It is also around this time that we first get some indication of Catherine's personal appearance which was described in the local press as 'slight, youthful, tall and pleasant looking'.

Later in the month Catherine, Sapio and her mother returned to Limerick. Presumably this was Sapio's time to show how much progress she had made and to get a renewal of his contract with Bishop Knox, which was due to expire in March 1840.

A concert was given on the morning of 15 January, 1840 at Swinburne's Great Rooms in Limerick. The announcement stated that the concert was 'Under the immediate patronage of the Honourable and right Reverend the Lord Bishop of Limerick'. The *Limerick Standard* newspaper made the following comments:

> . . . Miss Hayes, on making her appearance was greeted with loud and hearty applause. She appeared diffident at first, but shortly after

regained her usual firmness and self-possession. She has a splendid compass of voice from D in alt. to low G, and is, unquestionably, one of the most charming singers Limerick has ever produced.[23]

Some time later, the Dublin *Evening Packet* reported:

the rich and commanding tones of Miss Hayes' voice affords reason to hope that when matured by more extensive practice and under the able instruction of her talented master, she will take a first place among the principal vocalists of the present day.[24]

The Bishop and his friends were overjoyed with what they heard, and the Bishop held a party that evening at which the stars performed again. Sapio had his contract extended for another year of tuition. The shrewd singing master immediately setup a concert for 5 February which had the patronage of all the principal ladies of Limerick society, no fewer than 29 in all! Catherine sang arias and duets by Mercadante, Rossini, Bellini and Balfe. Once again, success reigned, and Sapio programmed a subsequent benefit concert for Catherine and himself for the afternoon of 11 February 1840. He also advertised his availability for singing lessons during his stay. This concert was well attended by the elite of rank and fashion, according to newspaper reports. Catherine returned to Dublin with her mother and Sapio some weeks later.

Towards the end of April, in Dublin, another concert was announced. This was to take place at the Rotunda on Friday, 1 May 1840. Sapio was the sponsor of this Grand Concert, and in addition to Catherine, a Mrs. Elliott would be performing. Catherine and Sapio sang the lively Rossini duet from *Semiramide* (1823) 'Se la vita . . . ', followed by Catherine singing a ballad called 'The Deserted' and closing with her singing the aria 'Il Braccio mio' by Giuseppe Niccolini (1762–1842), an early Italian operatic composer. A reviewer of Catherine's efforts stated that – 'the young lady was gifted with a voice of great compass'.[25]

The next concert she gave was on 13 May 1840 when she participated in Mrs. Joseph Elliott's annual concert at the Rotunda concert rooms. This was a particularly important concert for Catherine. For the first time, she would be singing with artists other than Sapio. Mrs. Wood (Mary Ann Paton) was the principal soloist. The opening number with Catherine was a Balfe quartet, 'Lo early beam', from the *Siege of Rochelle* (1835). She and Sapio then sang the duet 'Se la vita . . . ' from Rossini's *Semiramide*. Following this, Catherine, for the first time, sang 'John Anderson my Joe',

3. The announcement for a concert in January 1840, by the young Catherine Hayes, at Swinburne's Concert rooms, Limerick. (Author's collection).

a well-known Scottish song that she was to sing many times throughout her career. It was followed by a quintet from Wolfgang Amadeus Mozart's (1756–1791), *Cosi fan tutte* (1790). Catherine then joined in the musically complex and difficult Act I finale to Mozart's *Don Giovanni* (1787) with Mrs. Wood, Sapio and others. Catherine presumably sang Zerlina's music. This was a very significant evening for Catherine including a greatly expanded repertoire.

Another concert took place two nights later on Friday 15 May 1840, a benefit for the cellist, Mr. S.J. Pigott. Catherine, Mrs. Wood and Sapio again participated. At this concert, Catherine included the song 'Kathleen Mavourneen' for the first time. 'Kathleen Mavourneen' was written by Frederick N. Crouch (1808–96) to words by a Mrs. Crawford, possibly his first wife who was born in County Cavan. Frederick Crouch was born in England. He studied music with Nicholas Bochsa, the French harpist, and also the violoncello at the Royal Academy of Music. He later played in the orchestra at Her Majesty's theatre and at Drury Lane theatre in London. In 1849, he emigrated to America. After an unsettled career working at various occupations, he died in Maine in August 1896 in a state of poverty.

Catherine had good success at these concerts, particularly with her new ballad. The newspaper reviewer singled out the manner and feeling with which she sang the song, saying that she added much to the attraction of the evening. In time, 'Kathleen Mavourneen' became her signature piece. Over the next twenty years she would sing it at virtually every opportunity including using it as an encore for Queen Victoria when performing at a Buckingham Palace concert in London ten years later.

Crouch composed several other 'Irish' songs, but 'Kathleen Mavourneen' became his most popular ballad. He wrote it in 1838, and it was probably first published in a volume of 'Irish Songs' by D'Almaine, London music publishers, around 1840. There is little doubt that its great popularity during the nineteenth century was due to Catherine, who included it in so many recitals. Even the great Adelina Patti, (1843–1919) who was to become the highest paid and most sought after diva in Europe, Russia and America in the second half of the nineteenth century, sang it. There is a good possibility that the very young Adelina, who toured America in 1852 giving vocal concerts as a child prodigy ('La Petite Jenny Lind') under the direction of the impresario Maurice Strakosch, (1825–1887) may have attended one of Catherine's concerts and heard her sing this song.[26] In Baltimore in October 1852, Strakosch promoted the young Patti's concerts with advertising that stated she would sing 'all the bravura pieces of Malibran, Pasta, Jenny Lind and Catherine Hayes . . . starting with 'The Happy Birdling of the Forest' . . . a celebrated bravura song composed expressly for Catherine Hayes'.[27] Catherine sang 'Kathleen Mavourneen' many times during her concert tours in America. and over fifty years later, Patti felt that 'Kathleen Mavourneen' was important enough to include in the first group of vocal recordings she made, at the age of 62 in December 1905, in the early days of the recording industry.[28]

On 1 December, Catherine performed her final concert for the year 1840. This was a function sponsored by Herr Sedletzek, a prominent musician from Her Majesty's theatre, London. It was given at a private residence at 5 Gardner Row in Dublin. Catherine drew on her expanding repertoire of songs and arias and got good reviews. Pigott and Sapio also performed.

One of the most important events in Catherine's young career occurred shortly after. Early in the new year, she was invited to sing at another concert in Dublin. Sapio had arranged this when he dined with the principal performer and other members of the visiting party before their initial concert, which occurred on the morning of 7 January 1841. Their next concert was to be a J.P. Knight sponsored function at the Long Room of the Rotunda on Tuesday 12 January 1841.[29] The star of the evening was the celebrated Hungarian virtuoso pianist, Franz Liszt (1811–86), then only 29 years old and on his first tour of the British Isles. Other participants at the Knight concert included Mr. Pigott on the violoncello, John Parry, Miss Bassano, Miss Steele and J.P. Knight, all vocalists. Sapio, who had sung in the earlier concert, was also participating. Catherine was listed as 'Miss Hayes, a pupil of Signor Sapio'.

The evening opened with Sapio and the other vocalists singing in a quintet, 'Blow, gentle gales', by English composer Henry Bishop (1786–1855). Various vocal solos followed this, including arias from Mozart's *Don Giovanni* and 'The Wanderer', a Schubert song in which Liszt accompanied Miss Steele. Liszt then continued with his own arrangement of the 'Hexameron Variations' and the 'Grand Galop Chromatique'.[30] The addition of this last piece was a slight change from the published programme, which showed that the Grand Galop was scheduled to be played in the second half of the concert. Catherine and Sapio opened the second half of the concert with a duet, 'Dimmi che questo cor', by operatic composer Giovanni Pacini (1796–1867). Liszt and Pigott followed shortly after with a grand duet for pianoforte and violoncello.

The cello used by Pigott for this concert was a rare Stradivarius instrument, made in 1720. It was brought to Ireland from Spain in 1818 by a Dublin wine-merchant, and after a series of owners was offered for sale by Cramer and Beale in London in 1831 when Pigott purchased it.[31] After Pigott's death in 1853, the instrument eventually came into the possession of the great cellist Alfredo Piatti in London. Today the beautiful instrument is owned by Carlos Prieto, the Mexican cellist.

Immediately following the Liszt and Pigott performance Catherine sang 'Qui la voce' from *I Puritani*. After some solos from the other vocalists Liszt returned to perform his own variation on the finale from *Lucia di Lammermoor* which he had composed two years earlier. The evening closed with a Rossini quintet in which Sapio performed. This was Catherine's first exposure to the music of Donizetti's great opera, which had had its premier just six years earlier in Naples. Liszt's sensational performance of the music, which brought the house down, would leave a lasting impression on her.

Twenty-four-year-old Louis Lavenu (1817–59) was the conductor and manager for Liszt's tour. Lavenu had studied composition, pianoforte and cello at the Royal Academy of Music in London. He later composed several songs and went on to compose an opera called *Loretta – A Tale of Seville* which was first performed at the Drury Lane theatre in London on 9 November 1846 with some success. His father had been in a business partnership with Nicholas Mori (1793–1839), the violinist as music publishers in Bond Street, London. Louis Lavenu married Mori's daughter and eventually inherited the business. Lavenu didn't know it at the time, but he was destined to conduct Catherine's performances in many different cities around the world and to compose songs for her. This was the first concert in which Catherine would sing under his direction. She was 22 at the time. During this visit Lavenu had just celebrated his twenty-fourth birthday with Liszt at Morrison's Hotel in Dublin, where they were staying.

The press reported that the concert was attended by a 'brilliant assemblage of rank and fashion'. Liszt was the focal point of the reviews with only a mention of Hayes and Sapio, but it was an auspicious start to the new year for the young Catherine. This was her first experience of working with an artist of such international renown.

Reports appeared a number of years later that Liszt was so impressed with Catherine's performance that he immediately wrote a letter to Mrs. Knox, the Bishop's wife. It was claimed that Liszt stated, among other things, that 'he knew of no other voice more expressive than that of Miss Hayes, and that wherever he may be, in London, Paris or Italy he would always be happy to forward her in her profession'.[32] There is no evidence

---

**PROGRAMME OF
MR. J. P. KNIGHT'S
CONCERT,
On TUESDAY EVENING, Jan. 12, 1841,
AT THE ROTUNDO.**

Principal Performers :
**MONS. LISZT,
MISS STEELE, MISS LOUISA BASSANO,
MISS HAYES,** (pupil of Sig. Sapio,) **MR. J. PARRY,
SIGNOR A. SAPIO, MR. RICHARDSON,
MR. PIGOTT,** and **MR. J. P. KNIGHT.**

Part I.

GLEE—" Blow, gentle gales"—Miss Bassano, Miss Steele, Mr. Knight, Mr. Parry, and Signor Sapio, ...	Bishop.
Duet—" La ci darem"—Miss Steele and Mr. Parry, ...	Mozart.
Aria—" Batti, Batti"—Miss Bassano, (accompanied on the Violoncello by Mr. Pigott,) ...	Mozart.
New Song—" The Ship Launch"—Mr. Knight—[The 1st verse is descriptive of the building of the Vessel—the 2d of the Launch—the 3d of the Ship on her Voyage, ...	Knight.
Hexameron—Piano-forte—Mr. Liszt, ...	Liszt.
Song—" The Wanderer"—Miss Steele, accompanied by Mr. Liszt, ...	Schubert.
Solo—Flute—Mr. Richardson.	
Mr. Parry will sing his favorite Song, " Wanted, a Governess, ...	Parry.

Part II.

DUET—" Dimmi che questo cor"—Miss Hayes and Signor Sapio, ...	Pacini.
Song—" Go, forget me"—Miss Bassano, accompanied by Mr. Knight, ...	Knight.
Grand Duet—Piano-forte and Violoncello—Mr. Liszt and Mr. Pigott.	
Aria—" Qui la voce"—Miss Hayes, ...	Bellini.
Ballad—" Of what is the old man thinking"—Mr. Knight, (by desire,)	Knight.
Ballad—" They tell me thou'rt the favored guest"—Miss Steele, (by desire,)	Balfe.
Andante—Finale from Lucia di Lammermoor, and Galope Chromatique—Piano-forte—Mr. Liszt, ...	Liszt.
Mr. Parry will sing (by desire) his popular Song, " A Wife Wanted,"	Parry.
FINALE—Miss Steele, Miss Bassano, Mr. Knight, Mr. Parry, and Signor Sapio, ...	Rossini.

Conductor—Mr. LEVENU.

The Concert will commence at Half-past Eight o'Clock.
Tickets Five Shillings each ; to be had at the principal
Music Warehouses.
148

4. Catherine Hayes at the beginning of her career shared the concert platform at the Rotunda in Dublin with the thirty-year-old Franz Liszt and others. (Author's collection).

to show that Liszt actually wrote a letter along these lines. However, Liszt was known to be very helpful to fellow artists, particularly in their student or early years. Interestingly, Liszt did perform in Limerick during this period, so perhaps there was some communication or comment made to the Bishop or a family member on Catherine's progress. We will never know for certain.

As previously mentioned, Liszt and Lavenu stayed at Morrison's Hotel which was located at the eastern corner of Dawson and Nassau Streets, opposite Dublin University (Trinity College). It was a popular place for visiting artists to stay, a well-appointed hotel which was prominent in Dublin's history, both musical and political, to the end of the century, when it was demolished. The original proprietor, for whom it was named, was a former mayor of the city of Dublin. A few years later, when Catherine first returned to Dublin as an international celebrity, she too would stay at Morrison's – the appropriate place for a young visiting prima donna.

There is an interesting account of this Dublin visit by Liszt, Lavenu and other members of the party. John Parry (1776–1851), a Welsh harpist who was with the group, was also a humorist in addition to being a vocalist and song composer. He left a set of diaries covering his travels on the tour that are very amusing and include details of the philandering of Liszt and Lavenu in Cork, Dublin, Kilkenny and Limerick.[33] There is also an account of Parry taking Catherine to Pigott's music store at 112 Grafton Street so he could buy her the sheet music of one of his songs, only to find that that it was sold out. (perhaps they never had them in the first place!)

Catherine's concert activity increased sharply after this important January event. In early March she appeared again at the Rotunda, singing her regular repertoire. She also performed some of Donizetti's music for the first time – in a trio – 'Guai, se ti, sfugge, un motto', after which she sang an aria from *I Puritani* and a Scottish ballad. This was followed by another Anacreontic concert of sacred music on 5 April, during which she sang in a quartet from Mozart's *Requiem* with Sapio and others. She then sang Handel's great aria, 'Angels ever bright and fair', concluding with the equally famous 'With verdure clad' from Haydn's *Creation*. This was her first venture in oratorio. Despite her professional engagements, Catherine's studies with Sapio continued daily, mostly practising scales and sometimes learning new arias.

In early April she travelled to Belfast for another Anacreontic Society concert. This time she was the main attraction. Sapio accompanied her, with Pigott and a Mr. Murray. The concert was held in the Music Hall on Thursday, 15 April 1841. The sponsor was a Mr. J.T. May, who was also the conductor for the performance. Catherine returned to Dublin shortly afterwards.

The next concert, on 20 April, was again at the Rotunda. This time she sang a new cantata called 'Spirit of Music' composed by a Mr. Marsh, who was the conductor and sponsor for the evening. This was Stephen Hale Marsh (1805–88), who had studied with Bochsa at the Academy in London. Later in the concert Marsh performed one of his compositions for harp. Marsh later became an important musician in Australia, where Catherine would meet him again.

A concert was given on the last day of April under the patronage of the distinguished Duke of Leinster. Catherine, Sapio and a Mr. Frazier opened it with a trio from Balfe's new romantic opera, *Keolanthe*, which was the first time this music was performed in Ireland. The opera had had its premiere in London on 9 March 1841, just six weeks previously, with Balfe's wife Lina Roser in the principal soprano role. Catherine next sang Henry Bishop's 'Lo! hear the gentle lark', another new solo for her. Her busy schedule necessitated that she broaden her repertoire with each succeeding concert. In May two more concerts followed in quick succession at the Rotunda. At one of these Catherine joined in a duet with a former Sapio pupil, a Miss Hawes, and the critics liked what they heard.

By now Catherine's fee for each concert had gone from five English guineas to ten, a substantial sum in those days, particularly for a young lady who until quite recently had had such modest finances. Her determination and strength of character were finally paying off. However, the year would be even more eventful for her. It would bring her into contact with international superstars of the opera, which would greatly influence her thinking. For now, however, her focus continued to be concert singing.

During the time of the Liszt visit there had been considerable excitement in Dublin about a forthcoming visit by Giovanni Mario (1810–83), the handsome young Italian tenor. He had made his operatic debut in Paris in 1838 and was now all the rage in Paris and London. Mario, whose original name was Giovanni Matteo Cavaliere di Candia, was from a noble family and was born on the island of Sardinia. He was scheduled to arrive in Dublin in late August 1841 to perform in a number of operas, just as he was about to turn 31 years of age. Within a few years, Catherine and Mario would perform together at the Royal Italian Opera

House at Covent Garden to a glittering audience. The manager of the
Theatre Royal, Mr. Calcraft, made a formal announcement on 31 August
1841. Calcraft claimed that the new opera season would be the best ever
performed in Dublin, which was indeed to be the case.

Mario was making his debut in Bellini's *I Puritani* with Luigi Lablache
(1794–1858), Giulia Grisi (1811–69) and Lablache's son Frederick in the
leading roles. Lablache senior and Grisi had been creators in the original
production of the opera in Paris in 1835. The entire season promised to
be outstanding, with a strong focus on the music of Bellini and Donizetti.

Luigi Lablache was legendary throughout Europe at this point in his
career. He was born in Naples. His father was French and his mother
Irish. The mother's maiden name was Bietach which may have had its
origins in the Irish word 'Biatach,' possibly meaning 'food vendor' or
'public victualer.'[34] It is not known where in Ireland she was born.

Lablache was the most famous bass singer of the nineteenth century
and had created many operatic roles in the principal cities of Europe. He
was the singing teacher to Queen Victoria of England, for twenty years.
He was also on intimate terms with most of the major composers of the
day.

Later Giuseppe Verdi (1813–1901) would single him out to create the
bass role in I Masnadieri(1847) a new opera which had its premiere
performance in London with Verdi conducting.

Sapio possibly knew Lablache through his father. However, Sapio also
had met Lablache at the King's Theater, London when he was a performer
there some years earlier. Lablache sang in London from 1830 onwards.

Shortly after the basso's arrival in Dublin during the last week of
August, somehow Sapio managed to talk to Lablache about Catherine.
This was Lablache's first visit to Ireland, birthplace of his mother.
Lablache agreed to hear Catherine sing the following week. Perhaps his
mother's association with Ireland and the fact that she had a good soprano
voice made him predisposed towards hearing a young Irish soprano. Sapio
setup an appointment with Lablache at Morrison's Hotel for Sunday,
September 5, 1841. It was agreed that the conductor and composer, Julius
Benedict (1804–85), would be the accompanist.

At this time Sapio must have felt strongly that Catherine's talents were
more suited to opera than the concert platform, despite her timidity and
reserve. It also seems logical that he never would have risked offending so
important a person as Lablache if he did not really believe that he had a
star pupil with significant talent. He must also have recognized that she

needed further training and experience that was beyond his scope and capability. Whatever the reasons, in a few months the results of this audition would take Catherine on the next stage of her journey to becoming an important singer.

It's not certain if Catherine would have realized the significance of what was about to happen, given the fact that all along her primary interest was to sing in concerts, not opera. However, perhaps she too was beginning to think that her destiny was to be an opera singer given her level of proficiency with operatic arias and how comfortable she felt singing Italian music at this point in time.

She certainly had the opportunity to see opera in Dublin. A short Italian season had commenced in September 1840 with Giulia Grisi making her first appearance in Dublin as *Semiramide* in Rossini's opera of the same name. By this time, Catherine could afford to attend the opera if she wished to.

Catherine had learned a number of arias, but no complete opera. Certainly Sapio's residence at 1 Percy Place where he provided lessons would not have been suitable for student performances of this type.

Sapio's professional experience and his actions would suggest that by this time he fully recognised the level of her vocal capabilities. Singing concerts in Ireland would not help her to achieve her full potential. He decided to seek the advice of the experienced Luigi Lablache and take his direction, despite the potential economic loss to himself. A noble act on the part of Sapio. In any case, whatever feelings Sapio may have had about Catherine's future possibilities, it could only benefit her situation to have an audition with Lablache and possibly receive his endorsement. This would also be particularly helpful when he and Catherine met with the Bishop and his friends in Limerick to discuss Catherine's career path. The idea of Catherine wanting to change direction and go on the stage, a profession that was deemed morally dubious by the Church and society in nineteenth-century England, much less Ireland, was likely to meet with strong resistance in Limerick.

A tense Catherine and Sapio left Percy Place on Sunday 5 September to make the short ride to Dawson Street and Morrison's Hotel for a mid-morning appointment with Lablache. All week long Catherine had studied the coloratura parts of Elvira in Bellini's opera *I Puritani*. She knew the main aria 'Qui la voce' well, having sung it in concert a number of times. *I Puritani* was also one of the operas to be performed in the new season in Dublin, with Grisi, Mario and Lablache. She also studied the main arias from another Bellini opera, *La Sonnambula*, just in case she was asked to sing a second piece.

The lobby of Morrison's was comfortable, and it wasn't long before the huge figure of Lablache appeared with Julius Benedict, a slightly balding severe looking man of German origin who twenty years later in 1862 composed the opera *The Lily of Killarney*, based on the Irish born Dion Boucicault's play *The Colleen Bawn*. This ballad opera became a great favourite in Ireland and England over the next hundred years. Lablache's robust voice greeted Sapio. Catherine was startled at the sight of the 6'3" 47 year old Lablache who weighed over 250 pounds and had a lusty outgoing personality. Despite his size, Lablache made people feel at ease in his presence and no doubt he would also have been sensitive to Catherine's youth, timidity and reserved demeanour.

They proceeded to one of the music rooms at Morrison's, discussing the opera season and other subjects on the way. As Catherine was to recall many years later during an interview in Dublin, she nearly lost her nerve, she was so frightened when she was asked to sing. After a slight hesitation she chose 'Qui la voce' from *I Puritani*, an aria that takes about ten minutes to sing. Benedict accompanied her on the Broadwood piano. Lablache listened intently but said nothing. When she finished she looked at Lablache and then at Sapio, who made no comment. Benedict was also silent. Then Lablache turned to her and asked if she could sing the shorter but more difficult 'Vien, diletto, e in ciel la luna!', also from *I Puritani*, a piece that would provide more exposure for vocal flexibility and range. Despite the tension in the room she started this piece with greater proficiency and improved self-confidence. Again there was no particular comment. Next, at Lablache's insistence, she sang a duet with him from the same opera, probably the first act, second scene duet which starts with 'O amato zio, o mio secondo padre!' The session went on most of the morning, with Catherine becoming more relaxed and confident as she sang. She began to enjoy herself, realising that if Lablache was not interested in her he wouldn't have continued the exercise.

At the end of the session Lablache boomed forth that he was delighted with her performance, praising her technique and style, and assuring Sapio that she had all the talents needed to become 'the perfect vocalist in every sense of the word'. He invited her to be his guest at the Theatre Royal the following night, Monday 6 September, when Bellini's *Norma* (1831) would be performed for the second time that season. It would have Giulia Grisi, the greatest singing actress of the day, in the title role, Mario as Pollione and Lablache as Oroveso. Giulia Grisi's cousin Ernesta Grisi would be the Adalgisa of the performance and Julius Benedict was scheduled to conduct.

Giulia Grisi, the foremost protagonist of the role of *Norma* in Europe at the time, was 30 years old. She was to have a long career, most of which was spent performing in Paris, London, Dublin and various provincial cities in England and Ireland. She made one brief visit to New York. Originally Grisi had been under contract to the powerful impresario Alessandro Lanari of the Teatro della Pergola in Florence: however, after breaking her contract with him in 1832 she could never again sing in Italy. Earlier in her career she had sung the role of Adalgisa to Giuditta Pasta's Norma at the premiere of Bellini's masterpiece at La Scala Opera House in Milan on 26 December 1831. She was 20 years old at that time. Grisi created numerous operatic soprano roles, including Elvira in Bellini's *I Puritani* in Paris in 1835. She 'owned' the role of Norma during her lifetime, much like Maria Callas in the 1950s.

Grisi and Mario eventually paired up for life but never married. Grisi had been married in 1836 and was never able to get a divorce because she was a Catholic. Her husband DeMelcy outlived her. Mario and Grisi had three children. After a brilliant career that spanned thirty years, in November 1869 Grisi died, virtually alone, in a Berlin hotel room as a result of the after effects of injuries from a train derailment caused by a winter snowstorm. Her children were in the next room. She was on her way to meet Mario, who was singing at the opera at St. Petersburg in Russia. The Grisi and Mario relationship is one of the great romantic stories of all nineteenth century opera.

Grisi was at the pinnacle of her career and form when Catherine went to see her that September night in 1841 at the Theatre Royal in Hawkins Street, Dublin. Catherine later said that Grisi's performance that night changed her thinking forever and, in the process, her career. She also mentioned that this was the first opera she had seen. We will never really know how Grisi's portrayal of Bellini's tragic figure affected Catherine Hayes emotionally, but we do know that several months after this event Catherine and Sapio decided it was time to visit the good Bishop in Limerick to have a serious discussion about the idea of becoming an opera singer. Perhaps also around this time there had been some correspondence with Limerick outlining her plans, which may have hastened the need for a visit.

Meanwhile Catherine continued her studies with Sapio and gave concerts, primarily in Dublin. Early in August she and Sapio went to

Limerick to meet the Bishop. Then an unusual event occurred that suggests the Bishop, or more probably his wife, had a serious problem with Catherine's change in direction.

On Wednesday 10 August 1842, an advertisement in the *Limerick Chronicle* announced that Catherine would be sponsoring an amateur concert, featuring local Limerick vocalists. In addition, Catherine would be offering singing lessons during her stay at the residence of a Miss Maxwell at Cecil Street, Limerick. It seems that it was taking an undue amount of time to get the Bishop to consent to her change in career direction. Probably she decided to fill in the time with the concert and singing lessons. The delay in receiving the Bishop's consent might have been related to funding needs; however, it is more likely it was caused by concern over Catherine's choice of a theatrical life in opera, especially as the church was involved with the funding. There was also the increased expense to consider because her training for the opera would require her to study abroad, as Sapio and Catherine had decided that she should study with the foremost singing teacher in Europe, Manuel Garcia in Paris.

It is not clear how Catherine and Sapio came to make this choice. However, according to Garcia's biographer, Lablache had recommended Garcia.[35] Lablache was active in Paris and certainly would have known Garcia and his work, probably visiting his studio once in a while to listen to some of his students or possibly meeting him at the salons where so many musical personalities congregated. In any event Garcia was the choice and Paris was the city that Sapio and Catherine presented to Bishop Knox at that eventful meeting in 1842.

Shortly after the amateur concert in Limerick, Catherine received the consent of the Bishop to pursue an operatic career. Obviously Bishop Knox, who was a well travelled man, and his wife understood her resolve and determination. Lablache's endorsement most certainly further supported her case. The agreement was celebrated by a fundraising concert being announced for 14 August 1842 in Limerick.[36] Catherine had achieved her goal and would be going to Paris. Bishop Knox agreed to write to George Osborne, a musician and Limerick's most prominent citizen in the arts in Paris, and arrangements were made for her to study with Manuel Garcia. Catherine and her mother would also be able to stay with the Osbornes. It was probably good timing for Garcia too, as his prize pupil, Jenny Lind (1820–87), had just completed her training and would leave Paris to return to Sweden at the end of August 1842.[37] Catherine was scheduled to arrive six weeks later to start lessons.

Initially Catherine wanted to set off for Paris immediately, but this was not possible for a number of reasons. She returned to Dublin to prepare for her move to the musical capital of Europe. She gave one last private concert in Dublin in the home of Countess de Grey sometime early in September 1842.[38] Catherine and her mother were ready to travel to Paris by the end of month. Catherine mentioned much later that the money she had saved during her time in Dublin was sown into her petticoat before setting out for her long and dangerous journey to continental Europe. One wonders how heavy her petticoat, full of gold sovereigns, must have been!

On hearing about Catherine's planned departure, the well-known English writer, William Makepeace Thackeray, in his *Irish Sketch Book* written around this period, mentions in a solemn tone:

> And, finally, 'Miss Hayes will give her first and farewell concert at the Rotunda, previous to leaving her native country.' Only one instance of Irish talent do we read of, and that, in a desponding tone, announces, its intention of quitting its native country.[39]

Of course, as we know, Thackeray was not correct about Catherine's 'first and farewell concert' at the Rotunda!

In about four weeks time Catherine would turn 24. Her next stop would be Paris, the centre for artistic and musical talent in Europe in 1842.

CHAPTER THREE

Manuel Garcia and
the Student

PARIS AND MILAN 1842–1845

W HEN Catherine and her mother arrived in Paris in October 1842,
they proceeded to the Osbornes' apartment on the Rue St. Georges
in the 9th District, where many artists, writers and musicians lived.

Manuel Garcia (1805–1906) had his studio at No. 6 Square d'Orléans,
just a short distance from the Osbornes from 1841 to 1847.[1] The Square,
with its beautiful fountain dating from 1829, was built in the early 1820s
and still exists today. Its entrance is at No. 80 Rue Taitbout. The buildings
in the Square are now mostly used as professional offices.

Frédéric Chopin, the great pianist and composer was a resident of
No. 9 on the Square from 1842 to 1849. His mistress, Aurore Dupin,
Baroness Dudevant, who wrote novels under the pseudonym George
Sand, lived at No. 5 from 1842 to 1847.[2] During this same period Pauline
Viardot Garcia, Manuel Garcia's sister, lived at No. 2, as did the famous
ballet dancer Maria-Sophie Taglione (1804–84). Several other notable
musical and literary personalities of the day were also residents of the
elegant Square. Earlier in the 1820s, while Director of the Théâtre des
Italiens, Rossini had lived on the Rue Taitbout to the west of the
Square,and the popular composer Auber lived on the Rue St. Georges to
the east of the Square.

Paris at this time was very different from how it looks today. It would
be more than a decade before Baron Haussmann emerged as the new
prefect of the Seine and began his grand design for the city.[3] The
spectacular boulevards and some of the parks we know today were then a
vision of the distant future.

By the 1840s, the city had a population of almost one million people.
Its growth had been enormous during the previous thirty years, with

5. Number 6 Square d'Orléans, Paris (1998), where Catherine Hayes and Jenny Lind studied with the great singing teacher, Manuel Garcia in the early 1840s. (Author's collection).

strong migration from the provinces. During the post revolutionary period of the 1830s, the city became the focal point for Europe's Romantic age. Its cosmopolitan mixture of artists, writers, singers, musicians, poets and teachers of the arts gave it a unique flavour. Household names today, such as Liszt, Chopin, Berlioz, Wagner and others mixed with the best writers and poets in Europe, many of whom had settled in Paris by 1840 to pursue their craft in an environment that was conducive to creativity and success.

In the early 1840s, Paris became the central point for the national railway system in France. The city by this time was the centre of commerce for continental Europe, so it provided its residents with good transportation to and from other places in Europe. This was particularly important for musicians, given the fact that many of them made their living by touring.

Rossini had become one of the most important figures in the operatic movement since his arrival in Paris in 1824.[4] He composed several operas for the city, the last being the spectacular, lengthy *Guillaume Tell* in 1829, after which he virtually went into retirement, first in Paris and then in Bologna, returning to Paris in 1855 where he lived until his death in 1868.

From about 1827, the composer Giacomo Meyerbeer (1791–1864) emerged to establish French opera on a grand scale. His first success was *Robert le Diable* in 1831, followed by *Les Huguenots* in 1832. Meyerbeer's operas were mostly produced for the Paris opera at the Salle Le Peletier. The Italian opera – Théâtre des Italiens at the Salle Ventadour – primarily featured works by Rossini, Bellini, Donizetti and Mercadante. The Théâtre des Italiens, with its galaxy of operatic stars such as Rubini, Grisi, Lablache, Tamburini, Mario, Sontag and many others, was the focus for musical gatherings and social life in Paris during the 1840s. Verdi's music had not yet reached Paris. It would be October1845 before his first great Italian success *Nabucco* was performed in Paris.[5] By then Catherine had finished her training in Paris with Garcia and was studying and singing in Milan.

When the 24 year-old-Catherine Hayes took up residence in Paris, her surroundings must have caused her great excitement. The city's population was five times larger than Dublin, enormous when compared to her home town of Limerick. The language and culture were also very different. However, the Osbornes welcomed Catherine and her mother with open arms. Catherine didn't know it then, but this meeting with George Osborne would blossom into a life long friendship. He would participate in some of her most joyful and her saddest moments.

From the beginning Catherine recognised that Paris would be a challenge. First she would have to learn the language so that she could communicate, meet people and enjoy her surroundings. Manuel Garcia, however, could speak several languages including English, which at least would make singing lessons a little easier.

Manuel Patricio Garcia was born in Zafra, Spain, on 17 March 1805.[6] He first studied singing in Naples with Giovanni Ansani (1744–1826), then with Niccolo Zingarelli (1752–1837), and finally with his father, Manuel Garcia senior (1775–1832). His musical studies took place with François Fetis (1784–1871) in Paris, where his father was performing at the opera.

Manuel Garcia senior was an extraordinarily gifted person. In addition to being a composer, he was a singer and vocal teacher. He settled in Paris around 1820. He had three children, Manuel Patricio and two daughters, both of who became very famous opera singers – Maria (Malibran) Garcia, and Pauline (Viardot) Garcia. All of the Garcia children received vocal lessons and musical training from their father. Garcia senior was one of the most important operatic personalities of the nineteenth century. However, in time his three children also became very famous, through their musical accomplishments and contributions to the world of opera.

In his youth, Garcia senior had been involved with various musical groups, initially in Spain where he was born and later in France. He was a leading Rossini singer, having created the tenor roles in *Elisabetta, Regina d'Inghilterra* in Naples in 1815 and in *Il Barbiere di Siviglia* in Rome in 1816. After this he and his wife returned to Paris, where he became involved with the Théâtre des Italiens, which was then directed by the famous Angelica Catalani. He continued to sing and compose, sometimes visiting London to perform at the King's Theatre. On 1 October 1825, he set sail with his wife and three children – Manuel junior who was then 19, Maria, 16, and Pauline, 3 – from Liverpool, England, to New York, where they arrived on 7 November 1825.[7] Shortly after arriving Garcia set up the first Italian opera company in America, giving performances at the Park Theatre, starting with Rossini's *Il barbiere di Siviglia* on November 29. Garcia junior performed the part of Figaro. This was his operatic debut.

The Garcia troupe stayed in New York for almost a year, having achieved some modest financial success. When they decided to move on to Mexico City, the daughter Maria stayed behind to marry a French businessman named Francois-Eugène Malibran (1781–1836). In October 1826, the other members of the family sailed for Vera Cruz, Mexico, going on to Mexico City and staying there for two years. Sometime later Manuel

Patricio decided to leave the group because of certain differences with his father. He returned to Paris in December 1827. Eventually the family came together again in Paris when Garcia senior and the others returned there from Mexico early in 1829. Garcia senior died in Paris in 1832.

Manuel Patricio subsequently gave up the stage sometime around 1828. During this period, like many young men in their early twenties, he appeared to be unsure as to what he wanted to do with his life. He studied navigation and various other sciences and eventually, through the influence of his sister Maria Malibran who was now in Paris, he got a special position in a division of the French army that was assigned to Algeria in 1830. This experience gave him the opportunity to work at military hospitals, when he studied the anatomy and mechanism of vocal chords, probably on military casualties, which gave him the basis for his study on the physiological aspects of the human voice and larynx.

His first work on the subject of the voice was his *Mémoire sur la voix humaine*, submitted to the Academy of Sciences in Paris in November 1840.[8] This in turn led to his *Complete Treatise on the Art of Singing*, published in two parts, the first part in 1841 and part two in 1847. These writings earned him early recognition from the Academy of Sciences. His thesis subsequently became the standard reference work for vocal training in the nineteenth century, and indeed some of it principals are still used today in music schools around the world. Because of his achievements, he was invited to become a professor at the Paris Conservatoire in 1847. Early in 1848, he moved to London due to of the chaos and disruption caused by the revolution in Paris. Six years later he invented the laryngoscope – a scientific instrument used in its day for viewing the vocal chords in action. Later his writings and teaching techniques resulted in his becoming a professor at the Royal Academy of Music in London, a position he held until 1895. He died in London in 1906 at the age of 101.

By the 1840s, Garcia had established the foremost school of singing in Europe at his Paris studio. Ultimately his 'school' in Paris was managed by one of his pupils, Mathilde Marchesi (1821–1913), who in turn produced a long line of singers, many of whom became legends in their own lifetime.[9] Catherine Hayes was scheduled to meet this extraordinary man shortly after she arrived in Paris in October 1842, when she would commence her vocal studies. Garcia was 37 at the time.

A little over a year before Catherine's arrival at Garcia's studio on the Square d'Orléans in Paris, the 21-year-old Jenny Lind (1820–87) had come to Garcia in a state of vocal collapse.[10] It was probably the Italian baritone,

Giovanni Belletti (1813–90), who suggested she see Garcia. Belletti, who was 28 at the time, accompanied Lind from Sweden to France, where presumably he also had professional engagements. Initially Lind and Belletti met while they were singing together at the Royal Theatre in Stockholm where Belletti had been performing in the Italian repertoire since 1838.

By 1840, Lind had developed critical vocal problems, primarily caused by too much singing, bad technique and an over ambitious repertoire. When Jenny Lind came to Garcia for help, she had been singing in opera and operetta in Stockholm for almost four years. She had been singing roles such as Agathe in Weber's *Der Freischutz*, the title part in Bellini's *Norma* and Donna Anna in Mozart's *Don Giovanni*. These extremely heavy roles were much too taxing for a young light soprano voice.

On her departure from Sweden, Lind was given letters of introduction to a relative of the Swedish royal family then living in Paris. A reception was given shortly after her arrival and Manuel Garcia was invited to attend. Whether out of nervousness or extreme caution Lind elected to sing songs in her native Swedish language, accompanying herself on the piano. Garcia was not impressed. Her voice sounded worn, tired and rather hoarse. Garcia instantly reacted, stating that the voice was in such a condition that she should not have been singing in public, least of all to such a highly cultivated audience. Lind was totally shocked. However, Garcia's comment reinforced what she already knew – that she was in serious trouble vocally and desperately needed help. About a week later, a private meeting with Garcia was arranged for her at his studio to discuss her difficulties.

Garcia put her through a series of exercises culminating in the aria 'Perche non ho del vento?' with its difficult cabaletta, 'Torna, ah! torna, o caro oggetto', written by Donizetti for the opera *Rosmonda d'Inghilterra*, which was first performed at the Teatro della Pergola in Florence in 1834.[11] During the nineteenth century this piece (first sung by the soprano Fanny Tacchinardi-Persiani) tended to be associated more with one of Donizetti's other operas, *Lucia di Lammermoor*. It was the custom of some sopranos to replace Lucia's scena as we know it today – 'Regnava nel silenzio' and its cabaletta – with this brilliant six and a half-minute bravura aria, which ends in the vocal stratosphere, from the other Donizetti work.

Throughout most of her operatic career, Lind performed this difficult and taxing *Rosmonda* aria in *Lucia di Lammermoor* as a replacement for the original music. Later she was highly praised in London for her handling of its high tessitura and vocal requirements. However, despite the fact that she had sung Donizetti's demanding *Lucia* music many times the previous year, she apparently had great difficulty in dealing with the aria during this visit with Garcia. Being a stern disciplinarian, Garcia again reacted – perhaps he was frustrated that he had to listen to such an abused voice for a second time, simply as a favour to his Swedish friend and hostess – addressing Lind directly, stating that she had no voice left and therefore it would be useless for him to take her on as a student.

Many years later Jenny Lind mentioned to her friend and mentor, the composer Felix Mendelssohn (1809–47), that this moment – when Garcia made his predictions – was the lowest point in her life. It may well be that Garcia's pronouncements were a direct reaction to Lind's personality, which was generally considered somewhat arrogant and aloof. These were certainly two of her characteristics in later life. However, perhaps the experienced singing master saw through her personality at this point in time. In any event, Garcia stipulated that if he did take her on as a pupil she must initially be vocally silent for a period of at least six weeks, not singing a note and speaking as little as possible. There was nobody more fit to accept this challenge than Jenny Lind. Having agreed to the disciplines directed by Garcia, she turned her attention to studying French and Italian, knowing that if she was to be successful internationally as a singer she would need an understanding of these languages.

Around the middle of August, she again presented herself to Garcia at his studio on the Square d'Orléans, this time feeling more confident, given her period of rest. Garcia was satisfied with the improvement. The top of the voice was better, but the middle and lower registers still needed more work however. It was agreed that a course of two lessons a week with the maestro would commence, starting the last week of August 1841.

Over the next ten months, Lind would become Garcia's favourite pupil, appearing as the star at his student concerts. She learned rapidly, and studied with great determination and discipline. By July of 1842, Lind completely transformed, had finished her training with Europe's premier singing teacher. She decided to return to the Royal Theatre in Sweden, where she had been offered a contract. She gave her first performance as the vocally revitalised Jenny Lind on 10 October 1842 in Bellini's *Norma*, just two days before Catherine Hayes presented herself at Manuel Garcia's door at No. 6 Square d'Orléans in Paris. Lind was 22 and Catherine 24 at this point.[12]

Catherine Hayes and Jenny Lind were destined to cross paths many times during the next twenty years, in the major cities of Europe and

America. In Europe, they could be found sometimes singing the same role in the same opera in the same city on the same night! In America they tracked one another up and down the east coast and in the mid-west giving concerts in heavily packed halls and churches.

From the beginning, Catherine was acutely aware of Jenny Lind's talents. This was long before 'Lindmania' occurred in the major cities of Europe. Perhaps Garcia had instilled in Catherine some thoughts on following Lind's discipline and approach to her art. Whatever the reason, in some of her early correspondence Catherine specifically compared her voice to Lind's and even applied the Lind 'standard' when refusing to sing roles which she considered too heavy for her vocal style.

Jenny Lind was by far the most prominent Garcia student. Other successful students included his younger sister Pauline (Viardot) Garcia, who would later be a sensation in Paris, London, Dublin, St. Petersburg and other cities. Erminia Frezzolini (1818–84), a creator of Verdi roles at La Scala, Milan, was another. She also sang in Paris, Madrid, London and New York, in addition to her native Italy. Another of his students was Henriette Nissen (1819–75), a Swede who was a friend of Lind's and who became a singer in Paris, Berlin, St. Petersburg, London and Leipzig. He also taught German born Mathilde Marchesi (1821–1913), who in turn, using the Garcia technique would become the leading singing teacher in continental Europe in the second half of the century. Her successful students included such future prima donnas as Nellie Melba, Emma Eames, Susanne Adams, Mary Garden, Sybil Sanderson, Emma Calve and her own daughter Blanche.

Among others of note who studied with Garcia was Joseph Barbot, a tenor, who went on to create Charles Gounod's *Faust* in 1859 in Paris and later to become a professor at the Paris Conservatoire. Johanna Wagner was another, the composer Richard Wagner's niece, who would have a short career in Dresden, Hamburg, Berlin, London and other European cities. Her prominence probably related more to her famous uncle rather than to talents developed by Garcia.

Much later, in London, the Swedish soprano Christine Nilsson (1843–1921) took lessons from Garcia, as did the Irish bass A.J. Foli (Foley) (1835–99) who became a leading singer in London, Vienna, Dublin, New York, St. Petersburg and Sydney.[13] An American, Adelaide Phillips (1833–82) of Boston, was also a Garcia student in the early 1850s having been recommended to Garcia by Jenny Lind. However, Garcia's most important student in London was the baritone Charles Santley (1834–1922), who became very prominent in the last half of the century.[14] The French composer Charles Gounod added the baritone aria 'Even bravest hearts may swell' to his opera *Faust* for Charles Santley for an English-language production of the opera in London in 1864.[15] Santley also premiered Wagner operas in England, some with Foli, and created various roles in operas written by the Irish composer Balfe and by William V. Wallace (1812–65). Santley had a long and successful international career. As a young man he also sang with the by now well-established Catherine Hayes in the first complete English performance of Gluck's opera *Iphigenia in Tauris* in Manchester in 1860.[16] Santley became one of the few singers of the mid-nineteenth century period to live long enough to make vocal recordings some 43 years later in 1903.

Catherine Hayes was about to become another highly successful Garcia pupil. She studied with Manuel Garcia from October 1842 until March 1844. There is no known record of whether she performed during these years, nor is there any indication that Garcia permitted his students to perform publicly during their period of tuition. However, we do know that Garcia required his pupils to be proficient sight-readers of music and to be disciplined in their practice habits and the use of their voices. His thesis on singing with its endless pages of vocal exercises, supports the fact that an inept musician or a person who didn't sight-read could not have survived in his classes.[17] He expected a pupil to study the solfeggio and an instrument, in addition to singing and harmony. He believed that an understanding of harmony was essential for a singer.

At the time of Catherine's arrival in Paris in October 1842, the main operatic attraction was the Théâtre des Italiens.[18] The theatre building exists to this day in Paris and is currently used by the Banque de France as offices. During these early days in Paris in November, Catherine had the opportunity to hear Giulia Grisi again in *Norma*, this time with Henriette Nissen, a recent Garcia pupil, as Adalgisa. There was also Donizetti's *Lucrezia Borgia* with Grisi and Mario, an opera that Catherine herself would eventually sing in many different cities around the world. Other popular Donizetti operas at that time which would also enter her repertoire were *Lucia di Lammermoor* and *Maria di Rohan*. Lorenzo Salvi (1810–79), one of the tenors who was singing was destined to appear opposite Catherine when she made her London debut some years later. Just a few months after Catherine's arrival, Donizetti's new opera *Don Pasquale* had its premier at the Théâtre des Italiens in January 1843, starring Grisi, Mario and Lablache. It was a resounding success. These were exciting times for the young vocal student as she set out to become an operatic prima donna. She had come a long way from Limerick and those early days of dreaming about being a concert singer.

However, many hours of study with Manuel Garcia were still ahead before most of Catherine's dreams and ambitions would become a reality. Another year and a half would pass before she would enter the next phase of her professional career. During this time the little we know of her activity in Paris indicates that she mostly studied her vocal exercises, learned to speak French and possibly studied roles, although what those roles might have been we do not know. She did not visit Limerick during this period. In fact it would be quite a few years before she would set foot in Ireland again. Later in life, when being interviewed in Dublin and asked about her time spent as a student with Garcia in Paris, Catherine spoke of him with the greatest respect, saying specifically that 'he was the dearest, the kindest and the most generous of masters'.[19]

As 1844 approached, George Osborne told Catherine and her mother that he had accepted a post at the Royal Academy of Music in London and that he and his wife planned to move there in March of 1844.

Coincidental with this news, or perhaps because of it, came Catherine's discussion with Garcia in which he advised her that there was nothing more he could teach her. He recommended that she go to Milan, where she would have the opportunity to learn Italian and to gain professional experience as a singer. He also suggested that she should take coaching lessons with Felice Ronconi (1811–75), a prominent teacher in Milan who had excellent connections with the musical community in that city and with the music conservatory. Garcia probably had heard of Felice Ronconi through his older brother, the baritone Giorgio Ronconi (1810–90), whom he knew and who performed regularly in London and Paris during the 1840s.

Felice Ronconi's father Domenico had been director of the Italian opera in Vienna and a well-known singer in Russia and France. He had also been a teacher, first in Munich, then in Milan where he settled in 1829.[20] Felice's brother Giorgio was a celebrated baritone in Italy. Donizetti wrote a number of roles for him which premiered in major opera houses in Italy. Later Giorgio became one of the principal Verdi baritones throughout Europe and Russia. He created Verdi's *Nabucco* at La Scala and sang several other major Verdi roles. He also sang in the first performance of *Rigoletto* in England in 1853. Catherine would have the distinction of singing with him in the years ahead. Felice also had a younger brother, Sebastiano, born in Venice in 1814, who was a baritone and who performed regularly throughout Italy.

Felice studied vocal instruction with his father. He spent time in Munich and later became a professor of singing at Wurzburg and in Frankfurt, Germany. He subsequently taught in Milan from 1844 to 1848 and became a professor at the Milan Conservatoire. When revolution broke out in 1848 he went to London to join his brother Giorgio, establishing a studio there where he taught for several years. He eventually died in St. Petersburg in September 1875, where he had been a singing teacher and coach.

Garcia wrote to Felice Ronconi and made arrangements for Catherine to become his student. This was early in 1844. Catherine and her mother set off for Milan towards the end of March, just as the Osbornes departed for London. She would not see the Osbornes for another five years; however, when they next met, Catherine would be a renowned star of La Scala, Milan, and the leading opera houses in Florence, Genoa, Venice and Vienna.

At the time of Catherine's arrival in Milan in April 1844, Italy was split into several highly complex regions with greatly different controls and influences.[21] Passports were required for travel from one region to another. In the post Napoleonic period the Congress of Vienna in 1815 had created new territorial political boundaries in Europe. This had a significant impact on social and political life, which in turn affected opera houses and the censorship of new operas and librettos.

The major opera centres in Italy during these years were Milan (La Scala) and Venice (La Fenice), which were in the Habsburg Empire and controlled from Vienna. Both Milan and Venice also had several secondary opera houses. The San Carlo theatre, the premier theatre in Naples in the Kingdom of the Two Sicilies, was controlled by the titled Bourbon family. Tuscany's principal operatic centre was at the Teatro Pergola in Florence, which was managed by Alessandro Lanari, a powerful impresario during those pre-Risorgimento days in Italy. Genoa in the Piedmont region had the Teatro Carlo Felice, which was also important. Rome, controlled by the Papal States, had the Apollo theatre as well as several others. Beyond these locations there were other regional operatic centres.

La Scala was run by Bartolemeo Merelli (1794–1879), who was born in Bergamo, in northern Italy. He had been a music student of Simon Mayr (1763–1845), in classes that included the young composer Gaetano Donizetti (1797–1848). Merelli was an astute businessman who ran La Scala with a tight rein. His word was law. In time Catherine would come to know Merelli well and would sing under his management. Merelli ran the opera at La Scala from 1829 to 1850, where he staged Verdi's first opera. He also had a financial interest and partnership in the principal opera theatre in Vienna, the Kärntnertortheater, which was managed by one of his business associates, Carlo Balochino. After 1850 Merelli spent some time in Vienna. However, he eventually returned to La Scala, which he managed again from 1861 to 1863. He died in Milan in 1879.

In 1841, Merelli became very interested in the budding 28-year-old Giuseppe Verdi (1813–1901). He recognised Verdi's unique talent and potential, but he was also sympathetic to the young composer because of the tragic death of Verdi's young wife Margherita (1814–40) in June 1840 and of their two young children sometime earlier. However, his prime interest in Verdi was economic. As an experienced operatic impresario, he recognised Verdi as an important emerging talent and knew his compositions represented a real opportunity for profit. Merelli's erratic style of management ultimately resulted in the deterioration of his relationship with the composer, and by 1845 Verdi was virtually 'at war' with the La Scala impresario on matters relating to the quality of the production of his operas at La Scala.[22] In time, Verdi turned elsewhere – to Venice, Florence, Naples and Paris – to premiere his new works. He wanted no part of Rome and the Vatican, and it would be years before another of his works would premiere at La Scala, by which time Merelli was long since gone from the scene.

In those days the north of Italy as we know it today, including the provinces of Lombardy and Venetia, was controlled from Vienna by the Habsburgs, with Milan and Venice being the most important cities in the region. The Piedmont region was controlled by the House of Savoy, which also had jurisdiction over the island of Sardinia. The Parma area was a separate duchy and had its own opera house. Milan was an Austrian stronghold. It was also the most important city in Italy for the Habsburg empire, because virtually one-third of the empire's revenue came from the province of Lombardy.[23] In Italy the empire's holdings stretched as far as Milan in the west and Venice in the east. There were thousands of Austrian troops garrisoned in Milan around this time and its economy and social life were greatly affected by their presence.

Italy's leading operatic composers, Rossini, Donizetti and Bellini, had made Paris their place of residence several years earlier, because it was more conducive to their needs and did not have the censorship restrictions which prevailed extensively in the various Italian kingdoms, from Naples to Milan, from Venice to Genoa. By the time Catherine arrived in Italy, Bellini was dead, Rossini was in retirement and it wouldn't be too long before Donizetti was afflicted with an incurable disease. He too would die four years later. Of these three renowned composers Catherine would only have the privilege of meeting Rossini. However, she would also become friendly with two other established composers of the period, Federico Ricci (1804–77) and Saverio Mercadante (1795–1890). We do not know for sure if she ever met Verdi. However, any soprano in her position would probably have been interested to meet so famous a musical personality. They could have met in Milan or Florence in the mid 1840s, since both of them were in these cities around the same period. It is possible that Verdi may have seen her in an opera, since she was singing in Milan when he spent time there towards the end of 1845 and again during September 1846.

Verdi's first opera *Oberto* had its premiere at La Scala in 1839. He received a commission from La Scala's director to write three more operas. His next opera, *Un giorno di regno*, performed in 1840, was a failure and was withdrawn. Success came with *Nabucco*, his third work, which had its premiere performance at La Scala in March 1842, when Verdi was 28. It was an astounding success due in part to the choral piece, 'Va pensiero sull'ali dorate', which had strong nationalistic appeal to the people of occupied Lombardy. Even to this day 'Va pensiero' can rouse an Italian audience to a frenzy.

Curiously Verdi's destiny was probably determined by his opera *Nabucco*, as the recent loss of his family had caused him to renounce composition. The *Nabucco* libretto had first been rejected by the then popular German composer Otto Nicolai (1810–1849), who was living in Vienna. Merelli felt that the story had strong emotional appeal and should be set to music. And at his insistence, Verdi eventually agreed to read the libretto in 1841 even though he was still in a state of deep emotional depression. The scenes of the Hebrew slaves in chains on the banks of the Euphrates reflecting on their return to the homeland had such a strong emotional effect on Verdi that he agreed to set the libretto to music, and so the opera *Nabucco* was created.

Giorgio Ronconi sang the title role of *Nabucco* at its premiere at La Scala on 9 March 1842 and Verdi's future wife Giuseppina Strepponi (1815–97) sang the principal soprano role. After *Nabucco*, Verdi had another success at La Scala in 1843, *I Lombardi*, in which former Garcia pupil Erminia Frezzolini, then 25 years old, created the part of Giselda.

Frezzolini had also studied with Felice Ronconi in Milan some years before Catherine arrived there.

About the same time that Catherine and her mother arrived in Milan in April 1844, Emanuel Muzio (1821–90), Verdi's only pupil and assistant, also arrived there to take up his studies with Maestro Verdi.[24] Within a short time Muzio and Catherine would meet. Muzio was born in Parma and it was through the influence of Verdi's father-in-law Antonio Barezzi that Muzio managed to become assistant to Verdi in April 1844 in Milan. Over the next few years Muzio helped Verdi with the preparation of various operas, including *Macbeth* in Florence in 1847 and *I Masnadieri* for London in 1847. From the time of his arrival in Milan and for many years after Muzio would write detailed letters to Verdi's father-in-law, Barezzi, about Verdi's thoughts and opinions, both political and musical. Towards the end of 1846, one of these letters mentions Verdi's possible interest in Catherine for *I Masnadieri*.[25] This was an opera that Verdi had agreed to write for Benjamin Lumley (1811–1875), the London impresario who managed 'Her Majesty's theatre'. Verdi had also agreed that he would conduct the premiere. It would be his first visit to London and Muzio would accompany him.

Muzio by this time was more than just a pupil of Verdi; he travelled with him and also helped him with operatic productions. Muzio had a long active life that included becoming a conductor and travelling extensively in Europe, America and to places as far apart as Egypt and Cuba. It was also Muzio's privilege to conduct the first performance of Verdi's *Aida* in America in 1873, five years after its world premiere in Cairo in Egypt. He also had the distinction of conducting the first performance of *La Forza del Destino* in France in 1876. Muzio died in Paris in November 1890, eleven years before his famous Maestro would succumb in Milan in 1901.

When Catherine arrived in Milan early in 1844, Felice Ronconi was associated with Milan's Royal Conservatory as a professor of singing. However, Catherine studied with him privately, probably because she would have been too old to enter the Conservatory, even at her recently acquired 'theatrical age' of 18.[26] This was the same institution that had refused Verdi thirteen years earlier because the student composer was too old at eighteen! Ironically, the Conservatory now bears Verdi's name.

The Ronconi family name was famous in Europe, and as a result Felice's pupils included some of the best young talent in Italy, such as Erminia Frezzolini, who was now a professional singer, and Teresa Parodi (1827–?), who had just started studying with him. Parodi was a dramatic soprano from Genoa who became the protégée and adopted daughter of Giuditta Pasta. She later studied the role of Norma under Pasta's guidance. Later in London, Parodi became prominent in opera and shared the concert stage with Catherine. Parodi also performed in New York and other American cities in the 1850's. Ronconi's next prominent pupil was Matilde Marchesi, who arrived in Milan at Garcia's recommendation a few years later.

Ronconi's method of coaching included giving his pupils the opportunity to perform in public in the presence of various leading citizens, musicians and singers. This was a good grounding for the real world of performing in opera. He also had a close relationship with Giovanni Ricordi (1785–1853), the founder of the Ricordi Music publishing firm who sponsored musical concerts.

Catherine had been working with Ronconi for almost a year – studying operatic roles by Bellini, Donizetti and Rossini. By this time she had about five roles in her repertoire when she first appeared at a public concert in Milan early in 1845. The former prima donna Giuseppina Grassini (1773–1850), who was also an aunt of the reigning prima donna in London and Paris, Giulia Grisi happened to be present at this concert. Grassini was one of La Scala's leading performers during the 1790s, creating many operatic roles. In the early 1800s she sang for Napoleon Bonaparte after one of his victories in Italy and as a result was invited to Paris. She sang there at functions sponsored by Napoleon, much to the concern of his wife Josephine. Napoleon subsequently made her the director of the Paris opera. She also went on to sing at the Italian opera in London in 1804, after which she returned to the continent to sing first in Paris and then in Italy. Grassini died in her home town of Varese near Milan in 1850.

When Catherine sang at the concert in Milan in Februrary 1845, Grassini was 72 and had long since retired. However, she was still an important figure on the musical scene in Milan. Grassini was so impressed with Catherine's performance that she suggested to Ronconi that Catherine should be allowed to perform in opera. Grassini recommended the Marseilles Italian opera, where the director, Giuseppe Provini, was a personal friend. Ronconi felt that Catherine was about ready and agreed to Grassini contacting Provini to set up an audition. By coincidence, Provini was in need of a new soprano for his spring season, which was due to commence in May 1845 with operas by Bellini, Donizetti and Rossini, so, instead of asking Catherine to come to Marseilles for an audition, he went to Milan to meet her.

Provini arrived in Milan early in March 1845. After he had auditioned Catherine at Ronconi's studio he offered her three leading roles for the new season at the Théâtre Grand in Marseilles. Her partners for these performances would be established vocalists of the day. Her debut role would be Elvira in Bellini's *I Puritani*, which had had its premiere in Paris ten years earlier, with Giulia Grisi in the lead soprano role. Catherine was now progressing towards her goal. Before the year was over she would be singled out by the local musical press in Milan as Ronconi's brightest performer.

At this moment in time, Catherine must have thought back to the day a few years previously at Morrison's Hotel in Dublin when she had timidly suggested to Lablache that she would sing an aria from *I Puritani*. Now she found herself about to sing this beautiful but difficult opera on stage in costume before an audience. It seemed that all her dreams were coming true.

She spent the next few months preparing for her debut role. The second opera she had to sing in Marseilles was Rossini's *Mosè*, which was first performed in Naples in 1818. A year later, Rossini had made changes to his original score and in 1827 he again altered the score for a Paris production. The third opera she had to prepare was Donizetti's *Lucia di Lammermoor*, an opera she would sing in many of the great opera houses in Europe in the future.

When Catherine set out for Marseilles in April 1845 she was accompanied by her mother, and, while we don't know who else was with her, it is probable that Ronconi would have travelled with his outstanding pupil for her operatic debut.

The Marseilles Italian opera was the second most important centre in France after Paris. It was greatly influenced by its proximity to Milan and La Scala. The singers who performed there were generally seasoned performers who had built reputations in Milan, Venice, Rome and Paris. The first Verdi opera to be heard on French soil was *Nabucco*. It received its French premiere in Marseilles in August 1845 during this same season in which Catherine was about to make her debut. It was almost three months later before it was presented in Paris.

Catherine's debut as Elvira in *I Puritani* was scheduled for Saturday May 10 1845. Her Arturo for was tenor Andrea Castellan (1812–?), who was born in Vicenza, Italy, and who had just created the principal tenor role in Giovanni Pacini's opera *Lorenzino di Medici* the previous March in Venice. Castellan was also a frequent singer at La Scala. Adolphe Alizard

(1814–50), bass, was assigned the role of Giorgio in the performance. He was born in Paris and had a ten-year history of singing leading roles. During the same season and a few months after the *I Puritani* performance he was scheduled to sing the part of Zaccaria in the first performance of Verdi's *Nabucco* in France at the same theatre in Marseilles. The *I Puritani* baritone part of Riccardo was sung by Odoardo Ventura and the smaller bass part of Walton was sung by Angelo Alba, who had appeared in several Donizetti operas in Italy since 1840.

By this time Catherine had matured considerably. Her voice range was now almost two and a half octaves. She was able to speak French, having learned it during her year and a half in Paris, so Marseilles did not present too difficult a task. She also spoke some Italian but was not yet proficient at writing it. However, she was be able to communicate with director Provini and other members of the opera in Marseilles including the cast, who were either Italian or French.

Saturday 10 May soon came round. Catherine prepared herself all day feeling secure in her knowledge of the music but nervous about her impending stage appearance and all the things she had to remember relating to movement, entrances and exits and of course musical entry cues. Her mother was backstage and the opera house which held about 1,100 people was crowded to capacity, all anxious to hear the new prima donna. As she made her entrance in the duet 'O amato zio, o mio secondo padre' with Giorgio the bass, her mind must have flashed back to the time in Dublin a little over four years earlier when she sang this very same music for the first time with Lablache. She felt just as nervous now as she had then, despite all her years of study and training.

Later, when recalling these moments, Catherine would say that she felt a slight faintness, thinking perhaps that she would not be able to make it through the performance.[27] She awaited the reaction from the audience, however, just like the incredible Lablache audition in Dublin a few years earlier, there was nothing but silence from the audience – no recognition, no acknowledgement that they accepted her, nothing to tell her how she was doing, just a solemn silence. When she finished the twelve-minute scene with Giorgio she made her exit and was met by her mother in the wings, was assured her that she had done wonderfully; however, the lack of spontaneous applause – something Catherine had become used to at her various concerts – made her very confused. She had some time to gather her thoughts, as the next scene included the arrival of the tenor and his great entrance aria and quartet 'A te, o cara', in which she would join with the three other principals.

Still feeling faint and nervous at her next solo entry, 'Ah! . . . Son vergin vezzosa in vesta di sposa', she made a determined effort to overcome her nerves by singing these words with greater strength and conviction than she had ever done at rehearsal. Suddenly there was loud applause from all parts of the house. This immediately broke the tension and made her realise that her nervousness had prevented her from projecting her voice and artistry earlier.[28] The applause gave her the confidence she needed to build on her singing and performance. The audience continued to acknowledge her loudly, eventually showering the stage with flowers after her big aria 'Qui la voce' and at the end of the performance. Her debut night, which had started out as having the makings of a disaster because of her nerves and inexperience, turned into a triumph as she learned to conquer the problems most singers experience, particularly on opening nights.

The musical press reported briefly on this debut performance, recognising her youth, nervousness and ultimate recovery as the night went on, stating that 'Caterina Hayes a young prima donna of Irish nationality had high success . . . with a voice of delicious quality.'[29] And indeed her success was even greater with her next performances in *Lucia di Lammermoor* and in Rossini's *Mosè*. In all, she performed several times each week over the next three months. At the season's end, Provini, who had connections with the Italian opera in Paris, offered her a contract for the Théâtre des Italiens in that city.

Catherine, almost always the perfectionist, felt that she was not really ready for a Paris audience and decided to return to Milan to continue her coaching with Ronconi. At the time she made this decision she did not realise how important her return to Milan would be and how it would set her on a new road to success as a prima donna assoluta at Italy's most important opera houses.

CHAPTER FOUR

La Scala – Debut

MILAN, VENICE AND VIENNA 1845–1846

O N HER RETURN to Milan, Catherine found that Ronconi had scheduled her to sing at a concert, 'Mattinata Musicale', which was sponsored by Giovanni Ricordi, the founder of the music publishing empire of the same name. At that time, Ricordi had among other musical properties exclusive rights to publishing Verdi's operas in Italy. The concert was scheduled for Saturday 6 September 1845 at the home of Giovanni Ricordi. Other participants included the very young Angiolina Bosio (1830–59), soprano, Domenico Lorini (1820–?), tenor, and Domenico Coletti, a baritone who was the younger brother of Filippo Coletti, a prominent baritone and international artist.

The artists' repertoire for the concert included arias by Rossini, Bellini, Donizetti, Mercadante, Verdi, Nini and Salvi. We don't know who sang which composer's music but it can be assumed that Catherine, having just returned from her first success in Marseilles in *I Puritani* and *Lucia di Lammermoor*, in all probability sang arias from these operas. It also appears that as an encore, she sang an aria from Alessandro Nini's (1805–80) opera *La Marescialla d'Ancre* with the composer accompanying her on the piano. A week later the *Gazetta Musicale di Milano* reported on the concert as follows:

> C. Hayes, an Irishwoman, was the star who dominated, the voice and tone clear and well produced, nice and with a seductive figure. Voice agile, and pronunciation [of Italian] for a foreigner a great deal rare. Felice Ronconi's favourite and a favourite in Marseilles too . . . maestro Nini accompanied her in his music from *Marescialla d'Ancre*.[1]

Verdi was in Milan with Muzio during this period working on the score of a new opera, *Attila*. However, it's doubtful that he would have attended a student concert even if it was at the home of his publisher and friend Giovanni Ricordi.[2] Bartolemeo Merelli, director of La Scala, did however attend the concert and immediately recognised Catherine's talents. He offered her a contract for the La Scala season then in progress. Catherine was overwhelmed, and she spoke with Ronconi to seek his advice about her readiness for such a debut. Inwardly she felt that she had gained enough confidence to sing at La Scala, yet in Marseilles she had hesitated to accept director Provini's offer to perform in Paris – partially because she knew that Paris was then the pinnacle of opera in Europe and she had her doubts about appearing there without more experience in Italy. However, La Scala would be different and she would have Ronconi close by to help with her coaching, whereas in Paris she would have been on her own, except for her mother. In addition, Merelli was an important man and it would be difficult not to accept his offer. So she convinced herself that the time was right, she would sing at La Scala.

Later in the week it was decided that she should sing either a Bellini or, preferably, a Donizetti opera – one that suited her vocal style, ensuring that she would be successful. Merelli suggested Donizetti's *Linda di Chamounix*, which had been performed at La Scala the previous year and which he felt would be ideal for Catherine's voice and physical appearance.

Linda di Chamounix is a similar opera to Bellini's popular and lyrical *La Sonnambula*, which Catherine had learned the previous year. Eugenia Tadolini (b.1809) had created the title role in *Linda di Chamounix* in Vienna in May 1842.[3] Donizetti had written the role especially for Tadolini, who was 33 years old at the time. Later in the same year it had its first performance in Italy, but Tadolini did not take part. However, she did star in it again with great success in Naples in 1843 and at La Scala in March 1844, just before Catherine arrived in Milan.

The role of Linda was ideal for Catherine. It was lyrical, had hauntingly beautiful music with arias for the soprano, including a mad scene, and duets with the tenor. It was well within her range. She immediately set to work with Ronconi to learn the part completely before the first La Scala rehearsal. Catherine was always a fast learner, this was to be of great benefit to her throughout her career. Her debut date was set for 4 November 1845. Included in the cast was Elena d'Angri, (b.1821), the Pierotto a 24 year old contralto from Greece who had been singing regularly at La Scala since her debut there the previous year. Catherine would meet her again in Vienna and in London. The tenor, Giuseppe Sinico was cast in the role of Carlo. He had sung at La Scala earlier in the season, in Bellini's *La Sonnambula* and as Arnold in Rossini's *GuigielmoTell*, in addition to Almaviva in Rossini's *Il Barbiere di Siviglia*. The principal baritone part of Antonio was assigned to Achille De Bassini (1819–1881), who was then 26 years old. During the 1845 season at La Scala, De Bassini sang the title role in Rossini's *Guigielmo Tell*, Carlo in Verdi's *Ernani* and the Doge in *I Due Foscari*, which he had created the year before in Rome. In later years he created major roles in three other Verdi operas[4] and also sang in London and St. Petersburg. Other members of the cast included the distinguished young bass-baritone, Giuseppe Francesco Beneventano (1824–80), in the part of Il Prefetto, he was then 21 years old and had made his debut the year before in Naples in *Linda di Chamounix*, going on to sing extensively in Italy, Austria, Spain, England, America, Mexico and Cuba.[5] Beneventano and Catherine were scheduled to sing again at La Scala in the near future. Cesare Soares, a baritone, was the Marchese, a role he would repeat in other cities, including Donizetti's home town of Bergamo eight months later in mid 1846. While all of these performers were in the early stages of their careers, only Catherine was the true debutante that night in 1845 at Milan's greatest theatre.

The La Scala audience eagerly awaited the new prima donna on Tuesday 4 November 1845. The opening strains of the opera's short overture commenced, and shortly afterwards the chorus opened with 'Presti! al tempio!' followed by the entrance of Linda's mother and father, while Catherine waited anxiously in the wings for her entrance cue at the opening of the third scene. As Linda enters she reflects on her times with Carlo whom she loves. After the introductory verses she throws away her cares about the fact that they both are penniless and breaks into the sparkling cavatina 'O luce di quest' anima' as she thinks about their love and future together. This piece provided Catherine with brilliant music to display her vocal technique and set the mood for the evening's performance. This gem of an aria was not in the first performance of the opera in Vienna. Donizetti subsequently wrote it for Fanny Persiani for her performance at the Théâtre des Italiens in Paris in November 1842, after which it became a standard.[6]

This new production in Milan created quite a sensation. According to the *La Fama* newspaper, Catherine's performance revived memories of the role's creator, Tadolini, who was idolised a year earlier.[7] The *Gazetta Musicale di Milano* went on to feature Catherine's performance in an extensive front-page article, with her name in the headline.[8] The critic praised her singing and mentioned the fact that she was from Ireland.

During the next few weeks fifteen performances of *Linda di Chamounix* were given, Catherine sang in all of them.

Milan saw a great growth in foreign singing students during this period. There were several English born singers and students using Milan as their base while singing in Turin, Verona, Piacenza and various other towns in the region. There was regular coverage of the activities in the region in the English musical press, particularly when it related to 'English' performers.[9] The London musical press by this time was aware of Catherine's presence in Milan, sometimes calling her an 'English woman' and at other times calling her 'Irish' or 'a soprano from these islands'.[10] Shortly after her debut, the London *Musical World*, reporting on the event, incorrectly stated that the opera was *La Sonnambula*, not *Linda di Chamounix*. The critic went on to say:

> A Miss Hayes, a soprano vocalist, native of Ireland, has made a great sensation as prima donna at the Scala, in *La Sonnambula*.[11]

Catherine's professional career was now successfully launched. As her Linda performances progressed Merelli approached her about singing other roles including Rossini's *Otello* for the opening of the *Carnivale* season on 26 December 1845. Rossini's *Otello* had first been performed in Naples in 1816. Isabella Colbran (1785–1845), who would later become Rossini's wife, took the part of Desdemona at the premiere. The title role of *Otello*, a fiendishly difficult part, was for a tenor voice with an exceptionally high vocal range. The part of Desdemona is long and dramatic. Unlike Verdi's opera of the same name which had its premiere over 70 years later, all but one of the male roles in Rossini's opera are for tenor voices. Rossini's opera soon gained popularity and was performed in the major cities in Italy and, during the next six years, in the capitals of Europe. Manuel Garcia senior produced it during his New York opera season in 1826, taking on the role of Otello himself at its premiere in the new world.

Rossini's *Otello* presented a new challenge for Catherine. It was totally different from *Linda di Chamounix*, in terms of musical style, and from the other operas in her repertoire. The role of Desdemona did not require the same lyrical agility as Linda's music; however, overall the opera was much longer and more dramatic. Catherine would be required to be on stage for longer periods and to sing in extended solos and concerted numbers with the other principals.

Her training with Garcia had placed strong emphasis on musical skills and the ability to understand musical construction as it related to vocal technique. This would be helpful in learning a new and more musically complex opera. She consulted with Ronconi about learning the role. She felt that the part was within her vocal range and training and was excited at the thought of singing another major role at La Scala, particularly for the opening night of the *Carnivale* season. However, she was cautious, perhaps because her time with Garcia in Paris had immediately followed the Lind vocal crisis. She also had concerns about the dramatic aspects of the role. As her letters would later show, Garcia had instilled in her a strong sense of awareness of potential damage to the voice by singing the wrong music.[12] As a result, during her early years as a professional singer she consistently refused roles which she felt were outside her range or vocal style. Ronconi agreed to coach her for the role of Desdemona.

The *Carnivale* season in Italy generally started on 26 December and lasted until the beginning of Lent, a period of about six weeks or so. Each year it marked the opening of the new opera season at the major centres in Italy. It was the custom to start the season with a serious opera. In this 1845–46 *Carnivale* season at La Scala, Catherine would have the distinction of singing on the opening night in Rossini's dramatic opera, *Otello*. Fourteen performances were scheduled, But, despite the care and attention she had given to learning the role of Desdemona and despite Ronconi's coaching, it was not a successful undertaking for her. She was partnered by Giuseppe Sinico, who sang the part of Otello. Rodrigo was played by the tenor Giuseppe Perelli, and, strangely, the tenor role of Iago was performed by a baritone, Giuseppe Francesco Beneventano. This casting may have exemplified the problems that Verdi had encountered with Merelli and his productions at La Scala.

A few days after the performance, the *Gazetta Musicale di Milano* critic wrote an extensive article on the performances, in which he questioned the wisdom of adapting the tenor part of Iago to the basso cantata voice of Beneventano. Additionally, he went on to comment on Catherine's interpretation of Desdemona, saying that, while she sang well, she was not yet really ready for the role of Desdemona, and saying further that she did not have the volume or energy for the part.[13]

Sometime later the London musical press reported on this opening night and on Catherine in particular, saying that:

> Miss Hayes who made such a brilliant debut, a few months since, in *Linda di Chamounix* appeared as Desdemona, and made a decided fiasco . . . [14]

Catherine's next role for Merelli was in *Anna Bolena* by Donizetti, which took place on 20 January 1846. Catherine performed the part of Giovanna Seymour and Emilia Scotta sang the title role. There were a total of four performances of *Anna Bolena*. Since Catherine's role was secondary, there was not any significant press about her performance.

Federico Ricci (1804–77), an established composer who was born in Naples and who had composed his first opera jointly with his brother Luigi in 1835, had met Catherine during this La Scala season and was impressed with her performance in *Linda di Chamounix*. While Ricci had also written other operas for Naples, Venice and Trieste, his first venture at La Scala was in 1839 with *Un Duello sotto Richelieu*, which led to other new works in Florence and in Milan again in 1841.[15] By 1845 Ricci was well established on the operatic circuit in Italy; his name was also known in Paris and Vienna. Towards the close of 1845 he had suggested to Catherine and Merelli that he would like to write an opera for her based on a libretto by Francesco Maria Piave (1810–76), Verdi's friend and one of his librettists. Piave had written the librettos for *Ernani*, *I Due Foscari* and *Attila*, and in the future would produce librettos for *Macbeth*, *Rigoletto* and *La Forza del Destino*. Verdi and Piave remained lifelong friends.

The new Ricci opera would be called *Estella di Murcia*. The premiere was scheduled at La Scala for 21 February 1846, with Catherine creating the title role of Donna Estella, daughter of the Conte di Tavora. Other members of the cast included three of her partners from her debut night at La Scala – the bass-baritone Beneventano in the role of Don Enrico Paceco, Conte di Tavora, Donna Estella's father; De Bassini as Don Fernando, Sinico as Don Diego Tellez and Napoleone Marconi as Benedetto, a comprimario part. The opera had a dramatic text and was set in Spain in 1370 in the town of Murcia close to Toledo. However, it was not a great success with the La Scala audience, despite its cast and Ricci's reputation. It only ran for four performances. Ricci did manage to salvage his work by having enough influence with Merelli and his connections in Vienna to have it performed there a little over a year later with Catherine again in the title role. This time it ran for ten performances during April and May 1847. Apparently the Viennese audiences found it more interesting than their La Scala counterparts.

After her first premiere at La Scala, Catherine sang in Saverio Mercadante's (1795–1870) very successful opera *Il Bravo* on 11 March 1846, taking over the heavier soprano role of Teodora from Paulina Calcagno

ESTELLA

MELODRAMMA SERIO

DI FRANCESCO MARIA PIAVE

POSTO IN MUSICA DAL SIG. M.º

Federico Ricci

DA RAPPRESENTARSI

NELL' I. R. TEATRO ALLA SCALA

IL CARNEVALE DEL 1846.

Milano

TIPOGRAFIA VALENTINI E C.

Cont. de' Borromei, n. 2848.

PERSONAGGI — ATTORI

PERSONAGGI	ATTORI
D. ENRICO PACECO, conte di Tavora, gran Maestro di Calatrava	sig. *Beneventano G*
Donna ESTELLA, sua figlia	sig.ª *Hayes Caterine*
D. FERDINANDO, marchese di Villaflor	sig. *De-Bassini Ac*
D. DIEGO TELLEZ, marchese di Guescar	sig. *Sinico Giusepp*
BENEDETTO, suo scudiero	sig. *Marconi Napol*
LELIO, scudiero di Villaflor	sig. *Lodi Giuseppe*
FRANCESCA, governante di Estella	sig.ª *Ruggeri Teresa*

CORI

Cittadini di Murcia e Cavalieri Spagnuoli
Parenti ed amici di Paceco - Guerrieri Mori
Ancelle di Estella - Dame Spagnuole.

Comparse

Cavalieri - Scudieri - Paggi e servi di Paceco
Cavalieri - Scudieri e Paggi di Tellez
Scudieri - Paggi - Servi e Guardie di Villaflor
Paggi di Estella - Soldati Mori.

Scena la città di Murcia e suoi dintorni.

Epoca l'anno 1370 circa.

NB. Tra il primo ed il secondo atto corron tre mes
Si è scritto Paceco in luogo di Pacheco.

Le scene d'architettura sono inventate e dipinte dai sig
MERLO ALESSANDRO e FONTANA GIOVANNI; e quelle di
saggio dal sig. MERLO suddetto.

---

6. Programme for the opera *Estella*, which was especially written for Catherine Hayes by F. Ricci and premiered at La Scala, Milan during the 1846 season. (Author's collection).

who was indisposed. Catherine sang all five performances of the opera that season.

Mercadante was born near Bari in southern Italy. Over his lifetime he composed about 60 operas, many of which were very successful in their day. However he was eventually overshadowed by Verdi and, with the exception of *Il Bravo*, which premiered at La Scala in March 1839, and four or five other works, his operas are rarely heard today. Catherine came to know him personally. Her first introduction to his music, however, was the performance of *Il Bravo* at La Scala in March 1846. The cast once again included the baritone Beneventano, the soprano R. Basso-Borio was Violetta, Masset, a bass, sang the title role and the tenor Labocetta was Pisano. The opera had a good reception and Catherine moved another step forward in her professional career.

By now Catherine's name was known in Italy's major operatic centres. The English community in Milan, with whom she mixed freely, thought highly of her. A number of the English singers who were performing in Milan during this period were destined to linkup with Catherine again, in various parts of the world, as her career progressed.

Federico Ricci was so impressed with her performance in *Estella* that he told her he wanted to write another opera for her. Catherine realised the importance of this offer, so she graciously accepted. Over a year would pass before the opera would actually be completed. In the meantime, Merelli made arrangements for Catherine to travel to Vienna and to participate in the opera season there.

Catherine arrived in Vienna early in April 1846 having completed her season at La Scala. Her next performances would be at the renowned Kärntnertortheater, Vienna's premier theatre, where the audience was every bit as critical as that of La Scala. Today the famous Sacher Hotel stands where the theatre stood in those days. Four years earlier, in May 1842, Donizetti had arrived in Vienna to finalise arrangements for the premiere of his new opera, *Linda di Chamounix*, at the Karntnertortheater. Catherine was aware that Donizetti was well known in Vienna and his operas had been popular there for many years. For her debut role there she selected Donizetti's most famous opera, *Lucia di Lammermoor*. It was one of Catherine's most ambitious moves to date. She was now more self-assured and wanted to take on a soprano role that would give her scope to display her talents. Donizetti's great masterpiece was designed to do exactly that. It was almost a year since Catherine had last sung the opera, in Marseilles, so she needed to work with Ronconi before proceeding to

Vienna. She spent most of March perfecting the role so that she would be successful with her Viennese audience. Little did she know how successful she would in fact be in Vienna.

Catherine's debut in Donizetti's great tragic opera took place on Thursday 23 April 1846. Twenty-four hours earlier Jenny Lind also made her debut in Vienna at the Theater an der Wien, in Bellini's *Norma*.[16] Vienna was rich in talent that week.

The supporting cast for Catherine included Gaetano Fraschini (1816–87) as Edgardo.[17] Fraschini was born in Pavia and had made his debut in 1837 in Donizetti's *Gemma di Vergy*. He was one of the most renowned singers of the time and very much in demand. Composers eagerly sought him for new operas. He created several principal tenor roles in operas by the leading composers – Pacini, Donizetti and Verdi.. He was one of the new breed of tenors called 'tenore di forza' and was widely known in Italy as the 'tenore della maledizione' because of the dramatic manner in which he delivered Edgardo's 'curse' in the pre-nuptial scene in *Lucia di Lammermoor*. Later in his career Fraschini sang most of the major Verdi roles, including creating the tenor part in *La Battaglia di Legnano* in Rome in 1849 and Riccardo in the premiere of *Un ballo in Maschera* in 1859 in Rome. Other members of this distinguished Viennese cast of *Lucia di Lammermoor*, included Filippo Coletti (1811–94) as Enrico.[18] At the time of this performance Coletti was 35 years old. He too had created of important roles such as the principal baritone part in Donizetti's *Caterina Cornario* in Naples in 1844. In 1845 he created Guzmano in Verdi's *Alzira*. Agostino Rodas sang the bass role of Raimondo, Giulio Soldi sang the second tenor part of Arturo and Eliza Friedberg the role of Alisa, Lucia's attendant.

The Viennese audience would have to attend the opera two nights in succession if they wanted to be at the opening night for each of the prima donnas. Lind of course was by far the most famous, although the more desirable theatre in Vienna at the time was the 'Karntnertortheater. However, neither of the two prima donnas had to worry, as both houses were sold out. Reviews for Catherine's *Lucia di Lammermoor* indicate that she was slightly nervous at the opening but went on to offer an exciting performance. She gave fifteen performances of Donizetti's opera over the next twelve weeks. Jenny Lind triumphed as usual, though not competing directly with Catherine in the same opera. Manuel Garcia was well represented in Vienna during these extraordinary weeks and he would have been very proud of these two exceptional former students.

Catherine wrote to friends in Paris and Limerick to say that she was 'intoxicated by such unexpected success'. In addition to *Lucia di Lammermoor* she sang in Mercadante's *Il Giuramento*, a dramatic opera that had been composed for La Scala in 1837. There were five performances of this opera, the last of which was given during the third week in June 1846. Catherine's season ended very successfully in Vienna with a final performance of *Lucia di Lammermoor* on 29 June to a packed house.

Her first six months as a professional opera singer in 1846 had been a whirlwind of nonstop activity between Milan and Vienna. She decided to take a rest before her next appearance, which would be at La Scala in September. Catherine spent the next month in Vienna with friends. Jenny Lind stayed in Vienna until 27 May, when she departed for Frankfurt in Germany.

Since it was not uncommon for one prima donna to attend the performance of another, there is a good probability that Catherine may have seen Lind in *Norma* or one of the other roles she sang in *La Sonnambula* and *Der Freischutz*. After all, Catherine had heard much about Lind from Manuel Garcia and this would have been the first opportunity she had to actually see her perform. It was also, of course, possible though less likely that Lind paid a visit to one of Catherine's performances. Both of them would have many opportunities to meet and hear each other sing over the next fifteen years.

By this time Lind was very self-assured. Apart from her unique vocal talent, her two great mentors, Felix Mendelssohn (1809–1847) and the prominent operatic composer Giacomo Meyerbeer (1791–1864), provided stability for her and introduced her to important people in the musical world. By now Lind was greatly in demand at the major musical centres in Europe, but, for personal reasons, she had elected not to sing in Paris or Italy.

By the end of July Catherine was back in Milan. News of her success in Vienna had preceded her. Merelli was pleased, since he had reserved the opening night of the autumn season for her. This was scheduled to start in September with the four-act version of Rossini's *Mosè in Egitto*. The bass Ignazio Marini (1811–73), who was scheduled to play the part of Moses in the performance, was 35 years old and had been singing at La Scala since 1833. He was considered the best bass singer in Italy, after Lablache, who was now spending most of his time in London and Paris. Marini had created the title roles in Verdi's *Oberto* in 1839 at La Scala and in *Attila* in Venice in 1846. Throughout his long career, Marini sang extensively in Italy, Austria, England, Russia, and America and in Havana, Cuba. The

MOSÈ

MELODRAMMA SACRO IN QUATTRO ATTI

DA RAPPRESENTARSI

NELL' I. R. TEATRO ALLA SCALA

L'AUTUNNO DEL 1846.

Milano

TIPOGRAFIA VALENTINI E C.

Cont. de' Borromei, N. 2848.

PERSONAGGI	ATTORI
Mosè, Legislatore degli Ebrei	sig. MARINI IGNAZIO
Elisero, suo fratello	sig. POCHINI RANIERI
Faraone, Re d'Egitto	sig. DE BREUL STEFANO
Aménofi, suo figlio	sig. MEI LUIGI
Aufide, Uffiziale egizio	sig. MARCONI NAPOLEONE
Osiride, Sacerdote d'Iside	sig. LODETTI FRANCESCO
Maria, sorella di Mosè	sig.ª RUGGERI TERESA
Anaide, sua figlia	sig.ª HAYES CATERINA
Sinaide, moglie di Faraone	sig.ª JANNICH ANNA
Una voce misteriosa.	

CORI E COMPARSE

Ebrei - Madianiti - Egiziani - Sacerdoti d'Iside
Guardie e Soldati di Faraone.

La scena è in Egitto.

Musica del Maestro signor ROSSINI.

Le scene dell'opera e ballo per quelle d'architettura sono inventate e dirette dal signor MERLO ALESSANDRO; e quelle di paesaggio inventate e dipinte dal signor MERLO medesimo.

7. Programme for Rossini's *Mose* at La Scala, Milan featuring Catherine Hayes and other distinguished singers in 1846. (Author's collection).

complete cast included Catherine as Anaide, Marini as Mosè and the tenor Ranieri-Pochini as Elisero. The tenor Luigi Mei was in the role of Amenofi, with its high tessitura, and the baritone Stefano De Breul sang Farone. Tenor Napoleone Marconi was Osiride, with mezzo-soprano Teresa Ruggeri as Maria and Anna Jannich as Sinaide.

There was always great anticipation on the part of the public when it came to opening night at La Scala. Catherine went to the theatre early to look through the score and do some vocalising. La Scala in the 1840s was always heavily attended by the Austrian military in addition to the elite of Milan and this season was no exception. An air of excitement was everywhere after the hot summer months, at the start of the social season. Even in London the musical press covered events at La Scala in a weekly column. The Musical World reported:

> The Scala will open next week with *Mosè in Egitto*. The prima donna is to be *The Hayes*[19]

then reporting a week later:

> Miss Hayes, whom I dare-say you know is good . . . she is a first rate musician; but as to filling the Scala, it is entirely out of the question . . . Marini too, who has been there for years as primo basso, is exceedingly good, but rather passe . . . [20]

Around this time also the London press mentioned rumours that Catherine was also going to sing Bellini's *Norma* at La Scala, perhaps influenced by Lind's performance in Vienna; however, this never happened.

Despite the gloomy predictions of the London musical press about the vocal capabilities of the two principal stars, opening night was an enormous success according to the Milanese press. The *Gazetta Musicale Milano* reported that she sang the part of Anaide to perfection, and that it considered her to be a true artist.[21] A total of 21 performances of Rossini's *Mosè* were given that season, with Catherine singing the role of Anaide in all performances. It was an excellent start for her for the autumn and the new *Carnivale* season.

There is a slight possibility that Verdi may have heard her sing around this time, he was in Milan.[22] However, he generally kept far away from the theatre because of his ongoing feud with Merelli its director, although his assistant Emanuele Muzio does mention details of the *Mosè* performances at La Scala in letters to Antonio Barezzi, Verdi's father-in-law and benefactor.[23] It is more likely that Verdi would have heard Catherine at a salon, where the agenda was usually a mixture of literature, the arts, music and, of course, politics.

These salons or evenings 'at home' were social and political functions attended by Milan's elite and intellectuals. Clara Maffei (1814–87) was one of the most important hostesses in Milan and her salon ran almost continuously for fifty years from when she introduced it in 1836. She was a brilliant woman, enjoyed company, was well read and educated in world affairs. Italy was one of the few countries in Europe during the nineteenth century that tolerated women having this type of role.

Clara Maffei was a year younger than Giuseppe Verdi was and sixteen years younger than her husband Andrea Maffei. Visitors to her salon tended to be mostly politically oriented. However, since music of the period, particularly Verdi's, was intrinsically linked to the political movement, musicians and singers were also in attendance. Andrea Maffei, was an aristocrat and poet who specialised in translating English and German works into Italian.[24] He had met Verdi and was attracted to him not only because of the composer's music but also because of their mutual interest in Shakespeare and Schiller and the possible use of their works as operatic librettos. When Clara was introduced to Verdi she not only related to him personally but also recognised his potential politically, given the impact of his music on the people of Italy. She immediately extended an invitation to him to be a guest at her salon.

In June 1846 Clara Maffei had separated from her husband in order to keep her property free from his gambling debts. In the process, ironically, Verdi was asked to be a formal witness to their separation documents. Immediately after the separation Verdi and Andrea Maffei visited a spa at Recoardo, near Venice, where they discussed Verdi's options for two new operas, *Macbeth* and *I Masnadieri*, making decisions relating to the subject matter and location for the premieres.[25] Verdi returned to Milan immediately after this visit with Maffei. He remained a close friend of both Clara and Andrea all his life.

The other salon of significance in Milan which Verdi frequented regularly[26] was run by Giuseppina Appiani. She had started it in 1830 and continued it through to 1850. By the mid 1840's Giuseppina Appiani was a widow in her late forties with six children. Donizetti had been her lover, and with the departure of the composer to become music director in Vienna she turned her attentions to the young Verdi, who was now on a rapid rise. In contrast to the Maffei salon, the Appiani salon specialised in presenting the best musical talent of the day to its guests.

During 1846 Catherine was a prominent young singer in Milan and Vienna. The early part of the year she spent in Milan, from April to June she was performing in Vienna, and after that she returned to Milan. Catherine's name appeared with increasing regularity in the local musical press in Milan and other cities. She was in her twenties, spoke Italian, French and English and, given her personality and appearance, she would have been a very acceptable performer and at the Appiani salon.

On 24 September 1846, Muzio had written to Verdi's benefactor Barezzi to say that Benjamin Lumley was expected any day, and that Verdi was interested in 'l'Hayez', Fraschini and the older Lablache for *I Masnadieri*.[27] This probably meant that Verdi had heard Catherine sing, maybe at Giuseppina Appiani's salon sometime between August and September 1846. It was the end of September before Verdi eventually made up his mind that he would compose *Macbeth* for Alessandro Lanari, the Florence, impresario and *I Masnadieri* for Benjamin Lumley (1811–75), the London impresario. However, there still seemed to be some doubt, as on 4 December Verdi wrote to Lumley saying that he had *I Masnadieri* half-written and wanted to make sure that Lumley was agreeable to the subject. If so, Verdi would consider himself obligated, provided Lumley confirmed in writing the agreed cast of Lind and Fraschini.[28] Something had clearly changed between September, when Muzio wrote to Barezzi saying Verdi was interested in l'Hayez for *I Masnadieri*, and early December, when Verdi was now suggesting about Lind for the soprano role. The event which influenced Verdi was the arrival in Milan of Benjamin Lumley on 3 October.

Verdi had spent the latter half of 1846 in and around Milan. Early in October he had a meeting with Piave his librettist to discuss his new opera *Macbeth*. Andrea Maffei by that time had been assigned the libretto for *I Masnadieri*. Benjamin Lumley was a lawyer and a seasoned impresario and businessman. He arrived in Milan on Saturday 3 October 1846 with a well thought out plan to present to Verdi relating to the idea of composing the new opera for Her Majesty's Theatre in London for the following spring or summer.[29] At this meeting Lumley shrewdly suggested having Jenny Lind for the soprano role in *I Masnadieri*, even though Lind was not under contract to him at that time. The idea apparently fascinated Verdi, though he only knew Lind by reputation, never having heard her, since she hadn't sung in Italy and he hadn't yet travelled outside Italy, except for a brief visit to Vienna in 1843.

The set of events which apparently took place at this meeting raises several questions. If Lumley had not suggested Lind, would Catherine have premiered *I Masnadieri* in London? Or did Verdi have Catherine in mind only if *I Masnadieri* was to premiere in Florence? We don't know. However, given her popularity and high profile in Italy at the time there is a very good chance she probably would have been offered the premiere regardless of where it was to receive its first performance. Verdi and Muzio both thought well of her, as did the music critics in London and Milan.

Lumley's personal motivation was simple – he had a critical need for Lind to help his potentially ruinous new 1847 season in London. Several of his top singers, including Mario, Grisi and Tamburini, as well as the conductor and musical director Michael Costa, had defected to his new rival, the Royal Italian Opera at Covent Garden. The Royal Italian was due to start its first season on 6 April 1847, just a few days before Lumley re-opened his doors at Her Majesty's after a short recess. Lind would give him the drawing power he needed to make his season a success. However, at the time Lind still had contractual obligations to another impresario in London.

Lind had actually been planning to sing in England and had signed a contract in 1845 with Alfred Bunn of the Drury Lane Theatre. She chose to ignore her signed agreement when Bunn advised her that he wanted her to make her debut singing in an English-language production. Even though the contract with Bunn had now expired, he felt cheated and at this point was looking for compensation from Lind for non-performance. Lind had no plans to sing in London, given her situation with Bunn.

Immediately after his meeting with Verdi in Milan, Lumley went in search of Lind. He eventually met her in Darmstadt in Germany on 13 October 1846. He came prepared to convince the prima donna that she must sing for him in London. He had with him a long personal letter from Lind's friend Felix Mendelssohn to the prima donna, 'recommending that she consider Mr. Lumley's offer to sing in London' – Lumley had left nothing to chance.[30] Feeling that the Mendelssohn letter would certainly help to make Lind consider his offer, he made the proposition even more compelling by adding the opportunity to create a new Verdi role in London with the composer conducting. He felt certain he had the leverage he needed to get her to sign a contract.

Lumley's thinking was solid. Lind agreed to his proposition and signed a contract on October 17 in Darmstadt with a clause that required Lumley to handle any legal ramifications from the Bunn obligations. He also agreed to pay her among other things an enormous fee, of £4,800 pounds for the season from April to August 1847. Lind, apparently feeling pleased

HER MAJESTY'S THEATRE.
BY SPECIAL DESIRE,

———●———

The Nobility, Subscribers to the Opera, and the Public are respectfully
informed, that

On THURSDAY NEXT, July 22nd, 1847,

(IT BEING A SUBSCRIPTION NIGHT,) will be produced, An entirely new
Opera, composed expressly for Her Majesty's Theatre, by
Sig. VERDI, entitled

I MASNADIERI.

(The Libretto founded on the Drama of the Robbers of Schiller,) with new
Scenery, Dresses, and Decorations.—The scenery by Mr. Charles Marshall.

Amalia, - - - - .	Mdlle. JENNY LIND,
Carlo, - - - - -	Sig. GARDONI,
Francesco, - - - -	Sig. COLETTI,
Moger, - - - - -	Sig. BOUCHE,
Arminio, - - - -	Sig. CORELLI
Rolla, - - - - -	Sig. DAI FIORI,
Massimiliano, - - -	Sig. LABLACHE.

The Free List is suspended, the Public Press excepted.

₊ Pit Tickets may be obtained as usual at the Box-office of the Theatre, price
10s. 6d. each   Applications for Boxes, Pit Stalls, and Tickets to be made at the
Box-office, at the Theatre.—Doors open at Seven o'clock, the Opera to commence
at half-past Seven.

8. Programme for the London premiere of Verdi's opera *I Masnadieri*, July 1847, with the
composer conducting and Jenny Lind singing. (Author's collection).

with herself, wrote a letter on 27 October to one of her friends saying that
she was going to London, and that it was Mendelssohn alone that induced
her to go there!

Confirming the Milan meeting, Verdi wrote to Lumley on 11 November,
1846 stating that he wanted Lind and the tenor Fraschini. On 3 December,
Verdi wrote to Lucca his publisher for I Masnadieri, requesting him 'to
remind Lumley of the condition concerning the singers, which he
promised me verbally and in secret and to which I called his attention in
my letter of November 11. It is now necessary for Mr. Lumley to write
me a letter specifically assuring me I shall have those singers. . . .' 'Here
again are the conditions which have already been accepted: I am to write
I Masnadieri, and Lumley is obliged to give me from his company the two
singers he promised me.'

The implication here is that, when Verdi and Lumley met in Milan in early October, Lumley told Verdi he already had Lind under contract – which of course was not the case. Lumley's masterly actions in effect sealed Catherine's fate and denied her the possibility of being considered for the premiere of *I Masnadieri*.

Fraschini did not sing in the London premiere of *I Masnadieri* either. The English critics, having heard him in March 1847, didn't like him, and so Lumley replaced him with the newly arrived 26 year old tenor, Italo Gardoni (1821–82). Gardoni was to have a long and successful career.

When Lind finally performed in the premiere of Verdi's opera in July, Verdi is reported to have commented in his own language 'Canta ma non incanta', probably meaning that she didn't have the right temperament for his music.[31] Queen Victoria, Prince Albert, the Duke of Wellington and all London turned out for the Verdi premiere with Jenny Lind.

Despite the glamorous audience and the presence of Lind, *I Masnadieri* was not really a success in London. It only ran for three performances. Verdi turned over his conductor's baton (he used a baton in London, which was not the custom in Italy) to Irishman Michael Balfe after only two nights and within a week left town for Paris. He directed his faithful assistant Muzio to return to Milan. Lumley had paid Verdi a total of £1,200 to compose, direct and produce *I Masnadieri* for London, according to the musical press.

Over the next two years Lumley enjoyed great success with Lind under contract, creating 'Lind fever' in the British Isles. When Lind had completed her contract with him he signed a contract with Catherine to replace the 'Swedish nightingale'. This same pattern prevailed some years later in America when the great showman P.T. Barnum would do exactly the same thing! Once again, Catherine and Lind's paths crossed as they were destined to do many times in the years ahead. Catherine did, however, have the opportunity to premiere Verdi's *I Masnadieri* in another place at another time. She studied the principal soprano role with Verdi's assistant, Emanuele Muzio, in Milan, immediately after his return from the London premiere of the opera.

In Catherine Hayes' correspondence from around this period there is no indication that she was ever aware that she might have been under consideration for the premiere of *I Masnadieri*. She was aware that Lind had been signed for the London premier, but made no comment about it. She did, however, compare her voice and style to Lind's during this time, which probably explains why she agreed to perform Verdi's work despite her earlier decision to specifically exclude his music from her repertoire.

In Italy, Catherine's name now generally appeared with the Italian spelling of 'Caterina', with her last name being spelled correctly as Hayes. Muzio in his correspondence, however, used the spelling 'l'Hayez', probably because 'Hayes' was similar to a name which was prominent in Milanese circles, that of the painter and scenic artist Francesco Hayez who at that time was about to start working on the sets for Verdi's *Macbeth* in Florence. As time progressed Catherine's name appeared more and more on programmes and in notices in the Italian form of 'Caterina Hayez', even to the extent that sometimes she spelled it that way herself in her letters. In the Annals of La Scala her name today is shown as 'Hayez', even though it was spelled 'Hayes' on various La Scala operatic programmes of the period.[32]

The 1846 autumn season in La Scala continued with Donizetti's *Gemma di Vergy* and Rossini's *L'italiana in Algeri*. Catherine's next performance was in Rossini's rarely heard *Riccardo e Zoraide* in which she sang Zoraide. The first performance was on 13 October, followed by four additional performances. Immediately after this Catherine was cast in one of her favourite roles – *Lucia di Lammermoor*. This *Lucia* would have great significance for Catherine professionally and personally, because of the tenor engaged for the role of Edgardo – an Englishman named John Sims Reeves (1818–1900). About two months earlier this relatively unknown tenor – had joined the English colony in Milan, on the advice of his former singing teacher Giulio Bordogni of Paris, to gain experience in Italian opera.

John Sims Reeves was born in Woolwich in London.[33] He initially studied music with his father, who was a musician attached to a band with the Royal Artillery. In 1839 he made his vocal debut in Newcastle in the north of England in a small part in the opera *Guy Mannering*. Later he sang the baritone part of Dandini in Rossini's *La Cenerentola*. Between 1841 and 1843 he took lessons in London with Dublin born Tom Cooke. Cooke was a composer and singer who had studied music with Giordani in Dublin. He moved to London in 1813 and sang in opera at the Drury Lane Theatre. He subsequently became director of music there. At the time Reeves went to Cooke for lessons, Cooke was a well-known singing teacher, a member of the Philharmonic Society and the director of music at the Covent Garden Theatre. Under his tutelage Reeves graduated to secondary tenor roles. By now he realised that his voice was maturing, he was 24 years old and in order to advance his career and be able to sing in Italian opera he needed to go abroad to study. He had probably heard of Bordogni the singing teacher from the soprano Clara Novello (1818–1908), who had studied in France and Italy and who was the principal soprano at Drury Lane, where Reeves was singing.

Exactly when Reeves arrived in Paris is not really known perhaps sometime around July 1843. He may have stayed only a few months, since he was back performing in Scotland at the end of September. Descriptions of Reeve's voice from this time indicate that he had a powerful tenor voice with a good quality and a strong top.

After his return to England he continued to sing mostly in English opera or translated versions of Italian opera for the next two and a half years. On a recommendation from Bordogni, Reeves decided to go to Milan in 1846 to be coached in Italian opera by Alberto Mazzucato (1813–77), the head of the Milan Conservatory, who was also a composer and a reviewer for the Ricordi publication *Gazetta Musicale di Milano*. Mazzucato composed operas for La Scala and became a conductor and administrative director there. Prominent pupils of his included Arrigo Boito, a composer and Verdi's future librettist for *Otello* and *Falstaff*, and the Brazilian composer of Italian operas Carlos Gomez. Mazzucato had also translated Manuel Garcia's thesis on singing into Italian for use at the Conservatory.

Shortly after Reeves arrived in Milan around the middle of September 1846, Mazzucato introduced him to Merelli at La Scala.[34] After Merelli auditioned Reeves, he elected to use him for the part of Edgardo in *Lucia di Lammermoor*. A new production of the opera was scheduled for 31 October with the ever-popular Catherine Hayes (Caterina Hayez) in the title role. Whether or not Catherine was party to this decision we do not know. However, Merelli felt there was little possibility of failure with Catherine in the title role and given Reeves' musical ability and vocal strength – even though his Italian pronunciation left a lot to be desired.

When Catherine first met John Sims Reeves she was immediately attracted to him. He had a commanding appearance and an outgoing personality. He was a confident singer and dressed well. They were about the same age, spoke the same language, and interestingly, both their fathers had been musicians with British military bands. They had much in common. Reeves had worked his way up in music circles in England using his raw talent. He had achieved some success in London, but was ambitious and interested in learning all he could about Italian opera to better his career. Catherine had the Italian experience, spoke the language and was a popular singer in Milan and Vienna. She would soon be opening the *Carnivale* season at the Teatro La Fenice in Venice. She also had a strong interest in singing in London, where she'd never been and which was now fast becoming the musical centre of Europe.

Musically and vocally Catherine and Reeves made an ideal pair. They were both handsome, young and intelligent. Merelli was quick to seize the opportunity to present two foreign singers in one of the most popular Italian operas of the day. He felt assured of success. Rehearsals started, and the two singers worked well together.

During this period, the English Musical World, under their 'Foreign Intelligence' column announced from Milan that:

> Miss Hayes is going to Venice for *Carnivale*. She has met with so much success at Milan that Merelli has sold her! – for the period of the *Carnivale*, for as much as he gives for a [whole] year.[35]

In a later issue the London musical publication announced:

> Our countryman, John Reeves has been engaged at the Scala . . . he is reported to have a magnificent voice, and to sing remarkably well.[36]

Their performance on 31 October was electric. Merelli was ecstatic; he couldn't have asked for more. The chemistry between the two young singers was apparent to the audience from the moment Edgardo made his entrance. Reeves' vocal power filled the house, resulting in a spontaneous reaction from the audience. Catherine was breathless and yet had never sung better. It was one of those exciting nights that every impresario wishes could happen with greater frequency. They sang a total of nine performances of *Lucia di Lammermoor* to sold out houses, their performance growing better each night. Early in December the English press printed their report from Milan, saying:

> The English tenor Reeves, made a most successful debut a short time since at the Scala, in the *Lucia* with Miss Hayes, as Prima Donna. Certainly for a very long time past, there has been nothing here to equal their acting and singing, nature has done her part to aid them, both are young, both are handsome, both equally gifted with fine voices and a nice perception of the beautiful in their art, you can imagine nothing more perfect than the representation of their respective characters, it has been the only thing worth going to see at the Scala for a long time . . . everyone here is in despair at losing 'The Hayes', [La Hayez] who goes to Venice for the *Carnival*;

9. Catherine Hayes and Sims Reeves in Donizetti's *Lucia di Lammermoor* at La Scala, Milan in October 1846. (Author's collection).

Reeves however remains till the spring, and then goes to Vienna, where, in consequence of the great success he has met with here, he is accepted as primo tenore.[37]

The only negative comment by the local Milanese press about Reeves was on his Italian pronunciation, which they felt would be corrected with more experience. Even Emanuele Muzio wrote to Verdi's father-in-law Barezzi to inform him that the *Lucia* at the Scala was going very well.[38]

There is no doubt that Catherine's experience and reputation with the La Scala audience must have helped Reeves over his first-night nerves, something he suffered from all his life. In the not too distant future they would sing Lucia together in other cities; however, the magic of that night at La Scala made a lasting impression on the two young singers. In a strange twist of fate, some years later when Catherine was making an important debut in Dublin in *Lucia di Lammermoor*, it would be Reeves who would come to her rescue to turn the evening into a resounding success.

There seems little doubt that during these La Scala performances the two were emotionally attracted to each other, perhaps in part due the exhilaration of the passionate roles they played as lovers in Lucia, with its sweeping romantic music. The fact that as two young foreigners in Italy they had just conquered La Scala together would have fuelled their emotions during those eventful evenings.

It is doubtful that Catherine would have an affair at this point in time, although Reeves was certainly very charming. All her life Catherine was very reserved and private, rarely saying anything about her personal life. There are no letters from this period that reveal her emotions towards Reeves. Events later tend to corroborate that she did develop strong feelings for him even to the point of considering marriage. In any event, her mother travelled with her everywhere and would have been very protective of her. However, Reeves indicated in his memoirs that he had a good relationship with Catherine's mother. He describes her as 'a very pretty Irishwoman with a musical voice and a delightful brogue'.[39] Perhaps the mother might even have encouraged the relationship? The emotional attachment between the two which was apparent later probably started around this time in Italy and grew when they next met in London and Dublin, where they spent much more time in each others company. Unfortunately no correspondence between them survives.

Their last performance of *Lucia* at La Scala occurred around 20 November. In London the musical press made a final announcement

PERSONAGGI.

Lord ENRICO ASTHON.
  Sig. Badiali Cesare.

Miss LUCIA di lui sorella
  Sign. Hayez Catterina.

Sir EDGARDO DI RAVENSWOOD.
  Sig. Flavio Lazzaro.

Lord ARTURO BUCLAW
  Sig. Zuliani Angelo

RAIMONDO BIDEBENT educatore e confidente di
  Lucia.
  Sig. Lodi Giuseppe.

ALISA damigella di Lucia.
  Sign. De Rossa Zambelli Marietta.

NORMANNO capo degliArmigeri di Ravensvood
  Sig. Crosa Carlo.

Coro di Dame, Cavalieri e Congiunti di Aston,
  Abitanti di Lammermoor.

L' avvenimento ha luogo in Iscozia, parte nel castello di
Ravensvood, parte nella rovinata Torre di Wolferag.

L'epoca rimonta al declinare del secolo XVI.

LUCIA
DI LAMMERMOO

DRAMMA TRAGICO IN DUE PARTI
PAROLE
DI SALVADORE CAMMARANO
MUSICA
DEL MAESTRO GAETANO DONIZETTI

DA RAPPRESENTARSI

NEL GRAN TEATRO LA FENICE

La Stagione di carnovale e quaresima 1846–4

VENEZIA
TIPOGRAFIA DI GIUSEPPE MOLINARI
In Rugagiuffa s. Zaccaria N. 4879.

10. Programme for *Lucia di Lammermoor* at the Teatro La Fenice, Venice during the 1846–7 season, featuring Catherine Hayes in her most famous role. (Author's collection).

stating that Reeves continued to be a great favourite and that Miss Hayes was suffering from a severe cold, nevertheless, her singing was quite beautiful.[40] At the conclusion of this *Lucia* Catherine immediately left for Florence to discuss a contract for the following year with the impresario Alessandro Lanari. Earlier Lanari had contacted her to discuss the idea of working in Florence at his opera house. Catherine worked out the terms in principle with Lanari and promised to return in January when he had the contract ready. She did however have an obligation to perform further at La Scala during the 1847 autumn season. After her discussions with Lanari, Catherine left with her mother to travel to Venice for rehearsals for the opening of the *Carnivale* season at the famous Teatro La Fenice, one of Italy's oldest theatres, on 26 December 1846. She was scheduled to open the season with a new opera, *Albergio da Romano*, written by a young composer and a member of the nobility called Malespeno, who possibly was related to one of the directors of La Fenice. The opera was a fiasco, even with the presence of 'La Hayez.' and it didn't get even a second hearing.

Early in the new year, Catherine returned to Florence to finalise her contract details with Alessandro Lanari. On 9 January she signed an agreement, valid until 16 December 1848, under which she would sing for Lanari in Italy as a 'Prima Donna Assoluta' the most important title a soprano could achieve.

On her return to Venice Catherine was scheduled to sing *Lucia di Lammermoor* on 23 January, with a relatively non-distinguished cast except for the baritone. It included Lazzaro Flavio (a Spanish tenor whose real name was Puig) as Edgardo, Giuseppe Lodi as Raimondo and the baritone Cesare Badiale (1803–65) as Enrico. However, once again Catherine had great personal success in the role of Lucia. The local press in Venice reported that:

> . . . after her cavatina the enthusiasm was almost fanatical; the rondo finale created a hurricane of applause and bravos . . . at the end of the performance La Hayez was called before the curtain three times with the applause lasting a full ten minutes . . . La Hayez could not desire a more splendid triumph.[41]

At that time Venice had a strict law, imposed by the Viennese authorities, prohibiting any artist at any theatre from taking more than three curtain calls. After Catherine's next opera, which was *Linda di*

11a. The programme for *Lucia di Lammermoor*, the role in which Catherine Hayes made her debut in Vienna in 1846. (Courtesy Österreichisches Theatre Museum)

11b. Programme for Donizetti's rarely heard opera *Olivo e Pasquale*, which Catherine Hayes performed in Vienna in June 1847 (Courtesy Österreichisches Theatre Museum).

Chamounix, the excitement after three curtain calls was so great and the audience so insistent for her reappearance that the management became alarmed that a riot would ensue if 'La Hayez' did not appear a fourth time. Catherine would not disobey the law, however, without police permission, which the management eventually obtained. When Catherine appeared for the fourth time the audience covered her in flowers in a wild, uncontrolled display of affection.[42] After Catherine left the theatre that night and returned to her hotel she found a large crowd at the entrance. Once more there was spontaneous applause and requests for her to sing, which she declined to do, saying that she wanted to retire for the night.

On 13 March, after a delay of fifteen days due to Catherine being indisposed, Federico Ricci's new opera *Griselda*, which was written especially for Catherine, had its premiere. This was the opera Ricci had promised to write for her after she sang his *Estella* a little over a year earlier at La Scala. It was reported that this new opera was a real triumph, with all of the cast and the composer being loudly applauded. The review stated there was, among the more astonishing pieces in the first act, a cavatina by Griselda (Madame Hayez) – a beautiful melancholy piece, exquisitely sung.

Ricci was a popular composer around this time, and his opera *Estella* which Catherine had sung at La Scala the previous year was scheduled for the next season in Vienna, with Catherine in the title role again. Catherine stayed in Venice until the end of March, performing four operas in all for the season. During April the London musical press reported that Miss Hayes had been singing in a new opera by Ricci in Venice which had caused quite a furore. The review went on to say:

> she finishes her engagement with Merelli this Autumn and is afterwards engaged to sing at Rome, Naples and Florence . . . there has been no English singer who has made so great a sensation in Italy as Miss Hayes.[43]

Early in April, Catherine departed from Venice to join the many other distinguished singers at Vienna, where the season was already in progress. She would never again sing in Venice.

She returned to Vienna triumphant and confident about her opening night at the Kärntnertortheater, where she had been so well received the year before. On 10 April she opened in her most famous role, the lead in *Lucia di Lammermoor*. The cast singing opposite her could not be better –

Edgardo was played by the exciting Russian tenor Nicola Ivanoff (1810–80), who was then 37 years old. He had sung extensively in Naples, Paris, London, Rome and Milan as well as other Italian cities. He was a friend and particular favourite of Rossini, who had asked Verdi to write a special aria for him for the opera *Ernani*. The part of Enrico was sung by the baritone Felice Varesi (1813–89), who was 34 years old at the time of these performances and about to reach the pinnacle of his career. He had created the baritone role of Antonio in Donizetti's *Linda di Chamounix* in Vienna in 1842. Verdi also thought very highly of him and had insisted that Varesi create the title role of his new opera *Macbeth*, This had opened about three weeks earlier in Florence on 14 March, the day after Catherine had premiered Ricci's *Griselda* in Venice. A few years later Varesi sang the title role at the premiere of *Rigoletto* in Venice in 1851, and slightly later the part of Germont at the premiere of *La Traviata*, also in Venice.

It was a star-studded cast with lots of experience, and Catherine had the most important role in the opera. Success was assured. *Lucia* was performed about twelve times during the season with the same cast. The last performance took place around the middle of June. Reviews stated that 'Caterina Hayez, whom we know since last year, was happily a very pleasant Lucia. Her fine looking appearance, her good method, the climax and feeling showed during her performance, together with her acting, are the most beautiful qualities to distinguish this excellent young artist.'[44]

On 23 April, Ricci's opera *Estella* opened with Raffaele Mirate (1815–95) who was just 31, in the tenor role. Mirate had mostly sung in Naples, Paris and Milan; however, he was destined to create the Duke of Mantua in Verdi's *Rigoletto* in Venice in 1851. Later in his career he went on to New York and Boston, where he appeared with considerable success in several operas. The principal baritone part was taken by Filippo Colini (1811–63) who, at 36, was the oldest member of the cast. Colini was born in Rome, where he made his debut in 1835. Early in his career he sang mostly Donizetti operas in Palermo, Naples, Rome and Paris. When Verdi emerged as a leading composer after 1842, Colini sang the principal baritone roles in *Nabucco*, *Ernani* and various other Verdi operas. He created three Verdi roles including, Giacomo in *Giovanna d'Arco* at La Scala in 1845, Rolando in *La battaglia di Legnano* in Rome in 1849 and Stankar in *Stiffelio* in Trieste in 1857.

By now Catherine's success was so great that she felt she could never leave Vienna. She had a full social life and was very relaxed with the Italian singers – she spoke their language and knew many of their friends in Milan and Venice. A revival of one of Donizetti's earliest operas, *Olivo e Pasquale*, an opera buffo, was scheduled next. It had previously been performed there in 1836. On 17 June, Catherine played the part of Isabella while Colini was Olivo and buffo-baritone Cesare Soares sang the role of Pasquale. The young tenor Enrico Calzolari (1823–88), who had just turned 24, was also in the cast. He went on to have a brilliant career all across Europe, in Russia and England, where Catherine would meet up with him again. For Catherine the season ended with this Donizetti opera during the last week in June. She immediately headed back to Italy and Donizetti's home town of Bergamo, where she would next perform in one of his operas under the direction of one of his best friends.

In London during this period, Verdi, Muzio, Jenny Lind, Italo Gardoni, Lablache and other cast members were all rehearsing for the premiere of *I Masnadieri* which took place three weeks later on 22 July at Her Majesty's theatre under Lumley's management.

CHAPTER FIVE

The Prima Donna and Verdi's *I Masnadieri*

VERONA, FLORENCE AND GENOA 1847–49

W HEN CATHERINE arrived in Bergamo in early July 1847 the opera season which was under Merelli's direction was about to commence.[1] She opened on 9 August at the Teatro Riccardi in the title role of Donizetti's opera *Maria di Rohan*, a three-act work with strong dramatic content.[2] This was a new role for her.

Her young tenor partner from Vienna, Calzolari, appeared opposite her as Riccardo. Other cast members included the baritone Giovanni Battista Bencich as Enrico and Giuseppe Locatelli, the bass as di Suze. The conductor was Marco Bonesi, a close personal friend of Donizetti. Unfortunately by this time Donizetti was gravely ill in Paris, while his family and friends were endeavouring to bring him back to Bergamo. He did not return to his home town until 6 October, by which time Catherine was back at La Scala performing in his *Linda di Chamounix*.

Donizetti's *Maria di Rohan* had had its first performance in Vienna in 1843 with the soprano Eugenia Tadolini in the title role and Donizetti directing. Catherine was again following in Tadolini's footsteps, having chosen this opera as the appropriate work for her debut in Donizetti's birthplace. From the opening night through to the last performance on the third week in August she had one success after another, having to encore Maria's beautiful last-act aria and prayer, 'Avvi un Dio . . . Benigno il cielo arride' each evening.[3]

During her stay in Bergamo the mayor of the town, Guglielmo Lochis, gave a banquet to which she was invited as the special guest.[4] The famous tenor Giovanni Battista Rubini, who was also a native of the Bergamo area, now aged 53 and retired, was also present.[5] A few years later, at an interview in Dublin, Catherine mentioned that at the banquet Rubini sang the great aria 'Nel furor delle tempeste' from, *Il Pirata* especially for her. Rubini had created the tenor role at La Scala in 1827. After the aria he asked her to join with him in the Lucia di Lammermoor duet 'Sulla tomba che rinserra' and to the great enjoyment of all, she did.

On Saturday 28 August, before leaving Bergamo, Catherine gave a benefit performance, as was the custom then as part of the artist's remuneration. She first performed in *Maria di Rohan* and afterwards sang an aria from *Lucia di Lammermoor*, a trio from *Torquato Tasso* by Donizetti, the introduction of *Nabucco* (Abigaille's aria?) and a cavatina from *L'italiana in Algeri* by Rossini.[6] The London musical press was now reporting on her regularly. Early in September the Milan correspondent for *The Musical World* noted that some of the Milanese who had been to London and heard Jenny Lind were comparing the two, remarking:

> it was madness for either of them [Lind or Hayes] to attempt the grand lyric opera [*Norma*] in which Grisi has made so many triumphs, but they were both so supremely good in such operas as *Sonnambula*, *L'Elixir d'Amore*, &c . . . one man who spoke a little English who saw Lind in *Norma* [in London] said, 'I felt quite pitiful for her, for I had seen La Grisi the Saturday before.'[7]

The same journal a week later made mention that Catherine's benefit performance at Bergamo was an immense triumph and that she was received with cheers and the most rapturous applause.

With her season finished in Bergamo, Catherine left for Milan to start rehearsals in early September for the new season at La Scala. She did not know it then, but this was to be her last season ever at La Scala. The London musical press covering the various activities in Milan mentioned that Hayes would be singing in *Linda di Chamounix*. Catherine's first night was Saturday, 18 September. The cast included Eugenio Musich as the Visconte, Giovanni Corsi (1822–90) as Antonio and Amelia Poppi as Pierotto; the bass role of Il Prefetto was sung by Prosper Derivis (1808–80).

This time there was an indication from the London musical press representative that Catherine was having vocal problems. The report stated:

> she had a tremendous reception, however, the end of the first act showed that due to the size of the Scala her voice had sadly deteriorated since last season.[8]

There was also mention that Louis Jullien (1812–60), the London impresario from Drury Lane, had gone to Bergamo to hear her and had decided not to engage her. On this trip to Italy, Jullien was endeavouring to recruit prominent members of the English vocal community in the Milan area for his 'opera in English' venture in London and may have decided that Catherine's style was too continental for his needs. As it turned out his project failed miserably, but many years later he did have the pleasure of working with Catherine in London.

Catherine had now been singing continuously for almost two years, with very little time off. There were times when she sang as many as twelve nights in a row, without any break. This La Scala season was probably her first experience of vocal fatigue. Despite all the instruction on discipline and care for the vocal chords she had received from Manuel Garcia, her excessive activity had caught up with her and she needed a rest. However, her contract required her to sing in yet another new opera at La Scala – *Mortedo* by Vincenzo Capecelatro. This composer subsequently composed one other opera, that premiered at La Scala in 1850 with some success. In *Mortedo*, singing opposite Catherine were Giovanni Corsi (1822–90), baritone – who had a long career at La Scala where he sang into the 1860s – Eugenio Musich, tenor, and Carlo Bennati, second tenor. There were only four performances, since the new opera was not very popular with the audience. This was to be Catherine's last opera at La Scala. If she had realised this, she probable would have wanted to leave the audience with the memory of her most famous role – in *Lucia di Lammermoor*.

However, fate would also take a hand. Milan was by now a hotbed of political unrest. Within four months La Scala would completely close down because of the revolt against the Austrian rule. It would not reopen until December 1848, by which time Catherine was destined to be moving on to London, which was fast becoming the most important musical city in Europe.

On the advice of Ronconi, Catherine decided to move to Florence, given the political unrest that was brewing in Lombardy and Venetia. Ronconi himself was also planning to leave. Earlier, Catherine had met the impresario Alessandro Lanari, who operated from the Teatro della Pergola in Florence. Lanari was always on the lookout for young singers. Based on Ronconi's suggestion she initially went to Florence to discuss a contract around the end of November 1846. She then returned there between performances at La Fenice in Venice to sign a contract with the impresario on 9 January 1847.[9]

Alessandro Lanari's fame during the years 1839 to 1848 was as great as Merelli's of La Scala.[10] He had previously managed opera seasons at Venice and Senagallia. In those early days of opera most of Italy's best singers, including such notables as Giuseppina Strepponi (1815–97), Verdi's future wife, and the famous Giulia Grisi, had passed through his management at one point or another. However, like most opera company managers and impresarios of the nineteenth century, Lanari always seemed to be on the brink of bankruptcy. His years in Florence were important because of the number of new works he produced on behalf of Italy's leading composers. However, when he died in Florence in 1852 at the age of 65, he held the modest position of manager of a costume warehouse. A large collection of his letters to and from various people involved in the musical and operatic industry in nineteenth-century Italy (including Catherine Hayes), and other related material, exists in the national library in Florence.

When Catherine signed her contract with Lanari in January 1847 her strength of character once again came to the fore. She never again wanted her immediate family to have to suffer the pains of deprivation and hunger or to want for the essentials of life as they had in her early years in Limerick. As a result, Catherine's contract with Lanari had a clause that required him to provide 'adequate lodging in Florence' for both her mother, Mary Hayes, and her sister Henrietta, who would be joining them from Limerick. Lanari also signed Catherine as a *Prima Donna Assoluta*, the foremost rank in Italy for a soprano. The term of the contract extended to December 1848. However, perhaps the most significant clause in the contract was contained on the first page – where Catherine had inserted a statement that specifically excluded her from having to sing Verdi operas![11]

It was unheard of for a soprano in the Italian states to say 'no' to Verdi's music at a time when Verdi had already emerged as the most important composer in that part of Europe. To have it written into a contract with Lanari, one of the leading impresarios of the period was even more startling. Verdi's operas, *Nabucco, I Lombardi, Ernani, Attila* and *I Due Foscari* were being performed in various Italian cities with great success. The composer's potential which was to lead to *Luisa Miller, Il Trovatore, Rigoletto* and *La Traviata* in a few years, was apparent to most people in the profession. However, Catherine had decided that his music was not suitable for her voice. This was an amazing course for a young prima donna of the period to take, particularly at such an early stage in her

12. Programme for the Italian premiere of Verdi's *I Masnadieri* in Verona, December 1847. (Author's collection).

career. When it became public it made news. A few months later the leading London musical journal made reference to Catherine's inconsistency, in singing Verdi's *I Masnadieri* when contractually she had decided never to risk her voice by singing Verdi's music![12]

Once again Catherine showed her strength of character and decisiveness in matters relating to her career. This strength was particularly important during this period of her life. Her mother was her best friend and she had no other close associates other than Lanari, who was then almost 60 years old and besieged with business problems, the end of his career close at hand.

It is interesting to note that later in her career when her voice was more mature she did in fact sing in Verdi operas and perform his music at concerts. Catherine's primary reason for excluding Verdi's operas from her repertoire early in her career appears to have been that she considered Verdi's music too heavy for her type of voice. With the exception of *I Lombardi*, she was probably correct. Regretfully, she never actually sang this opera. In her correspondence with Lanari it is clear that she refused to sing not only Verdi's music but also the works of other composers for the same reason. In Florence in 1847 Lanari wanted her to sing in *Lorenzino di Medici* by Giovanni Pacini, but she rejected the idea, saying that it had been created by the soprano Barbieri-Nini, who had a different type of voice Catherine suggested Donizetti's more lyrical *Maria Padilla* instead.

Despite the clause in her contract about not being obligated to sing Verdi operas, in a letter she wrote to Lanari from around this period she rationalises why she would sing *I Masnadieri* – saying that Verdi had written it for Jenny Lind's voice and that Lind's voice and hers were of the 'same gender'.[13] Catherine had probably heard Lind the previous year in Vienna and understood Lind's style and voice, as it related to her own capabilities. In addition, because of the association she and Lind had with Garcia, no doubt Garcia would have compared Lind's voice and technique with Catherine's own vocal timbre.

Late in August 1847 in Milan Catherine met with Emanuele Muzio, Verdi's assistant, whom she had known for some time. She was in the process of preparing for the new La Scala season. Muzio had just returned from London and the premiere of *I Masnadieri* in the middle of August, hoping that Verdi would ask him to rejoin him in Paris.[14] In the meantime, Verdi had other interests and proceeded to Paris to meet with Giuseppina Strepponi, his lover, and to prepare a new version of his opera *I Lombardi* for the Paris stage under the name *Jerusalem*. Verdi had given

Muzio the responsibility of bringing the final *I Masnadieri* score to Milan to have Lucca one of his Italian publishers, print and publish it.

Through her association with Lanari, Catherine' had been signed to sing in *I Masnadieri* in Verona at the opening of the *Carnivale* season on 26 December 1847, about five months after the opera's London premiere. Lanari probably had acquired from Verdi the rights to premiere *I Masnadieri* in Italy during the period when he and Verdi were in negotiations over producing either *I Masnadieri* or *Macbeth* in Florence in the spring of 1847. Ultimately, as we know, *Macbeth* was selected for Florence, *I Masnadieri* for London.

In fact the Italian premiere of *I Masnadieri* was not only scheduled for Verona on 26 December, it was also scheduled to premiere simultaneously in Bergamo and Trieste. The Trieste performance was interrupted by a major fire in the area of the opera house and never finished. This was probably the first and only time a Verdi opera had its Italian premiere scheduled at three locations on the same night!

Meanwhile Emanuele Muzio had agreed to coach Catherine in the role of Amalia in *I Masnadieri*. In another letter to Lanari from around this time, Catherine reminds Lanari of the fact that she had 'studied the [*I Masnadieri*] part with Signor Muzio, maestro Verdi's assistant'.[15]

Her partner for *I Masnadieri* at the Teatro della Societa Filarmonica di Verona was Fortunato Borioni, tenor, as Carlo; Francesco was sung by the baritone Achille De Bassini, and the role of Massimiliano was taken by Giuseppe Romanelli.[16] Romanelli replaced Nicola Benedetti who became indisposed at the last minute. The first performance occurred on the opening of the *Carnivale* season, 26 December 1847 with great success. Local reviews indicate that the opera was well accepted by the audience, and La Hayez and other members of the cast sang well.[17]

The London musical press reported on Catherine's activity with increased frequency.[18] Even Henry F. Chorley, the cynical music critic of the London *Athenaeum*, devoted a whole column to Catherine's activities in Italy as provided by his Milan representative, saying:

> Miss Hayes has one great advantage, youth; another in having few faults to be unlearned. Her person is agreeable rather than striking; there's just that drawing- room good breeding in her demeanour which gratifies if it does not enchant. I have never heard any English or Irish Lady, so new to her profession, who was so thoroughly in the shape of an opera singer; and this says much for her steadiness of study and good taste in the selection of models [roles].[19]

There was now an expressed hope in the musical press that she would be coming to London soon, perhaps to sing for Lumley at Her Majesty's theatre.[20] She was referred to as 'this celebrated English vocalist'. An article featuring her achievements went on to say:

Miss Catherine Hayes, who has recently created an extraordinary sensation in Italy, has just completed her engagement of two years at La Scala, Milan, with eclat quite unprecedented. This charming young singer is now at Verona for the Carnival season, where success in Maestro Verdi's opera of *Masnadieri* has been most brilliant. On her first appearance on the stage (says the *Verona Gazette*), she was welcomed with a burst of applause which lasted several minutes. Her cavatina in the first act met with great admiration, but the air in the second act *Carlo vivi? . . . Oh caro accento*, produced such a tempest of applause that she was obliged to repeat it.' . . . The Hayes possesses a pure soprano of great extension, and her voice is so exquisitely sweet, so melodious and touching, that every heart is immediately captivated. Added to these rare qualities, she has a flexibility which enables her to execute the most florid and difficult passages, apparently without effort. Her style, intonation, and shake [trill] are all perfect. The grace and elegance with which she moves on stage, combined with the loveliness of her face and figure, enable us to aver with truth that she is unrivaled by any artiste of the present day.[21]

Obviously, Catherine wanted these performances of *I Masnadieri* to be her very best. In the event there was to be a comparison with Lind's premiere in London five months earlier so there is no doubt that she achieved her goal. During this same season in Verona there was some talk that Catherine would sing in another Verdi opera *I Due Foscari*, but this does not appear to have occurred.

Having completed her season at Verona, Catherine returned to Florence at the beginning of February 1848. Her timing was propitious, in view of the mounting political tensions in Milan and northern Italy, which would explode within six weeks. Milan was the focus in Italy for this revolt against the Austrians. Mathilde Marchesi, another Garcia pupil who was with Ronconi in Milan around this time, describes the historic events in her autobiography and tells us how musical life in the great city was affected.[22]

By now Catherine's focus was on Florence and the Lanari season at the Teatro della Pergola. The new season represented a variety of new opportunities for Catherine, including the local premiere of *I Masnadieri* with the same cast as in Verona, except that this time Nicola Benedetti performed the role of Massimiliano. On 17 March 1848 Lanari advertised that 'a new opera by Maestro Verdi, *I Masnadieri* will be on stage, and we'll have an excellent Prima Donna, new in Florence, the Irish [woman], Caterina Hayez . . . '[23] The reviews after the first performance indicated that Florence was not too impressed by Verdi's new opera; however, the principals all received good applause.[24]

Milan was in a state of siege by early March. La Scala was often empty except for rows of white-coated Austrians soldiers. News of a revolution in Vienna reached Milan, resulting in a local uprising breaking out on 14 March. Men and women took to the streets and windows respectively. Along the main thoroughfares women waved handkerchiefs or red, white and green flags. Up to 15,000 men marched to the Austrian government house to request that the Austrian police be disbanded and that a civic guard be formed by the citizens.[25]

The march was led by the highest-ranking Italian – the mayor – who paraded in a formal black suit with a tricolour boutonniere and an Italian flag carried beside him. The Austrians were so shaken that they immediately signed the document agreeing to the establishment of a civic guard. The insurgents, having got what they came for, also took the principal Austrian official as a hostage. On hearing this, the Austrian military declared war on the marchers. Barricades went up in street after street and the city ceased to function. Milan's five glorious days had commenced. La Scala closed down completely, not to reopen until the beginning of the *Carnivale* season on 26 December 1848.[26]

Bartolemeo Merelli of La Scala took off for Vienna, with the result that he was later accused of spying for the Austrians. Felice Ronconi, who had not immediately heeded his own advice to Catherine, found himself in hasty retreatæ out of Milan. He eventually made it to London where his brother Giorgio Ronconi was singing. Catherine had made the right decision at the right time.

The events in Milan sparked patriotism all over the Italian states. In Florence, between the performances of *I Masnadieri* and the next opera, a festival of lights was held at the Teatro della Pergola to celebrate the revolution in Milan. Participating were the baritone Achille De Bassini and the bass Ignazio Marini, both of whom were patriots from Lombardy. Catherine's Irish spirit no doubt compelled her to join in the festivities.

It was during this period that Catherine received an invitation from Angelica Catalani, the famous mezzo-soprano now in retirement in a villa in Florence. In an interview in Dublin in 1850, Catherine mentioned that Catalani commented after hearing her sing during her visit to Villa Catalani: 'What would I not give to be in London when you make your debut. Your fortune is certain.' Tragically, Catalani never heard Catherine sing again. On a visit to Paris in June 1849, two months after Catherine made her London debut, Catalani contacted cholera and died there, aged 69.

On 4 April 1848 in Florence an advertisement appeared in the *Gazetta* in which Lanari announced a new opera in three acts, *Gennaro Annese* by Gualtiero Sanelli (1816–61), who was then 32 years old. Sanelli had an unusual career. He was born in Parma in 1816 and travelled extensively with opera groups, sometimes as chorus master and other times as conductor. He spent time in Milan and various other Italian cities before going to Mexico and to the central American countries in 1841. Later he went to Paris and then to England, where he performed as a conductor. Ultimately he settled in Brazil, where he died in 1861. He composed eleven operas, none of which survives today.

The libretto of *Gennaro Annese* described the story as a melodramatic work in three acts. The opera is based on an insurrection which took place in Naples in 1647. Several other composers had used the event as the subject for their operas, the most famous work being *La Muette de Portici (Masaniello)* by the French composer Daniel Auber which was first produced in Paris in 1828.

The premiere of *Gennaro Annese* took place on 5 April 1848 at the Teatro della Pergola in Florence, with Catherine singing the leading soprano role of Adele. *Gennaro* was sung by Achille De Bassini. Other members of the cast included Nicola Benedetti, Angelo Brunacci, Francesco Rossi and Faustina Piombanti. Sanelli did not conduct the performance, although it is possible he may have attended.

The opera was well received by the audience at the Teatro della Pergola, whether because of the mood created by the activities in Milan coupled with a story involving a revolution, or the quality of Sanelli's music, it is hard to say. The reviews were excellent. Catherine was singled out for her performance: 'Caterina Hayes showed her great artistic abilities, and [as a result] she got extraordinary and astonishing applause.'[27]

It was on 8 April 1848 that the sad news of Donizetti's death was announced from his home town of Bergamo, where he'd been taken a few months previously by his nephew after he had lapsed into a coma in Paris. Donizetti was 50 when he died in the home of a friend in Bergamo.

GENNARO ANNESE

MELODRAMMA IN TRE ATTI

MUSICA DEL M.º GUALTIERO SANELLI

Da Rappresentarsi nell' I. e R. Teatro

IN VIA DELLA PERGOLA

LA QUARESIMA 1848.

Sotto la Protezione di S. A. I. e R.

LEOPOLDO II.

GRANDUCA DI TOSCANA

ec. ec. ec.

FIRENZE
TIFOGRAFIA GALLETTI
in Via delle Terme

PERSONAGGI

GENNARO, Popolano) Generali del Popolo Nap
TORALDO, Nobile)
   Sig. Achille De-Bassini.
   Sig. Angelo Brunacci,

ADELE, Sorella di Toraldo
   Sig. Caterina Hayez.

CORRADO, popolano
   Sig. Niccola Benedetti.

CALDORA, nobile
   Sig. Francesco Rossi.

ELISA, congiunta di Adele
   Sig. Faustina Piombanti.

CORI, E COMPARSE DI

Popolani, Nobili, Soldati, Donne attinenti ad
Senatori, Sgherri, Famigliari di Toraldo

Epoca — la metà del 1600.

Tanto la Musica che la Poesia del presente Li
sono proprietà del Sig. ALESSANDRO LANAI

---

13. Programme for the first performance of the opera *Gennaro Annese* by Sanelli, featuring Catherine Hayes. Florence 1848. (Author's collection).

It was his music more than that of any other composers that appealed to Catherine. Throughout her career she sang many Donizetti parts, always choosing his music for her major debut roles. Her favourite and most popular, of course, was *Lucia di Lammermoor,* which she sang at every opportunity. In April 1848, as Donizetti lay dying in Bergamo, Catherine was a few hundred miles away preparing for a performance of *Lucia di Lammermoor* in Reggio Emilia. It must have been a terrible day for her when the news of his death came through. Her resounding success in the role in early May was a fitting memory to the renowned composer who had died just three and a half weeks earlier. Sadly, as far as we know she never met Donizetti personally.

The chocie of Reggio Emilia as the location of this performance was related to Lanani's new problems in Florence. It seems that he had run into financial difficulties with the Accademia degli Immobili members, who were the owners of the Teatro della Pergola. On 27 March, 1848 Lanari wrote the members a long letter which outlined his position with respect to losses sustained over the previous three years, the lack of support funds from the Accademia, and his proposal and commitment for a new opera season.[28] In addition, an editorial appeared in one of the leading papers stating that the 'members of the Pergola theatre Accademia had met to discuss reopening the theatre, having appointed a commission to get an agreement with any impresario, except Alessandro Lanari'.[29]

Lanari's letter was written in response to mounting criticism and a notice that had appeared in the *Gazetta* in which some of the employees at the theatre had expressed their concern as to whether the opera would be able to continue through the spring of 1848. Presumably the employees hadn't been paid. The pressure of the political situation in the Italian states was taking its toll on the money available to support the opera and theatres.

In his proposal for a new season, Lanari detailed the economics and what he expected from the Accademia members in terms of financial assistance and the cast of singers he would present. Catherine and the soprano Rita Gabussi, who was the wife of Achille De Bassini, were listed as the prima donnas. Lanari gave the members of the Accademia four days to respond to his proposal, but he did not get his answer that quickly. In the meantime, presumably his cast of leading singers didn't wish to wait around, so Lanari resolved the problem by sending them to Reggio Emilia to give several performances of Donizetti's great favourite, *Lucia di Lammermoor*, over a period of about four weeks, after which they returned to Florence.

The first performance in Reggio Emilia was on 5 May with Catherine as usual performing the title role. De Bassini sang Enrico, and the 27-year-old tenor Lodovico Graziani, who had made his debut three years earlier in Bologna, sang the part of Edgardo. Reviews covering this performance showed that the cast continued to deliver a high standard vocally. Catherine was singled out once more:

> *Lucia* was a real triumph for Hayez, getting never ending applause all through the opera. Hayez is a proven singer, she has all the qualities of a real artist at the best level. *Lucia* is a perfect opera for Hayez, and it seems now that only a few women could equal her, particularly in the rondo, [which] she plays with extreme tenderness, and with a personal feeling that inebriates and ravishes you. The applause and calls were so many that the enthusiasm was indescribable.[30]

Before leaving Reggio Emilia she also performed in Sanelli's *Gennaro Arnese* with the same cast as in Florence.

Lanari's troubles at the della Pergola were still not resolved when the singers got back to Florence in June, so he set them up at a competing theatre, Real Teatro Degli Interepidi, where *Lucia di Lammermoor* was announced for 13 June, with the same cast as in Reggio Emilia.[31] Here they performed until the end of June. Other operas given during this period included Verdi's *Macbeth*, with De Bassini and his wife Rita Gabussi in the lead roles, and Rossini's *Guglielmo Tell*, with Francesco Cresci in the title role, Carlo Baucarde (1825–83) as Arnold and Adelaide Basseggio as Mathilde.

The review of the *Lucia* performance once again praised Catherine and the rest of the cast, saying:

> In *Lucia* again, Hayez performed in front of the public and she was proclaimed as a marvellous singer.[32]

Presumably Lanari's purpose putting the operas on at a competitive theatre was to put pressure on the members of the Accademia to accept his terms and for the season at the Pergola. However, his plan didn't work. The Pergola didn't re-open until September, and then without Lanari.

Lanari's troubles drifted on, without any resolution. The political situation in Italy continued to get worse and the remaining months of his season were badly affected. Eventually Catherine frustrated, made her decision to leave Florence and go to Genoa, where the situation was somewhat more stable. However, she still felt bound by her contract with Lanari. Whether or not he helped her to get a contract for Genoa we don't know, but she continued to write to Lanari after she arrived there in December 1848.

Catherine was now famous throughout the Italian states. Despite the closing of La Scala and the disruption in other cities, she was still in demand and was offered a contract for the *Carnivale* season which was due to start in Genoa on 26 December 1848.

Meanwhile, she also had to take care of the expense of moving her mother and sister to Genoa. Catherine was always good at saving money, even in the early days when she was giving concerts in Dublin she was thrifty. Her experiences in Italy had enabled her to save a considerable amount of money. This was now very important as it gave her a certain amount of stability, given the fact that there was very little work for her between the end of July and the start of the new season at Genoa in December. Catherine spent the next few months in Florence before going to Genoa. She took advantage of her surroundings to visit various places of interest and to spend time with some of the friends she had made. This also gave her an opportunity to get some rest in view of the fact that she had now been singing continuously for almost three years.

Even as she prepared to move to Genoa in the Piedmont region next to Lombardy, the political situation in Milan and the rest of Lombardy continued to deteriorate. A political fusion had taken place between 'freed' Lombardy and the leaders of the Piedmont region (Kingdom of Sardinia) immediately to the east. However, by August 1848 the Austrian army was back in possession of the city of Milan and what had promised to be a new order in Lombardy vanished with the return of Austrian rule.

Catherine, her mother and her sister arrived in Genoa at the end of November 1848. She immediately went into rehearsals at the Teatro Carlo Felice, preparing herself for the opening night debut on 26 December in *Lucia di Lammermoor*.

By now she was the most famous Lucia in Italy. Other renowned Lucias, such as Fanny Tacchinardi-Persiani who had created the role in Naples in 1835 had moved on to heavier soprano roles. Persiani was now primarily singing outside of Italy. In three years she would retire. Eugenia Tadolini, another great Lucia of the period, had by now being singing for twenty years. She too had moved on to heavier soprano roles in Verdi operas. Tadolini retired in 1851.

Catherine's presence in Genoa for the new season was anxiously awaited. The cast for opening night included the experienced tenor Raffaele Mirate as the Edgardo. Mirate and Catherine had sung together in Vienna the previous year. Other members of the cast included the baritone Luigi Vita as Enrico and the bass Francesco Monari in the part of Raimondo.

A review indicates that the performances were very successful. The reviewer went on to say:

> Hayez the famous singer got much applause; the tenor Mirate was considered at his best, and the basso Monari, from Bologna, who won good fame at Turin was no less successful.[33]

Catherine's contract with Alessandro Lanari ended on 16 December 1848. However, it was not her nature to ignore someone who had helped her. She wrote to Lanari on 30 December asking for his advice and to say that she had had a visit from a Mr. Fry who discussed the possibility of a visit to America.

This was William Henry Fry, an American operatic composer from Philadelphia, who was the European music critic for the *New York Tribune* based in Paris. It's not completely clear what Mr. Fry had in mind for Catherine, since his only opera of note, *Leonora*, which he had finished composing in 1845, had not had much success.[34] It is possible that he may have wanted to take her to Philadelphia to sing *I Masnadieri*, as there was mention of the opera in her correspondence and he did offer her a contract.

However, Catherine's focus was now on London. With its political stability, it had become the musical centre in Europe following the uprisings in Milan, Vienna and Paris in early1848. In addition, many of her contemporaries from Italy were now going there because of the disruption in the Italian states.

Catherine's season continued with the local premiere of Verdi's *I Masnadieri*, on 25 January, with Mirate as Carlo, Vita as Francesco and Monari as Massimiliano. Bellini's *I Puritani* followed, on 14 February, with the same cast. This was the first time Catherine had sung this beautiful Bellini score since her debut three years ago in the role of Elvira in Marseilles in May 1845. Her resolve to leave Italy was further reinforced when the Piedmont army terminated the armistice with Austria early in 1849. Within a week the Piedmont troops were routed and their King had abdicated and left Italy. The chaos had reached Genoa.

Before the *Carnivale* season finished in Genoa, either Edward Delafield, the lessee of the Royal Italian Opera in London, or his representative, possibly Frederick Gye, met Catherine in Genoa. She signed a contract and agreed to be in London by April 1849 for her debut at the Royal Italian Opera at Covent Garden. This would be in a Donizetti opera, *Linda di Chamounix*, the role that had brought her such success at La Scala three years earlier.

Catherina's years in Italy were drawing to a close. In another month she would have spent exactly five years in Italy learning her profession and advancing her career. She had achieved everything Manuel Garcia and Felice Ronconi had expected of her. She had sung in sixteen different operas by eight different composers and performed almost 100 times at La Scala alone in addition to her many performances in Vienna, Venice, Verona, Florence, Genoa and other places. In all, it totalled almost 250 operatic performances since she had first arrived in Milan in April 1844. She had also learned the language and wrote and spoke it fluently. She felt she was now ready for London.

She had partnered some of Europe's most renowned singers, and in her own right had gained fame and success, something she always knew she could achieve from her earliest days in Limerick. Her mother was proud of her daughter's achievements. Catherine had saved a considerable sum of money and taken care of her mother and sister, both of whom would accompany her to London. Her life was to take new directions after a period of time in England. However, she would return one more time to Italy to gain additional laurels in Rome, a city that she had not performed in during her early years.

Before leaving Genoa, Catherine had one more task to perform, which resulted in an amusing situation. Two American navy ships arrived in Genoa early in February 1849.[35] and Catherine was invited to give a concert each of them. Her mother and sister were also invited. Catherine's visit to the first ship, which had the senior naval officers on board, was to be followed by a visit later in the day to the second smaller naval vessel. It seems that the earlier visit was so successful that the American sailors, enjoying Catherine's company and particularly her mother's personality, wouldn't let them depart to the other ship. The fact that Catherine did not make it to the second vessel caused considerable disappointment for the crew.

If the truth were known, probably all of the Hayes ladies derived great pleasure from being able to speak English again, as it had been so long

MASNADIERI

MELODRAMMA

DA RAPPRESENTARSI

NEL TEATRO CARLO FELICE

Il Carnevale del 1849.

GENOVA
Tipografia dei fratelli Pagano.
Canneto il lungo, n.° 860.

PERSONAGGI

MASSIMILIANO Conte di Moor , Reggente
Sig. Francesco Federico Monari.

CARLO
FRANCESCO } figliuoli di lui
Sigg. Raffaele Mirate
Luigi Vita.

AMALIA , orfana , nipote del Conte
Signora Caterina Hayes.

ARMINIO , camerlengo della famiglia reggente
Sig. Francesco Galberini.

MOSER , pastore
Sig. Giovanni Garibaldi.

ROLLA , compagno di Carlo Moor
Sig. Timoleone Barattini.

Coro di Giovani traviati , poi Masnadieri
Donne — Fanciulli — Servi.

L'azione succede in Germania
sul principio del secolo XVIII , e dura circa tre anni

La Musica è di GIUSEPPE VERDI.

I Cori d'ambo i sessi sono formati dagli Allievi dell'Istit
di Musica , instruiti e diretti dal sig. M.° Paolo Carletti.
Suggeritore sig. Pietro Giannetti.
Macchinisti sigg. Ger. Novaro e Luigi Podestà — Attrezz
sig. Gius. Rollero — Capo-Sarto sig. Carlo Carrera — Ca
sarta Maria Merega — Berrettonaro sig. N.° Mazzini — Par
chiere Mich. Ferrando e figlio - - Calzolajo sig. G. B. Mosci

N. B. *I versi virgolati si ommettono per brevità.*

14. Programme for the local premiere of Verdi's *I Masnadieri* in Genoa 1849, featuring Catherine Hayes. (Author's collection).

since they had enjoyed that privilege outside the family. The fact that they were with the elite of the American navy in the Mediterranean probably also influenced them to stay where they were and enjoy the company and entertainment.

At the end of February, Catherine and her family left Genoa for England, arriving in London in mid-March. The London musical press announced her arrival on 31 March in a brief paragraph which also mentioned that the celebrated baritone Antonio Tamburini (1800–76) the tenor Lorenzo Salvi (1810–79) and others had arrived from St. Petersburg.[36] These two very famous singers were scheduled to perform opposite Catherine in *Linda di Chamounix* on her debut night at the Royal Italian Opera at the Covent Garden Theatre on 10 April 1849. It was an exciting time for her, she would be singing with some of the Royal Italian Opera's best singers in the most important city in Europe, exactly five years almost to the day from the time she first started working with Felice Ronconi in Milan.

She had been single minded in the pursuit of her profession, having taken virtually no time off for pleasure. She had managed to avoid the scandals and crises that several of her contemporaries had experienced. This was her first visit to London and she had no idea how she would be received. Only time would tell. In addition, Jenny Lind was also in town performing with great éclat.

Catherine looked forward to it all with a certain amount of anxiety and trepidation. She was confident that she would be successful professionally, but did not really know how the social side of her life in England would unfold, or how her mother, who was now 50 years old, would cope with the change. The move would also take her closer to Ireland, which she wanted to visit, a thought that gave her great pleasure.

Greater London at the time of Catherine's arrival had a population of about 2.5 million people.[37] In musical circles the very best of European talent had now settled there. In part this was due to the political instability that prevailed in Paris, Vienna and the principal cities of the Italian states. In addition, because of the size of London and its population there was a much greater demand for musical performances by its wealthy, sophisticated audiences. Industrial cities such as Birmingham, Manchester and Leeds had grown enormously in the previous ten years and each now had significant populations. The port city of Liverpool had also expanded with this industrial growth and to the north in Scotland, Edinburgh and Glasgow also saw great gains. This expansion and growth created a ready market for singers and musicians who wanted to extend their activities beyond central London. Also, across the Irish sea, Dublin – the second city in the British Empire – had a long established reputation as a major operatic centre with Cork, Limerick and Belfast in the north following close on its tail.

The transportation system was good throughout the British Isles with railways linking the major centres to cities in the provinces, which made it relatively easy and comfortable to travel.[38] The railway system in England and Scotland had grown dramatically during the first half of the century, and in Ireland a similar growth pattern prevailed.

All this industrialisation and expansion meant that London was also paying the best fees, outside of St. Petersburg in Russia, where the weather was permanently inclement and very hostile for the singer. However, competition in London was very fierce during those times; the rules were quite different from Milan and Vienna. There were three or more sopranos available for every operatic role and only two major operatic companies in London. To become indisposed could mean that a competitor was waiting in the wings ready to step into your role and displace you, as Catherine would soon learn the hard way. Despite all of these vicissitudes, Catherine eagerly looked forward to London with a strong sense that she was destined to make her life there.

CHAPTER SIX

The Royal Italian Opera – Debut

LONDON, 1849

EXCITEMENT prevailed among the Hayes ladies as they arrived in London around the middle of March 1849. None of them had ever been to London before. In Italy, no doubt Catherine would have heard about the London audience being super critical – in fact probably the most demanding in Europe. The music critics, and there were a number of very powerful ones, could make or break a career. It was all probably a little intimidating.

Catherine's mother, who was generally described as a women with a pleasant outgoing personality, was excited by being in London and particularly by her daughter's fame and publicity as she arrived in such a large and important city. The reality of what Catherine had achieved in such a short period of time became very clear to them on their arrival. However, for Catherine the ultimate test would be her debut night, and her reception by the audience and the reviews the next day. The Hayes ladies knew that if Catherine was successful in London she could go anywhere she wanted and earn fabulous fees, and that would give them all the security they had longed for from the earliest times.

For Catherine, in addition to first-night nerves, which normally accompanied a debut, there were also other anxieties. She was now using her theatrical age of 24, instead of her real age of 31! Even at this young age, the public knew she had almost five years of success on the continent in some of the most important musical cities of Europe. However, in England many looked upon continental experience, particularly Italian musical experience, with a certain amount of disdain. Even Verdi had felt somewhat uncomfortable during his first visit to England two years earlier. Additionally, Catherine's mother was now getting on in years, although was in good health. Catherine and her sister Henrietta, who was

33, were both unmarried, and neither had any marriage prospects on the horizon, which must have concerned their mother. For Catherine, there was the possibility of Sims Reeves, the suave erudite Englishman with whom she had collaborated at La Scala in October 1846. Reeves by now was a major figure on the London musical scene. Catherine wondered if he would remember her and if they would sing together again.

Accommodation for the Hayes family had been arranged by Catherine's long time friend and mentor from her days in Paris, George Osborne, who had taken up permanent residence in London with his wife since becoming a professor at the Royal Academy of Music a few years earlier.

However, perhaps the most important person in London from Catherine's perspective, was Jenny Lind. The publicity which preceded Lind's eagerly awaited arrival two years earlier at the beginning of 1847, fuelled by her delay in leaving Vienna, was only a prelude to what happened after her arrival. Lind's first performance in Meyerbeer's *Roberto il Diabolo* took place in May 1847 at Her Majesty's Theatre under Lumley's direction, with Michael Balfe conducting. From that moment onward, the phenomenon of Jenny Lind and the aura that surrounded her seemed to be everywhere – in London, Birmingham, Manchester, Liverpool, Glasgow, Edinburgh and even across the Irish sea in Dublin. If she wasn't singing in opera, concert or oratorio, the newspapers showed her attending charity functions at hospitals, orphanages and asylums, or giving donations to a favourite cause. Her name appeared to be in almost every newspaper and periodical.

Physically, Lind was five foot three inches in height;[1] she was considered plain and had a rather large nose and an introverted disposition. However, her secret in attracting attention came from her performances in the theatre, where her vocal technique and range, which was around two and a half octaves, up to a 'g' in alt., was fresh and exciting with a Nordic quality.[2] Musically, she probably had perfect pitch, which gave her high notes a brilliant silvery quality that was described by some as a sound which seemed to become disembodied from the singer while reaching out to every part of the theatre. Her cadenzas and florid style in the tradition of most Garcia pupils, were impeccable.

Later her friendship with the Bishop of Norwich, Bishop Stanley, and her involvement with religious music secured for her a pious halo that for the Victorians, dramatically separated her from her contemporaries. Lind had also publicly expressed a desire to leave the stage for the concert platform, which naturally received public attention. The Bishop encouraged her to take this course. In fact, her last operatic performance took place in London at Her Majesty's Theatre in Meyerbeer's *Roberto il Diabolo* during May 1849. It was the same opera in which she had made her London debut two years earlier. She never again sang in opera.

When Lind first completed her studies with Garcia in Paris in August 1842 she had first concentrated her performances in her native Sweden, and then mostly in Vienna and other cities in Germany and Austria. In Germany, she had developed a close friendship with Meyerbeer in Berlin and Mendelssohn in Leipzig. She had consciously elected not to perform in France or Italy. By the time Catherine arrived in London Lind had given almost eighty operatic performances in the two years she'd been there. Her repertoire primarily included the following: *Roberto il Diabolo*, *Lucia di Lammermoor*, *La figlia del reggimento* and *L'elisir d'Amore*; *La Sonnambula*, *Norma* and *I Puritani*; *Le Nozze di Figaro*; *La gazza ladra* and Verdi's *I Masnadieri*. Her six appearances in opera in Dublin were limited to music by Donizetti and Bellini. Lind's overall operatic career only lasted about seven years in Europe. She never sang in opera in America.

Lind was highly successful in every role she performed in London except Norma, which was considered a failure. This was primarily due to the fact that Giulia Grisi, who was also living in London, was considered untouchable in the role of *Norma*. However, Lind left her own indelible stamp on every one of her other roles.

Lind represented a formidable presence in London for Catherine, since the two were Garcia pupils and had similar voice styles and repertoires. Catherine wisely decided on *Linda di Chamounix* for her debut role, which did not create an immediate opportunity for the critics to make a direct comparison between the two singers. Fortunately, Lind was not scheduled to sing on 10 April, the night that Catherine was to make her debut.

Lind 'nights' at the opera in London generally created a clamour for tickets. Queen Victoria and her husband Prince Albert, both of whom were music enthusiasts frequently attended her performances. The Queen had been taking singing lessons from Luigi Lablache on a regular basis for years, and Prince Albert was a competent musician. Other admirers of Lind were the Duchess of Kent and numerous members of the aristocracy, including the famous Duke of Wellington, who even became her personal friend. A great sense of excitement prevailed when Lind performances were announced, resulting in long queues for tickets from early morning.

No other singer in London at the time generated such a frenzy of publicity. In some strange inexplicable way she seemed to enter uncharted waters with every new performance in London, creating more excitement each time, despite the fact that apart from Verdi's *I Masnadieri* every other opera she sang had been previously been seen and heard there. Catherine was acutely aware of Lind's magnetism and that there was the potential for comparisons to be made.

Apart from Lind, the London opera season of 1849 had a stellar array of talent and glamour lined up. Most of the greatest operatic names of the times converged on London having completed operatic or concert seasons at places as far apart as Havana, St. Petersburg, Moscow and New York. They also came in great numbers from the principal cities of Europe such as Paris, Vienna, Rome, Naples and Milan. The London musical press featured an ongoing listing of who was arriving, covering just about everybody of importance, including Catherine when she arrived in March. These arriving operatic luminaries were now a part of either the roster at the Royal Italian Opera at Covent Garden or that of the competing theatre, Her Majesty's, twenty minutes away at the Haymarket.

Benjamin Lumley at Her Majesty's, who was responsible for Lind's presence in London, now had two other new female stars. One was Marietta Alboni, a twenty-six-year-old, very large mezzo-soprano with a phenomenal range, who mixed her repertoire to include leading soprano roles such as Amina in Bellini's *La Sonnambula* with more traditional mezzo roles such as Cenerentola in Rossini's opera of the same name. Lumley's other newcomer was Teresa Parodi, a strikingly tall, good-looking 22-year-old dramatic soprano who had been a pupil of Giuditta Pasta (the original Norma) and who had also been a student with Felice Ronconi in Milan at the same time as Catherine.

On 10 April, Parodi made her debut with modest success in Bellini's opera *Norma*, the same night as Catherine's debut at Covent Garden. The undaunted Giulia Grisi – the greatest interpreter of *Norma* of the period- was scheduled to sing the same role a short time later at the Royal Italian Opera. In addition, Lumley's season also had Luigi Lablache and his son Frederick, a baritone, the soprano Erminia Frezzolini, the young tenor Italo Gardoni who was a great favourite, another good tenor, Enrico Calzolari, and the baritones Ronconi and Belletti. Even Felice Ronconi was now in London managing the chorus at Her Majesty's since the revolution in Lombardy had driven him out of Milan.

At the Royal Italian Opera at Covent Garden, apart from Catherine's debut, another new singer was Emilie de Meric, a contralto also making

304 THE MUSICAL WORLD.

Re-Appearance of Mdlle. ALBONI.

HER MAJESTY'S THEATRE.

The Nobility, Subscribers to the Opera, and the Public, are respectfully informed, that on

THIS EVENING (SATURDAY), MAY 12th, 1849,

will be performed Rossini's Opera, entitled

LA CENERENTOLA.

Angelina (under the name of Cenerentola) Mdlle. ALBONI.
Don Ramiro . . . . Sig. CALZOLARI,
Dandini . . . . Sig. BELLETTI,
Alidoro . . . . Sig. ARNOLDI,
Don Magnifico . . . . Sig. LABLACHE.

Director of the Music and Conductor - M. BALFE.

To conclude with the highly successful entirely new grand Ballet (in Five Tableaux), by M. PAUL TAGLIONI, (the Music by Signor PUGNI), entitled

ELECTRA; or, THE LOST PLEIAD,

In which

Mdlle. CARLOTTA GRISI,

Mdlles. Petit Stephan, Marra, Tommassini, Julien, Aussandon, Lamoreux, Mdlle. Marie Taglioni, and M. Paul Taglioni, will appear.

Applications for Boxes, Stalls, and Tickets to be made at the Box-Office of the Theatre, where Pit Tickets may be obtained as usual, price 10s. 6d. each.

Doors open at Seven o'Clock; the Opera to commence at Half-past Seven.

HER MAJESTY'S THEATRE.

GRAND EXTRA NIGHT, on THURSDAY NEXT, May 17.

It is respectfully announced that a GRAND EXTRA NIGHT, on the scale of former seasons, will be presented on THURSDAY, May 17th, when will be performed (for the last time) BELLINI's celebrated Opera of

NORMA.

Norma . . . . Mdlle. PARODI,
Adalgisa . . . . Made. GIULIANI,
Pollione . . . . Signor BORDAS,
AND
Oroveso . . . . Signor LABLACHE.

To be followed by the principal Tableaux of the admired Ballet of

FIORITA.

By M. P. TAGLIONI; the Music by Sig. PUGNI; the Scenery by Mr. C. MARSHALL.

PRINCIPAL PARTS BY

Mdlle. C. ROSATI, Mdlle. M. TAGLIONI, AND M. DOR.

The Selection will comprise the principal Pas of the Ballet, and the admired Tableaux of the Waterfall.—To be followed by a Selection from ROSSINI's Opera,

LA CENERENTOLA.

Including the celebrated Air, "Kallor se non ti speccio," by Sig. CALZOLARI; and the Scena and brilliant Rondo, "Non più mesta," by Mdlle. ALBONI.

Angelina (under the name of Cenerentola) Mdlle. ALBONI.
Don Ramiro . . . . Sig. CALZOLARI,
Dandini . . . . Sig. BELLETTI,
AND
Don Magnifico . . . . Sig. LABLACHE.

To Conclude with the admired Ballet of

ELECTRA; or, THE LOST PLEIAD.

(Omitting the first two Tableaux); the principal parts by

Mdlle. CARLOTTA GRISI,

Mdlles. Petit Stephan, Marra, Tommassini, Julien, Aussandon, Lamoreux, Mdlle. Marie Taglioni, and M. Paul Taglioni;

And comprising the admired Grand Pas de Deux d'Action, "La Lutte," Mdlle. CARLOTTA GRISI and M. P. TAGLIONI; and also the celebrated scene of the Restoration of the Lost Pleiad to the Regions of Light.

Applications for Boxes, Stalls, and Tickets to be made at the Box Office of the Theatre, where Pit Tickets may be obtained as usual, price 10s. 6d. each.

Doors open at Seven; the Opera to commence at Half-past Seven o'clock.

ROYAL ITALIAN OPERA,

COVENT GARDEN.

THIS EVENING, SATURDAY, MAY 12th, 1849,

Will be produced in its entire form (for the first time in this country), and with the most powerful *ensemble*, MEYERBEER's Grand Opera, in five acts,

ROBERT LE DIABLE,

With entirely New Scenery, Costumes, and Appointments.

Alice . . . Miss CATHERINE HAYES.
Isabella . . . Mademoiselle CORBARI.
Dama d'Onore . . . Madame BELLINI.
Elena . . . Mademoiselle WUTHIER.
Roberto . . . Signor SALVI.
Rambaldo . . . Signor LAVIA.
Alberto . . . Signor ROMMI.
Sacerdote . . . Signor TAGLIAFICO.
Eroldo . . . M. MASSOL.
AND
Bertramo . . . Signor MARINI.

In order to accomplish as perfect an *ensemble* as possible in the performance of this grand work, the Directors have the pleasure to announce, that M. MASSOL, Signor POLONINI, Signor MEI, Signor SOLDI, and Signor RACHE, have kindly consented to assist in the Choral combinations and effects.

In addition to the Orchestra,

A MILITARY BAND will be employed.

In the Fifth Act, the Chorus will be increased by

A DOUBLE CHOIR,

MR. COSENS PRESIDING AT THE ORGAN.

In the Second Act, the incidental

DIVERTISSEMENT

Will be danced by

Mdlle. LOUISE TAGLIONI and M. ALEXANDRE,

With a numerous CORPS DE BALLET.

In the Third Act, the BACCHANALE of the NUNS will be danced by

Mdlle. WUTHIER,

And upwards of ONE HUNDRED CORYPHEES.

COMPOSER, DIRECTOR OF THE MUSIC, AND CONDUCTOR,

MR. COSTA.

The Libretto edited and translated by Signor MAGGIONI.
The Scenery by Messrs. GRIEVE and TELBIN.
The Costumes by Mrs. BAILEY and Madame MARZIO.
The Properties and Appointments by Mr. BLAMIRE.
The extensive Stage Machinery by Mr. ALLEN.
The Ballet arranged by Signor CASATI.
And the SPECTACLE under the direction of Mr. A. HARRIS.

The Performances commence on Tuesdays at Half-past Eight, and on Thursdays and Saturdays at Eight o'clock precisely.

Tickets, Stalls, and Boxes (for the Night or Season) to be obtained at the Box-Office of the Theatre, which is open from Eleven till Five.

THEATRE ROYAL, DRURY LANE.

GERMAN OPERA, FOR TWELVE NIGHTS ONLY.

On MONDAY EVENING will be performed (for the first time these eight years) WEBER's Opera,

DER FREISCHUTZ.

Agatha . . . Mdlle. ROMANI,
Max . . . Herr ERL,
Caspar . . . Herr FORMES,

Supported by a Band and Chorus, each consisting of sixty performers.

Performances to commence at Eight o'clock.—Private Boxes and Places may be obtained at the Box-Office, and at Messrs. JULLIEN and Co.'s, 214, Regent Street.

Printed and Published, for the Proprietors, at the "Nassau Steam Press," by WILLIAM SPENCER JOHNSON, 60, St. Martin's Lane, in the parish of St. Martin's in the Fields, in the County of Middlesex; where all communications for the Editor are to be addressed, post paid. To be had of G. Purkess, Dean Street, Soho; Strange, Paternoster Row; Vickers, Holywell Street, and at all Booksellers.—Saturday, May 12th, 1849.

15. Catherine Hayes was scheduled to sing in Meyerbeer's grand opera, *Robert le Diable* in May 1849, However illness prevented her on the evening of the first performance. (Author's collection).

her debut on the same night. The tenor Lorenzo Salvi, who had just returned to London from Russia, was scheduled to sing with Catherine. The indispensable pair, Grisi and Mario, however were the mainstay of the Royal Italian Opera roster supported by Antonio Tamburini, also just in from singing in St. Petersburg. In addition, Fanny Tacchinardi-Persiani, who had made her operatic debut almost twenty years previously and was the creator of the title role of *Lucia di Lammermoor* under Donizetti's direction, was also announced, together with the ageing French prima donna Julie Dorus-Gras (1805–96), who would shortly be 44 years old.

The principal members of the cast for *Linda di Chamounix* on Tuesday 10 April included Catherine in the title role, de Meric as Pierotto, Salvi as the Viscount and Tamburini as Antonio, with Michael Costa conducting. There was great excitement about the new production of *Linda*, which was being performed at the Royal Italian Opera for the first time. Within a short period all of the leading publications were praising the performance and its prima donna; most of the space in the *Times* review (J.W. Davidson?) featured Catherine's performance:

> Miss Catherine Hayes, an Irish woman by birth, has for a considerable period enjoyed a high reputation in Italy, and has been the chief support of the Scala in Milan . . . Both debutantes [de Meric and Hayes] were successful. Miss Catherine Hayes singularly so. Her voice is a soprano not remarkable for power, but of a very sweet quality throughout, and capable of telling without the slightest effort. The middle and lower notes are exceedingly good, the latter especially so for a real soprano, which has nothing in common with a mezzo soprano; the higher notes, up to A flat are very pure and clear; thence to the D flat, the highest note we heard her sing, they bear evidence of fatigue; this may proceed from the excessive severity of Italian discipline, which taxes a singer until she is fairly worn out by reiterated execution. Miss Hayes's style of singing is artistic and graceful; she never forces her voice, but has abundance of energy at her command, which she uses legitimately, and without any tendency to exaggeration. Her intonation is generally perfect, although sometimes in attacking a high note there is a slight feeling of uncertainty. In the first scene, the uproar welcome she received from the attendance appeared to overcome her altogether and it was not till near the end of the well known cavatina 'O luce di quest' anima' that she entirely recovered her presence of mind; here

MISS. CATHERINE HAYES.   SIG. TAMBURINI.   MDLLE. MERIC.

SCENE FROM "LINDA DI CHAMOUNI," AT THE ROYAL ITALIAN OPERA.—THE MALEDICTION, ACT. 2.

16. Engraving of Catherine Hayes' debut night April 1849, at the Royal Italian Opera, Covent Garden, London in *Linda di Chamounix* with Tamburini and de Meric. (Author's collection).

however, an elegant cadenza introducing a clever and well executed shake, gained her great applause and an encore…In the grand scene with Antonio (Linda's father) Miss Hayes was excellent, and the mad scene that follows was sung with admirable effect, especially the well known bravura passage 'Non e ver,' where her execution of the chromatic passages was perfect, and the ascending trait with the violins, at the end, was accomplished with remarkable decision and brilliancy. In this, as well as the last scene, Miss Hayes gave evidence of a great deal of dramatic feeling, and a thorough familiarity with stage effect. In place of the duet which stands for the finale in Donizetti's score, she introduced a cabaletta, from an opera by Luigi Ricci, called [Il] *Colonello,* a work as unknown as its composer.[3] Although we cannot admire this air, we are bound to acknowledge the brilliancy and correctness of Miss Hayes's execution, which almost redeemed it from its natural insipidity. Nothing could be warmer or more unanimous than her reception by the audience, who applauded her enthusiastically and recalled her before the foot-lights after every act…her success was thoroughly deserved.[4]

Introducing an aria or special bravura piece from another opera to demonstrate a prima donna's skills or to close an evening was not uncommon in the nineteenth century, despite the questionable artistic value.

The infamous Henry Chorley, music critic of the *Athenaeum*, in a curt review reserved judgement, saying:

With the audience the success was unequivocal – Miss Hayes has to pass through a severer ordeal ere she can firmly hold the rank she aspires to. We shall reserve a definite opinion on her merits until she has overcome the timidity consequent on a first appeal to a London public.[5]

The review that appeared in the following Saturday's issue of the *Musical World*, possibly also written by the editor J.W. Davison or by staff member Desmond Ryan, stated:

Miss Hayes met with a most rapturous reception. The audience cheered her for several minutes . . . Miss Hayes has a soprano voice of very decided soprano quality. Its range is extensive, and its tone agreeable and telling throughout. It has been well cultivated, and, though not remarkable for extraordinary power or flexibility, is capable of giving the highest effects to that kind of dramatic vocalisation in which execution of roulades and ornaments is not the indispensable ingredient. The upper notes of Miss Hayes' voice are very clear and beautiful, as high as A; thence up to D flat they are less bell-like, and evidence those signs of fatigue that invariably result from lengthened practice on the Italian stage . . . the lower notes indeed, are the most beautiful we have ever heard in a real soprano. As a singer, Miss Hayes possesses the highest accomplishments of style, and a very remarkable facility of execution . . . suffice it that her success was one of the most decided and triumphant, and, let us add, one of the most really deserved we recollect since we have been in the habit of attending operatic performances.[6]

The *Examiner* reported that:

The Royal Italian Opera has been fortunate in the engagement of Miss Catherine Hayes, the young English (or more properly Irish) prima donna, who made her debut at Covent Garden on Tuesday. The great celebrity which Miss Hayes has gained in Italy gave rise to expectations from her first appearance here, which exposed her to a severe ordeal; but she met it triumphantly, convincing the public that she fully merits all the fame she has acquired. She is handsome, and her whole aspect and deportment made her a charming represen- tative of the heroine . . . Miss Hayes acted the part with captivating softness, simplicity, and tenderness; and in the concluding scenes, showed no small power of expressing strong passion. As a vocal artist, she is highly accomplished. Her voice is a pure soprano, has been highly cultivated, and its natural sweetness is enhanced by the purity and equality of its tones. Its volume is not great, but its clear and penetrating quality enables it to 'fill' every part of a large theatre. Taking her for all in all, she is certainly one of the most delightful performers of whom the modern musical stage can boast.'[7]

One of Catherine's home town papers, the *Limerick Chronicle*, also reported on her debut using excerpts from the *Times* (London) and the *Morning Advertiser* (London) to describe her performance and a footnote to remind its readers that the distinguished lady was a native of Limerick![8]

Despite the reserve of the *Athenaeum* music critic it was apparent that her success was complete on her debut night. Added to her jubilant reception that night was an extra surprise – her sponsor Bishop Edmond Knox of Limerick was in the audience to witness the success of the young Limerick girl he had so kindly helped many years before. Catherine saw the Bishop from the stage and between the acts, she visited him in his private box. Falling on her knees she wept with emotion and gratitude for all he had done to make that night and her career possible.[9] It was their first meeting since she had left Limerick almost ten years previously. It was also destined to be one of their last. On Thursday 26 April, the Bishop attended a function held by Queen Victoria at St. James's Palace in which he presented his niece Isabella Knox to the Queen and Prince Albert. Shortly after that he left for the provinces on his way back to Limerick via Liverpool. On 3 May, aged 77, he succumbed to pneumonia in Birmingham. Short obituaries appeared in the *Times* and in the *Examiner* within a few days.[10] Then, on 10 May, the *Times* published a scathing full-column obituary. The writer began by saying:

> In ordinary cases we abstain from anything like comment upon the actions of those who have just passed away from amongst us, when their actions cannot be spoken of in terms of praise and their memory with regret. In the case of Dr. Knox, however it is in the discharge of a public duty we break through our usual system. With the memory of the individual we would deal as lightly as possible; but the public consequences of his omissions, rather than his acts, survive him, and must be productive of permanent evil.[11]

The writer goes on to make a personal attack on the Bishop for his absenteeism from Limerick during a time of need [the Great Irish Famine], mentioning the fact that he was paid almost £5,000 per year from the diocese but chose to spend most of his time in Italy. The entire obituary castigates the Bishop for his lack of involvement in his parish, the decay of the cathedral building in Limerick and the infrequency with which he visited his home base. Strangely there was no mention whatsoever of how the Bishop had made it possible for Catherine Hayes to be appearing at Covent Garden that same week. Ironically this obituary appeared in the *Times* the very week she was making great news as the new prima donna at the Royal Italian Opera. Her success and her presence in London would never have been achieved without the help and support that was provided by the good Bishop of Limerick.

Catherine's next great challenge was a series of performances of *Lucia di Lammermoor*, the first on Thursday 26 April; the next performance was

17. Portrait of Catherine Hayes around the time of her return to Ireland as an international prima donna. Published London 1850. (Courtesy of the National Library of Ireland).

on Saturday 28 April, and there were several others over the next few weeks.

Catherine's partner for *Lucia* was the star tenor, Mario, then 38 years old and in his prime. It must have been an interesting and exciting experience for Catherine. She had first seen Mario in Dublin in *Norma* that eventful September night in 1841 when she had been invited to the opera by Luigi Lablache. Now she was singing opposite him in the lead role. Antonio Tamburini sang the part of Enrico. The young Entimio Polonini, who had just arrived from Havana having completed the operatic season there, sang the bass part of Raimondo. The Times reporting on her Lucia was highly complementary, saying:

> Miss Hayes has a very graceful conception of the character of Lucia. Her acting is full of gentleness and resignation. When Enrico, her brother, shows her the letter which discovers Edgardo's supposed falsehood, and further on, when writhing under the malediction of her lover, she is overwhelmed with despair, her demeanour rather betrayed the evidence of intense suffering than of vehement passion. Her mad scene, too, depicted the wreck of a gentle nature; there were no violent outbreaks – no sudden bursts of rage; it was throughout a soft and touching picture. In her singing, Miss Hayes gave further evidence of those artistic accomplishments which we have found occasion to praise. Her first cavatina 'Perche non ho' was delivered with equal brilliancy and refinement; the largo was sung with great feeling, and the long note that preceded the cabaletta was sustained with utmost ease, the gradual increase and diminution of power being exquisitely managed; in the cabaletta the scales were even and finished, and the fioratura (of which there was rather an excess) developed both neatness and invention.[12] In the long scena of the second act Miss Hayes exhibited a more happy combination of the dramatic with the vocal art than we had observed in her Linda; the one did not interfere with the other, but each played, as it were, into the other's hands. Her delivery of the theme and rondo was somewhat slow and over elaborated, but in other respects the entire scene was a piece of clever and highly finished execution.

The reviewer continued on to say

> the applause throughout was liberal and unanimous; the success of Miss Hayes was complete, and she more than once re-appeared with Mario before the footlights.[13]

The music critic at the *Examiner* was not able to attend and elected to use the review from the *Daily News* to inform his readers of Catherine's performance with the following:

> Miss Hayes appeared in Lucia, one of the parts on which her reputation was chiefly founded in Italy and Germany [Vienna]. It was a very fine performance, and was completely successful. We have already described the qualities of her voice and the peculiar features of her style. Her powers were more severely tried than in her previous part of Linda. The music demanded much more vocal exertion, and the character is one of the most tragic on the musical stage. But Miss Hayes was equal to all it exigencies; and, with the exception of Jenny Lind, she is, on the whole, the most natural and interesting representative of *Lucia* that we have seen. Her reading of the character differs much from Jenny Lind's. She has more softness and less passion; and in the final scene her madness does not rise to that terrible violence which terminates in death. Her manner of singing the air in that scene 'Alfin son tua' was exquisitely beautiful.[14]

The *Musical World* commented that:

> Miss Catherine Hayes made an immense impression in *Lucia*. She sang with the utmost feeling and energy, and acted with the greatest delicacy and gentleness, which betokened a thorough appreciation of the character. Her first cavatina 'Perche non ho', was rendered with exceeding brilliancy and finish; and some daring cadences at the close, executed with singular precision and skill, elicited a storm of applause. In the mad scene she refrained from all extravagance, and depended more for her efforts on intensity of feeling than any exuberance of display. Nor was she less impressive on this account. The reality of the scene became more apparent, and those who, at some ill-judged show-off, would have raised the hand and lifted up the voice, were silent and felt the more. We were highly pleased with Miss Catherine Hayes throughout this trying and oft-mistaken part, and pronounce her performance a very great improvement on her Linda...Miss Catherine Hayes's success was triumphant.[15]

The six-and-a-half-minute aria 'Perche non ho del vento' and its cabaletta, which Catherine sang in the second scene in this performance of *Lucia*, replaced Donizetti's original music 'Regnava nel silenzio' and belonged to Donizetti's opera, *Rosmonda d'Inghilterra*. The opera *Rosmonda* was composed in 1834, a year before his *Lucia di Lammermoor*. In 1842, Garcia had used this difficult piece as a training exercise for Lind during her study period. However, the aria was introduced into *Lucia* by the prima donna Persiani around 1837, with Donizetti's approval, after she had sung in the first performance of *Rosmonda* in Florence in 1834 under Lanari's management.[16] Catherine apparently was aware that Lind normally sang the aria in her *Lucia*, and elected not to be outdone by the great Lind in London. Original librettos for Catherine's performances in Italy during the 1840s show that she usually sang the original music 'Regnava nel silenzio' in the second scene of *Lucia*, not the *Rosmonda* aria and cabaletta.

Two nights after Catherine's first Lucia, on 28 April, Jenny Lind was also featuring in *Lucia* at Her Majesty's while Catherine was singing the same role at Covent Garden. This was the first time this season that Lind was performing *Lucia* in London. Queen Victoria and Prince Albert elected to attend the Lind performance. Two days earlier the Queen had also attended Jenny Lind's *La Sonnambula*. This time the Queen and the Prince brought a large number of the royal family and visiting royalty from Germany with them. The Duke of Wellington and Lady Wellesley were also in attendance.

Lind's Edgardo for the evening was Italo Gardoni, the young tenor who had sung several performances with Lind in London. Filippo Colette was Enrico. Catherine had sung with him in Italy. Michael Balfe was the conductor. The opera was scheduled to commence at 8 pm.

At the Royal Italian Opera, Covent Garden, where the opera was also scheduled to start at 8 pm the cast included Catherine as Lucia, Mario as Edgardo and Tamburini as Enrico, with Michael Costa as the conductor. In attendance were the Duchess of Cambridge and her party, which included visiting royalty from Germany and other countries. The Duke and Duchess of Bedford, who held the patent to the theatre, occupied the royal box at Covent Garden for the occasion. There were also several members of the Irish aristocracy present.

The *Times* reviewed the Lind opening night saying:

> The opera house was exceedingly well filled on Saturday and the reception of Mdlle. Jenny Lind in *Lucia di Lammermoor*, was a continuation of the wonted enthusiasm. The first aria, 'Perche no ho del vento', was one of those delightful combinations of a natural

gift and a finished cultivation by which this most fascinating of vocalists exercises such a potent charm over her hearers. She was never in better voice, the gushing forth of rich melodious notes never seemed more spontaneous, and the profuse ornaments were never executed with more surprising facility. The interview with the brother in the second act, the trembling agony with which she reads the forged letter, and the histrionic eloquence which she throws into the cabaletta 'Se tradvimi' produced a great effect; but, as usual, her chief triumph was obtained by the mad scene, which was illustrated with all that phrenetic rage, and with that wild leap of insanity which, as we have said, really gives the distinctive character to her Lucia . . . Mdlle. Lind was called at the end of each of the two first acts, and twice at the conclusion of the mad scene, when Her Majesty joined in the applause.[17]

The *Musical World* critic didn't feel quite the same way as the *Times* reporter, saying that:

Our opinion of her performance in this opera has been given on more than one occasion. It is not altered. She sings the cavatina, 'Perche non ho' to perfection, and the duet with Enrico as well as it can be sung; her singing in the mad scene also is occasionally exquisite, especially in the aria; but her acting throughout is a glaring mistake – one of the most glaring ever made by any artist on any stage . . . shall we record the 'ovations' paid to the 'Nightingale?' Heavens forbid. They would take up too much space that might be devoted to more interesting matters. The house was crowded, but not so full as on Thursday previous [*La Sonnambula*].[18]

In seems a strange that there was not some element of comparison of the two, given the circumstances. Of course the Lind 'legend' was already in place, Lind was in a class by herself, and to suggest that any other singer might compare to her at that point in time was probably not a consideration for the London critics.

The two prima donnas had many similarities. They both had studied with Garcia (who was now living in London), they had vocal styles and techniques that were similar (Verdi also thought so for *I Masnadieri*), they were around the same age and sang the same roles. In fact Catherine was scheduled to sing the part of Alice in Meyerbeer's *Robert le Diable* on Saturday 12 May (advertised as 'produced in its entire form for the first time in this country') at the Royal Italian Opera. Lind was also scheduled to sing the same role (advertised as *Roberto Il Diavolo*) at Her Majesty's Theatre on 10 May. Great publicity and fanfare was attached to the Royal Italian Opera version because of the fact that it was claimed to be the first complete version of the opera ever to be performed in London. It would be left to the music critics in Ireland to tread the dangerous ground of making a comparison between the two singers, given that country's predisposition to the native born prima donna.

Meanwhile, on 8 May a 'morning' concert (1.30 pm) was arranged at the Royal Italian Opera at Covent Garden. Virtually the full roster of the opera participated. Catherine sang the principal aria from *Linda di Chamounix,* which was encored. She later sang a duet with de Meric, also from *Linda.* Others participating in the concert included Mario and Grisi, the baritones Ronconi and Tamburini, soprano Madame Dorus-Gras, the tenor Salvi, the contralto Mdlle. d'Angri and basses Marini, Polonini and Tagliafico. Michael Costa conducted the concert, which was described as 'somewhat long' but also as a success with the audience.

It was now almost a month since Catherine had made her debut in London. She had survived the critics and was making good progress towards acceptance in London musical society. Her schedule for the next few months included many more operatic appearances and a variety of concerts. She was also booked to participate in the Birmingham music festival in July.

The pressures of her work were starting to take their toll, as they would many times during her career. As the time drew near for her debut in the new role of Alice in *Robert le Diable* she was not feeling at all well; whether it was the London weather exhaustion or from her heavy schedule we don't know. She did not want to miss singing this important role or risk disappointing her audience. Queen Victoria and her entourage were also scheduled to attend the opening night. All her attention was given to the task in hand – Meyerbeer's grand opera in its original form, which was scheduled for 12 May. All the leading newspapers and the *Musical World* had advertisements announcing her forthcoming performance in the opera. However, by midday on the day of the performance she was suffering from a bad sore throat. It was impossible for her to go on that night. She advised the theatre management who immediately looked for a substitute. The obvious choice was Julie Dorus-Gras, who had performed in the premiere of *Robert le Diable* in Paris in 1831. When Dorus-Gras was approached about going on as a substitute for Catherine, the ageing

French prima donna advised that she only knew the opera in French and that, if she did appear, it was on condition that she would sing every performance of Meyerbeer's opera that season. Frederick Gye and the other members of the management were desperate and had no option but to agree to her conditions. A notice of Catherine's indisposition was inserted into the programmes that first evening.

The theatre management did not immediately tell Catherine Hayes about the Dorus-Gras agreement, and it was several days later that Catherine learned of the fact that she would not be appearing in any of the *Robert le Diable* performances. This came as a great shock to her. She was incensed, since nothing like this had ever occurred in Italy or Vienna. The London rules were very different from anything she had previously experienced. She felt cheated and decided to go public, writing to the Post: 'declaring her entire astonishment at the part being taken from her in so unceremonious a manner'.[19] Catherine's illness stayed with her for almost three weeks. Meanwhile Dorus-Gras sang the remaining performances of *Robert le Diable*. Catherine never sang this Meyerbeer opera anywhere afterwards.

Catherine's first performance after her illness, occurred on 29 May, when Lucia was given with the same cast as previously. Next on 30 May, there was a morning concert at the Royal Italian Opera in Covent Garden, with Grisi, Catherine, Dorus-Gras and Persiani as the female performers and Mario, Salvi, Tamburini, Ronconi and Sims Reeves and others comprising the male side. This was the first time since her arrival in London that Catherine appeared on the same concert platform as Sims Reeves, however they did not sing together. Sims Reeves had just joined the Royal Italian Opera having made his debut there on 22 May, in La Sonnambula with Persiani in the role of Amina and Tamburini as Rudolpho. Catherine attended this performance not only because of her interest in Persiani, but also because it was Sims Reeves' debut at the Royal Italian Opera – a step that brought him closer to her.

Next came a formal request and invitation from Buckingham Palace to selected members of the Royal Italian Opera and Her Majesty's Theatre to perform at a state concert for Queen Victoria and her guests on 2 June at Buckingham Palace.

Over 570 guests were invited to the concert. In addition to the Queen and Prince Albert attendees included the Duchess of Kent, the Duke and Duchesses of Cambridge and various other members of the Royal family, visiting Royalty from Germany and the Netherlands, and members of the aristocracy and clergy.

The singers from the two Italian opera companies included: Giulia Grisi, Marietta Alboni and Catherine Hayes; Mario, Italo Gardoni, Filippo Coletti and Luigi Lablache. Michael Costa the conductor was the accompanist.

The first part of the concert started with the beautiful quartet 'Mi manca la voce' from Rossini's *Mosè in Egitto*, with its opening harp accompaniment and soprano vocal line. Catherine, Alboni, Mario and Gardoni were the performers. Catherine's first solo came a short while later when she sang an aria completely unknown today called 'Oh vanne pompe' from *La marescialla d'Ancre*, a tragic opera by the composer Nini which was first performed in Padua in 1839. This is an aria she later sang at several concerts; obviously she felt it suited her voice. This was well received. During the second half of the concert Catherine, Luigi Lablache and Italo Gardoni performed a trio from Mozart's *Il Flauto Magico* (The Magic Flute), sung in Italian and called 'Dunque il mio ben'. Since Lablache was Queen Victoria's singing teacher, presumably he had some say in the pieces selected for the concert and must have felt that the Queen would like the Mozart trio. It was not something that Catherine would normally have sung.

There were various encores given by the performers during the concert. For her encore, Catherine chose to sing 'Kathleen Mavourneen', which she had not sung since her early days in Dublin. It is interesting that she decided this was the appropriate moment to sing the Irish song once again. Could it have been her sense of humour, or perhaps the desire to make a point about her nationality, that made her select this song as an encore for the Queen of England and 500 royal guests at Buckingham Palace? Perhaps it was her mother (who would not have been present) who suggested it as a possibility, should she be asked for an encore. She must have brought the music with her so that Michael Costa could accompany her, therefore it is reasonable to assume it was not an impulsive decision. In any event, it was probably the only time during the nineteenth century that anyone ever sang an Irish song in Buckingham Palace for Queen Victoria!

Whoever or whatever prompted the idea, it pleased the audience. Following the concert Queen Victoria made a note in her diary as follows:

> The concert was a very good one, but hardly so much as the last. Grisi's voice has sadly gone off. Alboni sang beautifully and Miss Hayes very nicely & with much feeling, & a good method. Mario was in excellent voice.[20]

Quite some time later, when Catherine spoke about this concert during an interview in Dublin, she mentioned that:

> The Queen entered into conversation with her, complimenting her on what the Queen was pleased to term her 'deserved success' and Prince Albert and the Duke of Cambridge both paid her flattering attention.[21]

Catherine's prominence on the London musical scene prompted one of the leading management agents and music publishers, Cramer & Beale of 201 Regent Street, to sign a contract with her. Shortly after the Buckingham Palace concert, Cramer & Beale published the sheet music of 'Kathleen Mavourneen' with a picture of Catherine and a headline that said 'Kathleen Mavourneen, Ballad sung by *Miss Catherine Hayes* at Her Majesty's Concerts, Buckingham Palace.'

With Cramer & Beale as her agents she now found she was heavily in demand. Her next activity brought her into new musical areas on the concert platform in early June, when it was announced that she would appear at a grand musical festival of upward of 800 performers sponsored by the London Sacred Harmonic Society! The festival was in central London at Exeter Hall, which was built in 1831 for the performance of sacred music. Exeter Hall was located on the site of the Strand Palace Hotel today.[22] It was demolished in 1907. Haydn's *Creation* was the featured work, with Catherine singing two famous pieces for the first time: 'With verdure clad' and 'On mighty wings'. Her Italian training equipped her perfectly to sing this type of music. Reviews next day said:

> The Society gave a very effective performance, the first and second parts of Haydn's Creation last night, with a band [orchestra] and chorus numbering little short of 800 performers. The principal vocal artist of the evening was Miss Catherine Hayes, who sang for the first time at Exeter Hall. The two airs 'With verdure clad' and 'O mighty wings' were delivered with equal judgement and taste; in the first the high notes were taken with clearness and certainty, in the last the florid divisions were executed with great neatness and decision, and in both a purity of style was evinced, which showed that Miss Hayes knew how to appreciate the distinction between sacred and dramatic music. The audience received her with great favour, and an encore of 'With verdure clad' was demanded, but Miss Hayes judiciously refrained from responding to the compliment.

Catherine's innate musical abilities once again came to the fore in Exeter Hall. Her training and her years in Italy in opera should naturally have pushed her to respond to the encore requested by the audience; however, guided by her judgement and intellect, she knew that for this sacred music it would not be appropriate. Repeatedly her common sense on the concert platform would prevail, so that she rarely ever ventured outside the realm of good taste, even when the mood of the moment tended to dominate.

Several concerts followed quick in succession. The next concert was at Exeter Hall again, followed by one at Covent Garden with the usual performers from the Royal Italian Opera. As an encore Catherine again sang 'Kathleen Mavourneen'.

In mid-June she performed at the Hanover Square Concert Rooms with her old friend and mentor from her days in Paris, George Osborne, as her accompanist. This was quickly followed by a performance of Handel's *Messiah* with Sims Reeves and Sir Henry Bishop conducting. This was her first time working with Sims Reeves since her arrival in London. By now Catherine and Sims Reeves had renewed their friendship. It was only natural that the two singers who had been drawn together in Milan should continue the relationship in London.

Towards the end of the month Julius Benedict, who had accompanied her during her audition with the great Luigi Lablache in Dublin eight years earlier was the conductor for a grand concert that had all the best singers in London performing, including Catherine. This concert was scheduled at Her Majesty's Theatre for 22 June. It would be Catherine's first time singing at that important theatre.

By early July Catherine was in rehearsal for her next operatic engagement. This would be one of the most important performances of her life. Three months previously the premiere of Meyerbeer's grand opera *Le Prophète* had taken place in Paris with a star-studded cast, including Pauline Viardot-Garcia, the sister of Manuel Garcia junior and one of the finest musicians and most important singers in Europe. Now Viardot-Garcia was in London for an Italian version of *Le Prophète* at the Royal Italian Opera. Meyerbeer was supervising the overall direction and translation from his home in Paris. Pauline Viardot-Garcia was also very much in control of all aspects of the performance. Catherine was scheduled to perform the principal soprano role of Berta in this London premiere sharing the stage with Mario and Viardot. The new production was set to premiere on 24 July, at Covent Garden. This was to be the biggest event of the entire London musical season.

Rehearsals went well. By the time Viardot arrived most of the rehearsals were finished. The first night drew near and everything appeared to be in place. The musical press provided extended coverage of the upcoming event. Catherine was on tenderhooks as the first night grew closer. This was one opera she would not want to miss, given the disappointment she had experienced over the earlier Meyerbeer work. However, she had two more important concert engagements before the opening night of *Le Prophète*. The first was on 6 July at Covent Garden with Sims Reeves and the Italian tenors Mario and Salvi. Other performers included Tamburini, Polonini and Marini. At this concert Catherine included a song, 'Why do I weep for thee?', which was especially written for her by William Vincent Wallace, the Irish composer of the opera *Maritana* and other works. Then, on 11 July, the renowned Sir Henry Bishop gave a concert in the Hanover Rooms with Mario, Catherine, Parodi and Tamburini performing. On 21 July, at Covent Garden, after a performance of Rossini's opera *La Donna del Lago*, in which Giulia Grisi sang the principal role, Catherine, the tenor Salvi and the baritone Tamburini performed an act from *Lucia di Lammermoor*.

Then came the opening night of *Le Prophète*, on Tuesday 24 July. It was sung in Italian and it was the most spectacular operatic production in years. Next day the *Times* dedicated more than two columns to the review, which mostly focused on the stage settings, the grandeur, scope and originality of Meyerbeer's score and how the story and music are integrated into a work of monumental proportions. The critic commented on the unique performance of Pauline Viardot-Garcia as Fides, saying:

> Madame Viardot's impersonation of Fides is one of the highest exhibitions of dramatic and musical art that has been witnessed on the lyric stage . . . we have no time to enter into details at present about Madame Viardot's singing, but it is enough to say that it was admirable throughout.[23]

The same *Times* critic went on to say:

> Mario's *Prophète* was one of the most picturesque and forcible of his personations. In the coronation scene his aspect and bearing were highly impressive, and he wore his robes with all the dignity of an Emperor . . . nothing could be better than his singing in the fourth and fifth acts.[24]

Reviewing Catherine as Berta the writer said:

> We must be content to mention that Miss Catherine Hayes was a
> very graceful Berta, and sang her music with unfailing care.[25]

The *Musical World* also gave considerable coverage to the event, praising:

> the duet 'Della Mosa un di', a melodious and simple composition,
> sung with Berta [and Fides], which was most beautifully vocalized
> and chastely acted by Mdme. [Viardot] Garcia, effectively assisted by
> Miss Catherine Hayes . . . Miss Catherine Hayes pleased us much
> more in Berta than in any part in which she has yet appeared. She
> sang with admirable effect, and acted with considerable feeling and
> energy. This young lady, too, in a future number, shall meet with
> more attention . . . At the fall of the curtain . . . Pauline Garcia and
> Mario appeared twice, and showers of bouquets were thrown on the
> stage. A separate call was then made for Miss Catherine Hayes, who
> was received with loud cheering.[26]

Meyerbeer's opera was such a success that the original plan of giving a
total of nine performances was extended to twelve, to satisfy demand.

For Catherine the reception she received for this first-night performance of *Le Prophète* in London must have been completely rewarding
for all the years of hard work and study, from her earliest times in Dublin
to Paris and Milan.

However, despite the initial success of the new work, Catherine's vocal
health came into question once again during the sixth performance of *Le
Prophète* on Tuesday 7 August, when the *Musical World* reported:

> On Tuesday the *Prophète* was repeated for the sixth time.
> Unfortunately, Miss Catherine Hayes was attacked with hoarseness,
> and could not sing a note. An apology was made for the fair artist,
> who undertook to appear in the necessary portions of the opera, but
> was compelled to omit all the music. Although thus curtailed of some
> of its fairest proportions, the performance did not fail to create the
> usual admiration and excitement . . . The seventh representation of
> the *Prophète* took place on Thursday. Miss Catherine Hayes had not
> entirely recovered; she was enabled, however, to sing the duet [with
> Fides] in the first act, though by no means with her previous effect.
> We confidently anticipate a complete restoration of her powers to

Thursday. Aug: 2ⁿᵈ 1849.

2. Tuesday. Aug. 14ᵗʰ 1849.

{ NB. Brought out Tuesday July 24, } with tremendous success.

Gal: with John, Red Cloth, Harvey & Boy. Flemings !!! specially "coronation" Marie's Blossom quite upset us.

2. Gal: with Tweedie & Cleveland being the eve of departure for Wales.

ROYAL ITALIAN OPERA
COVENT GARDEN.

This Evening will be presented MEYERBEER'S New Grand Opera,

LE PROPHETE

Fides, (Mother of Jean of Leyden)	**Madame VIARDOT.**	
Bertha, (Betrothed to Jean of Leyden)	**Miss CATHERINE HAYES.**	
Jean of Leyden, (The Prophet)	**Signor MARIO.**	
Count d'Oberthel, ...	**Signor TAGLIAFICO.**	
Sergeant, ...	**Signor LAVIA.**	
Peasants, ..	**Signor ROMMI** and **Signor SOLDI.**	
Giona, ...	**Signor POLONINI.**	
Mathisen, Signor MEI,	**Zaccaria, Signor MARINI.**	

(The three Leaders of the Westphalian Revolt.)

In the Second Act, the Incidental

Divertissement

Will comprise the PAS DE LA REDOWA and PAS DU GALOP, in which **Mademoisee WUTHIER, and Signor CASATI will dance.**
And also the celebrated

QUADRILLE DES PATINEURS.

The following New Scenery has been painted for this Opera, by Messrs. GRIEVE and TELBIN.
Act 1.—Scene 1. *A Landscape near Dordrecht.*
Scene 2.—*Interior of a Dutch Auberge.*
Act 2.—*A winter scene in the environs of Munster, in which will be danced the original* QUADRILLE DES PATINEURS.
Act 3.—Scene 1. *A Public Place in Munster.* Scene 2. *Interior of the Cathedral of Munster with the Coronation of Jean of Leyden.*
Act 4 *A Prison Vault in the Palace of Munster.* Scene the Last. *Grand Banquet Hall in the Palace of Munster.*

COMPOSER, DIRECTOR OF THE MUSIC, AND CONDUCTOR, MR. COSTA.

The Scenery by Messrs. GRIEVE and TELBIN. The Dresses by Mrs. BAILEY and Madame MARZIO. The Appointments by Mr. BLAMIRE. The Machinery by Mr. ALLEN. The Spectacle arranged by Mr. A. HARRIS.

The Performances commence at half-past Eight on Tuesdays and Thursdays and Eight on Saturdays.

Tickets, Stalls, and Boxes (for the Night or Season), to be obtained at the Box Office of the Theatre, which is open from Eleven to Five.

ELLIOT. Printer, 14, Holywell-street, Strand

18. Playbill for the London premiere of Meyerbeer's grand opera *Le Prophete* at Covent Garden, London July 1849. (Courtesy of V&A Theatre Museum, London).

> Miss Catherine Hayes this evening [Saturday 11 August], when the
> eighth performance of the *Prophète* will be given . . . The houses have
> been very full every evening since the first night of the *Prophète*.[27]

The last performance of Meyerbeer's great opera occurred on 14
August when the entire cast went all out for a great finale. The *Musical
World* had a few words to say about Catherine at this final performance:

> Miss Catherine Hayes, who has recovered from her severe indis-
> position, went through the character of Berta with undeviating care
> and correctness, although in many places (especially in the last trio),
> the music is painfully high for her voice.[28]

Catherine's appearance on stage in *Le Prophète* despite her vocal
difficulties was a lesson learned from the Dorus-Gras experience. She had
learned the hard way and no one was going to deprive her of her role in any
opera again, despite her vocal problems. No one did replace her, and she
completed all of the performances. Her relationship with Pauline Viardot-
Garcia was warm and friendly. Many years later she mentioned that Pauline
had been very helpful to her in terms of interpretation of the role of Berta.

The memory of Pauline Viardot-Garcia's portrayal of the role of Fides
and the great aria 'Ah mon fils' made an indelible impression on
Catherine. This was an aria that the young prima donna would bring into
her own repertoire and sing in many cities around the world, sometimes
in French, sometimes in Italian and other times in a slightly higher key
than the original music.

Cramer & Beale held the rights to publish the music of *Le Prophète* in
England.[29] However, Chappel & Co., another London publishing house
apparently was allowed to capitalise on the great success of *Le Prophète* by
advertising and selling the sheet music for the main arias and duets,
including 'O, quale incanto' (Miss Hayes) and 'Della mosa un di' (the duet
by Viardot and Miss Hayes).[30]

Even though she had barely recovered from her illness, Catherine still
found herself committed to a benefit concert for Augustus Harris, the
manager of the Drury Lane Theatre. This concert was only important in
one respect for Catherine: it would put her in touch with two artists, one
of whom she had met previously and the other of whom she was meeting
for the first time. Both of these artists would play an important part in
Catherine's future career. The first was Louis Lavenu, the conductor for
the concert. This was the same man Catherine had met with Franz Liszt

in Dublin eight years earlier. The other was Josef Mengis, usually referred to as 'Herr Mengis', a Swiss-born tenor who was now singing baritone roles. Mengis was destined to accompany Catherine to Ireland when she returned there three months later. Both of these men would be a member of her party when she embarked for America two years later, Lavenu eventually travelling with her to many foreign destinations.

Immediately after the Royal Italian Opera season ended on Friday 24 August, Catherine was scheduled to travel to the provinces. Her first stop was Liverpool, where she sang at the Liverpool Festival inaugural concert to celebrate the opening of the new concert hall on 27 August; other principal vocalists included Marietta Alboni, Grisi and Mario, Lablache and Sims Reeves. This was immediately followed by a performance of Mendelssohn's *Elijah* and another concert. On the morning of 30 August she performed in Handel's *Messiah*.

The next series of concerts took place in Birmingham, where the important Birmingham Musical Festival was scheduled, starting on 4 September. New artists joining the group included Henrietta Sontag (reappearing after retirement), Jetty De Treffz and Madame Castellan. In quick succession there were a number of performances, including the *Messiah* with Catherine and Sims Reeves, a concert of sacred music and a concert of miscellaneous music primarily by Rossini, Bellini, Donizetti, Meyerbeer, Auber and Mozart. Catherine for the first time sang 'Casta Diva' from Bellini's *Norma*. The *Times* representative at the festival reported that, among other things, "Casta Diva' from *Norma*, [was] vocalized with great brilliancy by Miss Catherine Hayes.' Later Catherine sang 'Angels Ever Bright and Fair' and a duet from Rossini's *Mosè in Egitto*, 'Qual assalto', with Mario. The concert then continued with a septet by Haydn in which Catherine participated.

During this festival Catherine also sang the grand 'Softly sighs' from Weber's opera *Der Freischütz*, the *Times* critic reporting: 'Miss Catherine Hayes exhibited a great deal of musical refinement, and vocalized the concluding allegro with great energy and brilliancy.' She also sang 'Kathleen Mavourneen' as a set piece or as an encore. From this period forth this melodious song would become a signature for most of Catherine's career.

She then travelled to Liverpool, where she was joined by various new performers. She also gave concerts at Sheffield, Newcastle, Leeds and Manchester, finishing up towards the end of October. Catherine's plans then called for her to make her first visit back to Ireland, in early November.

After Catherine left London for the northern provinces there were economic rumblings at the Royal Italian Opera, Covent Garden, that would have a great impact on many of the singers, but not Catherine. Edward Delafield the director, despite his artistically successful season, now found himself in a financial bind with his debts greatly exceeding his receipts for the season. As a result he filed for bankruptcy. His debts exceeded £45,000 (sterling) a phenomenal amount of money for that period. Edward Delafield had little experience in the theatre and had spread his resources thinly, with investments in Covent Garden and two other theatres, Drury Lane and the Lyceum, while his business experience was actually in brewing. The net result was that his theatre career was over.

His creditors included virtually every level of employee at Covent Garden, as well as costume and jewellery suppliers and a host of other vendors. He owed large sums of money to his company of singers, covering payments for their final engagements of the season, including £900 to Pauline Viardot-Garcia, £374 to Mario and £700 to Giulia Grisi. He also owed £1,200 to Madame Dorus-Gras, almost her entire salary for the season (£1,500), which meant that she had sung the part of Alice in *Robert le Diable*, which she so ruthlessly took from Catherine, for nothing! In addition, Delafield owed tenor Sims Reeves £450, and £320 to the conductor Michael Costa. He owed nothing to Catherine: wisely, her contract, which she had signed in Genoa in the early part of the year, had demanded full payment of £1,300 up front for the season. As a result she was not listed as a creditor in the Delafield bankruptcy proceedings which were in court in early September 1849.[31]

Catherine's first six months in England had been exhilarating. She now realised that there were opportunities for her besides singing in opera. As time went on she was drawn more towards the concert platform, where she was the principal soloist and there were fewer pressures in terms of her performance requirements. Perhaps the example set by Jenny Lind a few months earlier, announcing her departure from the operatic stage, had made an impression on Catherine. In the meantime she was committed to sing in opera in Ireland, where she was scheduled to arrive in early November 1849 after an absence of seven years. She looked forward to this next journey with great pride and satisfaction.

CHAPTER SEVEN

Return to Ireland

DUBLIN, LIMERICK AND CORK 1849–1950

A T THE TIME of Catherine's return, Ireland was in the midst of one of the worst tragedies of nineteenth-century Europe – the Great Famine. The potato blight that caused the Famine originated in America and first appeared in Europe in Belgium in June 1845. It subsequently spread fast, first to England and then to Ireland, where it manifested itself in the autumn of that year.

The potato was originally brought to Ireland from Peru in the sixteenth century, probably via Spain. However, exactly when and how it first arrived in Ireland is not really known.[1] By the middle of the nineteenth-century an estimated three million of Ireland's eight million population were dependent on it for their daily food.

In 1845, the British government, represented by the 38-year-old arrogant and self-righteous Assistant Secretary to the Treasury, Charles E. Trevelyan, (who had sole responsibility for the Irish relief measures), was impervious to the potential threat to the Irish people. Early warnings by the British press about the grave danger the blight posed to Ireland, given its dependence on the potato for food, were ignored. Early in 1846, the House of Lords in London seemed to have as its focus on the reinstatement of the eviction process in Ireland and the increasing crime in places such as Limerick, Tipperary and Clare. Even strong protests by the Quakers (Society of Friends) in Ireland relating to the potential disaster were ignored.

The powerful Anglo-Irishman the Duke of Wellington (who was born in Dublin) was out of touch and a little late when he admitted in the House of Lords on 31 March 1846 that he 'had been entirely wrong in supposing, last November, that the famine in Ireland was exaggerated.'[2]

While the Famine peaked in 1847, its effect continued to be felt in Ireland until the end of 1852.[3] According to the census taken in 1841,

Ireland's total population was just over eight million people. As the Famine was nearing its end in 1852, the population of Ireland was fewer than five million. Most died from starvation, sometimes on the roadside eating grass (many of these were children), others were fortunate enough to be able to emigrate to America, Canada, Australia or even England.

Dublin with its strong economic base, its large Anglo-Irish population and military establishment tended to be sheltered from the difficulties that prevailed in much of the rest of the country. Strangely, cities such as Limerick and Cork, both hard-hit disaster areas, were somehow able to support operatic entertainment, as Catherine was about to find out.

Catherine arrived in Dublin from Liverpool on 4 November 1849. accompanied by her mother. Her sister Henrietta probably also accompanied them. Catherine immediately proceeded to Morrison's Hotel at the eastern corner of Dawson and Nassau Streets, where she had auditioned with Luigi Lablache a little over eight years previously. Now she was returning as a visiting prima donna and guest. Tenor Sims Reeves and a group of other singers and musicians were also staying there, having completed a week of opera in English at the Theatre Royal. Reeves and some members of his party had stayed on an extra night so that they could attend Catherine's operatic debut before returning to England. For Reeves it was a payback in some small way for the support she had given him at his very nervous La Scala debut three years earlier. Reeves' decision played a significant part in Catherine's success that special evening.

In the years since Morrison's Hotel was built in the early part of the century, it had become the place of choice for visiting dignitaries of many professions. The actor Edmund Kean had stayed there in 1824. In December 1838, a special dinner attended by one hundred gentlemen at a cost of one guinea each was given in its main dining room in honour of Michael Balfe's early operatic successes and his first return visit to Dublin.[4] Franz Liszt used the hotel during his stay in January 1841. Giovanni Mario and Giulia Grisi also stayed there on their first visit to Ireland in August 1841. According to one source, Mario and Grisi first became lovers during this stay at Morrison's.[5] In October 1848, Jenny Lind, Michael Balfe, impresario Benjamin Lumley and other members of Lind's party stayed at the hotel, Balfe and Lind had actually danced together in one of the hotel's music rooms during one evening's festivities.[6]

The hotel was an important meeting place for all types of personalities. In addition, many of the great singers, actors and musicians of the nineteenth century who visited Dublin enjoyed the hotel's renowned hospitality and its close proximity to the Theatre Royal in Hawkins Street. Later the hotel also played a part in the downfall of the famous Irish patriot, Charles Stewart Parnell, who was arrested there in October 1881.

Morrison's was a Dublin landmark. It had been built in 1819 by Arthur Morrison (or Morrisson), who had previously owned a smaller hotel in South Frederick Street. He subsequently became Mayor of Dublin in 1835. Two years later he died and the business passed on to members of his family.[7] At the end of the century, in May 1899, Battersby & Co., a leading firm of Dublin auctioneers, sold off the historic hotel's contents, including several pianos.[8] The building was demolished in early 1900 to make way for commercial offices.

Catherine's arrival at Morrison's with her mother in November 1849 must have given her great personal satisfaction. However, her focus was surely on her first return appearance in her native country, which was scheduled with the Philharmonic Society in Dublin on Monday 5 November at the Antient Concert Hall in Brunswick Street. Dublin's elite turned out to hear the young soprano sing. The Viceroy and Lady Lieutenant, Prince George of Cambridge, Chief Justice Blackburne and Chief Justice Doherty were in attendance, also the Countess of Clarendon and many others.

Catherine's programme opened very ambitiously with the cavatina 'Casta Diva' from Bellini's *Norma*. Could it be that she wanted to let the audience know that she was now capable of singing this difficult and exacting music from the first opera she had ever seen eight years earlier in Dublin? This was followed by arias and duets from *Linda di Chamounix* and *Le Prophète* in which the English born Elizabeth Poole (1820–1906) sang the mezzo-soprano parts. Catherine closed the concert with 'O luce di quest' anima' from *Linda di Chamounix*. The Vincent Wallace song, 'Why do I weep for thee?', which she had also sung in London earlier in the year, followed the operatic arias. Her success was a foregone conclusion. Representatives of the press who were present at this first concert give us an interesting insight into her overall performance and her personal appearance during this period:

> The reception of Mademoiselle Hayes was, beyond conception, enthusiastic. But on last evening, the peals of applause that greeted each glorious effort of our Irish soprano, were worthy of the theatre during the Lind epidemic. Miss Hayes sang an air 'Why do I weep for thee?' a rapturous encore followed; but instead of repeating the

song, she whispered to Mr. Benedict, the pianoforte president, who
forthwith struck a few chords of the sweet Irish ballad 'Kathleen
Mavourneen', the audience were at once stilled into silence, and the
fair vocalist broke forth in a tone of wild and plaintive melody,
rendering the sweet and heart-breaking music of this exquisite
melody with a degree of pathos, feeling and taste, that kept the
audience as if spellbound: these, together with the recitative and
cavatina, 'O luce di quest' anima', from Linda, form[ed] her crowning triumphs. Madlle. Hayes, in person, is extremely prepossessing,
she is somewhat thin, but eminently graceful and symmetrical in
figure. Her eyes are large and lustrous and the expression of her
features, which are regular, is full of intellectuality. The fine
enthusiasm in voice and manner that marked her rendering of the
Irish ballad, seemed to win every heart, and cause every hand to
applaud her.[9]

Another publication's reviewer said:

it was therefore but natural to find, that, when Miss Hayes came
forward and was greeted with loud plaudits of such a brilliant
audience, she became agitated; and if, in the few first bars of her aria
from *Norma*, her voice had a slight degree of uncertainty in its tones,
the secondary doubt thus created soon gave away to pleasure, and
that to wonder and delight, at the fine executive skill and clear telling
soprano accents of the artiste . . . while now, if her lowest register is
not all through very round, it includes some most effective notes,
and the upper range is remarkably distinct, musical, and flute-like,
with a resonant and buoyant freshness quite charming. Her singing
created a most decided sensation. The concert passed off with
remarkable eclat, and the vice-regal party remained until its
termination.[10]

Catherine's return to Ireland must have created many mixed emotions
for her. She knew her appearances would be welcomed and she was
confident enough to understand that her performances had to be the very
best so as not to disappoint. Additionally, she was aware that Jenny Lind
had appeared in Dublin the previous year, creating a sensation while
performing two of the roles that Catherine was about to undertake.
There would obviously be comparisons.

Why Catherine picked November for her return to Ireland is difficult to say. Perhaps her timing had something to do with a simple desire on her part. Coincidentally, it was exactly four years to the very day since she had made her La Scala debut. In any event, the fact that she did arrive in November had an unfortunate impact on the quality of the other singers available for her performances.

By the middle of the 1840s the Italian opera seasons in Dublin were managed by the Cramer & Beale agency of London. The Dublin season started around the middle of August or early in September and lasted about two weeks (Lind's performances in October 1848 were an exception, but she was not managed by Cramer & Beale). The timing was generally related to the end of the season in London, which meant singers, became available for performances in the provinces, which included Dublin. Prior to Catherine's arrival, the Italian opera season had concluded at the end of August, so Catherine's arrival in November meant that the quality of singers available for her performances was secondary at best.

For her debut role in Ireland she had selected her most famous portrayal, *Lucia di Lammermoor*, which was scheduled to take place on 6 November at the Theatre Royal in Hawkins Street. Unfortunately for her, she did not get the opportunity to select the other members of the cast. The theatre manager John William Calcraft (whose real name was J.W. Cole), an experienced professional theatre manager, had made that decision with her London agents, Cramer & Beale. However, just prior to her return to Ireland she had sung concerts in England with some of the singers who were scheduled to appear with her in Dublin. Additionally, the conductor was Julius Benedict, the well-known musician who had accompanied Jenny Lind during her visit the previous year and whom Catherine knew intimately.

The eventful night arrived, and Catherine was ready and waiting in the wings. On her entrance she received a standing ovation which lasted for several minutes. She managed to compose herself and to sing her introductory lines. Edgardo, a tenor named Paglieri, made his entrance in a hesitant discordant manner, immediately causing a hissing and booing from the audience. In the next few minutes it became painfully obvious that Paglieri was either ill or so incompetent that he would not be able to continue. The Dublin audience reacted again, this time Catherine herself could not continue and so the curtain had to be lowered.

Sims Reeves and some of his friends occupied a box in the theatre. The audience, recognising him, started to chant his name with the idea that he would step in and sing the part of Edgardo. The theatre manager Calcraft then appeared, saying that Mr. Reeves had been approached and had declined to sing. This did not stop the crowd; they continued to call Reeves by name, until he relented and turned to the house and announced that 'he would sing for the sake of the public, but not to satisfy Mr. Calcraft'. Catherine impatiently waited in the wings, wondering if her first performance in Ireland as a prima donna would end up being a disaster. The minutes slipped by before she realised what was happening in the house: Sims Reeves would be her Edgardo, assuring her of great success. The audience reacted to Reeves' agreement with a loud cheer. It took another thirty minutes before Reeves had donned a costume and prepared himself for his entrance in the second scene.

However, all nerves were tense and, as he crossed the back of the stage, Reeves made a comment to Benedict which irritated the conductor and caused him to walk out. Fortunately, the musician Louis Lavenu, who was with the Reeves party that evening, agreed to take over the job of conducting the performance, and so the opera commenced, more than an hour late.[11] The rest of the performance went off without a hitch. Tenor Paglieri was nowhere to be seen for the remainder of the evening, but he later felt strongly enough about the incident and the way Calcraft had treated him to write a letter of protest to one of the local newspapers.

Reviews of the performance initially focused on the Paglieri incident, then went on to say:

> our audience feel proud in appropriating and claiming as their own the magnificent natural powers – the pure voice – the matchless musical skill – and the rare dramatic genius evidenced in the performance of our young Irish *prima donna*. As she came out before the audience in the first act and commenced the recitative the whole house rose *en masse*, and the cheering and waving of hats from the pit and galleries, and of handkerchiefs from the box circles, continued for many minutes before the fair artiste could commence the music of her part. Owing, doubtless, to some natural excitement at such a delighted and flattering reception by the metropolitan audience of her own country, our fair *prima donna*, seemed at first rather agitated, and a slight tremor seemed to pervade her glorious tones as they fell on the ear in the opening passages. This however, wore off, and as she proceeded her splendid voice expanded in soft and brilliant power, thrilling on the ear delightfully.

19. Portrait of Sims Reeves as Edgardo around the time of his performance in *Lucia di Lammermor* in Dublin November 1849. (Author's collection).

The reviewer continued with:

> At length, the curtain rose again, and Mr. Reeves came on from one
> side of the stage, and Miss Catherine Hayes from the other. The two
> eminent artists met and greeted each other cordially and gracefully,
> amidst the pealing and deafening thunder of applause from the
> entire house. We need not dwell upon the magnificent singing of
> Miss Hayes and Mr. Reeves throughout the opera. They were called
> for at the conclusion of every separate act, and greeted with the
> enthusiastic cheers of the entire house. We cannot but advert to the
> really magnificent acting of Miss Hayes in the Opera. Her
> conception of the character and feeling of *Lucia* was about the most
> exquisitely classical piece of histrionic presentation, apart from the
> superb singing – that we have witnessed for a long time.[12]

It was also around this time that a rumour was circulating in Dublin
that Reeves and Hayes were engaged to be married![13] There is no
evidence that their relationship ever reached that degree, but a strong
relationship did exist between the two during this period and would
continue through the next year. Interestingly, on the night when Reeves
took over the part of Edgardo in Dublin, his future wife, Emma Lucombe
(1823–?), a minor singer, was with him in the theatre having performed
with him the previous week. He married Lucombe a year later. Reeves
and Hayes were destined to sing together in *Lucia* again the following year
in London. The day after the eventful Dublin *Lucia* performance Reeves
left for Belfast, having repaid his artistic debt to his favourite Lucia.

Catherine's next opera was Bellini's *Norma*, on 7 November. This was
a very audacious choice on her part, given her experience and the fact that
Giulia Grisi had given her famous portrayal of the tragic Norma the
previous season at the very same theatre. However, her confidence in her
vocal technique and the fact that she knew her audience gave her the
courage to perform this difficult and demanding Bellini work.

Adalgisa in this performance was Elizabeth Poole, a young mezzo-
soprano who had considerable experience singing in London. Poole had
appeared with Maria Malibran in the first performance of Balfe's *Maid of
Artois* in London in 1836. She had also sung in the premiere of Balfe's
Bohemian Girl in 1843 and the first performance of Wallace's Maritana in
1845 in London. The Pollione was a tenor called Herr Damcke of the
Grand Opera in Berlin. This was possibly Berthold Damcke, who was

born in Hanover in 1812. The Oroveso was Signor Burdini, an Irish born singer named Burdine with an Italianised name, Flavio was Signor Galli and Julius Benedict was the conductor.

One of Dublin's leading newspaper critics seemed to be inclined to 'ramble' in his review of her *Norma*. His comments first relate to her performance in *Lucia* the previous night and her style and handling of its dramatic elements as they relate to the requirements for the role of *Norma*. This review provided an interesting insight into the audience's acceptance of Catherine as *Norma*, a famous Grisi role. The reviewer stated:

> our audience of Tuesday night were completely taken by surprise, and stricken mute in absorbed delight by the magnificent display of tragic genius, naturalness, and truth, presented by Catherine Hayes in the character of *Lucia di Lammermoor*. The same audience often before listened with delight and applauded with ecstasy the gorgeous roulades and brilliant cadenza of Madlle. Lind in the tragic scenes of the opera; but it was the music they admired and the music alone. It was for such a display of dramatic genius evinced in the passionate excitement, the utter *abandon* and thrilling despair of the heroine of the piece, as rendered by Miss Hayes, that such enthusiasm as that displayed on Tuesday night was reserved. Who that was present can forget the sensation produced by her acting in the well-known scena, where Lucia has been made to sign the marriage contract that separates her from Edgardo for ever, and where he rushes in to upbraid her broken plight? None who witnessed the glorious conceptions and magnificent rendering of the very spirit of this deeply touching scene by Miss Hayes, will wonder at the anxiety of all to see her perform again.
>
> Her Norma of last evening was a grand piece of acting, whilst in the rendering of its divine music she brought a tribute of applause as warm and enthusiastic as ever greeted the most famed and gifted of any of her great musical contemporaries. The Norma of Grisi was said to be perhaps her best operatic character: but it was remarked, that it was as the high soul'd priestess, stern and high minded, the Druid Medea contemplating the death of her off-springs, and breathing the vengeance of scorned and slighted woman. Jenny Lind's Norma, on the other hand, was declared the most beautiful in the tender and more subdued passages, where the

courage and lofty pride of the Druid priestess is merged in the tenderness of the mother and the remorseful memory of the still loving woman.

Catherine Hayes, as all who witnessed her magnificent performance of the character on last evening will admit; is great in both aspects of the part. Nothing could possibly be finer in taste than her conception of the scene in the second act, whilst her readings of the music were perhaps as pure and powerful as any we have ever heard. Miss Hayes was called before the curtain repeatedly, and greeted with enthusiastic plaudits of a densely crowded audience.[14]

Between the acts, apparently a piano was pulled out and she sang 'Kathleen Mavourneen' to satisfy the house, which was packed to capacity. This was a common occurrence in Dublin during the nineteenth century.

On Saturday 10 November she performed her benefit concert, which was the custom at the time. This concert started with highlights from *Norma*, followed by the closing scene from *La Sonnambula* by Bellini. The theatre was completely sold out, 'from the pit to the ceiling' according to one critic. During the evening she sang a song especially composed for her by Julius Benedict for the occasion and called 'The Return to Erin'. The words of the song seem particularly appropriate for Catherine Hayes, given the incredible number of places she visited during her short career.

The Return to Erin

As a child to its mother returning,
Long absent, its anguish now o'er
So my fond heart with rapture is burning,
Dear Erin, to see thee once more.
When far, far away on the ocean,
I have sighed for my dear native shore,
And prayed, with the purest devotion,
For the day I should see it once more.

In sunnier climes, the glad smile
Of kind friends oft had banish'd a tear:
But my heart they could never beguile
From the lov'd ones that welcome me here.
Nor distance, nor years can e'er sever

The strong links that bind me to thee;
I may roam through the wide world, but ever
Will Erin be dearest to me.

As a further encore she sang 'Kathleen Mavourneen' and then completed the evening concert with the finale to *La Sonnambula*. There was an outpouring of applause and appreciation, and bouquets of flowers were flung on the stage in profusion, according to one critic.

Limerick and Cork, where her next performances were given, were cities that had a strong tradition of classical music. Both cities had sophisticated audiences and were on the circuit for visiting musicians, singers and other performers since the 1830s. Limerick's cultural and business interests had been supporting several newspapers for many years. Cork also had about three newspapers during this period. Their critics generally had a good knowledge of music and the vocal scene in Dublin, frequently reporting on operatic performances from there and, indeed, occasionally reporting from London and other places further afield.

Immediately after this benefit concert Catherine, accompanied by her party of singers and her mother, set off for her native city, Limerick, where she was scheduled to sing in concerts sponsored by Corbett & Sons, starting on Monday 12 November. The Hayes party stayed at Cruise's Hotel, which must have given her great satisfaction when she reflected on her upbringing and early childhood. She was joined in Limerick by some of the singers who had performed with her in Dublin, including Elizabeth Poole, Damcke and Burdini. Benedict once again was the accompanist.

The first concert took place in Limerick's Theatre Royal on 12 November. The theatre had a capacity of 870 seats, all of which were completely sold out three days ahead of time. Demand was so strong for tickets that a 300% premium was being offered for first-night seats. By the morning of the first concert people were crowded around the theatre hoping to get a glimpse of the prima donna as she went from Cruise's Hotel to the theatre later in the day. The excitement was unparalleled and detachment of police was brought in to manage the crowd.

According to one report a total of 900 people actually attended this first concert. There was also mention that 1,100 people actually attended the second concert! In any event, Corbett, sensing the need for additional space yet having concern for overcrowding and safety, opened as many doors as possible so that those who were unable to buy a ticket might at least get to hear the famous Limerick prima donna on her first return visit to her native city. Her schedule only allowed her two days in Limerick before going on to Cork for another concert, then to Waterford, and back to Dublin.

The concert opened with a trio by Poole, Damcke and Burdini, which was well received. The tension as the crowd awaited Catherine's appearance could be felt everywhere in the house. When Julius Benedict appeared on the stage with Catherine on his arm, the house arose 'en masse' with a spontaneous burst of applause from an estimated 900 people. The reception lasted ten minutes. Nothing like it had ever been experienced in Limerick previously.

Given her experience in Italy, Austria and England, Catherine kept her composure and acted like a professional. She bowed to the audience, acknowledging their feelings and at the same time trying to control her own. When the nervous excitement calmed down she composed herself once more and calmly nodded to Benedict that she was ready to start. Bellini's wonderful 'Casta Diva' (*Norma*) was her first piece that evening. The reviewer for the *Limerick Chronicle* reported:

> she delivered the first notes of the 'Casta Diva', with an intensity of feeling and sound that at once assured the audience of the presence of a cultivated singer and artist. This cavatina presented some exquisite points of vocalisation, the embellishments introduced in the first delivery of the thema were chaste and judicious, and the florid passages accompanying the *refrain* were splendidly intonated. In the resumption of the theme, the alterations were delivered with unerring nicety, and in the *Cabaletta* 'Ah bello a me ritorna', the *mezza voce* delivery of the phases was erotically delivered. Her final shake on the 7th or leading note, ending with a rapid flight in *fioritura* was most brilliant, and drew down the prolonged plaudits of the audience.[15]

After some songs from the other performers, Benedict exhibited his own talents on the piano. Catherine returned to sing a song 'Always with me' written by 'Walter Maynard', an alias used by Willert Beale, a junior partner with Cramer & Beale, her London agents. She followed this with 'Kathleen Mavourneen' and a new song 'Home of my heart – my native land', composed for her by Dubliner Richard Frederick Harvey. By mid December, S.J. Pigott of 112 Grafton Street, the Dublin music publishers, were advertising the availability of this new song as sung by 'Miss Catherine Hayes'. At the end of the concert the applause lasted for over fifteen minutes.

And so her first return visit to Limerick as a fully established prima donna at the peak of her form was very satisfactory in every respect, except that Bishop Knox, her mentor and the person who had made it all possible, was no longer there.

The following night she gave her next and last concert that year in Limerick. Her success of the previous night resulted in such a demand for the Tuesday night that people were offering a premium of one pound over the normal sale price of tickets – without much success! By seven o'clock every seat and all of the standing room in the theatre was filled to capacity. Her first piece was Bellini's 'Ah non giunge' from *La Sonnambula*. Various songs followed this, including a new song written for her by a local Limerick resident called '*The Coquette*'. The music and words were by a Miss E. Jervis of Limerick city, and the audience received the piece with great pleasure.

During this time the Theatre Royal in Limerick was owned by a Joseph Fogerty. He had leased it to Corbett & Son, who were the promoters for Catherine Hayes' visit. Fogerty was so enamoured with Catherine Hayes that many years later he wrote a book called 'Caterina' roughly based on the social life in Limerick during the middle of the nineteenth century. In general terms, the story was centred around a visiting prima donna called Caterina – presumably Catherine Hayes.[16]

Reports of this visit to Dublin and Limerick make no mention of Catherine seeing Antonio Sapio, her original singing teacher, who ten years earlier had shown so much faith in her and provided the grounding for her eventual success. As a result we must assume that Sapio had either died in the meantime or was living outside of Ireland.

During her stay in Limerick, Catherine wanted to give a concert in aid of the city's poor. Mayor William Monsell was to have headed up the committee, but it appears that time ran out and it never happened. Instead of giving the concert, Catherine made a donation of twenty pounds, which a Mrs. Gabbet distributed to two hospitals and the city dispensary. This was the first of many efforts that Catherine made to help the poor and the underprivileged in many parts of the world. The poverty she and her family had experienced in her early days in Limerick was never far from her thoughts.

Catherine and her party left for Cork, promising everyone in Limerick that she would soon return to perform in opera. In Cork, she opened her concert on the evening of 14 November with 'Casta Diva'. A reviewer made reference to a slightly unsteady start which he attributed to nerves or to her voice being unsettled (she had only arrived from Limerick that afternoon). She seems to have settled by the time she sang the duet 'Meet again' by Bishop with Elizabeth Poole. The Wallace song 'Why do I weep for thee' was next and then 'Kathleen Mavourneen'. She closed with 'O luce di quest anima' from *Linda* to much applause, and as an encore she gave the bravura finale 'Ah! Non giunge' from *La Sonnambula*.

The next day a newspaper reviewer made the following comments on her personal appearance, vocal timbre and capability:

> The personal appearance of Miss Hayes is most attractive; and were we inclined to be at all poetical in this age of iron realities, we might regard her as the impersonation of the grace, and delicacy, and innocence of Irish modesty and Irish beauty. She is eminently feminine in features, and there is a certain willowy gracefulness about her figure which is sufficiently perceptible when standing on the formal platform of a concert room, but which must be peculiarly attractive on the stage. She is the fairest blond [?] that can be imagined; and her expression is full of soul and feeling, more than of intellect.

The reviewer continued with:

> Miss Hayes' voice is a rich soprano; but many of her lower notes are of the finest *contralto*, very rich and very deep. Her facility is great; in fact, equal to any operatic requirement. Her articulation is admirable, and her reading is most correct, and full of expression. That is as fair an idea we can give of a vocalist who undoubtedly takes her proud position amongst the foremost of her art, and who may fearlessly sing by the side of Grisi and Lind.[17]

Catherine and her party travelled on to Waterford where another concert was given before returning to Dublin where she decided to rest during the holiday period. She had been singing continuously for several months. Her next series of concerts were scheduled for London early in the new year.

On 7 January Elizabeth Poole and Eliza Birch joined Catherine for a concert at the Beaumont Institution in London. Eliza Birch was a new participant at one of Catherine's concerts. She had known Catherine from her student days in Milan where Birch was a member of the English community and studying with Felice Ronconi. The Beaumont evening was followed a week later by a concert at Exeter Hall on the Strand, in which several other singers including Lablache sang. The eminent musician and pianist Sigismond Thalberg (1812–71) also shared the platform. Julius Benedict was the conductor. Two weeks later on 26 January Catherine was the principal vocalist at a Sacred Harmonic Society concert which was conducted by Michael Costa and featured excerpts from Mendelssohn's *St. Paul*.

The following week saw her in Edinburgh for the first time. Her anticipated arrival was announced with a notice that stated:

> Miss Catherine Hayes – We are glad to notice that this lady is to appear here in a few days. The sensation she has created wherever she has sung is very great, surpassing the warmest anticipations. The *Musical World* writes of her as follows: 'Her voice is a pure soprano, of surpassing sweetness, but not lacking in power. There is but one singer with whom Miss Hayes can be at all compared, and that is Jenny Lind. There is about her the same gentleness of deportment and captivating manner – always natural – always graceful. Her figure is faultless, and her countenance full of sweetness, and is powerfully expressive.'[18]

Catherine's first concert in Edinburgh was on Wednesday 13 February – the Reid Commemoration Concert at the Music Hall, an important annual event in honour of a General Reid who was the founder of the Chair of Music at the University of Edinburgh. A reviewer of the concert reported:

> The great star of the evening was Miss Catherine Hayes, a lady of whose extraordinary vocal attainments we have already spoken in the highest terms. Her voice is a fine soprano, very powerful and highly cultivated, and abounding in sweetness and expression. Her countenance and figure are remarkably pleasing, and the audience appeared to be quite captivated with her gentle and graceful manner, combined with such surpassing talent.

The reviewer went on to say:

our pleasure was changed into absolute delight if not more, when in kind compliance with the hearty recall, the first notes of our own beautiful song 'Annie Laurie' met our ear. The audience were in perfect rapture; the song was given with all that intensity of feeling and pathos which is so generally awanting amid the brilliant shares of the talented foreign singers. The song was called for a second time, and was received with the same enthusiastic applause as greeted it at first.

She followed this up as the featured vocalist, again at the Music Hall in George's Street, on 15 February 1850. Other members of the party were Elizabeth Poole and a Mr. Travers who had also been a student in Milan when Catherine was there. He had sung with considerable success under the name of 'Traversi' in Turin, Verona and other places but not at La Scala. The principal bass in the group was Entimio Polonini, an established young Italian singer with La Scala and north American experience. Also in the party was Herr Mengis, the Swiss tenor turned baritone whom Catherine was destined to have in her company in baritone support roles during her travels over the next three years.

The music performed at this concert varied somewhat from her recent activity in Ireland. She started off with an aria, 'O vanne pompe', from the opera *La Maresciella d'Ancre* by the composer Alessandro Nini. She followed this with Wallace's song 'Why do I weep for thee?' The second half of the concert included the Bellini duet 'Mira O Norma' with Elizabeth Poole then Catherine sang Lady Duffren's beautiful 'Terence's farewell to Kathleen', after which came an aria from *Lucia di Lammermoor*. For encores she sang 'My last thoughts are of thee', a song composed for her by Willert Beale (her agent) under the alias Walter Maynard, 'and ye shall walk in silk attire' and finally the bravura aria 'Ah non giunge' from *La Sonnambula*. In all, a lengthy programme, considering that there were five others sharing the platform with her. The evening also included music by Rossini, Donizetti, Cimarosa, Balfe, Benedict and Wallace. Catherine's singing was reviewed on 18 February, with the following comments:

> Her voice is a soprano of a clear and flexible quality, moderately powerful, and is managed with much freedom; To these qualities Miss Hayes unites the advantages of personal appearance in an eminent degree, with a manner lady–like and agreeable . . . Miss Hayes's solo performances were received with loud and repeated acclamations.[19]

From Edinburgh she and her party set off for Belfast, crossing the North Sea the next day to Ireland. A concert was scheduled in Belfast for Tuesday night 19 February at the Music Hall. Here she was received with great acclaim. Members of Bishop Knox's family residing in the area attended her performance.

A new opera season was next scheduled in Dublin starting Thursday 21 February. The opening night saw her in Donizetti's *Linda di Chamounix* for the first time in Ireland. A second performance of *Linda* occurred two nights later. This time her supporting cast was considerably above the levels of her earlier experience in Dublin. Catherine was Linda, Elizabeth Poole played Pierotto, Travers played Carlo; Polonini played the Marchese and Mengis performed Antonio. The conductor was a Signor Vera.

The orchestra leader was the 39 year old Richard M. Levey, a Dubliner whose real name was O'Shaughnessy. He had adopted the name of Levey while studying in London because the locals had difficulty pronouncing his real name. He was an eminent violinist and the orchestra leader for over forty years at the Theatre Royal, Dublin. In 1880 Levey co-authored (with J. O'Rorke) a historic and exceptional book called *Annals of the Theatre Royal, Dublin*, which chronicled the 60-year history of this famous Dublin theatre and its incredible operatic seasons during most of the nineteenth century.[20] The Theatre Royal was destroyed by fire in February 1880. It was rebuilt twice: first in 1897 and again in 1935. The third Theatre Royal in Hawkins street was finally closed and demolished in 1962.[21]

Catherine's reappearance created the same sensation as her previous performances in Dublin. One reviewer provided an interesting perspective on the emotions of the first evening at the moment of her entrance:

> When, in simple rustic garb, this most charming of all representatives of the fair and gentle Linda advanced from the back of the stage, a peal of welcome burst forth, such as was not heard since, as the Druid [*Norma*] Priestess, Miss Hayes's return, after innumerable Continental ovations, was crowned here with a new triumph, more glorious, and, we are sure, more gratifying to her, than all the splendid successes of the past. Again and again, gracefully and with evident deep feeling, did she bow her acknowledgments. Again and again was the applause renewed till we might almost have fancied that the audience did not require Miss Hayes to sing, but merely to appear before them, mutely but with appealing eloquence of look and gesture, expressing her gratitude for their boisterous cordiality.

At length, and with difficulty, silence was rendered, the opera proceeded, and, after a brief but brilliant recitative, the beautiful 'Oh! luce di quest anima' displayed all the dulcet sweetness of tone, pure and perfect vocalisation, and exquisite expression which have won for Miss Hayes the title 'The Irish Jenny Lind.' . . . Her voice is, if possible, clearer, richer, more resonant than before; the resulting perfect tone and the dazzling brilliancy, with which the most difficult or involved passages are achieved reminding her enraptured hearers strongly of Jenny Lind, and not reminding them as a more servile imitator might, but as a close similarity, created by the possession of the same great gifts, the same winning grace, the same glorious genius . . . her acting too, like that of Adelaide Kemble, so unexpected in a great vocalist, increased the enthusiasm of the audiences.[22]

Norma followed on 25 February, *La Sonnambula* on the 26th, *Linda di Chamounix* again on 28 February and *Lucia di Lammermoor* on Saturday 2 March. All four operas achieved the same great success and excitement as at the earlier performances.

Her Amina in *La Sonnambula* was compared to Jenny Lind's by one of the reviewers:

Many of our readers, doubtless, will remember the first appearance of Jenny Lind as Amina, and the instant feeling her trip in upon the stage, expression her bright face created, that she looked the artless and happy village girl better than any former representative of the part. A similar sensation was created by the entrance of Catherine Hayes, who's animated greeting of her dear companions and bounding elasticity of step reminded us strongly of her compeer, as did the clear and flute-like beauty of her pure soprano, when heard in the delicious 'Come per me sereno'. There is something singularly prepossessing in the appearance of Catherine Hayes as Amina. Her figure is so graceful, her face so fair and so winning in expression, and her exquisitely fresh and purely natural acting, so pleasing from the absence of all effort, the very perfection of the *ars celare artem* that characterises it, peculiarly adapt her to represent, truthfully and beautifully, the innocent village maiden.[23]

A brief review of her in *Lucia* was particularly interesting:

It is really an impossibility to convey, in written words, any idea of the consummate tenderness and feeling of her acting, or the purely perfect beauty of her singing in this very arduous character.[24]

On March 8 she was scheduled for *Lucia* but could not perform as she had taken a fall on the stage the previous night and was suffering from a stiff neck and backache. She did agree, however, to sing various Irish songs rather than disappoint the audience, and Elizabeth Poole agreed to present a concert version in English of Donizetti's *Daughter of the Regiment*. This pleased the crowd and the show went on.

Throughout her career Catherine rarely disappointed an audience unless she was seriously ill. As time went on however, she did seem to have repeated problems with sore throats and colds. It was truly quite remarkable that she didn't experience greater vocal problems, given the frequency of her performances. Perhaps Garcia's training and Ronconi's coaching had enabled her to conserve her resources in some way despite the number of performances she gave.

In anticipation of her departure for Limerick and Cork the *Dublin Evening Packet* crafted an editorial summarising her visit, and once again making a comparison to Jenny Lind. This comparison is worded in a very poetic nineteenth-century manner and as a result it has been quoted in many publications since:

Miss Hayes is about to leave our metropolis, to the regret, we venture to say, of every one who can appreciate genius and grace. Her successes here almost mark an epoch in Irish theatricals, and are honorable alike to her audience and herself. For they prove, not only that the Irish taste can still distinguish and delight in the charms of perfect vocalism, but that, unlike our English neighbours, who invariably neglect their native singers, we feel our interest in art increases, when the artist is one of ourselves . . .

It is the fashion to compare Miss Hayes with Jenny Lind. We venture to think there is no resemblance than that of a common excellence. The power of Jenny Lind consists in a lucid and brilliancy of tone which makes every note tell, and cause her singing to appear more like the mechanism of an instrument than the articulation of a voice; the triumph of Miss Hayes is in the combination of sweetest sounds into a stream of melody, which gradually sheds itself into the heart. The one, like a gem, flashes upon the sense, and emits a thousand rays, each glorious in itself; the other, like a flower, is redolent of soil, and gradually diffuses sweetness around. Or we might compare the foreign artist to one of her native landscapes, basking in splendor, and clear in its outline and objects beneath a starry sky: Miss Hayes's beauties are those of our own clime, with its features of tenderness melting into light, or darkening into shade. The charm of Miss Hayes's acting too is its exquisite sensibility. She has not the art of 'gorgeous tragedy', with its lofty declamation and sublime majesty. Her figure is too gracile, her voice is too tender, and it would seem her mind is too gentle to impersonate the sterner forms of female character. But no one who has seen it can forget her delineation of Lucia's love and sorrows; the almost painful truthfulness of her Linda's madness; and the unspeakable pathos of her Amina. Every look, tone, and gesture, she makes happily subservient to her beautiful conceptions of these characters; and, through the entire impersonation, wears a look of the most perfect grace.[25]

As was customary, she held a benefit performance on Saturday 9 March, choosing *La Sonnambula* for the evening. After the performance she sang two Irish songs to satisfy the audience's demands for more. As a finale to the evening the manager, Mr. Calcraft, announced that she had agreed to return to Dublin for two more performances after her Limerick engagement. With this her season ended, for the time being. On Monday a notice appeared in local Dublin newspapers to the effect that Catherine Hayes would return by popular demand and sing on 21 March in *La Sonnambula* and in *Linda di Chamounix* on 23 March, with a special concert between these dates.

She arrived in Limerick by rail on Sunday and stayed at Cruise's Hotel again. It was reported that:

> at every station along the railway line excited crowds thronged the carriage containing our gifted countrywoman, eagerly welcoming her back again to her native place; and at [the] Limerick terminus several hundred ladies and gentlemen were awaiting her arrival, anxious to do homage to the Irish Queen of Song. Indeed, it's impossible to describe the fervent welcome she received. Her entry into Limerick, as *Prima Donna* of an Italian company, formed an event in the musical history of 'the City of the Violated Treaty'.[26]

She was joined by a Mr. (later Dr.) John Joy who was the representative of Cramer & Beale. He had also supervised her performances in Dublin. Over the next year Mr. Joy would have a strong influence on her activities, eventually leading to dissatisfaction on her part and a split with Cramer & Beale.

On Monday 11 March she appeared in *La Sonnambula* and on Tuesday in *Norma* to great acclaim. Immediately afterwards she travelled to Cork, where she sang *La Sonnambula* on Thursday 14 March. *Norma* came next on the 15th. *Linda di Chamounix* was performed on Saturday the 16th. This was the first performance ever of *Linda di Chamounix* in Cork city. A concert consisting of selections from *La Sonnambula* took place on the following Monday. The critics again praised her highly, saying:

> her exquisite melody and finished acting, where all is perfectly natural, and told with the most trilling [sic] effect . . . several bouquets were thrown on the stage, and accepted with a winning grace and courtesy by Miss Hayes, and amongst them was one entirely composed of Shamrocks – an expressive compliment to one of Ireland's most gifted daughters on the eve of the national festival [St. Patrick's Day].[27]

She then departed for Dublin, by rail. In Dublin, as previously announced, she first appeared in *La Sonnambula* on 21 March. The following day a concert was given in the Antient Concert Rooms in Great Brunswick Street. The first half of the concert was devoted to sacred music. Catherine sang from Handel's *Messiah* and Mendelssohn's *Elijah* and *St. Paul*. Her contribution to the second half of the concert, which focused on popular songs and operatic arias, was three Irish songs. On Saturday night she again sang *Linda di Chamounix*, concluding her season.

Dublin's leading newspaper of the period, *Freeman's Journal*, summed up the impact of her visit to Ireland during a period of such difficult times.[28] The following is a brief extract from a review which allocated a full column of the newspaper to praising her talents and personality:

> the engagement of Miss Hayes, now just concluded, has been in truth one of wondrous and unexampled success. Its history amongst circles constitutes a theme of astonishment as well as gratulation [sic] – astonishment at such an amazing succession of overflowing houses in a time of such general depression [the Great Famine], and in the midst of what is usually known as the 'close[d] season' for

theatre and operatic representation; and gratulation [sic] in the evident combination of popular musical taste, and popular recognition of native genius . . . At the conclusion of the opera, trice had she to come forth, whilst the entire house seemed to join in one cheer of delight and approbation. Ladies from the boxes showered wreaths and flung bouquets on the stage at her feet; never perhaps was there beheld in that theatre such an exciting scene. The fair vocalist then came out and sang, amidst death-like silence and enwrapt attention of an audience, her sweet ballad of 'Kathleen Mavourneen': cheer after cheer accompanied the encore which followed. The gifted vocalist again came forth, amidst renewed cheers, and sang 'Kathleen's Farewell' by John Duggan and Mr. Levy . . . and amidst the reiterated peals of cheering that thundered from all parts of the house, a beautifully woven Shamrock wreath was thrown from the boxes and alighted at the feet of the fair Irish songstress . . . our Queen pressed the emblem of her country to her heart, and retired amidst the reiterated cheers of the audience.

And so Catherine finished her first full season of opera in Ireland. Her success was phenomenal and brings to mind 'Sutherland nights' at Covent Garden 110 years later.

Her ability to maintain her voice and performance quality throughout was interesting, given her schedule and the primitive modes of travel in those days. From the time of her return to Ireland in November 1849 until 23 March 1850, she had given almost 50 performances of opera and concerts in six cities, including a quick side-trip to London and Edinburgh for some concerts. The credit for her survival and staying fresh for each performance must in part be given to her own strong will and determination. However, Manuel Garcia's firm grounding in vocal technique must also have played an important part.

On 24 March, Catherine and her mother departed on the steamer for Holyhead, travelling from there by train to London. Before arriving in London she gave a concert in Cheltenham. Later in the week she went to Her Majesty's Theatre in London for rehearsals for the new opera season. It was the first time that she would perform under the direction of the theatre's musical director, Michael Balfe, and for the impresario Benjamin Lumley. She was scheduled to perform with Sims Reeves again in *Lucia di Lammermoor*, and to sing in several concerts with a number of her peers.

Benjamin Lumley's actions this season were destined to sow seeds of 'discontent' in Catherine – causing her to gradually move away from opera to the concert platform.

Perhaps also she was influenced in some way by Jenny Lind's similar action some time earlier.

In any event, towards the end of the year-end she would return to Ireland briefly to perform in opera again. After that she returned to Italy for a three-month season at the Rome opera. These performances would be her final operatic appearances anywhere for many years.

Jenny Lind's Influence

ENGLAND, IRELAND AND ITALY 1850–1851

EARLY IN 1850, P.T. Barnum and Jenny Lind had entered into a contract for her to visit America in September of that year. Barnum had agreed to pay Lind the enormous sum of $150,000 in addition to all of her expenses, the cost of a maid, a secretary and a companion; all to be paid in advance. Julius Benedict was scheduled to accompany her; his fee $25,000, while respectable, was modest when compared to Lind's. The baritone Giovanni Belletti, Lind's close friend from her early days in Sweden would only receive a paltry $12,500 for his services.[1]

Lind's part of the bargain included a commitment to perform about 120 concerts in America. In August 1850 she left Liverpool on board the New York-bound Collins Line ship, the *Atlantic*, a paddle steamer whose sister ships were breaking records by crossing the Atlantic from Liverpool to New York in around ten or eleven days.

These were also the early days of the Cunard Line's new service on the Liverpool to New York run. As a result there was great competition and excitement in terms of the speed of the paddle steamers, and how quickly they could make the crossing. Lind chose the faster line. Her departure from Liverpool was celebrated with a concert the night before and there was a special ceremony at the departure dock during the boarding process. She had reserved the most luxurious cabin on the ship – after all, Barnum was paying for it!

All of this activity was reported daily in the press on both sides of the Atlantic as the Barnum promotion machine moved into top gear. This was probably the greatest publicity campaign ever launched for any singer. Catherine was very conscious of Lind's high profile. She seemed to believe that her destiny was in some way linked to Lind's, either through time, place or vocal genre, which was perhaps the result of Garcia's early influence and the dominance of his prize pupil on the principal musical stages of Europe.

Lind's arrival in New York was destined to be sensational, as Barnum had created such an aura of excitement in anticipation of her arrival. A reported 30,000–40,000 people were at the pier as the *Atlantic* cruised into its berth, downtown on New York's lower east side, slightly after noon on Sunday 1 September 1850. Lind ushered in a new era for the prima donna in America.

What Catherine's thoughts may have been early in 1850 about Lind's plans to go to America later that year we don't know. Her immediate focus was her upcoming performances of *Lucia* starting 2 April, with Sims Reeves as Edgardo, Belletti (Lind's partner for America) as Enrico and Frederick Lablache (Luigi's son) in the role of Raimondo. Michael Balfe was the conductor.

A reviewer of the season's opening night with Catherine and Sims Reeves in *Lucia di Lammermoor* at Her Majesty's which was classified as a 'reopening night' (after the Lenten theatre hiatus), described the evening's entertainment:

> The performance of *Lucia di Lammermoor* in such excellent style, with two English singers in the principal characters, is a great argument in favour of the vocal talent of this country. Miss Catherine Hayes, who made her debut at the Royal Italian Opera last year, and who made her first appearance at Her Majesty's Theatre last night, is a charming singer, neat and finished in her execution, and with a voice which, without being extremely powerful, is uniformly sweet and melodious. Her acting, without being violent, is animated and expressive; her manner is thoroughly feminine, and there is something both in her tones and her gestures which really gains the sympathies of an audience.
>
> Edgardo was the character, which first introduced Mr. Sims Reeves to the London public, when he appeared as one of the English operatic company at Drury Lane Theatre, under the spirited management of M. Julian. The energy and passion which he throws into this leading part, and which animate him both as a singer and an actor, went very far in establishing the position he now holds in the public estimation. . . . The greatest enthusiasm was displayed in favour of the two English vocalists. And they were repeatedly called in the course of the evening.[2]

Another newspaper reviewer stated the following:

The joint appearance of an English prima donna and an English prima tenore on our Italian stage is without parallel, we believe, except in the single instance of Billington and Braham, some half a century ago. Last night, *Lucia di Lammermoor* was produced, with Miss Catherine Hayes in the character of Lucia, and Mr. Sims Reeves in that of Edgardo; and both performers achieved a triumph of the most brilliant description. Both of them had performed those characters separately, but never before [in London] with such striking effect: and in regard to Miss Hayes, we can now understand how it was that her Lucia excited such enthusiasm at La Scala and other principal theatres in Italy. She is certainly the sweetest, the most graceful, the most interesting representative of the character we have ever seen. In the most impassioned scenes, she did not reach the tragic power of Jenny Lind, particularly in the scene of Lucy's madness and death, which the great actress rendered terrible as well as pathetic. Miss Hayes's whole picture was in a softer and more subdued tone, more true to nature, and fuller of delicacy and feeling. In respect to vocal performance too, she was equal to Lind. Her voice was never loud, but fell rich and full upon the ear, and, even in the softest passages, its pure and ethereal tones were distinctly heard throughout the theatre. She sang exquisitely in tune, and rose to the extreme altitude of the scales without effort or the slightest degree of shrillness. Her execution of every vocal phrase was finished and refined; and the delicacy of her taste was shown in the style of her embellishments, which were graceful and imaginative, without being forced or overcharged.[3]

The magic of the partnership which was born at La Scala some years before obviously had the same impact on the London music critics. However, Lumley was looking for something bigger for his theatre.

Ever since the commencement of the Royal Italian Opera seasons in 1847, Benjamin Lumley had continued to have problems at Her Majesty's Theatre. Lind's arrival in London that year had given him the initial boost he needed to combat the competition. However, she was now gone from Her Majesty's and the competition at Covent Garden was stronger than ever. Lumley had already featured Catherine in one of her best roles, but he felt he needed something more.

He decided that he needed to strengthen his season with a 'big' name so that the desired ticket sales would be achieved. He sought out the former operatic star, German born Henriette Sontag. She had married a Count Rossi, a prominent Sardinian diplomat, in1830, after which she had retired from the stage.

Timing as always for Lumley was propitious. Count Rossi was deep in financial difficulty for a variety of reasons. Rossi had also lost his job as a diplomat due to the King of Sardinia's abdication. Lumley was aware of these things when he approached Sontag about coming out of retirement to sing for him in London. The vivacious Sontag looked remarkably youthful, despite her age (she turned 45 in January 1850) and the fact that she had made her London debut as far back as 1828. Her musicianship, personality and stage presence were outstanding, since she had been part of a theatrical family.

After a period of hesitancy on her part, which was partially due to the fact, that she might lose her title of 'Countess' if she did in fact return to the stage, she eventually agreed to consider Lumley's proposition. Given her husband's change in fortune and the need for independent financial security, she ultimately agreed to come to London for a singing engagement. As usual the impresario was remarkably persuasive and successful in achieving his goal. Additionally, his music director Michael Balfe was a friend of Sontag's, which also proved helpful. During his days as a vocalist, Balfe had actually made his Paris debut as Figaro in Il *Barbiere di Siviglia* singing opposite Sontag.

Lumley knew from experience that Sontag's presence had the potential to generate full houses for his new season in 1850. This prompted him to offer her all the star roles. Thus, Lumley's decision was based purely on potential financial gain, which of course is always foremost in the minds of most theatre managers. Despite Catherine's success in *Lucia* and the plaudits she received from the critics, Lumley elected to virtually ignore her, even though at that time she was the best young artist in his company.

This was a very competitive time in London. The foreign singer was always better 'box office' over native talent, as tenor Sims Reeves found out all too often over a fifty year career in England. Lumley was not prepared to risk a 'native' born singer as the season's leading prima donna, so logically it was Sontag who filled that role for the season's new productions of *I Puritani*, *Linda di Chamounix*, *La Sonnambula* and *Don Pasquale*. These were all operas that Catherine had the vocal stamina and musical ability to perform with great success, yet she did not sang in any of them that season.

There's no doubt that Lumley's decision significantly affected Catherine's career, as it crystallised her thoughts with respect to her future as an opera singer in England. If she had any doubts before this season, Lumley's actions convinced her that she had to change course.

During April and May, Catherine also sang the principal soprano part in Mendelssohn's *Elijah* at Exeter Hall. This was followed by Haydn's *Creation*, and a performance of Handel's *Messiah* before the Royal Society of Musicians in the Hanover Square Concert Rooms which was conducted by Michael Costa. She found herself constantly in demand for oratorios and concerts.

Following Lucia, her next role at Her Majesty's was the unlikely part of Cherubino in Mozart's *Le Nozze di Figaro*, which had its first performance that season on 18 April, with Sontag singing Susanna, Belletti as Figaro and Coletti as the Count. Reviews of the performance the following day primarily centred on Sontag, with a secondary mention of Catherine's role as follows:

> Miss Catherine Hayes, though her singing is not altogether effortless, was highly successful in the expression of deep emotions, which she threw into that most impassioned of airs, 'Voi, che sapete', which was deservedly encored.[4]

The *Dublin Evening Packet* reported on her performance using the reviews of several London, newspapers including the *Morning Chronicle* and the *Sun*. The *Chronicle* recorded the following:

> The novelty was the first appearance of Miss Catherine Hayes in the difficult part of Cherubino, one so foreign to her usual range of characters. She gave a very charming, arch, and graceful rendering of the character of the madcap young page – one in the highest degree intelligent from first to last. Her 'Voi che sapete' was sung with exquisite feeling, and was enthusiastically *encored*.[5]

The *Sun* critic said:

> Miss Catherine Hayes appeared for the first time in the character of Cherubino, and has won for herself golden opinions by her graceful, tasteful, and artiste-like manner of rendering the music of Mozart. . . . Miss Catherine Hayes was last night submitted to this test, and the success she achieved was most triumphant. Never have we heard that most impassioned of airs 'Voi che sapete' as thrillingly, so beautiful, so faithfully rendered as it was by Catherine Hayes, and

never was [an] *artiste* greeted with a more enthusiastic encore than she was at its conclusion. A bouquet was thrown to her from one of the boxes, and seldom, indeed, has [a] bouquet been so well merited.[6]

During the spring and summer months Catherine also participated in a variety of concerts in and around London. Many of these were with Sims Reeves, which may have been by design as they seemed to enjoy performing together. Some of these concerts took place at Her Majesty's Theatre, when Sims Reeves partnered Catherine in duets.

The first of these large-scale concerts at Her Majesty's occurred on Monday morning, 13 May. Sontag's name received top billing, followed by Catherine, and various other singers, including Teresa Parodi, Ida Bertrand and Madame Giulani. Tenors in the company included Calzolari, Reeves and a new one, Carlo Baucarde from Florence who was then just 25 years old. Baritones and basses included Belletti, Coletti, Frederick Lablache and the indomitable Luigi Lablache, who was now 55. Balfe was the conductor.

The concert opened with Beethoven's *Eroica* symphony, after which Belletti, Parodi and Giulani sang a trio from *Fidelio*. Catherine came next and was partnered with the mezzo-soprano Ida Bertrand in a duet 'Di conforto un raggio solo' from the first act of *La Vestale* by Mercadante. This was immediately followed by Sontag's first solo – Henry Bishop's ballad 'Home Sweet Home' from his 1823 opera *Clari, or The Maid of Milan*. Catherine next appeared with Sims Reeves in the second part of the concert singing a duet, 'Dolce offerta grati accenti', from Rossini's *Guglielmo Tell*. This was followed by a trio from the same opera, in which Catherine, Sontag and Parodi joined forces, possibly with Catherine singing Jemmy's (Tell's son) music and Sontag Matilde's. The third part of the concert also had a 'Trio for Three Tenors', in which Baucarde, Calzolari and Reeves performed from Rossini's *Armida*. Sontag then sang a song especially written for her in Paris, 'Swiss Airs' by Eckert. Then came a major scene this time from, from Gluck's *Armide*, with Catherine and eleven other singers, including Luigi Lablache.

Catherine, always proud of her Irish heritage and in sharp contrast to the other musical selections of the day, followed with her favourite ballad, 'Kathleen Mavourneen', accompanied by Balfe at the piano. The concert closed with the finale to the first act of Spontini's *La Vestale*, involving virtually every singer present and a full chorus. Sontag was the only vocalist who did not participate in this extravagant finale.

HER MAJESTY'S THEATRE

A

GRAND CLASSICAL, DRAMATIC, MISCELLANEOUS, CONCERTED

MUSICAL ENTERTAINMENT

WILL TAKE PLACE

On MONDAY MORNING, MAY 13th, 1850,

Selected from the following Authors : —

WEBER, SPOHR, CHERUBINI, SPONTINI, ROSSINI, GLUCK,
MERCADANTE, CIMAROSA, BEETHOVEN, RICCI, ZINGARELLI,
PURCELL, BISHOP, ECKERT, MOZART, and MENDELSSOHN ;
And embracing many highly interesting Novelties.

ON THIS OCCASION WILL APPEAR

Madame SONTAG,

Miss CATHERINE HAYES, Madame GIULIANI,
Madlle. IDA BERTRAND, AND Madlle. PARODI.
Signori CALZOLARI, SIMS REEVES, AND BAUCARDE,
COLETTI, BELLETTI, LORENZO, F. LABLACHE,
M. MULLER, AND Signor LABLACHE.

SUPPORTED BY ALL THE INSTRUMENTAL AND CHORAL
RESOURCES OF THE THEATRE.

THE WHOLE UNDER THE DIRECTION OF

Mr. BALFE.

Amongst other Novelties, **Madame SONTAG** will have the honour to sing the

SWISS AIRS BY ECKERT,

(Composed expressly for her, and sung with the most enthusiastic success, at
the Concerts of the Grand Conservatoire of Paris) ;

The Grand Scena from

OBERON,

The admired Ballad,

"HOME, SWEET HOME!"

And the celebrated Hymn,

"HEAR MY PRAYER,"

With FULL CHORUS by MENDELSSOHN.

In addition to which will be presented,

A TRIO FOR THREE BASSES,
A TRIO FOR THREE SOPRANOS,
AND
A TRIO FOR THREE TENORS.

20. The programme for a major concert at Her Majesty's Theatre, London May 1850, with
Michael Balfe conducting. (Courtesy V&A Theatre Museum, London).

The overall concert programme, which lasted four hours, was intriguing for London in 1850 and for its variety and selections. The concert included music by Beethoven, Weber, Mozart, Spohr, Rossini, Bellini, Mercadante, Ricci, Zingarelli, Spontini, Cherubini, Cimarosa and others. The programme selection seems quite remarkable given the lack of music by Italy's two most prominent composers, Donizetti, who was immensely popular, and Verdi, who by now had great influence all across Europe, although to a lesser extent in London. Reviews the next day stated:

> Beethoven's magnificent Symphony in E flat, the *Eroica* which was performed entire, gave solidity to the concert . . . the manner in which it was played was highly creditable to the band [orchestra] and its talented conductor, Mr. Balfe.[7]

Sontag's performance, apart from songs, also included the *Oberon* aria 'Ocean thou mighty monster', which she sang in German. She was well received and an encore was requested. An extensive review of the concert included the following comments about Catherine's singing of the Irish ballad:

> Miss Catherine Hayes sang the ballad of 'Kathleen Mavourneen' with charming taste and expression, and was loudly encored.[8]

Catherine returned to Her Majesty's Theatre on 27 May, with Balfe again on the podium and the virtuoso pianist Thalberg participating as special guest. This time the programme did include various Donizetti pieces. Verdi, however, was only represented by the aria 'Sempre all' alba' from *Giovanna d'Arco*, which was sung by Teresa Parodi. Sontag in typical style dominated, and was featured with 'Let the Bright Seraphim' from *Samson* by Handel.

Many of the singers from the previous concert participated. The 'Trio for Three Tenors' was repeated by Baucade, Reeves and Calzolari. Catherine only sang two items: 'Voi che sapete' from *Le Nozze di Figaro* and a ballad called 'The Joy of Tears' which was composed for her by Balfe. This song which was described by one reviewer as written 'in the composer's happiest manner', was well received by the audience. Thalberg's contribution included his variations on Donizetti's *L'Elisir d'Amore* and on *Lucrezia Borgia*. Another concert followed, on 30 May.

Perhaps the real event of the season occurred in the audience at one of these concerts when the celebrated prima donna Giuditta Pasta, now 53 and in retirement for many years, made her entrance into the theatre. It was announced that Pasta was on a short visit to London. However, it wasn't long before there was advertising in the *Times* announcing that Pasta would sing a final 'farewell' concert in addition to giving a performance of Donizetti's *Anna Bolena* at Her Majesty's, in which her former pupil Teresa Parodi would participate.[9] In the past, *Anna Bolena* had been one of her greatest roles, ever since she created the title part in Milan in 1830.

On 31 May Catherine participated in a performance of the *Creation* by Haydn. However, she did not sing in any more operas at Her Majesty's that season. She was scheduled for another series of *Lucia* starting 4 June, but illness prevented her. Erminia Frezzolini, who had just joined the distinguished Lumley company at Her Majesty's, substituted for her and completed the series with considerable success.

Catherine was once again advertised to sing on 6 June in the premiere performance of a new Fromental Halévy work, *La Tempesta*, with a libretto written by Scribe the prominent French writer. Michael Balfe was to be the conductor. This was postponed, however, because of the need for additional rehearsals. When the premiere finally occurred two days later on 8 June, Catherine's assigned part of Spirit of the Air was sung by a Madame Giulani. Catherine was either indisposed or she had had second thoughts about singing such a small role opposite Sontag, who was the featured star of the performance. There was only a very brief one-line comment on Madame Giulani's performance as the substitute for Catherine, in the review that followed two days later. Halévy and Sontag received virtually all of the coverage in a review that extended to two full columns in the *Times*.[10]

Over the next weeks Catherine was advertised to sing in several concerts, the most important of which was on 21 June and titled 'M. Benedict's Morning Concert'. The concert was under the patronage of 'Her most Gracious Majesty The Queen and His Royal Highness Prince Albert'. The concert, however, started in the early afternoon, not the morning. Balfe was on the podium as conductor.

Catherine's first appearance at this concert was in a large scene from Gluck's *Armide*, with many singers, including the two Lablaches, baritones Coletti and Belletti, tenors Calzolari, Gardoni and Baucade and, on the female side, Parodi and Frezzolini, with Sontag featured at the head of the list. There was also a 'Trio for Basses' in which Coletti, Belletti and Luigi Lablache sang from Luigi Ricci's comic opera *Chiara di Rosenberg*, which was first performed at La Scala in 1831. The first part of the concert closed-out with Mozart's *Ave Verum*, with Sontag, Catherine and Parodi, the three tenors and the basses again participating, and a chorus. Catherine did not perform any solos until part three of the concert. Most of the singers including Catherine sang in the finale to the second part of the concert. This was a religious piece called 'Alla Trinita beata' composed under the title *Laudi Spirituali* in AD 1546. The composer was not named.

The concert included other soloists and instrumentalists among whom was George A. Osborne, Catherine's friend from her student days in Paris. Osborne had composed a piece for two pianos which he and his former student, Charles Halle, played on one piano while Julius Benedict and Lindsay Sloper were at the other. The premiere of the Osborne composition opened the third and final part of the concert. This was followed by Catherine singing the Irish ballad 'Terence's Farewell', after which she contributed to the final vocal piece of the evening, which was Gluck's *Le Dieu De Paphos*.

Donizetti was featured prominently at this concert with several of the vocalists contributing arias. Sontag and Frezzolini sang a duet from his opera *Maria Padilla*; this was the first time these two singers had appeared together. Once again no Verdi music was performed.

Catherine's limited participation could have been because of her recent indisposition, which was probably a cold or sore throat, both of which she seemed to suffer from with greater frequency during those years in England. It was certainly unusual for her not to have performed more solos at this type of function. Around the same time the tenacious Jenny Lind was touring England in a series of final 'Farewell' concerts, in preparation for her departure for America.

A fourth and final concert was advertised, in which all of Lumley's stars were to perform for the last time. Sontag was again positioned as the lead artist, followed by Parodi, Catherine and Frezzolini. Sims Reeves was also scheduled to participate and Balfe was the conductor. Just before the curtain rose Catherine and Sims Reeves could not be found. It seems they had elected to be absent from the concert without giving advance notice to the manager. An announcement was duly made with no explanation given to the audience or the press, much to the surprise of everyone.[11]

There is little doubt that during this period the relationship between the two singers had reached its peak. They had been together off and on for almost a year in London and they shared the operatic stage and the concert platform regularly. Catherine's demeanour in England had always been very decorous. There was no scandal or innuendo reported at any time in the press about her personal life. However, this absence from the scene was noted by the press the following day with a certain amount of puzzlement. For Reeves there was also the need for discretion because of his relationship with the soprano Emma Lucombe. He had appeared in several concerts and operas with Lucombe, and things had to be fairly advanced as they were eventually to marry. In any event, it was during this period that the relationship between Reeves and Catherine must have started to erode, presumably because Catherine realised that nothing would come of it.

She did sing with Reeves again several times, but almost a year would pass before their next meeting took place. They were to remain life-long friends. They empathised with each other, realising the limitations placed upon them by English conventional opinion that foreign born was better than native talent. At the concert which they missed, Teresa Parodi sang Catherine's arias. Indeed, the non-appearance of Catherine and Reeves must have been a disappointment for Balfe, also – among other things, they were scheduled to sing a duet from his opera the *Siege of Rochelle*. It would have been the first time the two of them had sung Balfe's music together.

In mid-July Catherine left for Birmingham, Manchester, Liverpool and other places in the north of England, before arriving in Edinburgh in October. In Edinburgh, she gave two concerts at the Music Hall in George's Street, on 12 and 14 October 1850. After Edinburgh she crossed to Belfast for more concerts with the Anacreontic Society. While in Belfast she stayed with relatives of the late Bishop Knox at their home, 'Hollywood House'. From there she went to Dublin, where the press announced that after this Irish tour 'Miss Hayes would depart for Rome, Italy'.

She was scheduled to perform in Dublin in eight nights of opera over a two-week period at the Theatre Royal. Her first performance was on 21 October in Bellini's *La Sonnambula*. This was followed the next three evenings by three Donizetti operas, *Linda di Chamounix*, *Lucrezia Borgia* and *Lucia di Lammermoor*. She also performed in Bellini's *Norma*. This season was her first appearance anywhere in *Lucrezia Borgia*. It was also the first time this Donizetti opera was performed in Dublin. The reviews stated:

As we anticipated, the production, for the first time in this city, of Donizetti's opera of *Lucrezia Borgia,* on Thursday night, caused one of the most overflowing audiences ever beheld in Hawkins Street [Theatre Royal] to assemble. The *Freeman* [*Freeman's Journal*] thus speaks of the crowd and crush:- To say that the Theatre Royal was crowded would give but a faint idea, indeed, of the awful *melee* that characterised the assemblage of the pit and gallery audience. The house, as viewed from the stage, presented the same awful appearance which characterised its interior on the night of Miss Hayes's benefit on the occasion of her last visit to Dublin. The pit literally swarmed, the galleries seemed ready to yield beneath the accumulated masses of spectators, crowding and crushing to the front, and the boxes, both dress and upper circles, seemed inconveniently crammed. Hundreds had to retire without being able to obtain standing room in any part of the house; and the patience and good humour with which the crush was borne was indeed marvellous . . . at the outset we would be inclined to remark that the character of Lucrezia is not one at all suited to Miss Hayes, by whom Amina, Linda and all similar parts, are so truthfully represented. But true genius overcomes many difficulties, and in the highly-wrought scenes – when giving the poison cup to her son – when startled with horror at finding him among the guests at the fatal banquet – when, in broken tones of agony and remorse, disclosing his birth – when prostrate in all the abandonment of sorrow – her acting exhibited dramatic power that evidently astonished the audience. *Saunders'* [newsletter/newspaper] justly says: . . . Miss Hayes sustained the leading character with great dramatic judgement, truth, and pathos, but we would rather see her in the more winning and touching characters of Amina or Linda. The whole representation was, however, an evidence of genius, of genius adapting itself to circumstances that might at first be justly regarded as somewhat alien to the disposition of the artiste, and her last scene was exquisite, allowing as it did the display of the more affectionate sympathies of our nature. The appealing fondness of her manner, the burst of emotions as the word 'Figlio' was repeated again and again told at once with the house. From the charming opening aria, 'Come e bello' interpreted by Miss Hayes with all the purity of expression and brilliancy of execution that distinguish her vocalism, to the concluding scene, in which the agony of despair is so finely expressed, her interpretation of the music was characterised by blended delicacy of taste, truth of expression, and beauty of ornament. The applause at times grew, into absolute tumult, and on the falling of the curtain, when loaded with bouquets, she again

158   *Catherine Hayes*

came forth, accompanied by Sig. Bordas and Herr Mengis, the scene
in [the] pit, boxes, and galleries, exhibited an amount of enthusiasm
without precedent, even in any of her former engagements. Her
concept of the character of *Lucrezia* is very fine, and the embodiment
of that conception, from first to last, was essentially dramatic, original
and effective. We did not think Miss Hayes could command so large
an amount of sustained energy as she displayed during the terrible
banquet scene, and are quite convinced that the enthusiastic gratification expressed at its termination by the audience was as much an
expression of delight at the evidence of improved health and strength
its delineation proved, as of merely selfish pleasure in the enjoyment
of singing and acting, unsurpassed for beauty and power.[12]

Her final performance of *Lucrezia Borgia* created a unique situation for
her. The following is a report from one of the Dublin newspapers:

An unusual scene occurred on Saturday night during the performance of the grand tragic opera of *Lucrezia Borgia*. Miss Hayes, in the
midst of her performance, and after one of the most exciting acts of
the opera, was called before the curtain again and again, but still the
uproar of applause in the pit and galleries was not quelled. At length
the fair vocalist was obliged to try the charms of music, and to
comply with a stentorian shout for 'The Harp that once through
Tara's Halls' which she actually sung in full costume, and
surrounded by the bewildered tenor, baritone and chorus, also in
complete dramatic habillment [sic]. The progress of a serious opera
stopped for the performance of an Irish ballad! It was, in truth, an
incident without precedent, and equally without precedent were the
roars of gratification that followed; one ardent gentleman in the
middle gallery shouting with a voice that was heard above all the
tumult, "Musha! God bless you, Catherine darlin".'[13]

During this visit to Dublin she was interviewed by *Dublin University*
(now Trinity College) *Magazine* for the November issue, an extensive
article profiling her career to date and providing some insight to her
thoughts and ambitions for the future.[14] The article showed her as a
somewhat serious person, intent on her career – a person obviously driven
by deep ambition.

Between her operatic performances at the Theatre Royal she gave a
concert 'For the Benefit of the Poor' on Friday morning 25 October at the

Antient Concert Rooms in Brunswick Street, during which she sang 'Ah! mon fils' from Meyerbeer's *Le Prophète*, next came 'Come e bello' from *Lucrezia Borgia*. During the second half of the concert she sang a song composed by Louis Lavenu called 'Those happy days are gone' and after that Schubert's 'Ave Maria'. She also performed a duet, 'O meine Geliebte' by operatic composer Otto Nicolai. While this piece was advertised by its German title, she and her partner, the Swiss baritone Josef Mengis who was fluent in English, in all probability sang it in English. The proceeds (one half of the net receipts for the concert) were distributed by the Archbishop of Dublin, the Reverend Dr. Murray and the Protestant Archbishop Dr. Whately. The beneficiaries were St. Vincent's Hospital, the Coombe Lying-in Hospital and the St. Vincent de Paul Society for the relief of the Dublin poor. Similar concerts were announced for Limerick and Cork.

As Catherine prepared to depart for the provinces the Dublin daily press was reporting on Jenny Lind's activities in America, with a long article featuring Lind's ability to draw large crowds and contribute enormous amounts of money to charity.[15] Catherine could not escape the Lind phenomenon, even in her home country and despite her own strong presence.

After the conclusion of the opera season in Dublin in early November Catherine and her company of artists, including Bordas, Mengis, Paltoni and Macfarren travelled to the provinces to give concerts in Wexford (4 November), Waterford (5 November), Clonmel (6 November), and later to Kilkenny and Galway, offering a similar programme to the Dublin concert. This was her first appearance in all of these towns. This part of her tour was managed by Mr. John Joy of Cramer & Beale. It was Mr. Joy's responsibility to take care of the advance concert and performance details in Ireland, and he had advertised her planned concerts in the local newspapers. Sadly, next to the notice of her concerts, advertising featuring 'Emigration' ships to New Orleans and Savannah in the New World also appeared, in response to the needs of a people suffering from the Great Famine.

In Wexford her arrival was heralded with a number of advance notices and an extended article on her background most of which was extracted from the Dublin University Magazine article which had just been released.[16] Jenny Lind's activities in America's New England were also being reported at the same time. In anticipation of Catherine's visit to Wexford a notice in an earlier issue of one of the newspapers also reflected on Jenny Lind, saying:

> If there be a Jenny Lind in Yankee land, we are happy to say that there
> is a Catherine Hayes mania in Wexford . . . although we worship
> genius, from whatever clime or country it proceeds, our *native land*
> shall always hold the first place in our heart of hearts.[17]

After Catherine's performance on 4 November the reviewer said the
following regarding her concert at the Theatre Royal (the same theatre
that has hosted the annual Wexford Opera Festival since 1951):

> The Theatre on Monday evening was overflowing from 'pit to roof-
> tree [sic]', and the Dress circle presented a galaxy of beauty and
> fascination which made us proud indeed of our still happy and
> model shire [county] . . . The concert which opened with the beau-
> tiful trio finale 'Guai se ti sfugge un moto' from *Lucrezia Borgia*,
> which was artistically and beautifully executed by Signor Bordas,
> Herr Mengis and Madame Macfarren. Signor Paltoni next came
> forward and gave his aria from Rossini, with great fervour and feeling
> – followed by the most enthusiastic acclamation, accompanied by cries,
> or rather vollies [sic], of impassioned anticipation for Catherine Hayes
> – when slowly and pensively she came forward in all her native
> grace, simplicity, and purity of heart and soul, the sweet and
> glorious 'Star of the Night'. An audience more enthusiastic was
> never, perhaps, assembled within the walls of a Theatre or Concert-
> room; and although the applause that greeted the first appearance
> of Catherine Hayes in Wexford was absolutely deafening, it
> continued at intervals till the close of the magnificent French
> Cavatina – 'Ah mon fils' – when it gathered into a perfect tempest,
> which literally swept the house, and at once proclaimed her triumph
> as the Irish Queen of Melody and Song.
> She also sang the Irish ballads, 'Kathleen Mavourneen' and 'The
> Harp that once through Tara's Halls'. . . . [This] was sung by
> Catherine Hayes on this occasion with much more Irish feeling and
> pathos than ever we heard breathed into it before, even by Moore
> himself.[18]

The reviewer concluded in a long column that provided some
comments on her voice among other things. Of particular interest was
the closing paragraph, which referred to a sonnet, written in Italian by
one of the newspaper staff to commemorate Catherine's visit to Wexford
and forthcoming trip to Rome. On presenting the sonnet to the prima

donna, it was reported that the response was: '[she] will place it amongst her fondest memorabilia.'

On 5 November she appeared in the Town Hall in Waterford, where the concert commenced at 8 pm. The next day she departed by rail for Clonmel in Tipperary, where on Wednesday 6 November she performed at the lecture room of the Mechanics' Institute before an audience composed of 'the rank, and beauty, and fashion of Clonmel and the surrounding neighbourhood'. A review stated that:

> Long before the hour appointed for the commencement of the concert, the rolling of carriages towards Anglesea Street, evidenced the desire of their occupants to possess the seats best adapted for hearing . . .
>
> Mr. Lavenu appeared leading forth the world famous songstress, who with delicacy of feeling and becoming simplicity, bowed to the immense auditory. A pause for a moment, and then in tones of enthusiastic gladness they bid *cead mille failthe* [sic], to the fair young girl that stood blushing before them. A silence as of the grave followed, and stealing over the soul came the first low notes of Bellini's beautiful and touching cavatina [*Norma*] 'Ah! bella, a mi ritorna' – notes that undulated, like the sighing of the summer wind, and while exciting to the utmost the imagination by the magic of their melody, they found response in the heart by the sweetness of their delicacy, and as they rose and fell with graceful ease, and as the conclusion approached, when she displayed in a wonderful manner that enchanting shake which she so naturally possesses, the feelings of the audience which had been nerved to over-tension found – a vent in a hearty and prolonged burst of applause which was again repeated on Miss Hayes withdrawing from the stage.[19]

Speaking of the 'thrilling pathos' left by her performance of the song 'Kathleen Mavourneen' the Clonmel critic went on to say:

> The flute-like tones of her noble voice were heard distinctly, though low and soft and again they rose clear and swelling, concluding with that exquisite shake to which we have referred. The depth of feeling evidenced throughout the varied emotions which this beautiful melody evoked all were expressed so truthfully, that the sentiments were re-echoed by her auditory and all felt the influence which she exercised and which will leave an impression on memory's tablet which length of time cannot obliterate.[20]

Catherine next visited Cork and here she performed in La Sonnambula (8 Nov.), Lucrezia Borgia (9 Nov.), and Lucia di Lammermoor (11 Nov.), to packed houses at the Theatre Royal and at the same time adding the role of Norena in Donizetti's Don Pasquale (Nov. 12) to her repertoire. Reviews once again were highly complimentary:

> Last night, a house crowded in every available corner beheld the Irish prima donna once more performing the heroine in that inexhaustible favourite, La Sonnambula.
>
> The enthusiasm with which Catherine Hayes was hailed, when she made her appearance as Amina in the opening scene, is absolutely indescribable the whole house rang with the shout of welcome and the denizens of the pit, in the height of their excitement, flung up their hats in the air, and strained their throats with cheering. Nor were the boxes much behind any other part of the house in the warmth of their greeting.
>
> We thought last night that Catherine Hayes's voice had much improved in volume and softness of tone; and during the whole opera not a note emanated from her lips suggestive of harshness – each individual song and recitative was one unbroken tide of clear, flowing melody, not equalled we thought even by any of the previous performances [the previous year] of this matchless vocalist.[21]

Another newspaper reviewer in addition to complimenting Catherine on her style, acting and beautiful voice, went on to say the following about her personal appearance and overall deportment:

> Catherine Hayes possesses soul, a soul of exquisite feeling, if she is to be judged of by the expression which she imparts to her operatic singing, and the pathos of her ballad performances. Then her person is singularly attractive. Her profile is almost severely beautiful, which imparts a dignity and a nobleness to her assumption of lofty tragic characters, such as Norma, Lucrezia, and others of that class. Her figure is slight, but admirably formed, and all her motions are free and graceful. Indeed it is quite impossible that Catherine Hayes could be *un*-graceful, or that any gesture of hers could happen to be awkward. A word as to her acting. It is nature, it is truth, it is like reality as what is not positively real can be. Catherine Hayes seems instinctively to comprehend the character which she personates, and

to enter into all the feelings, emotions, and passions, which she is called on to depict and represent.[22]

Returning to Limerick for a brief visit and short rest she gave two concerts, one being a charity concert for the poor of her home town. The Dublin papers reporting on her Limerick activity stated:

> the concert for the poor was extremely well attended; that the fair vocalist exerted herself to the utmost, and that the performance passed off with unequivocal success.[23]

In Limerick an admirer called W.C. Desmond wrote a seven-stanza poem titled 'La Perla Del Teatro' (The Pearl of the Theatre) in advance of her visit and this was featured in one of the local newspapers.[24] Other publications reported on her visit with equal enthusiasm, reinforcing all the pronouncements of reviewers in other places. The song 'Kathleen Mavourneen' was once again singled out for the manner in which it was delivered: 'thrilling expression, deep pathos with the same cantabile gracefulness'. During this stay in Limerick she was admitted into the Limerick Harmonic Society.

After Limerick she travelled to Galway, where she appeared at the Theatre Royal on Saturday 16 November. Galway was slightly different from the other places she had visited during this period, as it was not on the regular circuit for travelling performers, so her visit there had special significance for the local community. In closing his review one reporter who attended the concert let his emotions get out of hand when it came to expressing his reaction to the evening:

> We would have walked one hundred miles to catch the soul-inspiring notes of music and patriotism which flowed from the lips of Catherine Hayes, while singing the most beautiful of our national melodies. The next song was the aria 'Ah non giunge' [*La Sonnambula*] which electrified the audience, as it was rendered by Miss Hayes's soprano voice, which is of such immense compass, great power, and exquisite sweetness . . . [25]

A few weeks after her departure from Galway, one of the local newspapers featured a short notice, presumably information provided by Mr Joy the tour manager:

Miss Catherine Hayes, our fair country woman leaves London for Rome in a few days, and proceeds from thence to Russia, being engaged to appear at St. Petersburg [Italian Opera Season] and Moscow. She will visit the New World early in the ensuing season, accompanied by Mr. Joy.[26]

It would have been logical that Catherine may have been considering a visit to Russia, where many of the leading operatic artists of the day performed at the Italian Opera in St. Petersburg, and where they were paid fabulous amounts of money. However, there is no record that she ever actually visited Russia at this or any other time.

Two days later she departed for Kilkenny for a concert on Tuesday 19 November. Kilkenny, like Galway, was slightly outside the regular circuit of visiting artists. However, Franz Liszt and Louis Lavenu (Catherine's accompanist for this tour) among others had visited it in 1841.

The weather on the evening of Catherine's concert was apparently quite inclement. The concert took place in the Common Hall of the County and City Courts. Kilkenny apparently did not have a theatre, or at least not one big enough to accommodate everybody who wanted to attend Catherine Hayes' concert. According to the press the hall was not well suited for the occasion, being cold and insufficiently lit for an audience that amounted to about 300 people including the aristocracy, the military and the most respectable of the mercantile and trading classes.

Kilkenny's two newspapers had representatives in attendance and reported on the event. On Catherine's first appearance of the evening, one of the reviewers stated:

> at length she came forward to sing her first cavatina, 'Ah! Mon fils'. She was received with a perfect storm of applause, during which the prima donna gracefully acknowledged the compliment, and then turning to the director, Mr. Lavenu, the accompaniment began. Whilst it was playing, she stood immoveable [sic] as some fair statue of grave modesty. It ceased, and she began to sing. – What a voice – what a voice was there! How sweet, penetrating, rich and full! What volumes of enchanting sound issued from that shrill warbling throat and delicate heaving chest!
>
> But she had too much the soul of music in her to keep that passionless expression long – her eyes were raised, her countenance dilated – and then she poured forth, sweet as the trill of the nightingale, that almost unearthly shake, bubbling and melting forth

like honey, and dying away into the softest whispering echo of vocalisation the moment that delightful music ceased, she resumed her grave and calm expression. Thunders of applause broke on every side, whilst the very roof of the concert room re-echoed with sound of applauding hands – ancora! ancora! ancora! the demands for an encore were not resisted – she yielded.[27]

The reviewer for the other newspaper seemed to have a slightly different view of the outcome of the evening stating as follows:

An operatic or concert performance, wherein artists of reputed fame appear, is by too many, in localities where such occurrences are rare, looked forward to, as some extraordinary exhibition, the like of which is not less to please, than to *astound* the hearer . . . We would not be justified in attributing any want of due appreciation of musical ability to the people of Kilkenny. From the cradle to the grave, the genius of music is with them – more particularly with the operative classes. But, somehow or other, there was not, at the concert on Tuesday evening, that warm enthusiasm which we would expect to see manifested on an occasion in which Catherine Hayes alone might be expected to appear . . .

   . . . one of the party is reported to have said that 'the day was coldæthe place was cold and *the people* were cold.'

   . . . for travelling to a concert in 'rain everlasting;' being then placed in a rather long hall, badly lighted, with unneighbourly, and chilling flag stones to stand on one may not feel quite brimful of exuberance when a concert opens even with a Hayes.

The writer appeared to have a good understanding of vocal art when he went on to discuss the evening. Initially, he was contented to compare her to Jenny Lind, then modified his opinion slightly to describe Catherine's voice as a 'mellifluous, sweet voice, which trembles, or soars or whispers, or startles you with the manifold beauties of its resources, its power, its compass'.[28]

With the Kilkenny concert over, she returned to Dublin for three nights of opera commencing on 20 November at the Theatre Royal. In quick succession she performed in *Lucia di Lammermoor*, followed by two performances of *La Sonnambula*, after which she immediately prepared for her journey first to England and then on from Falmouth to Italy and Rome, where she was scheduled to open the *Carnivale* season on 26 December.

It would be many years before Catherine would set foot on Irish soil again. However, for now, she felt well pleased with her visit. She had been to places in Ireland she had never visited before, she was in good voice and had never had to cancel a performance during her visit. She had saved significant amounts of money and was looking forward to Rome, where she had not performed previously, and of course to returning to Italy, which had now become more tranquil since the upheaval of 1848.

She had signed a contract with Beale of Cramer & Beale for her visit to America in the autumn of 1851. She was to be accompanied by Mr. Joy (later Dr. John Joy) as tour manager, the baritone Josef Mengis and Louis Lavenu as music director, together with one other artist. Her mother and sister Henrietta would also travel with her to America.

Jenny Lind's success in America had spurred Catherine on to visit the New World, where she felt there were significant financial opportunities. This would happen after she had completed her operatic engagements in Italy early in 1851, followed by a series of concerts in England during the summer months, including participating at the Great Exhibition in July 1851 in Hyde Park. In September she would embark for America.

CHAPTER NINE

New Accolades and New Places

ITALY, ENGLAND AND AMERICA 1850–1851

WHILE TOURING in Ireland in 1850, Catherine was under contract to Cramer & Beale of London. She had discussed the idea of visiting America with T. Frederick Beale, one of the partners, earlier in 1850. Her success in Ireland, which was very profitable for Beale, prompted him to increase his offer to her for the year 1851. His new offer not only covered an agreement for an American tour, it also included a provision for a return to Ireland to sing in opera again. Mr. Joy presented the new contract to her while she was still travelling in Ireland.

The plans to visit America were firmed up and her departure was set for September 1851. Concidentally, this was exactly one year after Jenny Lind's departure for America from the same port on the same shipping line. However, unlike Barnum's deal with Lind, Catherine settled for far less with Beale.

Beale's initial commitment to her for the American tour was £500 per month, plus one sixth of the profits of the tour with all expenses to be covered by Beale. Three artists would accompany her: tenor Augustus Braham, a former military man and the son of the famous John Braham, the Swiss baritone Josef Mengis and Louis Lavenu as musical director. Mr. Joy would be the manager of the group. Although Catherine couldn't have known the association with Mr. Joy would contribute to major business problems for her during her early days in America. Her contract had a penalty clause that, in the event that, either Beale or Catherine was in breach of the terms of the contract at any time, payment of £3,000 had to be made to a bank in London, upon which the agreement would be terminated. Catherine had no experience in dealings of this type, although she liked Beale and trusted him and in general, the terms of the contract appealed to her.

When compared to Lind's financial arrangements with Barnum, Catherine's deal was extremely modest. In addition, the artists who were to accompany her were nowhere near the quality of those that accompanied Lind. As time would prove this would directly reflect on her in America, yet she did not request any changes to be made. Presumably, Beale had made these decisions because of cost. However, on the face of it, the offer represented significant earnings for a singer in the 1850s, and, given the opportunity to receive a percentage of the profits, it could make her a very rich woman.

Little is known about her earnings during this period in England and Ireland, except for limited information that has come to us from some of her personal correspondence. In major cities such as Liverpool, Manchester, Dublin and possibly London, she appeared to earn about twenty guineas (£21) per concert or for an oratorio. It was probably double that for an operatic performance. A gold guinea was a unit of English currency that was primarily used for professional fees – one guinea was equivalent to one pound one shilling sterling.

Assuming that this was her fee, she probably earned about £350–400 monthly during this period of her career, less whatever expenses she might have had to pay for transportation and Beale's commission, etc. Therefore, the offer from Beale was reasonable and had the potential to greatly expand her basic earnings. It also provided her with the opportunity to move away from the highly competitive musical scene in London and direct her career towards concerts, which had a greater appeal for her. She signed the contract for an 1851–52 American tour with Cramer & Beale in November 1850, just as she was about to embark for Italy.

At the end of November, she set off for Rome, travelling via England where she made a brief stop in Cheltenham for a concert before going on to Falmouth for the boat to Italy. On her arrival in Rome in the middle of December she immediately went into rehearsal for the *Carnivale* season at the Teatro Apollo which commenced on 26 December. Her principal roles included Elvira in *I Puritani* and the title roles in two Donizetti works, *Lucia di Lammermoor* and *Maria di Rohan*.

After opening the season in *I Puritani*, in which her partners were tenor E. Naudin and the baritone A. Ottaviani, she sang in a number of concerts before her next opera appearance, which was *Lucia di Lammermoor*, followed by *Maria di Rohan*. The season lasted until the middle of March.

It was no coincidence that, during the same period in Italy, the great talent of the 37 year-old Giuseppe Verdi was again hard at work – this time in Venice. Verdi was at the Teatro La Fenice where he was in the final stages of rehearsals for the premiere of his new opera *Rigoletto*, which had its first performance on 11 March 1851. Unfortunately, Catherine was still firm about Verdi's music not suiting her voice, consequently she had not been performing any of the composer's music. The role of Gilda in *Rigoletto* probably would have been ideal for her. As it turned out, later in life she did sing excerpts from this and other middle period Verdi works. However, the unique opportunity missed in Italy in March 1851 was enormous.

Meanwhile, about 350 miles away in Rome, Catherine's success singing Donizetti's music was quite phenomenal, so much so that the British press in London picked up on the sensation she had created – featuring her in a special report from Italy which also covered the overall operatic scene and saying:

> The managers [in Rome], are in despair at the restrictions by the authorities respecting modern operas the majority of which are prohibited for political or religious reasons. Verdi's *Ernani*, *Lombardi*, *Nabucco*, also the works of Bellini, Donizetti, Rossini, etc., have been completely changed in words. Miss C. Hayes after her great success in *Puritani* made her appearance in *Lucia* with immense 'furore'. She sang the part six times with the theatre crowded every night. She was recalled 5–6 times after each act. Her next character to be Maria di Rohan.[1]

A further report went on to say:

> *L'Italia Musicale* and *La Fama* record in the most eulogistic terms the triumphant reception in Rome of Miss Catherine Hayes; her last character was *Maria di Rohan* of Donizetti in the opera of that name . . .[2]

Catherine visited royalty and was the toast of the town at receptions given in her honour. In early March, she gave her final performance of *Maria di Rohan* at the early hour of ten o'clock in the morning, followed by excerpts from *Linda di Chamounix*. She gave two additional concerts in the homes of Princess Borghese and Princess Doria and was the guest of the Duchess Salvati.

Her success in Rome was so complete that a deputation consisting of members of the nobility recommended that she be awarded a diploma from the Accademia di Santa Cecilia, Italy's oldest and most distinguished musical award. The report on her last performance went on to state:

The season has closed. The last opera was *Maria di Rohan*, in which Catherine Hayes appeared for twelve successive nights. Nothing could exceed the sensation her singing and acting created. The enthusiasm by the audience knew no bounds. The proudest of aristocracies have paid Catherine Hayes the most marked attention. She has been honoured of being invited by the Princess Borghese, by whom she was introduced to the most distinguished of the noble ladies present. She has also been honoured with the diploma of 'Sona della Pontificia Congregatzione ed Accademia di Santa Cecilia' one of the oldest music societies in Italy, the last named artist enrolled in it being that of Maria Malibran.[3]

A formal diploma document was issued on 5 March and signed by eight members of the Accademia di Santa Cecilia. Two days later, Catherine followed up with a personal letter to the Accademia thanking its members for bestowing such an honour on her.

With the fanfare over and her season successfully completed, Catherine left Rome for England on Friday 25 March, feeling very good and wondering if she should consider going back to live and work in Italy. She and her mother, who had shared in her success in Rome, no doubt discussed how she could possibly use it to her benefit in England or America.

It was also during this period while Catherine was in Rome, that her London agents, Cramer & Beale, decided to take advantage of the publicity by running an advertisement featuring Catherine and Lind and various English songs which they had published.[4] Interestingly, the advertisement had placed Catherine's name above Lind's and went on to say:

Miss Catherine Hayes
and
Mdlle. Jenny Lind

The only English Ballads sung by the above distinguished vocalists, 'Take this Lute' by Benedict; 'Oh, summer morn,' by Meyerbeer; and the 'Lonely Rose' by Balfe sung by Mdlle. Lind; 'Those happy days are gone' by Lavenu; 'Why do I weep for thee,' by Wallace; 'O sing to me' by Osborne; and 'My last thoughts are of thee' by Maynard [W. Beale],' sung by Miss Hayes.

Shortly after Catherine's return to England around the beginning of April 1851, she was approached by John Henry Wardwell, a New Yorker who had been involved in the New York musical scene, possibly as a piano salesman or a dealer's representative.[5] Wardwell, apparently, was professing to represent America's greatest showman, P.T. Barnum, in Europe.

Catherine was later to find out that Wardwell was a person of questionable character. On this occasion he led Catherine to believe that Barnum was interested in offering her a contract to visit America for a concert tour, at a fee of £1,000 per month – virtually double what Beale had agreed to. However, his backer was in fact a New York-based associate who preferred to remain anonymous and who, seeing Barnum's success with Jenny Lind, hoped to make large profits by exploiting another singer of the same style in the New York area. This was Wardell' intention when he contacted Catherine on her return from her highly publicised performances in Rome early in 1851.

Catherine was probably aware of the fact that Lind, now six months into her contract with Barnum, was becoming disenchanted with the association. Information about Lind's dissatisfaction had already started to circulate in England. Lind, always conservative and religious, at least outwardly, felt repulsed by the Barnum relationship. She had come to realise that Barnum was better known as a manager of 'freak' shows such as the 'Fijee Mermaid', 'Tom Thumb, the Midget' and a variety of other unusual characters than as an impresario and manager of serious artists. She rightly felt that this association was not suitable for her and many of her friends agreed.[6]

In New York in April 1851, Lind was already considering a break with Barnum with the idea that she would manage the balance of the tour on her own, or possibly use the services of 28-year-old William Avery Bushnell. Bushnell was a Connecticut-based professional manager and former schoolteacher, who had been handling Lind's arrangements under Barnum's aegis. After much harmful publicity, including openly trading letters in the press, Lind's break with Barnum finally occurred in June 1851. She wrote him a letter stating that she wished to be released from her contract and that she was prepared to pay whatever penalty was incurred. Lind had performed a gruelling concert schedule for Barnum over the previous nine months, from Canada to Cuba, from New Orleans to Chicago and many places in between. She had completed 93 concerts in all and received over $175,000 for her efforts, while Barnum pocketed more than $500,000.[7] Lind paid a penalty of $25,000 to Barnum for the termination of her contract.

It was around the same time that John Henry Wardwell arrived in London, probably in early spring 1851. His mission was to make contact with potential Lind 'replacements' for the New York scene. Catherine was an obvious choice. Her vocal style and repertoire were similar to Lind's, and she had high visibility in the media. It was a logical choice for Wardwell to approach Catherine immediately on her return from Italy.

From Catherine's perspective, the results of her reception in Rome and the publicity she had received in England, along with the intriguing offer which Wardwell implied was from Barnum, prompted her to ask for a meeting with Beale to discuss the contract she had signed for America. She felt she needed to reopen negotiations because she was now worth more. Beale always liked Catherine and had been very helpful to her. In addition, he was sensitive to her point of view and really didn't want to lose her. Beale agreed to increase her base fee to £650 per month and to pay the travel expenses for her mother and sister and for all of her dresses and other apparel. All other terms and conditions of their original agreement were to remain unchanged.

Catherine notified Wardwell that she had signed a final contract with Beale on 30 April 1851 and that no further discussion was possible.[8] Wardwell accepted her decision for the time being, however, another plan was soon forming in his mind which he developed more fully over the next two months.

With her plans for America firmed up for the autumn, Catherine concentrated on the immediate future and her concert schedule for the summer months, including those at the Great Exhibition of 1851, which was an enormous event starting in London in July.

The Exhibition palace was of unprecedented proportions, style and structure, designed by Joseph Paxton and made of glass and steel. The Crystal Palace, as it was called, was built in Hyde Park in central London. The Exhibition itself was unique in the history of Europe. The Palace was designed to house the many exhibits that were indicative of the expansion and growth of the industrial age in Europe. A few years after the close of the Exhibition, the Crystal Palace building was removed to a new location on the outskirts of London at Sydenham in Kent. It remained at this location until 1936, when a fire started in the interior and, sadly, the entire structure was destroyed.

Meantime, to coincide with the start of the Great Exhibition a long series of concerts and oratorios were scheduled at various locations around London throughout the summer months. Catherine was taking part in many of these musical events and was partnered on several occasions with the now married Sims Reeves. Early in May, she and Reeves performed in Mendelssohn's *Elijah*, and this was repeated later in the month.

On Monday morning 19 May 1851, she was featured in a concert at the Hanover Rooms in London. She received ecstatic reviews from one of London's leading critics:

> The grand morning concert by the distinguished vocalist last Monday at the Hanover Rooms attracted an immense auditory, thus establishing the popularity of this young and gifted prima donna. The sensation produced by her vocalisation was very great –it was quite a Lind *furore*; and it was perfectly justified by the ability developed by her in a variety of schools, She first sang the cavatina of *Fides* (in French), 'Ah! mon fils', from Meyerbeer's *Prophète*, with impassioned feeling: this air brought out the compass of her fine voice, and the hearers were evidently astonished at the richness of her lower notes. Her next essay was in the 'Casta diva' of *Norma* and neither Grisi nor Lind in a concert-room, ever created a more thrilling effect in this cavatina than did Miss Hayes. The slow movement was rendered with the highest dramatic sentiment; and the *cabaletta* was characterised by a series of roulades, executed with the utmost certainty and brilliance . . .
>
> We learn that Miss Catherine Hayes, at the close of the season, will depart for America, to sing in opera as well as the concert-room. After the brilliant career of the vocalist in Italy, after being *prima donna* both at Her Majesty's Theatre and the Royal Italian Opera, and after immense success in the provinces at our great festivals, and in Ireland, her success in this Transatlantic trip cannot be doubted.[9]

Her next vocal concert took place on the evening of the same day with a performance of Handel's *Messiah* at Exeter Hall sponsored by the Sacred Harmonic Society, with Michael Costa as musical director. A second performance of the *Messiah* was given about a week later.

Before the official opening of the Great Exhibition at Crystal Palace, Catherine had concerts and oratorios to perform in Liverpool, Manchester and other northern cities. In late May, she was a last minute substitute for soprano Louise Pyne at a concert in Liverpool. She kept the integrity of the printed programme intact by singing for the first time pieces, that were new to her – one from Daniel Auber's popular opera

Masaniello; the other an aria from Rossini's *Semiramide*. Her handling of this programme as a last-minute substitute, with little or no time to learn these new pieces, was indicative of her musical ability and talent.

At the end of May and throughout June she travelled extensively, performing in oratorios and concerts with Sims Reeves and other singers. There was a particularly important, very prestigious concert given by the City of London on 13 June in conjunction with the Literary & Scientific Institution. She and Sims Reeves performed at this event to great acclaim. Two weeks later she and Reeves performed *Elijah* again.

In July, she took time off to rest and plan her trip to America. She went to Trouville in France, travelling there via Le Havre. Her mother and sister accompanied her. She felt exhilarated when she contemplated her next move and what it would mean to her to visit America, both emotionally and financially.

Unknown to Catherine, while she was out of the country Wardwell approached Beale, presumably on the instructions of his New York contacts. The full details of their arrangements only became known much later, other than the fact that someone in New York was looking to create another 'Lind type promotion' – the implication of course being that it was Barnum, given the fact that Lind had just severed her agreement with the showman.

On 25 June 1851, Wardwell, described as a 'Merchant', signed a contract with Beale in which it was agreed that Wardwell would have full rights to Catherine's performances and those of the other artists or the tour in America. The deal gave Beale £1,800 per month for Catherine's services, a significant profit for his firm. Wardwell also agreed to pay Beale all expenses, up to and including the return of the artists to England after the tour was over, and a percentage of the receipts from each concert. In effect, Beale made a considerable amount of money on the deal without any perceived risk whatsoever. Each of the contracting parties agreed to post a performance bond for £4,000 to guarantee the terms of the contract. All of this was done apparently without first consulting Catherine. The ramification of this agreement became explosive later in New York.

Whether or not Barnum was involved in this arrangement is not known. However, it seems very unlikely, given the problems that arose in New York with Wardwell and his associates, and given the excellent relationship that developed between Catherine and Barnum a year later.

On her return from France to England, Catherine started a series of farewell concerts similar to Lind's the previous year. She generated great excitement wherever she went. During the first week of September 1851, one of the leading London weekly publications reported on the furore surrounding her farewell concerts in August in Manchester and Liverpool, where Jenny Lind had appeared the year before. Strangely, again there was no direct comparison to Lind – only an implied one. It was reported from Manchester that:

Upwards of 9,000 persons have attended the three farewell concerts of Miss Catherine Hayes at the Free Trade Hall on Thursday, Friday and Saturday; and habituated as I have been to the enthusiasm of the audience in many countries, rarely do I recollect a greater impression to have been made by the vocalisation of any *artiste* than by the 'Swan of Erin.' At the first concert, she was encored in 'Ah mon fils' from Meyerbeer's 'Le Prophete,' in Wallace's ballad 'Why do I weep for thee;' in the '*Sonnambula*' finale, 'Ah! Non giunge,' and in 'Kathleen Mavourneen:' at the second concert, she was recalled after 'Casta Diva' from Bellini's *Norma*, and encored in Lavenu's graceful ballad, 'Those happy days are gone,' in Donizetti's polacca from Linda, 'Oh, luce di quest' anima,' and in Knight's ballad, 'The Grecian Daughter,' substituting for the latter, 'Bonnie Prince Charlie,' the second time. At the third concert the encores were for 'Ah, mon fils,' sung again by general desire, as also 'Kathleen Mavourneen.' On returning after the demand for the repetition of the last mentioned air, Miss Katherine [sic] Hayes gave the 'Ah! Non giunge.' The last piece rendered by Miss Hayes, was Donizetti's 'Havvi un Die' from *Maria di Rohan*, at the end of which a most exciting scene was witnessed, the assemblage of upward of 3,000 persons recalling Miss Hayes, and giving her a tremendous ovation as a farewell from Manchester. I never heard this gifted vocalist in finer voice; her improvement, since she sang at two Italian Opera-houses, is quite surprising; it is no longer the timid vocalist, but the thoroughly accomplished *artiste*, capable of moving the masses, the most intensely dramatic and highly finished style. Her ballad singing is perfection – her 'Kathleen' is one of those exquisite interpretations in which the intellect and sentiment of the exponent are equally apparent . . .

Continuing, the reporter said:

The tariff at these farewell concerts of Miss Hayes was, of course, at an advanced rate, but still the 'people' were here in force; and delightful was it to watch their quick appreciation of the beautiful in art – their sensitiveness, as a fine point of vocalisation or execution was developed – their deep and breathless attention to the music – their outbreak of rapturous admiration at the close, unshackled by conventional forms . . . [10]

A report of her concerts in Liverpool followed:

> Great as was the excitement at Manchester concerts, the last night at the Theatre Royal, at Miss C. Hayes's farewell concert, was if possible, greater. The house was filled to overflow – the orchestra was turned into high-priced stalls after the overflow from the boxes. On her entrance the audience rose *en masse*, and cheered for some minutes. Every time Miss Hayes came on the stage, the enthusiasm was renewed. She sang 'Ah! mon fils,' Wallace's ballad 'Why do I weep for thee,' 'Ah! Non giunge,' and 'Kathleen Mavourneen,' in each piece being vehemently encored; for the 'Kathleen,' she substituted 'The Harp that once through Tara's Halls,' and after this melody, again did the excited auditory exact the presence of the 'Swan of Erin,' to bestow a parting cheer; and such a cheer it was, prolonged for several minutes, one lady throwing some present on the stage, amidst the *bouquets*. Miss Hayes is evidently one of those singers whose sensibility is acute under the effect of applause; she sang in a manner as she has never been heard to sing in London; in the 'Ah! Non giunge,' in the encore, I could scarcely believe her to be the same vocalist. More daringly beautiful cadenzas were never essayed with a more positive brilliancy and finish; there was one long-sustained shake, articulated in the most marvellous style. Miss Hayes most assuredly will quit this country with the suffrages of the northern amateurs, for no *artiste*, has ever created a greater *furore* by her vocalisation in Manchester and Liverpool.
>
>   . . . . Many visitors to Miss Hayes have arrived from various parts of Ireland and from London to bid her adieu. The Adelphi Hotel has been besieged by her friends, and a farewell dinner will be given this day to her. The *Pacific* leaves to-morrow afternoon.

Her departure on Wednesday 3 September from Liverpool for New York on the Collins Line ship *Pacific* was equally exciting and reported on as follows:

21. Catherine Hayes age 32, published by James McGlashan of Dublin, 1850. (Courtesy of the Huntington Library, California).

There were upward of 200 passengers on board, and, curiously enough, Miss Hayes occupies the state berth prepared for Mdlle. Lind [Lind actually sailed on a sister ship, the *Atlantic*] in this gorgeous palace. At two o'clock, the tug with the Post office bags having been signaled, the friends of Miss Catherine Hayes quitted the *Pacific* to return to land, giving three tremendous cheers at parting, in which passengers joined heartily, Miss Hayes being, on the paddle-box with Captain Nye and waiving her handkerchief as long as the tug was in sight . . . the Americans on board were in high glee at having Miss Hayes on board . . . Miss Hayes is accompanied by Dr. Joy, the director of the tour, Mr. Augustus Braham, Herr Mengis and Mr. Lavenu, the composer, who will act as accompanist and conductor. [Her mother and sister were also on board.] Miss Hayes's first concert will take place on board the *Pacific*, for the benefit of the crew.[11]

The fact that Catherine chose the Collins Line for her journey to New York was probably in part related to Lind's same choice a year earlier. However, during this period the Collins Line which was operated by a New York based company, was in direct competition with the Cunard Line between Liverpool and New York. Cunard's service had started slightly earlier. The American government supported the Collins Line, through a lucrative mail contract. The Collins Line had four ships, the *Atlantic*, *Pacific*, *Arctic* and *Baltic*, which offered the greatest luxury in terms of staterooms and modern conveniences such as electric bell service and steam heat. They also offered the best rate between the two continents. Their first ship, the *Atlantic*, was launched in 1849.

The Collins Line ships were large by the standards of the day and extremely fast. A leading American marine architect, George Steers built them to a radical new design. He had previously designed the racing yacht *America*. During these early days, The Collins' skippers soon broke Cunard's record (*Europa*) of eleven days and three hours for crossing the Atlantic. The Cunard, caught off-guard by its competitor's speed, was unable to respond immediately. This led to fierce internal competition among the various Collins Line captains for new Atlantic speed records, since the Cunard captains were, for the time being anyway, incapacitated.

This was a time when industry on both sides of the Atlantic was in a period of rapid growth. Speed and luxury were strong selling points. These new ocean going paddle steamers were the talk of the east coast of

America, and when the news of their speed records posed a great challenge to British pride as a seafaring nation.

There was great prestige in being able to sail on one of the Collins Line ships and it was only natural that this appealed to Catherine as a *prima donna*. The fact that T. Frederick Beale was paying her expenses and those of her mother and sister must have added to the pleasure. The duration of Catherine's crossing was indeed impressive, though not a new record, primarily because of bad weather. The *Pacific* only took ten days and seventeen and a half hours to arrive in New York from Liverpool.

Henrietta Sontag and other prima donnas who followed Catherine to America during the next few years almost all travelled on Collins Line vessels. However, the glory days of the Collins Line were short-lived. Almost five years later, in January 1856, the *Pacific* (the vessel on which Catherine had travelled to America) and all aboard disappeared in the Atlantic while sailing from Liverpool to New York. Two years after that tragedy, for a variety of reasons including a reduction in its subsidy from the American government, the Collins Line collapsed financially, never to recover.[12]

Meanwhile, Catherine's plan to visit America had been mentioned with great fanfare in the New York press during the summer. One journal, drawing on a report by a Liverpool paper, painted an interesting personal portrait of Catherine in typical rambling nineteenth-century prose. The writer was possibly 'influenced' by Wardwell and his associates. In any event, the article reported that:

Catherine Hayes possesses more than ordinary claims to the sympathy of the Americans. It is not alone her resplendent talents, her exquisite voice, her magnificent singing, and the grace and beauty of her person, which will direct her to their affection and enthrone her there. Two other circumstances will tend to place her in the lofty position she is destined and entitled to occupy. The first of these is the strict decorum of conduct by which her artistic career has invariably been regulated. Catherine Hayes is, in short, 'a good girl' and a 'lady,' in the highest acceptation of these terms. Although young, lovely, and celebrated, her character is not only beyond the possibility of reproach, but beyond the pale of suspicion. Calumny itself, with its perverted vision, and its hundred crooked tongues, has never dared to sully her whiteness. The snow on the peak of Slieve-Donard [Mourne Mountains, County Down, Ireland] is not more pure and spotless than the name of Catherine Hayes . . . Catherine Hayes will go to America with a powerful and especial recommendation, apart from genius, acquirement, or conduct. She is an Irishwoman, and will be received with open arms by universal America.[13]

In anticipation of her arrival another journalist contributed to the growing excitement about her presence in New York, predicting that:

Her presence would create a considerable sensation, for thousands of her countrymen – and indeed of all classes – are eager to welcome one so good and famous. We hear that salutes will be fired at various points in the Bay, and bands of music will greet her as she passes the several islands [in New York Harbour], to say nothing of a grand serenade from the musical societies on the night of her arrival.[14]

Unfortunately, Catherine arrived in New York on Sunday 14 September 1851 at eight in the morning, virtually a day late because of bad weather. Her arrival time was not the best for a rescheduled reception. The weather was overcast and it was raining. Sunday morning generally meant that most people were in church or on their way there. Her arrival and reception, which had been anticipated by the media, was nothing like Barnum's well-orchestrated event for Lind. The fanfare was rescheduled for the next day at her hotel. After a greeting from a modest crowd, Catherine made her way to the Astor House hotel on 12th Street. This was New York's most luxurious hotel, it had been built during the 1830s and had a variety of special services including running water! Here she planned to rest from her trip and prepare herself for her first concert, which was scheduled for 23 September at Tripler Hall. Jenny Lind was not in town, as she was touring in the New England area.

One reporter was quick to provide a personal description of Catherine's appearance, shortly after her arrival:

. . . the very personification of all that is graceful and elegant in woman: her eyes, dark blue, her teeth dazzling white, her finely formed lips slightly parted as though always anxious to speak some kind thing; her hair neither golden nor auburn, but with that changeful color which sparkles in the folds. Her face highly expressive . . . of kindness – goodness of heart.[15]

According to reports, it was a disappointing arrival for Catherine, and, given the combination of the lack of crowds, the rain and the gloomy weather, she wasn't happy with her first day in the New World. However, during the next few days she seemed to recover her spirits. Crowds had descended on her hotel (5,000, according to one report; 10,000 reported by another) and the Musical Fund Society delivered its planned fanfare.[16] She also decided to attend the opera which was taking place at Castle Garden, the spectacular theatre that extended out via a 300-yard promenade walkway from the Battery in downtown New York.

Castle Garden, formerly known as Castle Clinton after one of New York's governors, had originally been built as a fortress for the war of 1812 to guard against a British invasion which never happened. Later the city acquired it and made it into a summer resort for swimming and entertainment.[17] Towards the end of 1844, it was converted into a theatre with a seating capacity for about 5,000 people. It was the theatre where Jenny Lind had made her first Barnum managed appearance a year earlier on 11 September 1850. Marti's Havana Opera Company from Cuba, run by Francisco Marti y Torrens, gave many performances of Italian operas there from 1847 onwards. A number of years later, the small island on which Castle Garden stood was absorbed into the Battery area through landfill. Today the Castle Clinton National Monument stands on the same site at the Battery in downtown New York.

When Catherine decided to visit the theatre, Bellini's *I Puritani* was being performed with Angiolina Bosio, Lorenzo Salvi, the baritone Cesare Badiale and bass Ignazio Mariani, all of whom she knew personally, having performed with them in Milan, London and elsewhere. It was the final week of the Italian opera season at Castle Garden.

New York had various venues where Italian opera was performed. In addition to Castle Garden, there was the Astor Place Opera House, which was located between Broadway and 8th Street at Astor Place from 1847 until 1852 when it closed permanently. The renowned impresario Max Maretzek (1821–97) operated his Italian opera company from the Astor Place location for a number of years before moving on to Castle Garden and then to the Academy of Music, which opened in 1854.

Another location for Italian opera was Niblo's Garden, located at Broadway and Princes Street, which was run by Dublin-born William Niblo (1789–1878) who in 1828 initially established it as a resort with beautiful walks and a relaxed family atmosphere. It had a concert hall which later became a theatre. In 1854, the Academy of Music on 14th

Street and Irving Place opened its doors with a performance of *Norma* featuring the great European stars Mario and Grisi on their first visit to America. Earlier in the same visit, these two superstars had made their first appearance in the New World at Castle Garden, at the Battery.

For the next months, Catherine embarked on a series of concerts in New York and in towns and cities on the east coast of America. Her schedule basically duplicated Jenny Lind's of the previous year. At the time of Catherine's first concert on 23 September in New York, Lind had returned to New England, performing concerts which had been arranged for her by William Avery Bushnell, Barnum's former employee whom she had hired as manager.

Shortly after Catherine's arrival in New York one of the leading newspapers reported that:

> We understand that a coalition of forces has been effected between Catherine Hayes and [Max] Maretzek's troupe, the invincible manager having the general direction of affairs, these affairs pertaining first to concerts, with the possibility of operatic representations later in the season.[18]

Could the impresario Max Maretzek have been one of the parties behind the Wardwell negotiations in London? Probably not, although a Maretzek family member who was a harpist joined Catherine in several of her concerts in New York and Boston over the next month. However, Maretzek, in his memoirs written some years later, said that he knew Wardwell, but, when he had not paid Maretzek some fees which were owed him in relation to artists participating in Catherine's tour, assumed that Wardwell and his associates were unethical opportunists working for some silent partners.[19]

In Max Maretzek's memoirs there is a long letter to his close friend Michael Balfe which throws some light on the situation. Maretzek wrote to Balfe, who was in Italy, on 5 September 1855. The letter refers to a New York newspaper report that Balfe would replace him (Maretzek) as director of the opera at the Academy of Music. This letter covers a variety of Maretzek experiences and philosophies about his dealings with operatic agents in New York and warns Balfe against individuals posing as operatic agents and 'would-be Barnums', should Balfe visit New York. There is also a reference to how many talented artists were induced to come to America based on 'the Barnum success with Lind'. This leads into an extended description of Catherine Hayes' trials and tribulations with John Henry Wardwell and his anonymous New York backers in 1851. It makes for very interesting reading and corroborates many of the details that have appeared from time to time in various sources about this period of Catherine's career. The following are brief extracts from this letter to Balfe written by Maretzek in 1855:

> Among others was your beautiful, spiritual, and genial country-woman Catherine Hayes. She was engaged by an association of such would-be Barnums, who as I believe, intentionally placed at their head an inexperienced and inoffensive *entrepreneur* of the name of Wardwell. I say, intentionally, for they kept sedulously in the background. It appears to me, now when I reflect upon it, like a hungry set of wolves draping themselves in a sheepskin. They borrowed Mr. Wardwell's name, that they might the more readily and easily 'humbug' [P.T. Barnum's phrase] the public, and take in Catherine Hayes.
>
> However from a pecuniary point of view, this enterprise utterly failed. Remember, that I am not now speaking of the failure of the Irish soprano. Since she divorced her interests from theirs, it has been told to me that she has succeeded, and I have every reason to believe this . . . finally, these speculators were purely without the slightest genius. They attempted to follow in Barnum's course, by faithfully planting their feet in the footprints he had left behind him. His tactics were sedulously and most indiscreetly followed with scrupulous exactitude. They forgot that he had already worn them out. Their effect had been already lost. Thus, one of their greatest errors was the attempt to proclaim the 'holy immaculacy' [sic] of their prima donna. She may have, in truth, been everything, which P.T.B. had proclaimed Jenny Lind to be, but this 'puff' had succeeded for Jenny, on the score of its rich unexplained novelty. The 'Prince of Humbug' [P.T. Barnum] had been accustomed to deal with in all sorts of curiosities, and this time he had discovered a new one. In the repetition of the 'puff,' however, its attraction had been lost.
>
> . . . Not a doubt now exists upon my part, my good Balfe, but that Catherine Hayes could have stood the test of the severest criticism. As a vocalist, she might, without losing a single laurel, have been named with almost any one of her contemporaries. No such blundering attempt was needed, to drape her excellencies with the

mantle of morality which, to tell the truth, had somewhat soiled in the hands of its original inventor [Barnum], and frayed its edges upon the person of her [Lind] for whom he had in the first place sharpen it.[20]

Maretzek goes on to mention how Wardwell arranged with him to borrow his artists from the opera (baritone Belletti and tenor Lorini) for concerts in New York and Boston for $5,000 a month and how Wardwell never paid him. He also mentions that at this point Catherine Hayes decided to break her contract with Cramer & Beale, presumably because of Wardwell and Dr. Joy's bad management of her financial arrangements. This breach of contract eventually involved Catherine in a significant lawsuit with Cramer & Beale in the courts in New York and London and with another party called Mr. Nicholas K. Anthony who was probably Wardwell's 'behind-the-scene' backer. It also had a much more long-term effect on Catherine's career, which she would only learn about several years later in England.

To add to Catherine's woes during these early days in New York, Dr. John Joy, her tour director and Cramer & Beale representative, totally ignored her problems with the Wardwell takeover. Dr. Joy elected to immerse himself in the 'local nocturnal New York scene where he was seen night-after-night on the town indulging himself on oysters and champagne and in the company of freeloaders from the press' – all at Catherine's expense. Dr. Joy indignantly wrote to the press to defend his position. Subsequently the 'legitimate' press, after recognising the squandering of Catherine's earnings, asked the question:

> 'How much did it cost Dr. Joy to manage all the newspapers of New York'? One report speculated that the manager had spent about $30,000 in oyster houses and on freeloaders and that Catherine had only been paid about $4,000 for the more than twenty concerts, she had given over an eight-week period. The report went on to say that Catherine Hayes has been the victim of musical jobbers and management speculators, under a series of contracts, lettings, sub-lettings, sales and re-sales. Catherine Hayes had been the victim of troops of organized speculators in musical popularity almost without a parallel in musical affairs in this continent.[21]

By the end of the year end Catherine had sorted out her problems with her managers. Dr. Joy was given his return fare to England and was never heard of again. She retained Wardwell for a short time at least, until someone else entered her circle who would have a profound influence on the rest of her life.

Catherine spent a little over a year in the eastern part of the United States. In the New York area, where she gave her first concert on 23 September 1851 at Tripler Hall, she gave 23 concerts, more than in any other city. She took time off to go to east Brooklyn on 6 October to visit an orphanage, where she sang 'The Harp that Once through Tara's Halls', by Irish composer Thomas Moore, to the children.[22]

During this first year in America she sang concerts in about 45 cities in the east and in Canada. Her programme changed very little from city to city. There was very little artistic growth, as her goal, like Lind's, was financial, not artistic. Lind had paved the way and Catherine's itinerary was a blueprint, sometimes almost overlapping in the same cities.

By the end of 1851, Lind was planning to return to Europe. In addition, a series of events would occur that would change her life and direction. She was planning to marry a German musician, Otto Goldschmidt, but had informed no one. Goldschmidt was a competent pianist from a prosperous Jewish merchant family in Hamburg. He and Lind had met and spent time together earlier in Europe. Lind brought him to America when Benedict, her original accompanist and conductor, had elected to return to Europe earlier in 1851.

Lind's mother had died in October 1851 in Sweden. However, she only received word of the event in late December, when she was scheduled to give a farewell concert in Metropolitan Hall (formerly Tripler Hall) in New York on 30 December. Despite the fact that Lind was not particularly close to her mother (Lind may have been born outside marriage, she was raised by someone other than her mother), she decided to cancel the performance. Catherine had given a concert at the same venue the night before, and she gave another on 31 December, the night after Lind was scheduled to appear.

In February 1852, to everyone's surprise, Lind married Otto Goldschmidh just outside Boston.[23] He converted to her faith at the wedding ceremony. There was an outpouring of emotion in newspapers and the musical press in America and Europe, many articles running along the same lines – people were resentful that the unknown Otto Goldschmidt had taken away 'their Jenny'. There had been a widespread feeling that 'Jenny Lind belonged to everybody'. Lind gave a few more concerts as Lind-Goldschmidt and eventually returned to Europe in May 1852.

The structure of the Lind and Hayes concerts was very similar, although the music selection of the two prima donnas differed slightly. Lind usually sang works by composers such as Weber, Mendelssohn,

Meyerbeer and Handel, occasionally including an aria by Bellini or Donizetti and usually some Swedish or German songs for variety. Catherine sang music by Donizetti, Bellini and Meyerbeer, occasionally including an aria from a Handel or Mendelssohn oratorio. She also featured Irish songs or occasionally a Scottish song between arias. The selections chosen by the sopranos were appropriate for them, given their individual backgrounds, talent, training and musical experience.

Lind had superior supporting artists in Salvi and Belletti, resulting in a more pleasing concert overall. Two of Maretzek's artists from his Italian opera troupe, Cesare Badiali and Ignazio Marini, joined Catherine's concerts, as did harpist Madame Bertucca-Maretzek.

During Catherine's dress rehearsal in New York, before her formal debut, one reviewer 'lauded her magnificent voice and her capacity for great passion and feeling'.[24] A later review, this one from the *New York Daily Times*, was very reserved, perhaps because it was one of the paper's early issues (#6), as it had only started publishing that month. The following were the critics comments:

> The first concert of Miss Catherine Hayes was given at Tripler Hall last evening. At this time, we shall not attempt a criticism of the performance. The Hall was as full as we ever saw it, and the audience appeared to be composed of our first citizens. The reception of Miss Hayes, was enthusiastic in the extreme. At least three bushels of boquettes [sic], were thrown upon the stage, and stacked in one high pile in front of her. Her rendering of the Cavatina from the *Prophete*, was applauded, but the wildest enthusiasm followed the ballad 'Why do I weep for thee' [Wallace]. The following 'The Harp that once through Tara's Halls' was her opening song in the second part. It was unsatisfactory to us, but the audience appeared to receive it with wildest expressions of joy and satisfaction. There was however too much embellishment to suit us, and we were forced to compare it with the chaste, unadorned, and yet highly finished manner in which Jenny Lind sang the same class of ballads.
>
> . . . In fact the whole concert was highly successful, and its results must be taken as evidence of the strong hold Miss Hayes has upon the public.[25]

Catherine also sang 'Kathleen Mavourneen' and 'Ah! non giunge' from Bellini's *La Sonnambula* at this first concert.

Another reviewer took a slightly different approach to her first concert, using rather 'flowery' nineteenth-century English:

> Miss Hayes has a voice of very unusual range, being a high soprano, with which is combined, like something distinct in itself, a most voluminous and rich casket of contralto tones. The various registers throughout the entire scale are at the points of transition well blended, the voice on the whole being symmetrically developed, but having by nature rather a pyramidal structure, (in point of volume) broad and strong at the base, and tapering at the summit. In respect of school, and vocal management, Miss Hayes is thoroughbred; and in all ornate and florid embellishments, she is equal to the best. These being her materials for song, the use of them must, upon the constitution of the artist's own soul, express the quality of her emotive nature. And here we have to do with a tender and susceptible organisation, and one of most delicate fibre. This stamps her entire style, and makes *pathos* the leading characteristic of her performance. Miss Hayes is consequently a tender, pathetic, *moving* singer, as distinguished from a startling, tragic, dramatically exciting one.

The writer, after outlining some thoughts on ballad singing and the importance of the words versus the music, continued:

> Miss Hayes either finds this *too* unwelcome, or else she doesn't understand the true nature of the ballad, and lacks a correct impression of the true manner of singing it. Her delivery of the text was so indistinct, and her change of the vowels from the proper sound (to suit her musical purpose of producing a good tone) so strange and marked, that she makes the words, or the sense, of inferior importance, thus giving the ballad an operatic or musical expression, rather than a poetic and intellectual one . . .
>   . . . Miss Hayes sings best in the operatic style . . . Her exquisite 'Ah, mon fils!' proves this.[26]

Catherine was frequently criticised for adding ornamentation and trills to songs such as 'Kathleen Mavourneen' and 'The Harp that once through Tara's Halls', which must have seemed out of place with the overall tonality of these beautiful ballads. However, she was rarely criticised for her diction. It must also be remembered that her training was in the Italian *bel canto* style and the time she spent in Italy made her highly

22. Sheet music cover of a song composed especially for Catherine Hayes by Walter Maynard (Willert Beale), London 1850. (Author's collection).

susceptible to adding ornamentation to anything she sang since it was the expected of the singer, particularly a prima donna.

While in New York she met the Irish priest Father Theobald Mathew (1790–1856), 'The Apostle of Temperance', who was on a fund raising visit to America for his temperance movement. No doubt, the 'Good Father' saw Catherine's prominence among the New York Irish as an opportunity to raise more funds, despite their different religious upbringing. The Tipperary born priest had opted to have P.T. Barnum handle his tour, which brought him to many of America's important cities.[27] In the process, Father Mathew was so convincing that the great P.T. Barnum became one of his strongest supporters, even producing a temperance newsletter on behalf of the movement. It's also possible that Catherine may have met Barnum through Father Mathew.

During Father Mathew's final stay in New York, a special fund raising event had been planned by a local organisation. However, the event turned out to be a total fiasco with the good Father refusing to accept the paltry amount ($168) offered to him after all the promoters 'had been paid'. This was when Catherine stepped into the breach to offer a charity concert.

As a prelude to setting up a concert for Father Mathew, Catherine wrote a letter to Wardwell which was published in the *New York Daily Times* on 30 September 1851 as follows:

> The following correspondence between Miss Hayes and her business agent, has been furnished us. The proposition to give Father Mathew a benefit, is worthy of the woman and the artist and we feel confident the public will nobly respond:

> ASTOR HOUSE, Sept. 30, 1851

> Dear Sir: Will you favour me at as early a day as possible consistent with your arrangements already made to announce and prepare, on my account a concert, as attractive as any of the present series of musical entertainment, the proceeds of which I wish presented to the Rev. Father Mathew, my warmly esteemed countryman, as my humble recognition of his disinterested and noble efforts in the cause of benevolence and of humanity.

> I shall be happy to confer with you on the best means of carrying out this objective, in which I feel assured the good citizens of New York will gladly cooperate.

> I remain, dear Sir,
> Yours very truly,

> Catherine Hayes

> J. H. Wardwell, Esq., &c., &c.

Wardwell responded positively manner and his letter was published beneath Catherine's. With the momentum going for Father Mathew, E.K. Collins of the Collins Line next offered Father Mathew a free passage home to Europe., which he accepted 'for the steamer of October 25'.

Around this time Catherine was supposed to perform at a Maretzek managed concert at the Astor Place Opera House. For some reason this was postponed and never rescheduled, despite the fact that it had been advertised.

After her New York concerts, Catherine travelled to New England, where she performed with her troupe with considerable success in Boston, Lowell and other places in Massachusetts. She travelled to Boston on 14 October by the Fall River line from New York. Apparently she was scheduled to take the New Haven train from New York but at the last minute, because of the pleasant weather, decided to go by boat. This disappointed many of her fans, who were assembled for the midnight arrival of the train – however, her arrival by boat occurred at 9 am the following morning. The local press recorded that she disembarked:

> looking refreshed, elegantly attired in a rich travelling dress and carried in her hand a magnificent bouquet. The arrival depot was crowded with people anxious to get a glimpse of the fair songstress . . . she passed through a file of eager gazers, to a splendid barouche drawn by four horses, bowing her thanks to the crowd, she was whirled away to the Winthrop House for her stay in the city.[28]
>
> Her mother and sister accompanied her as did Dr. Joy, now described as her 'private secretary' and Mr. Wardwell as her 'concert manager'.

Catherine had a happy stay in Boston, where she was well received. It was only after returning to New York some time later that she realised that Wardwell's financial dealings there had not been in her best interests. However, in general she was quite satisfied with her American tour, enjoying the reception she received and all the new experiences.

CHAPTER TEN

An Irish Welcome in America

BOSTON, WASHINGTON, SAVANNAH
AND NEW ORLEANS 1851–1852

CATHERINE'S first concert in Boston was at the Tremont Temple on
14 October, 1851 where her programme included the usual Irish
songs and operatic arias, similar to those she had sung in New York. After
the concert at 11 pm, the Germania Musical Society gathered outside her
hotel (The Winthrop House) to welcome her. There was an initial display
of fireworks, after which members of the musical society played various
numbers, concluding with the Irish air 'The Last Rose of Summer'.
Catherine came out on the balcony to great cheers from the large crowd
that had gathered, and said a few words of acknowledgement about how
grateful she was for the many honours which had been heaped on her
since her arrival in the country.

On 15 October, she arrived in Providence in Rhode Island for a concert
at Howard Hall, before returning to Boston for another concert the next
night. In anticipation of her evening concert in Providence, the local
newspaper featured the following short article:

> Catherine Hayes – The musical people of our city are of course
> ready for the concert this evening. Catherine Hayes, we believe,
> divides with Jenny Lind the empire of song, and numbers as many
> admirers. It is certain that the interest, which her concerts excited,
> from the first in New York, continued unabated, and that many
> persons attended every one, and even followed her to Brooklyn.
>
> The New York Mirror closes a notice of the fair Irish girl with the
> following deserved compliment to Mr. Wardwell – 'Of Mr. Wardwell,
> the American Manager of the 'Swan' is not necessary to speak. He
> makes friends wherever he goes; and we take the liberty of
> commending him and his [sic] to the best services of our Boston
> brethren, whom for the once we envy, for they are to take from us
> both Katy Hayes and Anna Thillion.'[1]

The New York media meanwhile reported Catherine and Jenny Lind's activities, reporting that:

> Jenny Lind's concert in Buffalo [15 October] was well attended, the church being quite full, and she was received with great enthusiasm. Her farewell concert takes place tomorrow evening, at the Baptist Church.[2]

Immediately under this announcement the following appeared in relation to Catherine's first concert in Providence:

> The Concert of Catherine Hayes last night [15 October] created the greatest enthusiasm, and the Hall was densely crowded. Several hundred applicants for tickets were refused admission. Gov. Allen, ex-Gov. Anthony, Maj. Burgess, Judge Brayton and many other distinguished officers of the State, with their families, were present.[3]

She returned to Boston where she was scheduled to give a concert on Saturday 18 October; however, she suddenly became ill and had to reschedule it for the following Tuesday. New York also reported on her illness and recovery and the rescheduling of the Boston concert for Tuesday 20 October. Boston, glad to see her back on track reported extensively on her return performance as follows:

> The indisposition from which this accomplished artist was suffering has proved to be of no great moment, save that it induced her to postpone the concert which has been announced . . . Indeed, she was in far more efficient and brilliant voice than we have yet heard her. And much as we have previously relished her singing, we must fairly own that last night she exceeded our previous impression of her singularly in the power of her voice as she had on her first appearance in this city done in the sweetness and delicacy of its tones . . . the Tremont Temple was crowded in every seat. Just at the moment of the entrance of the orchestra, the Hon. Daniel Webster [1782–1852] and family, escorted by Mr. Wardwell and his assistants, proceeded up the center aisle of the Temple to a front seat which had been reserved for the distinguished visitor.[4] Before Mr. Webster had reached his seat, the entire audience had risen to their feet, and cheer after cheer, and peal after peal of applause, testified the overwhelming enthusiasm which his presence created. Bowing his

PROGRAMME

of

MISS CATHERINE HAYES'

GRAND CONCERT.

PART I.

OVERTURE—Fingal's Cave,	MENDELSSOHN.
GRAND SCENA—" Oh! 'tis glorious sight, (Oberon)	WEBER.
MR. A. BRAHAM.	
CAVATINA—" Ah mon fils," (Prophete)	MEYERBEER.
Miss CATHERINE HAYES.	
ARIA—" Il Bivacco,"	BATTISTA.
HERR MENGIS.	
" The hill of Lochiel,"	A SCOTCH BALLAD.
MR. A. BRAHAM.	
DUETT—" Quanto amore," (L'Elisir d'Amore.)	DONIZETTI.
MISS CATHERINE HAYES AND HERR MENGIS.	

PART II.

OVERTURE—Semiramide,	ROSSINI.
" John Anderson, my Joe, John,"	A SCOTCH BALLAD.
Miss CATHERINE HAYES.	
SONG—" The Bay of Biscay"	DAVEY.
MR. A. BRAHAM.	
ARIA—" Lorsque mon maitre est en voyage,"	BOILDIEU.
HERR MENGIS.	
SCENA AND ARIA—" Havvi un Dio," (Maria di Rohan)	DONIZETTI.
Miss CATHERINE HAYES.	
SOLO on the Violin.	
" Erin is my home,"	IRISH BALLAD.
Miss CATHERINE HAYES.	
GRAND FINALE INSTRUMENTALE.	

Conductors, Mr. LAVENU and Mr. G. LODER.

A Grand Orchestra of more than Forty Performers, the most talented resident in New York, have been engaged.

The Grand Pianoforte employed at this Concert, is from the Manufactory of Mr. J. Chickering.

23. Programme for a Catherine Hayes concert in Tripler Hall, New York, October 1853. (Courtesy Derek Walsh collection).

thanks, Mr. Webster took his seat, and during the evening, was one of the most attentive listeners.

The great and leading gem of the evening, was of course, the Air from the *Messiah* – 'I know that my Redeemer liveth.' . . . It was to the rendering vocally one of the finest pieces of music which Handel ever wrote, that Catherine Hayes addressed herself and most triumphantly did she succeed. As she stood before us, and we felt ourselves carried away by the magic of her vocalisation [sic], we lost sight of the concert room; and as we heard the rush of streaming notes that rose from her lips, we confess that we were absolutely carried away by the devotional fervor [sic] which was expressed in them. Indeed we must say that Catherine Hayes is one of the greatest singers we have ever listened to; and we believe that there are but few of those who were most coldly disposed towards her, that were present last night, and heard her sing 'I know that my Redeemer liveth' who would not now be disposed to acknowledge this.

. . . the last thing which she gave us was the Rondo Finale from the *Sonnambula*. Nothing could well have exceeded the beauty of her reading of the 'Ah! non giunge' and as peal after peal of rapture burst from those who listened to her, her triumph was of the most complete order.[5]

Another report appeared in the same paper stating that:

The performances of Tuesday evening at the Tremont Temple were exceedingly gratifying to a very large audience. The Swan of Erin fully sustained her high and well-deserved reputation. Comparisons will naturally and necessarily be made between her and Jenny Lind; but they may and should be made without unkindness or disparagement to either. They both excel in their peculiar style. They are both accomplished vocalists. The most enthusiastic admirers of the Swedish Nightingale – and the writer of this article is among the number – must acknowledge that Miss Hayes possesses great power of melody, and is highly trained and disciplined in vocal science. 'I know that my Redeemer liveth' was a graceful and ravishing exhibition of her talent, and was warmly appreciated by the crowded assembly; and so was 'Bring me wild flowers' and also Bellini's lovely gem, 'Ah! non giunge.' Miss Hayes sings very sweetly, and has a voice of fine discrimination, enriched with a clear and varied volume in its delicate intonations.

. . . . When she was singing her last song, knowing from report[s] the natural diffidence and dove-like timidity of this beautiful enchantress, I could perceive her enthusiasm rise in swelling notes, after each pause she made among the drowning thunders of applause, and she retired with the lightsome step of graceful emotions. Her accomplishments as a vocal artist are of the first order.[6]

Immediately after this Boston concert Catherine returned to Providence for a concert on Wednesday 22 October; after which a lengthy report appeared. The following is a brief extract:

Miss Catherine Hayes' Second Concert – It would be wrong to allow the musical entertainment like this to pass away without a word of acknowledgement of its great excellence . . . we feel it to be equally a duty and a pleasure to express our admiration, in general terms, of the second and last entertainment given by Miss Hayes, in our city, and to say that, in point of variety, beauty, and intrinsic worth, it surpassed in our own humble opinion and in the opinion of some of the most professional men and amateurs among us, any concert that has hitherto been given in Providence.

. . . If anybody had any doubts after the previous concert – and we do not know that anybody had – of the justness of the very high eulogiums [sic], which have been bestowed, in other cities upon the talent and genius of Catherine Hayes, they must have been effectively and entirely dispelled after hearing her sing on Wednesday evening. We dare not trust ourselves in any remarks on her several exquisite pieces – 'I know that my Redeemer liveth,' 'Casta Diva,' 'Ah mon fils!' 'Bring me wild flowers,' and 'Kathleen Mavourneen' – for, if we once begin to talk about these things we shall not know when or where to stop.[7]

While Catherine appears to have had a very successful visit to Providence, her performance was not up to one reviewer's standards. On Saturday 25 October, a long column and a half review appeared which wandered through various classical quotations and references to demonstrate why Catherine Hayes' performance should not be viewed as first rate. In general, this review compared her negatively to Jenny Lind. What prompted it is not known, since Catherine had no plans to return to Providence. The writer was probably the newspaper's editor given the amount of space he allocated to his criticisms. He obviously thought very highly of Jenny Lind and resented the opinions expressed by local patrons about her coldness as a singer, as compared to Catherine. Written by a well-educated, travelled person, who obviously had a good knowledge of singing, this review it is important because of its finely articulated description of Catherine's voice and style in relation to Lind's attributes. The writer compares Lind's northern Germanic unemotional delivery, which he prefers, to Catherine's warmer more lachrymose Italian style, the one virtuoso, the other schooled and more conservative. This is the first time detailed description of how the two singers differed vocally. The following are extracts from the review:

> We may say that the comparison of Jenny Lind and Catherine Hayes is as vague and unmeaning as that of Raphael and Carlo Maratta. The two singers have nothing in common but fine cultivation. Both voices are soprano. But while Jenny Lind's is much the richest and fullest of the two and of a far more magnificent tone, that of Catherine Hayes is, perhaps, as flexible, and has contralto tones in which Jenny Lind's is entirely deficient – Jenny Lind's cultivation, also, is much more perfect. Her shake is crisp and distinct and brilliant to a degree unrivalled by the low and gurgling liquidity of that of Catherine Hayes, and the electrical precision with which Jenny Lind drops upon the unrelated notes below, is unsurpassed by any singer in the world. But the whole impression of the two singers precludes any other than mechanical comparisons.
>
> . . . The voice of Catherine Hayes is a pure soprano, of a quality both sweet and sympathetic, and having, although in no remarkable degree, what the French critics call *une larme dans la voix*, – a tear in the voice. It is extremely smooth and flexible, but of no great volume or richness – Her musical cultivation is exquisite and accurate. In singing, she evinces an academic precision which is delightful, as far as it goes, because it assures you against failure. She will not undertake what she cannot do. Her singing is also refined and graceful in sentiment, and her delivery is delicate and smooth. The *refinement* of the whole impression she leaves, is very remarkable. But it is rather the refinement of a miniature painting than the delicacy of truly great art. Its studied elaboration leaves upon the mind the impression which, in social manners, we call *maniere*, too mannered. Hence, you feel that it is only accomplished talent and not original genius. The impression of refinement goes so far, that you feel while hearing her that every musically

accomplished lady who has a fine voice ought to sing quite as well as she . . . thus her singing seems to be more of an accomplishment than an art, as we say of a young lady's painting that it is an accomplishment, although we do not say so of Titian's . . . This of course is the great imperfection of Catherine Hayes, considered as a true artist . . . But Catherine Hayes is an academic singer, rather than a genuine artist. By which we mean that she aims to achieve results by following certain traditional rules of her art and not by trusting herself to an individual instinct, which genius does, and hence is what we call original or creative . . . It will be seen that we have spoken of Miss Hayes from an artistic point of view. No one questions the pleasure of hearing her sing. But music is art. It has other and higher ends in view than drawing our tears. Yet we complain of singers if they do not excite this lachrymose tendency, as if that were condemnation or *criticism*. All the patrons of the circulating library complained that Jenny Lind did not make them cry. Of course she did not. Neither would the Parthenon, or the Apollo, or the Venus; neither Raphael's Transfiguration, or St. Peter's, or any other great work of art make you cry or want to cry, except incidentally.

The writer then goes on to conclude his criticism by comparing Catherine to various other singers of note, ending with the following:

Catherine Hayes is doubtless the most pleasing singer we have had among us except Jenny Lind . . . We hear of Grisi, of Alboni, of Sontag, and of Jenny Lind . . . Miss Hayes has never been ranked with the first singers of Europe. Partial friends and interested critics have naturally celebrated her praises. We, too, praise the sweet singing of Catherine Hayes; and if the impetuous reader concludes from these remarks that we do not enjoy this singing, because there is better to be heard in the world, either he is singularly obtuse, or we are remarkably obscure.[8]

All in all a fascinating piece of writing. Catherine returned to Boston for a concert on 23 October and for a final one in that city, on Sunday evening, 26 October, which was sponsored by the prestigious Handel and Haydn Society of Boston. This last concert was given at the Melodeon. Earlier, this society had met with the intention of discussing a concert which would feature Catherine Hayes singing works by Handel and Haydn. The secretary of the society, Joseph G. Oates, was designated to approach Miss

Hayes and he reported to the Board of Trustees on 17 October saying that 'He had had an interview with Miss Hayes' Manager (Mr. Wardwell) and that his proposition was to pay all of the expenses of the Society and give us two hundred tickets, if we should supply the chorus.' The society felt this was 'a most advantageous arrangement'. Unlike her earlier concerts, which had multiple-level ticket prices, all entrance fees for this concert were fixed at $2 per ticket.

The concert programme was entirely made up of music of Handel and Haydn, with three exceptions. Obviously, Catherine must have chosen to include a sacred song called 'Searcher of Hearts' by her friend the Irish composer William Vincent Wallace, which she sang as her second number. A Mendelssohn chorus and an aria from *Elijah* were also included in the programme.

Other pieces which she performed in the first half included 'And there were Shepherds' (*Messiah*) and 'I know that my Redeemer liveth' (*Messiah*). In the second part of the concert she performed 'With verdure clad' (*Creation*), followed by a trio 'On thee each living thing awaits', (*Creation*), in which Catherine was joined by tenor Braham, and bass-baritone Mengis. Choral pieces from the *Messiah* and the *Creation* preceded each solo. Louis Lavenu conducted the evening performance.

Reviews the next day were extensive, although slightly critical of the placement of the Wallace piece next to Handel's music. The reviewer went on to say:

> We have it in our power but to reiterate our previously expressed convictions, that in sacred music Catherine Hayes is a singularly great artist. She sings it with a purely devotional and religious fervor [sic] which we have rarely listened to, and more especially does she do this with the works of Handel. Rarely, indeed have we heard anything at all approaching her delivery of that grand air of jubilant and conscious faith, 'I know that my Redeemer liveth.' We have now listened to her twice as she delivered this air, and we confess ourselves unable to suggest an adverse criticism on it. The mighty, and possibly somewhat bare character of much of the melody of Handel, is merged in this strain of singular majesty. The sacred song which was written by Wallace was somewhat unwisely placed in the first part. The words which are by General Morris, are beautiful . . . the melody which Wallace has wedded to these words is very exquisite, but it was somewhat unluckily placed in the midst of

Programme

∽ OF ∽

CATHERINE HAYES'
GRAND CONCERT.

PART I.

OVERTURE, ... HANDEL.

RECITATIVE AND AIR,—"Comfort ye my people,"(Messiah) HANDEL.
Mr. Augustus Braham.

SOLO, on the Piano Forte, ... BOULANGER.
M. E. Boulanger.

CAVATINA,—"Ah Mon fils," (by particular request) . MEYERBEER.
Miss Catherine Hayes.

AIR,—"The Trumpet shall sound," (Messiah) . . . . . HANDEL.
Herr Mengis.

AIR,—"Deeper and Deeper still," (Jeptha) . . . . . . HANDEL.
Mr Augustus Braham.

AIR,—"I know that my Redeemer liveth," (Messiah) . . . HANDEL.
Miss Catherine Hayes.

PART II.

NEW OVERTURE,—(Zanoni) . . . . LAVENU.

ARIA,—"Il Bivacco," . . . . BATTISTA.
Herr Mengis.

BALLAD,—"Bring me wild flowers," . . . . LAVENU.
(COMPOSED EXPRESSLY FOR)
Miss Catherine Hayes.

SOLO, on the Flute, ... BOEHM.
Mr. Kyle.

SONG,—"When other Lips," (The Bohemian Girl) . . . . BALFE.
Mr. Augustus Braham.

RONDO FINALE,—"Ah non giunge," (La Somnambula) . BELLINI.
Miss Catherine Hayes.

ARIA,—"Se la vita vuoi godere," . . . . TADOLINI.
Herr Mengis.

GRANDE FINALE INSTRUMENTALE.

Conductor, ... Mr. LAVENU.

A GRAND ORCHESTRA, including the GERMANIA MUSICAL SOCIETY, is engaged.

The GRAND PIANOFORTE employed at this Concert is from the Manufactory of
J. CHICKERING, Esq.

24. Programme for a Boston concert by Catherine Hayes in October 1851. (Author's collection).

Handel's music, where it was overweighed by the comparison which necessarily suggested itself between the modern operatic composer and the undisputed master of oratorio.

The reviewer concluded by saying the following about Catherine:

> That she is a great singer of all serious music, whether operatic or in oratorios, is certain – much greater indeed than we had supposed her to be while reading the eulogiums passed upon her in New York. The extent of her voice places nearly the whole of [the] *contralto* music within its range, and enables her to sing the whole of the music of the *mezzo-soprano* with admirable power. In her higher portions of its register, it is occasionally somewhat weak. We have mentioned these points simply to show how absurd it is to force a comparison upon her with another singer [Lind], whose voice is so totally opposed to hers in its character, and to explain to our readers why we have neglected to draw comparisons when it appears to us that none could legitimately have been made. As a vocalist, setting voice aside, she is a singularly well cultivated one, and well indeed does she deserve that success which has attended her here and in New York since her first appearance upon our shores.[9]

Artistically Catherine's stay in Boston had worked out well. However, she was not satisfied with the financial returns, including the deal Wardwell had made with the Handel and Haydn Society. In fact, one report said that the entire Boston arrangements were a complete financial loss.

Catherine left Boston and headed south, giving concerts in Springfield and Hartford. At the request of Governor Seymour, she visited two state institutions, in Hartford, one a children's deaf and dumb asylum. When Catherine entered the classroom, the teacher made a sign to the girls to turn around their blackboards, all of which had the name 'Catherine Hayes', much to Catherine's surprise and delight.[10] Her other visit was to the Retreat for the Insane. In New Haven, she gave one concert in Brewster's Hall before returning to New York, where she arrived at the beginning of November.

In New York, her first return performance was advertised for Monday 4 November at Tripler Hall. Catherine changed the day when she realised it conflicted with the opening night of Maretzek's Astor Place Opera House, which by contract had to schedule its performances on Mondays, Wednesdays and Fridays.[11]

Also advertised was the benefit concert for Father Mathew on Wednesday 5 November. Catherine left this concert date as planned, despite it conflicting with the opera. As it turned out both venues were well attended. In addition, Father Mathew, not feeling any pressure to depart on 25 October as previously planned, had decided to stay on for the concert. He occupied himself in the meantime with administering 'the pledge' after Mass in Brooklyn on Sunday 2 November. He also indulged in similar activities at other churches in the greater New York area. Father Mathew departed New York on 10 November after a dinner where he gave an emotional speech in which he acknowledged:

> . . . my gifted and amiable countrywoman, Miss Catherine Hayes. Never will I forget the sympathy felt by that noble-minded lady, or the spontaneous generosity (too characteristic of her Irish heart) which prompted her recent grateful and substantial complement [concert]. Never will this noble act be forgotten by Fr. Mathew, and when this earthly pilgrimage is over, when his stewardship ceases, and he is called to the state of future existence, long may her honored [sic] name be pronounced with gratitude and respect by the sons and daughters of that beauteous Isle which she loves so well . . . [12]

In New York, the nagging problem of Wardwell's financial mismanagement continued to trouble Catherine. She made the decision to discuss with him the idea of cancelling the Beale contract, which would require her to pay a cancellation fee. This was initially accepted by Wardwell but subsequently rejected, probably because of his backer, Nicholas K. Anthony's potential exposure to penalties.

On independent advice Catherine decided to go ahead and break the contract anyway, advising Beale directly instead of through Wardwell, and agreeing to a forfeit of £3,000, which was equivalent to $15,000. Her actions apparently caught, Nicholas K. Anthony off guard, leaving left him with an obligation to pay Beale significant cancellation fees, over and above forfeit of the performance bond. The additional penalty amounted to the equivalent of six months' fees, which apparently Wardwell had not comprehended at the time of signing the sub-contract with Beale. However, Wardwell had signed over the sub-contract to Anthony when he returned to New York, which perhaps explained his slightly cavalier attitude when Catherine first suggested the break with Beale.

When the news got out about Wardwell's convoluted deal and Catherine's subsequent actions the newspapers in Boston and New York and even the musical press in London had a field day. Nothing like this had ever happened before in New York. Catherine severed all relations with Wardwell and on 15 November a newspaper report in New York confirmed both this and her cancellation of the Beale contract, saying:

> Like Jenny Lind, she pays forfeit, but unlike the Swede, we doubt not she will fall into more competent, at least, into more successful hands, than she has parted from. Her admirers, of whom she has many in New York and in England, will renew the interest they have heretofore taken in her success on the announcement of the new programme.[13]

Ten days later there was a notice in the *New York Daily Times* to the effect that: 'Nicholas K. Anthony as assignee of Wardwell's had commenced court action against Thomas Frederick Beale a music dealer of London, for damages in the amount of £4,000 pounds sterling, for alleged breach of contract relating to the concerts of Catherine Hayes.' Obviously, Mr. Anthony had decided to go on the offensive.

Meanwhile, Jenny Lind continued to give sold-out concerts in various upstate New York towns, and in Toronto and other parts of Canada. She then moved west, down Lake Erie, and on to Cincinnati and Louisville, before returning to upstate New York. Presumbaly she was oblivious to or uninterested in the state of Catherine's contractual affairs, having experienced something similar herself earlier in the year with P.T. Barnum.

Catherine gave a final concert in Tripler Hall on Saturday 8 November, which was well received. Afterwards she immediately set off for upstate New York to sing first in Albany, then Utica, Syracuse and other towns in the area. Lind, having left that part of New York, was now headed for Boston, where she was scheduled to give a series of concerts in New England, starting 25 November in Boston.

The fact that Lind and Catherine's schedules didn't clash with each other leads one to wonder if Bushnell, as Lind's manager, may have been in contact with Catherine to agree on itineraries. If so, this would have been the beginning of a relationship, which would have a very important outcome for Catherine. There was also a rumour around at this time to the effect that Lind had purposely moved out of the New York area on Catherine's arrival as a special gesture to ensure Catherine's success. If this was in fact correct, then it would be reasonable to assume that there must have been a relationship between the two singers of which the public and the press were unaware.

Two weeks after Catherine's concert in New York's Tripler Hall, the very young and diminutive Adelina Patti (1843–1919) – she was only eight years old – gave her first public concert at the same venue, with great success. Patti became the greatest prima donna of the second half of the nineteenth century. She lived well into the twentieth century, making her first phonograph recordings when she was in her sixties in 1905. One of the songs she recorded was 'Kathleen Mavourneen', no doubt influenced by the popularity the song had achieved through Catherine Hayes.

After Boston, Jenny Lind ran into trouble in Providence. She was scheduled to sing a farewell performance at Howard Hall on Monday 8 December with ticket prices set at $2, $3 and $4. (Catherine's ticket prices had been $1 and $2.) There was a public outcry about the Lind pricing, resulting in cancellation of the concert. The cancellation announcement was initially related to the tenor, Salvi, being 'indisposed', however, a few days later the following report appeared:

> Jenny Lind was advertised to give a concert in Providence last Monday evening, the arrangement broke down under the prices demanded for tickets, which were two, three and four dollars. The refusal of the people to pay such outrageous prices for concert tickets is evidence that their senses are returning to them.[14]

After New York State, Catherine first went back to Providence, then she went to Philadelphia where the Musical Fund Society had invited her to give two performances. The first performance set for 6 December she cancelled due to illness. Her next performance occurred on 9 December at the Musical Fund Hall. The programme included some new additions, including a duet with Mengis 'Quando Amore' from Donizetti's *L'elisir d'Amore*, and a song, 'The Happy Birdling' which had been composed for her by Vincent Wallace. Ticket prices were $1 and $2. The review the next day once more praised her execution and style:

> The concert of Miss Hayes, last evening, attracted a brilliant assemblage of the taste and fashion of the city, and the room was filled to an extent that was barely consistent with comfort. The first appearance of the fair *debutante* was the signal for the most cordial and prolonged applause; and when the audience had sufficiently settled into quiet, she commenced her introductory cavatina, 'Ah, mon fils,' from *Le Prophete*, of Meyerbeer. It was sung with great taste and power of execution, and the pathetic passages were uttered

with rare eloquence of expression, which has distinguished the 'Irish Swan' over all contemporaries. Her second effort was the celebrated scena and aria, *Que la Voce* from '*I Puritani*.' This delicious morceau was delivered with admirable skill, and the singer moved through Bellini's music with grace and ease that captivated all hearers. It was a selection well adapted to the tender sweetness of her voice and the simplicity of her style. The ballads embraced in the second part of the programme were all rendered with a felicity peculiar to Miss Hayes. One of them was a song composed by Wallace, called 'The Happy Birdling,' which was given with rare art. The caroling of a little bird is prettily imitated and the miraculous trill with which it was concluded electrified the audience, and drew forth enthusiastic cheers, which lasted several minutes.[15]

Continuing on, Catherine next went to Baltimore, where she was scheduled to perform at the New Hall of the Maryland Institute on 17 December and again on 19 December. Her concert was attended by an estimated 2,300 people.

Immediately following her into Philadelphia came Jenny Lind, still charging high ticket prices and now being managed by a Mr. C.S. Seyton, who apparently had replaced Bushnell. The high ticket prices affected attendance and the concert was not considered successful, even though she raised enough to contribute $1,000 to a young singer named Adelaide Phillips who wanted to go to Europe to study.

Catherine returned to New York on 20 December feeling totally exhausted from her concert and travel schedule. She was still deliberating on her financial problems with her manager and the need to determine her future plans. She chose Staten Island as her retreat for a few days while she thought about this. Her mother and sister accompanied her.

On Saturday 23 December 1851 both Lind and Catherine and their respective parties, checked in to the Union Palace Hotel in New York City for the Christmas holiday.[16] This was the last time that these two great pupils of Manuel Garcia would be in such close proximity. They knew each other well. Perhaps they spent some time together or even dined together over the holidays – we'll never know. Unfortunately, neither one left any direct thoughts or opinions of the other.

Catherine went back to work almost immediately, with her first return concert on Christmas Day, 25 December, at the former Tripler Hall, now renamed Metropolitan Hall by its new lessee. This series was announced as 'Her Last in New York' before going to the southern states. The initial concert was followed by performances on 27, 29 and 31 December. She changed her programme slightly this time around by adding the Scottish song 'Annie Laurie' and the Irish song 'The Last Rose of Summer'. Catherine's ticket prices remained at $2 for reserved seats and $1 at the door.

Jenny Lind announced her farewell series of concerts in America to commence on 30 December at the Metropolitan Hall, with five additional concerts set for early January at the same location. Lind's ticket prices had came down slightly, to $3, $2 and $1.

Lind's concert advertisement ran above Catherine's in the Amusement section of the *New York Daily Times* on 27 December. Both singers offered thirteen pieces for their respective programmes, including orchestral numbers. Catherine's concert that same day added George Loder, an experienced and first-rate musician and composer, as a second conductor to Lavenu. Loder was an Englishman whom Catherine knew from her days in London. Catherine's programme consisted mainly of works by Rossini, Donizetti and Bellini, as well as a number of Irish songs. The majority of the pieces to be performed had been heard at one of her earlier concerts in New York.

However, Lind's programme for her concert three days later was quite spectacular in its variety, with music by Beethoven, Mozart, Weber and Haydn in addition to Meyerbeer, Bellini and Donizetti, and some Scottish songs. She was scheduled to sing six solos, including a beautiful aria, 'Oh! mie fedeli . . . Mala sola', from Bellini's *Beatrice di Tenda*, which was ideal to show off her incredible top notes.

Catherine, in response to the scope of Lind's programme, decided to mount a much stronger offering for her 29 December concert. In addition to Lavenu and Loder, she added the talents of her friend William Vincent Wallace, who was a highly influential member of the New York Philharmonic, a well-established composer of operas and a significant personality in New York and Europe. She also varied the music for the programme considerably by including works by composers such as Linspainter, Boildieu, Spohr, Weber and of course Wallace, in addition to Rossini and Meyerbeer. Lavenu, who was a competent composer, had written songs for her previously and now wrote a special song 'Greeting to America', which she was scheduled to sing for the first time that evening.

On the morning of 30 December it was announced that Jenny Lind had received notice the previous evening that her mother had died in Sweden in October and as a result she had decided to withdraw from all further concerts in the United States, including the concert scheduled for that evening.

Catherine's performance of the 29th received excellent reviews, with one critic saying:

> . . . and we came very near [to] saying genius, of the woman. There is such a charm in the style and fire in the manner that even the Swede [Lind] might borrow to advantage.

There was one final request on Catherine's schedule before she left town for the south. This was from the President of the Board of Education and the Superintendent of Schools in New York for a matinee performance for the children of the New York public school system. It appears there was concern that the children did not have any exposure to music because of the cost of concert tickets. The officials stated that 'Catherine Hayes is the first great artist who has felt this and adapted the means for hearing her to the purses of the younger part of the community.' Catherine's concert took place at the Metropolitan Hall on Wednesday afternoon, 31 December. Tickets were free. We don't know what she sang for the children since there was no report on the performance, however we can be sure that 'Kathleen Mavourneen' was one of the numbers.

Over the holidays William Avery Bushnell, Lind's former concert manager, met with Catherine. The proposal he made for handling Catherine's concert tour was very satisfactory from her perspective. In effect, he would become her advance man, going into the cities she planned to visit seven to ten days ahead of her arrival to set up the concert hall and, the orchestra or piano as needed. He would also release information to the local newspapers about Catherine, including her biographical details, successes and current activity.

There was a maturity and confidence about Bushnell, whom she had previously met in Boston, that pleased Catherine. She did not know it then, but he would provide everything she wished for – the guidance, the stability and above all the friendship which she longed for, both in business and in her personal life. He would also become something much more – but that was a long way off.

William Avery Bushnell was born in Lisbon, Connecticut, in 1825. He came from a distinguished family who were direct descendants of the original Bush family, settlers who came from England in the seventeenth century. A few years after William's birth, his family, which included his mother and father, a brother and two sisters, all moved to Rome, New York, where his father had been appointed a church minister. Probably around 1847, William moved back to Connecticut to the Bridgeport area where he became a school-teacher. He later went to Long Island, New York, involving himself in managing and organising political campaigns for a local politician. When this no longer suited him, he returned to Bridgeport, where he met P.T. Barnum, who took a liking to him and appointed him as an assistant. When Barnum contracted with Jenny Lind in 1850, Bushnell helped him setup her tour of US east coast cities. He subsequently became her manager for a short period after Lind broke with Barnum in June 1851. When Bushnell met Catherine in December of that year, he was actually out of work. Bushnell was married to a woman from Connecticut at this time. He subsequently divorced her a number of years later. It is not known whether they had any children.

In mid-January, as planned, Catherine arrived in Washington with her mother and they checked in to Brown's Hotel. Her first concert was set for 16 January, at a place called Carusi's saloon, which apparently was the only location Bushnell could find available at the time. At the next concert on the following night, Saturday the 17th, Catherine had the distinction of having the 13th President of the United States, Millard Fillmore, and his wife and family in attendance.[17] President Fillmore had been Vice President and had succeeded to the presidency on the sudden death of President Zachary Taylor the previous July.

After two more concerts, Catherine and her party left Washington to go south to Richmond later in the week on the boat *Powhatan*. However, they ran into heavy ice and the boat had to turn back, so they took alternative transportation by land. Her concert schedule continued at the same pace as before. After Richmond she went on to Wilmington and Charleston (Hibernian Hall) in South Carolina, and from there to Savannah (St. Andrew's Hall), where the good citizens insisted on a second concert before she left for Augusta, Georgia. After that she travelled to Montgomery and Mobile in Alabama, before arriving with great ceremony in the city of New Orleans.

Bushnell had gone ahead to New Orleans, which had an estimated population of about 125,000 at this time. The Irish in the city represented around 25 per cent of its total population. Next to New York, New Orleans had the largest port in the country. It had a good diversified economy, supported by its port.

On his arrival, Bushnell negotiated the donation of a brand new Boston Chickering Piano, the premier instrument of the day for concerts, compliments of Parson's Music store on Camp street. Catherine arrived on Thursday 12 February and proceeded to the St. Louis Hotel.

Bushnell had done his job well, getting almost daily publicity about her before her arrival, and saturating the city with notices of her concerts. He had reserved the Armory Hall, a large concert hall, for the first of five scheduled appearances, starting on Monday 16 February. Catherine was already seeing the benefits of Bushnell's organisational skills.

New Orleans was a very sophisticated city, with a strong social structure and an elite lifestyle. There tended to be some division between the French Catholics and the Irish Catholics, much of which was related to Sunday sermons being in French instead of English. The city had a long history of operatic performances, going back to the end of the previous century. Its citizens were well versed in opera having had their own resident company for many years. In fact, New Orleans had been the location for numerous operatic premieres in America. The city also received visiting operatic troupes from Cuba on a regular basis. Rossini, Bellini and Meyerbeer's music were particularly popular during the time Catherine visited the city.

Surprisingly, despite the audience, Catherine's programme changed little from her concerts in other cities except that she sang the Meyerbeer arias from *Robert le Diable* in French instead of her usual Italian. What did change, however, were her ticket prices, presumably at the suggestion of Bushnell. Ticket prices were now became $3, $2 and $1, depending on the position of the seating. All seats were numbered, which was a relatively new innovation. Reservations by seat number brought better order to the arrival and seating process at the theatre before the start of the performance. In addition, librettos containing translations in English, French and Italian of all of the songs and arias were now being offered at the door, at a cost of $0.25 each, with the obvious economic benefits to the prima donna. This was also something Lind had done at her concerts, no doubt under Barnum's or Bushnell's influence.

For this initial series of concerts in New Orleans, Catherine decided not to put together an orchestra to support her performances. This was strange, given the number of talented and musicians available in the city at the time, and the fact that most of her other concerts in the larger cities had an orchestra to support her.

She no longer had Braham as the tenor in her party, as he had stayed behind in New York. Also, George Loder had left, making his way to

California, where Catherine would meet him later. However, she had added some new members to the group. Now included were a pianist by the name of Eduard Boulanger, a pupil of Chopin (possibly the father of Nadia and Lilli Boulanger), and a violinist, Ferdinand Griebel, generally known as Herr Griebel, in addition to Menges, Lavenu, and the American flautist John A. Kyle.

New Orleans was bustling at the time of her arrival. On Monday 16 February, Rossini's opera *Semiramisde* was being performed at the New Orleans Theatre. The French Opera season had just commenced with *The Queen of Cyprus* by the famous French composer Fromental Halévy (1799-1862). A new theatre was also in the final stages of completion and scheduled to be opened the following April.

The review of Catherine's first concert was very positive; however, it did mention the lack of the orchestra and the need for greater musical support in such a big hall. There was also a nice description of her personal appearance:

> There was a brilliant attendance of ladies. We missed the orchestral display usual in grand concerts, wherein vocal performances have a part . . . But we were content to hear Miss Catherine Hayes, though it be always with a piano accompaniment. Her personal appearance immediately disposes in her favour. She is of a well-proportioned and elegant figure, a little above the ordinary standard of woman's height, with a complexion of the most delicate and dazzling purity, aquiline and spirited nose, thin and well chiseled lips, of a rosy tinge, fine teeth, eyes large, well-formed, of a deep, clear blue colour, and soft, languid look, eyebrows lightly drawn and prettily arched, an elegantly shaped head, a face a little too broad to be called regularly oval, but bearing the stamp of gentleness, delicacy and lady-like purity; hair in abundance, of that deep, rich, chestnut tint which every flash of light transforms into a golden glow, and which the old Italian masters were so fond of painting . . . Miss Hayes's success here as an artist may be considered as complete . . . her voice is as clear as the tones of a silver bell; the lower notes are very soft and rich.[18]

Two nights later when reviewing the second concert the same source classified her as 'standing in the front ranks of vocal musicians'. For her third concert a large segment of the audience consisted of military personnel, including the Emmet Guards and the Louisiana Grays all in uniform. Also in attendance were members of several Irish charitable societies, with their badges and other insignia. The large gilt harp of the Shamrock society was as prominent [an] object of attention'. Speaking of her voice the writer went on to say:

> . . . the power she possesses in so remarkable a degree of dwelling on a succession of long, even notes, was signally displayed in the sacred air, 'I know that my Redeemer liveth.' We think she surpasses Jenny Lind in it.[19]

One of the most dominant personalities among the New Orleans Irish at the time was Father James Ignatius Mullon. Father Mullon was born in Ireland, in Londonderry, and as a young man came with his family first to Maryland, where his father founded a school.[20] After a stint in the American navy in the war of 1812, the young Mullon decided to become a priest. He was ordained in Cincinnati, where he practised for a while before being assigned to New Orleans in 1834. He was the hero of the Irish in New Orleans, not only because of his lectures, which were in English, not French, but also because of his energy and personal magnetism. His sheer physical size added to this, giving him an immediate presence.

Father Mullon's mission in life was to complete the construction of the Gothic church known as 'St. Patrick's' which had commenced some years before. A fund of over $100,000 had been raised to cover the cost. The project had been plagued with a series of mishaps, including a spire that had a precarious lean! Some of the parishioners believed the 'patron saint' had forsaken the project. The original architects, James and Charles Dakin, were Irish brothers, but the committee overseeing the project had dismissed them. They were replaced by another Irish architect, James Gallagher, who was from Dublin. Now known as James Gallier, he was to become a very famous designer of buildings in New Orleans and his work can be seen to this day in many of the city's public buildings.

Father Mullon pursued his mission with an energy and will that were dauntless. He also established a school where Catholic orphans could be educated and taken care of. His energies reached everywhere, even to improving the female orphans asylum that was run by the Sisters of Charity.

Catherine's arrival presented an ideal opportunity for the mission driven Father to test his powers of persuasion. Catherine was a Protestant, but a concert of hers at St. Patrick's would generate a significant amount for the church's building fund. Catherine's visit didn't quite coincide with

St. Patrick's Day, 17 March, which would have been a good excuse for Father Mullon to request a favour. However, not being bashful, he took the direct approach of using the leverage of the Irish community and city leaders. He and one of his assistants, Father Flanagan met Catherine and Bushnell at her hotel, the St Louis. Father Mullon made his request, suggesting in the process that it would be good publicity if the whole idea of the charity concert was announced as 'her decision'. Bushnell couldn't resist. It had the smell of success. The outcome was a resounding 'yes' from Catherine, with Bushnell setting the time and date for the 'Sacred Event' in the partially constructed St. Patrick's.

On the morning of the concert the leading newspaper ran an article outlining the events which had led to the planned 'Sacred Concert' that evening:

> Concert at St. Patrick's – A sacred concert will take place at St. Patrick's Church this evening – the proceeds to be employed in aid of the completion of that grand edifice. The grand attraction of the evening will be Miss Catherine Hayes. She has volunteered her powerful assistance to the uses of the church, and the melodies which have been entrancing all hearts at the Armory Hall during the week will tonight fill the vast walls of the holy temple with divine music. One of the first acts of Miss Hayes, on her arrival here, after a succession of triumphs in other cities, was to undertake, in the most graceful manner, this act of unaffected generosity, which will not fail to be warmly appreciated. The unfinished state of St. Patrick's Church – in design one of the most imposing in our city, where so many of her own countrymen and women worship – being made known to her – she immediately placed her services at the disposal of Father Mullon for a concert in aid of the completion of the building. This zealous pastor – indefatigable in the service of his flock, and considerate for the interests of his warm-hearted countrywoman – has selected this night [Saturday] as best calculated to assemble a large audience, and least likely to interfere with the other arrangements of Miss Hayes. The spacious church will, we doubt not, be thronged in compliment to the charming songstress, and in sympathy with the object of her munificence.[21]

The 'Grand Sacred Concert' took place as planned on Saturday 21 February in St. Patrick's with Catherine singing from Handel's *Messiah*, 'I know that my Redeemer liveth', and from Haydn's *Creation*, 'With verdure clad'. Josef Mengis also assisted, along with the choir of the new Philharmonic Society.

Next day, Sunday, one of the newspapers reported that:

> After the concert, the Irish volunteer companies and charitable societies marched down to the St. Louis Hotel to serenade their accomplished country-woman, Miss Catherine Hayes. There was a very large crowd present. Lehman's fine band took up a position in St. Louis Street in front of the hotel, and executed several choice pieces of music. Miss Hayes appeared on the balcony, accompanied by several of her friends, and waived [sic] her handkerchief in token of her thanks for the handsome compliment paid to her. Her appearance was greeted with loud and enthusiastic cheering. There were over two thousand persons present, the majority of whom remained on the grounds until a very late hour.[22]

St. Patrick's Church at Camp and Girod streets still exists in New Orleans today. It is now designated a national monument by the US National Trust – thanks in some small part to the efforts of Catherine Hayes.

All her life, time and time again, Catherine offered her services free of charge for charitable causes. Religious denomination didn't seem to matter, which illustrates her sincerity and character in a century of terrible religious prejudices.

Unlike Lind, Catherine's style and personality did not permit her to promote her charitable acts. It would not have been in character for her to use the difficulties of others to her own advantage. Perhaps as a result, the memory of her generosity has long since faded, even in terms of memorials or other forms of recognition, except in a few cities far from her birthplace. Catherine seems to have had a special place in her heart for children, especially those children who were abandoned or orphaned, no doubt a direct reflection of her own early childhood in Limerick, when her father left her mother and family to fend for themselves, never to be heard of again.

Anna Bishop (1810–84), another prima donna, from England, arrived in town via riverboat from St. Louis around the third week in February. Bishop was several years older than Catherine. She had extensive operatic experience in Italy and arrived in New Orleans with her lover (described as her musical director) and accompanist, the famous French harpist

Nicholas Bochsa, to give concerts. Bochsa and Catherine's musical director Louis Lavenu also knew each other from their days in London, where Lavenu had been a pupil of Bochsa's. Bishop had a wide operatic repertoire (she had also premiered a Lavenu opera in London) and a remarkable talent for languages – she spoke several fluently. She gave her performances in operatic costume to add drama to the evening's entertainment. Catherine would do the same when she reached San Francisco later in the year.

Bishop gave her first concert on Thursday 26 February, in the Armory Hall. Her programme was quite varied, covering a wide range of operatic arias and songs. Interestingly, she included one of Catherine's most popular Irish songs, 'The Harp that once through Tara's Halls'. Bishop's ticket prices were $2 and $1, with multi-lingual librettos selling at the door for $0.20 each.

The following evening, Catherine sang her last official concert at the Armory Hall. In the process, she made a conscious decision to 'repay Bishop the favour' by singing 'Home Sweet Home', which was a very famous song that had been written by the husband Bishop had abandoned some years before – Sir Henry Bishop. It was also the first song that Bishop had sung at her concert the previous evening. Competition among prima donnas is not new!

Catherine's venue changed for two additional concerts, the first of which she gave on 1 March. She also added a new assisting artist – an experienced bass called Pietro Novelli who had been a member of the Astor Place Opera Company in New York. Catherine's new location was at the New Orleans Theatre, where a full orchestra was at her disposal. Ticket prices were kept at the same level as the Armory Hall, $3, $2 and $1, despite the addition of the orchestra.

The second evening at the same location she performed another charity concert, again influenced by Father Mullon. The proceeds were distributed among the Orphan Boy's Asylum; the Home for Indigent Widows and emigrants from the 'Old Country' who needed aid! Around this time, the effects of Ireland's Great Famine still continued to bring many Irish to New Orleans and other US cities.

On Thursday 4 March, the French Opera performed Halévy's opera *Charles VI* at the New Orleans Theatre. In the audience, sitting near by to each other, were Miss Catherine Hayes and Mrs. Anna Bishop. The reporter who observed the situation said that the 'talent who was performing [Mme Widemann] was evidently warmly appreciated by that which was listening!'

Catherine Hayes now took time off to rest and enjoy the unique hospitality of New Orleans, the surrounding area and the friends she had encountered. She didn't perform any further charity concerts for Father Mullon With his need temporarily abated, the good Father Mullon, probably felt that the Protestant prima donna had done her bit for Rome!

On 6 March, Catherine set off up the Mississippi river by steamboat to perform in mostly one- and two-night concerts in Baton Rouge, Natchez, Jackson and Memphis. In addition, patrons on the Mississippi steamboat had the pleasure of her talents at an evening concert between Natchez and Memphis. Then, leaving the great Mississippi around Cairo, she transferred to an Ohio river tributary to get to Nashville, where she gave two concerts.

After Nashville, she took a few days to explore the spectacular Mammoth Cave area in south-west Kentucky, something tourists do to this day. Lind had done the same the previous year. Continuing up the river, she arrived in Louisville, where she gave two concerts. Cincinnati saw her next on 4 April. Bushnell had checked in to the relatively new Burnet House Hotel, at Third and Vine streets, the previous week.

Once again, Bushnell's expertise paid off. Despite bad weather, all four concerts at Smith & Nixon's new hall sold out, due to his good advance promotional activity. The local press referred to Catherine as 'one of the greatest living vocalists'. Tickets to her concerts in Cincinnati sold for $2 and $1 and multi-lingual librettos were sold at the door for $0.15 each. Local market values had obviously different economics. The review of her first concert said:

> it was a succession of brilliant triumph, each more brilliant than the past. Miss Hayes is slightly above medium size, rather delicately proportioned, with a quite pleasant but not beautiful face. Her manner is easy and graceful, and her dress almost severely simple.[23]

After Cincinnati she continued by riverboat to Wheeling and Pittsburgh, giving concerts in both cities. Cleveland was the next stop on her itinerary, where her troupe arrived by rail on 21 April for three concerts. Her arrival was announced with an amusing comment: 'Bushnell, the Barnum of Catherine [Hayes] is among the troupe.' At the end of her stay, one reviewer had the following to say about her:

> Miss Hayes is not only a sweet singer, but her every expression and appearance denote her a sweet girl also. She has a modest and most

winning look, which with her fine voice, and agreeable manners, and more than ordinary personal beauty, make her an object of much interest, and combine to make her concerts deeply interesting. She does not astonish like Jenny, but she pleases you far better – Her melody seems to come from a heart attuned to it by nature, and not forced upon it by humdrum rules of written music.[24]

In addition, one of her many admirers addressed a lengthy poem to her, the Cleveland newspaper published it.

The Hayes group left immediately afterwards on Monday 26 April, taking a Great Lakes steamer to Buffalo in New York State, with a short stop at Dunkirk on the way north. The ice on Lake Erie had broken up a few days earlier, enabling boat transportation between the towns on the Lake to be resumed as the winter season drew to an end. In Buffalo, according to the local media, she created a 'Lind like' furore at her first concert. This was familiar territory for Bushnell, and he worked it well.

After Buffalo she went to Montreal and from there to Toronto, where she performed in the St. Lawrence Hall, afterwards going to London in Ontario and from there down to Detroit, where she appeared on 18 June. Her gruelling itinerary, similar to Lind's the previous year, continued with her arrival in Chicago for concerts on 21 and 23 June, then on to Racine and Milwaukee in Wisconsin and after that to St. Louis.

Her next recorded appearance was quite a distance away, in Binghampton, New York, performing in the Methodist Church on 12 and 13 July. The local newspaper in Binghampton commented as follows:

The greatest criticism, as between Miss Hayes and Jenny Lind, is that the former excels on the low notes and the latter on the high notes. We have only to say, we have heard Jenny twice and Miss Hayes once, and 'taking it, all in all' we prefer Catherine Hayes.[25]

Amusingly the editor of *Dwight's Journal of Music* in Boston commented in response the above: 'That settles the question, forever, we presume!'[26]

Catherine's tireless energy and Bushnell's exceptional planning skills took the whole party on this incredible journey without any mishaps. It was a distance of over 4,000 miles using steamboats, rail, secondary river transportation, coach and steamers on the Great Lakes. It was a phenomenal undertaking, in pre-civil war America, that required intensive planning, strong personal discipline and a good constitution. Given the conditions along the way – weather, river pirates (there were river pirates!), primitive transportation, accommodation, food and personal hygiene needs – it was an extraordinary journey. Catherine could never have contemplated it without William Avery Bushnell, something she fully appreciated.

While Catherine was performing in US mid-west towns and cities, legal proceedings in her contract dispute with Thomas Frederick Beale were moving ahead in London, England. Beale had tried to collect her deposit of £3,000 from the London bank, based on the fact that Catherine had broken her contract. Beale had gone to court to get approval to have the bank release the funds. In an effort to stop him, Catherine initiated a counter lawsuit for a restraining order against the Union Bank of London, with co-defendants named as Beale, Wardwell and his backer Anthony, to protect her £3,000 deposit.

Catherine's lawyer argued that, as Beale only paid her £650 per month, while he was receiving £1,800 per month from Wardwell for her services, he had not acted in good faith. This meant that, the agreement was unfair, and her deposit of £3,000 should be returned to her. Catherine also claimed that she had not known about the contract between Beale and Wardwell. Beale, in his defence, claimed that she knew of the agreement ahead of time, as he had discussed it with her in her home in London before her departure to America. Beale also claimed that Catherine and Wardwell had colluded to replace his contract with the prima donna with a direct agreement with Wardwell, in which she would be paid more. The case became even more complicated when Anthony entered the fray with various counter claims. The judge eventually ruled in favour of Beale because Catherine was not prepared to complete an affidavit that she had not been in collusion with Wardwell. Catherine had to forfeit the deposit and pay the legal fees. It was a bitter lesson for her.

The long-term ramifications of the dispute with Beale ended up costing her much more when she arrived back in London several years later. Beale was the most powerful concert agent in London, and he ostracised her because of the dispute. On her return, she initially had to make do with setting up concert arrangements on her own or through friends in England and Ireland. This limited her opportunities and earnings. However, by then she was a wealthy woman.

When Catherine returned to New York in 1852, it was not to give concerts but to meet with the legendary P.T. Barnum. The meeting had been arranged by Bushnell, who was interested in seeking the great showman's advice about a possible tour to California for Catherine.

Bushnell was not personally familiar with the west, as Lind had not gone further west than St. Louis. The trans-continental railway was many years away from completion. Barnum invited Catherine, her mother and her sister Henrietta to stay at his home Iranstan, (so called because of its Eastern design), in Bridgeport, Connecticut. He also invited the three ladies to attend the wedding of his eldest daughter Caroline, to a David W. Thompson in October.[27]

By now, the east coast of America was alive with musical activity. The arrival in New York in September of the vivacious Henriette Sontag on board the Collins Line ship *Arctic* was only the beginning of a long stream of musical talent from Europe. One of the century's greatest stars to be, Adelina Patti, was not too far away in Baltimore, during the early days of October 1852, preparing for another concert. Her manager Maurice Strakosch was advertising the diminutive Patti as 'La Petite Jenny Lind', with copy that said:

> the not yet eight year old [she was actually nine by then] musical prodigy would sing the bravura pieces of leading prima donnas *Lind, Sontag* and *Catherine Hayes* . . .

Patti's first concert in Baltimore took place on 5 October 1852. The programme opening number was featured as 'Happy Birdling of the Forest . . . a bravura song, composed expressly for Catherine Hayes by W.V. Wallace'. This was followed by a Lind number. Tickets to the Patti concert sold for $0.50 each! A remarkable price when compared to the cost of a 'Patti ticket' fifteen years later.

In the meantime, in Bridgeport, Barnum not only embraced the idea of a California tour for Catherine, but, with his usual vision and exuberance, he expanded on the idea by suggesting that it would also be logical on such a trip to include Mexico – and perhaps even Cuba on the return. He pointed out that Lind's visit to Havana had been very successful and profitable two years earlier.

Catherine immediately took to Baraum, perhaps seeing in him a reflection of the father and warmth she had never known. In his inimitable manner, he volunteered to underwrite the project, and also said that Bushnell could have two of his assistants to help with the tour. Catherine could hardly believe the great man's generosity, knowing the significance and value of having the Barnum name attached to such an enterprise. Elated, she decided to make a trip to Boston to outfit her wardrobe for the journey to the Far West – a place where Jenny Lind had not been!

Bushnell's influence had again prevailed, as it would many times over the years as he managed Catherine's travels to Latin America, the far corners of the Pacific and back to Europe. She appreciated his insight, boldness and solid business acumen and grew closer to him as time went on.

One day when preparations for the Barnum wedding were under way, the great man happened to be in downtown Bridgeport having a shave, when he got news that his home, *Iranstan* was on fire. He rushed back to the house to find Catherine, her mother and sister out on the lawn where the Irish prima donna had all of her trunks lined up (along with the wedding gifts). Catherine had made sure that all her belongings were far away from the inferno-like flames which were engulfing the beautiful *Iranstan*, which was almost totally destroyed.

While Catherine was in Bridgeport, Barnum asked her to give a charity concert for the benefit of his new venture, the erection of the entrance gateway and an adjacent stone tower for the Mountain Grove Cemetery. Barnum was the owner of the land on which the cemetery was built. Catherine willingly obliged. The cemetery, which still exists today, is where P.T. Barnum and several of his business associates are buried.

Catherine and her mother spent a week in Boston stocking up on new clothes for their journey. They returned to Bridgeport to attend the re-scheduled wedding of Barnum's daughter later in October.

The California press reported on the agreement between Barnum and Catherine, saying 'her arrangement with Mr. Barnum is for sixty concerts, to be divided between California, Mexico and Cuba.'[28] The Barnum machine was in operation once again.

The Hayes party departed New York for California on the *SS Illinois* on 20 October 1852.[29] There were 600 passengers on board. It is also possible that Bushnell brought his wife along, as there was a Mrs. Bushnell listed on the passenger manifest. However, we don't know if in fact this lady of the same name was his wife.

The route they took to California was via Panama. The *SS Illinois* arrived in Aspinwall, which was named after one of the railroad builders but later changed to Colon, in memory of Columbus. The cross-Panama railroad was started by a group of Americans in 1848, but it wasn't completed until 1855. In fact, a large number of railroad personnel and workers were on the same boat as Catherine and her party en route to Aspinwall.

GRAND MUSICAL EVENT.
MAURICE STRAKOSCH

Has the honor to announce to his friends and to the public in general, that he has engaged
SIGNORINA ADELINA PATTI,
not yet eight years of age, yet styled the most wonderful Vocalist of the age, universally called
LA PETITE JENNY LIND.

This extraordinary musical prodigy sings with the most astonishing perfection, purity of style, and with incomprehensible ease, all the Bravura pieces of
MALIBRAN,
 PASTA,
  JENNY LIND,
   SONTAG,
    ALBONI,
     CATHARINE HAYS,
      ANNA BISHOP, and
       TERESA PARODI.
exactly as they were composed for them, and with all the variations by the above-named celebrities.

SIGNORINA ADELINA PATTI
WILL
GIVE HER FIRST GRAND CONCERT,
IN THIS CITY,
On TUESDAY EVENING, Oct. 5th,
AT THE
NEW ASSEMBLY ROOMS, Hanover street,
on which occasion she will be assisted by
MISKA HAUSER,
the great Violinist, and
MAURICE STRAKOSCII,
the eminent Pianist and composer.

Signorina ADELINA PATTI will sing the following brilliant English and Italian ballads, cavatinas and variations:

1. "The Happy Birdling of the Forrest," a celebrated Bravura Song, composed expressly for Catherine Hays,...W. V. Wallace.
2. "Ah, Non Giunge," the grand rondo finale of the opera of La Sonambula, as sung by M'lle Jenny Lind, ————.————....Bellini.
3. "I am the Bayadere," Madame Anna Bishop's famous ballad.
4. Jenny Lind's Echo Song—exactly as sung by the incomparable Queen of Song.

MISKA HAUSER and MAURICE STRAKOSCII will perform some of their best and most popular compositions. Vide the bills of the day.

☞ Doors open at 6½ o'clock. Concert to commence at 7½ o'clock.

☞ Price of admission FIFTY CENTS.

Tickets to be procured at the principal Music Stores and at the door on the evening of the Concert. o2-3t

25. Advertisement for the eight year old Adelina Patti's concert in Baltimore in 1852 when she sang musical selections of Catherine Hayes and other prima donnas. (Author's collection).

At Aspinwall, Catherine's party went over-land to Panama City where they boarded the *SS Oregon* bound for San Francisco. They left Panama City on 4 November and steamed north, with a brief stop in Acapulco, Mexico. They avoided a stop in San Diego because of storms and bad weather. Their arrival in San Francisco on 20 November was announced the next day in the local press.[30]

Their journey west had taken them about a month. California brought new challenges and enormous earning opportunities. Catherine was the first major European operatic star to arrive in San Francisco. According to the press her initial appearance was looked forward to with great anticipation.

On arrival in San Francisco, Catherine found another soprano performing there, with considerable success, she was Eliza Biscaccianti, (1824–96) who was from Boston. The American Biscaccianti was known as the 'American Thrush'. She had studied in Italy with Giuditta Pasta and others and had performed opera there, but not at leading theatres. She had actually arrived in San Francisco from the eastern States the previous March.[31] In addition to performing in opera at the New York Astor Place Opera House, she had also sung in other cities, mostly to mixed reviews.

Biscaccianti, who was six years younger than Catherine, had followed Lind and Catherine on their east coast concert circuit to places such as Boston, Providence, Baltimore and New Orleans. In New York and California, she had been managed by Catherine's friend, the musician and conductor George Loder who had settled in San Francisco earlier in the year.[32] Biscaccianti's husband Alessandro was a cellist whom she later divorced. She was the daughter of a prominent pianist Sophia Hewitt (Ostinelli), and an Italian violinist, Louis Ostinelli. On her mother's side, the Hewitt family had a long line of distinguished musicians who had been residents of New York. By the time Catherine arrived in San Francisco, Biscaccianti had been giving regular concert and operatic performances in the area with reasonable success. However, shortly after Catherine's arrival Biscaccianti moved on to South America, to join an Italian opera company in Lima, Peru.

California brought great changes for Catherine, not only from a professional point of view but also in her personal life. She was to make decisions there that would change the course of her life. Some of these were quite daring and adventurous for someone of her nature, no doubt a reflection of the greater influence Bushnell was now having on her life.

CHAPTER ELEVEN

The Pacific Pioneer

CALIFORNIA, CHILE, PERU AND AUSTRALIA 1852–1854

SAN FRANCISCO in the early 1850s was booming. The gold rush days that started in the Sacramento area in 1848 were in full swing. At the time of Catherine's arrival in November 1852, San Francisco was in its early days of development. The editorial in one newspaper commented on the number of people arriving from the Atlantic (east coast), stating that it was the largest in many months. The paper also mentioned the clipper ships arriving daily, taking 116 days from Boston, or 131 days from New York, depending on weather. There was mention of other ships coming from France and China – creating a problem with the amount of merchandise thrown on the market, but anticipating a brisk business.

The population of San Francisco by the end of 1852 was somewhere close to 45,000. It had grown very rapidly since gold fever struck four years earlier.[1] There were nine daily newspapers and various weeklies, in addition to a monthly magazine.[2]

The town still had a long way to go in terms of development; it had no paved streets or proper lighting. The few sidewalks that existed were made of wood, with the result that on rainy day – and there were many – there was mud everywhere. The city lacked a public water supply and sewerage system. It would take another fifteen years before the transcontinental railroad would come through and twenty years before the first cable cars arrived. The San Francisco that existed when Catherine arrived was part of the rough and raw western frontier. Most people were there for gold. There was a large influx of people, of all nationalities, entering the town on a regular basis to seek their fortune. Catherine was one of them.

Fire was the city's greatest concern, due to the many wooden buildings. Extensive fires had occurred in 1851 causing great devastation. Because of this, most new buildings were being constructed of brick, which was less hazardous and more durable. Local fire departments were manned by volunteers, many of whom were Irish born. There was no formal or professional fire department.

For Catherine, this rugged environment must have represented a dramatic change from the sophisticated lifestyles and salons of London, Milan, Vienna or even New York, however eager she may have been to seek out financial opportunities. Her arrival in this western outpost of civilization must have made her question her reasons for being there. However, when she was ready to depart, her financial position clearly answered that question – she was now a reasonably rich woman, having earned somewhere around $30,000 during her stay in California![3]

As if to challenge Catherine on her arrival in San Francisco, the reigning prima donna, Eliza Biscaccianti, gave a concert on 22 November at the new Musical Hall which featured three of Catherine's standard pieces – 'I know that my Redeemer liveth', 'Ah, non giunge!' from Bellini's *La Sonnambula*, and the Irish song 'Kathleen Mavourneen'! Tickets to this Biscaccianti concert were sold at $3 and $2. The advertisement announcing the concert included a statement to the effect that 'Street Lamps [presumably lit by oil] will be placed in front of the building for the accommodation of carriages.'

Biscaccianti was quite successful in San Francisco, where she featured a wide range of Italian operatic arias and songs in her recitals. She had created a new level of musical appreciation in the town. She also performed in Sacramento and various other places, including the mining camp areas. Her husband had proposed an Italian Opera be started in San Francisco, to be supported by artists from the Italian Opera in Lima, Peru. Naturally, he wanted his wife to be its principal prima donna. However, the concept never materialised.[4] Later, in January 1853, Biscaccianti and her husband sailed for Peru, where she joined the Italian opera company in question. This was an important pioneering group, the largest on the west coast of South America at the time, including some of Catherine's friends from her early operatic days in Milan.

Bushnell was not the advance man for promotional activity in San Francisco, possibly because his wife from Connecticut accompanied him on the ship to California. Instead, one of Barnum's other agents, probably Henry Stanford, did the preliminary work in San Francisco. Bushnell and George Wells (Willis?), another Barnum agent, both arrived on the same boat as Catherine and her party – the *SS Oregon*.[5]

For Catherine's first performance on Tuesday evening 30 November at the American Theatre at Sansome and Halleck Street, the weather was damp and drizzling. This theatre was very large with a seating capacity for about 2,000 people. Ticket prices were $5, $3 and $2, with numbered seating and an usher to help guests locate their seats. The lobby of the theatre had on display a diagram showing the location of all numbered seats, a new feature for theatres in San Francisco. Catherine had an orchestra to accompany her and George Loder, who was also conducting Biscaccianti's concerts a few blocks away at the San Francisco Hall, was her conductor.

The following is an extract from the review of Catherine's first concert in the 'Far West'. Which appeared the day after the concert:

> . . . it [her debut] has been looked forward to with considerable anxiety, both on the part of those who accompanied the fair artist to these distant shores from the theatre of her achievements in the east, and by our citizens, to whom she is introduced crowned with honors, which even 'the Lind' might envy. Miss Hayes has been even represented as contesting the palm with this most glorious of living singers.
>
> . . . To say that the American Theatre was filled would only be to confirm the expectation of every one who has heard of Catherine Hayes. The house had been re-arranged and put in excellent order for the reception of so large a company . . . Several minutes before the opening of the concert, all the vacant places in the dress circle and parquette were filled, and one of the most intelligent and respectable audiences ever assembled within the walls of a theatre in this city awaited the appearance of the star of the evening.
>
> . . . Long and loud were the cheers and applause, which greeted her *entree*. She acknowledged again and again the enthusiastic testimonial, and again and again the audience cheered and applauded. Silence having been restored, Miss Hayes sang the sweet plaintive invocation, the 'Ah mon fils,' one of the most touching gems of Meyerbeer's music. It was while standing at the foot-lights, amid the storm of applause, that our citizens had the first view of Miss Catherine Hayes.
>
> . . . Miss Hayes is about thirty years of age. She is a graceful, queen-like person, of medium stature, with a fair oval face. Her features are regular, hair bright auburn, eyes blue, and her face wears an intellectual expression without much animation. She dresses with taste, and her manner is perfectly easy and self-possessed; her gesticulation appropriate and graceful.[6]

The *Alta California* did not consider her rendering of 'Casta Diva' from Bellini's *Norma* successful. The reviewer felt it was not delivered in the correct Bellini style. In the audience that night was the other prima donna of the moment, Eliza Biscaccianti, who was seen to join 'warmly in the testimonial of greetings showered upon the stranger artist'. The reviewer closed with the following comment:

> There was much enthusiasm, and altogether too much noise and uproariousness [sic]. Some young *Sons of Erin* became so excited as to toss their hats and money on the stage, which, however enthusiastic it might seem, could not but be regarded as exceedingly bad taste.[7]

The advertisement for Catherine's second concert contained a notice to the effect that she would give a total of six concerts in San Francisco, after which she would leave for Mexico on a steamer departing on 15 December. The reviewer of this concert was highly critical of her performance, saying:

> Miss Hayes will doubtless confine herself to ballad singing during the remainder of her stay in this city. Her success in Italian music is certainly problematical, and notwithstanding the fame which has preceded her, a discerning public will not be slow to perceive that extravagant expectations have been encouraged concerning her operatic singing...her voice lacks strength and freshness for Italian and what is termed 'classical' music...The selection from sacred music 'I know that my Redeemer liveth' which was sung by Miss Hayes last night was in every respect a disappointment.[8]

It's quite possible that Catherine's voice was undergoing a darkening process, as she got older. She had just turned 34 at the time of this second concert in San Francisco. Several of her reviews over the past year had indicated that the strength of her voice seemed to lie in its lower register. In fact, one reviewer actually felt that it was more a mezzo-soprano than a soprano voice. A number of the critics had referred to a 'pyramidal' effect, meaning that the voice was broader in its bottom register and tended to 'thin out' as it got higher up the scale. This also may account for the fact that during the past year virtually every one of Catherine's concerts had opened with the mezzo aria 'Ah mon fils' from Meyerbeer's *Le Prophète*, although we don't know what musical key she sang it in.

Additionally it had been two years since she had last performed in a complete opera, so it's quite possible that she had not continued Garcia's vocal exercises with the discipline normally required for opera performances. It's also possible that when she did sing a soprano aria such as 'Ah non giung,' from *La Sonnambula*, or an aria from *I Puritani*, she may have transposed it. This would probably have reduced 'the brilliance' of these pieces as far as the listeners were concerned. However, we don't actually know how she handled her music and vocal pieces.

Whatever the cause, during this period in San Francisco either she was having some vocal problems or else she was just tired and this affected her vocal health. The critic who said that her voice was no longer able to handle operatic arias could not have been correct, as some months later she performed opera successfully with the Italian group in Peru. Much later in her career she continued to sing some of her most successful operatic roles and arias before highly sophisticated European audiences. At that time, she also took on important new Verdi parts, something she had completely avoided when she was younger, and certainly not something a fading prima donna would venture into if she was concerned about high notes.

Regardless of the vocal difficulties perceived by one critic, there was a great demand for tickets to her concerts and Bushnell took advantage of the situation by creating a ticket auction, the first of its type in San Francisco. This was held on 3 December, with a 'professional auctioneer' officiating. It seems that the Fire Chief, Captain George Green of the Empire Engine Company (who was a butcher in the Pacific Market), was so enthusiastic about his countrywoman that he actually paid $1,125 for one seat – an unheard-of amount, then or now![9] He also purchased tickets for his entire engine company for $19 for each company member – also a phenomenal amount in those days! Catherine's third concert, on Saturday 4 December, saw the entire Empire Engine Company turn out in full uniform for the evening. Fortunately, there were no fires that evening! Also in attendance was the Knickerbocker Engine Company. Both of these esteemed groups elected to escort Miss Hayes to her hotel at the conclusion of the evening.

The reviewer for the *Daily Alta California* newspaper still had difficulty with Catherine's singing, particularly of operatic arias,[10] but three nights later he said that her singing had improved, giving her a better review after her fourth concert, which he erroneously described as her fifth. Her next concert was postponed due to hoarseness and indisposition and was rescheduled for three nights later. The reviewer once again noted his dissatisfaction with her rendering of two of her most famous pieces, 'Ah non giungi!' and 'O luce di quest anima', saying that 'all who have heard them must unite in pronouncing [they are] quite beyond her powers!' A benefit concert was announced for the Fireman's Charitable Relief Fund for the following Thursday and another ticket auction was held with similar success.

On 15 December, a notice appeared in the leading newspaper requesting that Catherine extend her stay in San Francisco. It was signed by sixty of the city's most powerful and prominent citizens, a number of whom had become her close friends. Catherine's response was also recorded in the same issue of the paper as follows:

San Francisco, Dec. 15. 1852

Gentlemen: – I acknowledge, with pleasure, the receipt of your flattering letter, requesting me to prolong my stay in your city beyond the 16th inst.

It conveys to me another most gratifying evidence of your kindness and friendship. I assure you, gentlemen, that it will afford me very great pleasure to defer my departure from San Francisco, where my reception has been among the most warmhearted and cordial of my life.

I have submitted your letter to the gentlemen entrusted with the management of my concerts, and am happy to say they have acceded to your request and my own inclinations.

I have the honor to remain, gentlemen,
Your obedient servant,
Catherine Hayes

To the Hon. C.J. Brenham and others.

Catherine did not depart for Mexico but continued to sing in the San Francisco area, giving several more concerts.

The support and backing that Catherine received from San Francisco's leading citizens was unanimous, despite negative reviews. Consequently, she and Bushnell made the decision not to provide free tickets to her next concerts for the reviewer from the *Daily Alta California* newspaper. The newspaper recorded the incident for posterity by saying simply:

Neither the rain nor the mud prevented a large attendance at the American Theatre last evening to listen to Miss Hayes. The program [sic] embraced several new pieces, each of which was executed in a manner that drew forth ample and frequent testimonials of pleasure from the audience. Mr. Mengis was in good voice, and the entertainment passed off smoothly.

In consequence of admission tickets not having been furnished to this office, our reporter did not take his seat to report on the concert.[11]

Catherine's motivations for continuing to perform in San Francisco were more related to the financial rewards than to the sentiment expressed by the town's leaders. A report appeared in a New York newspaper in early January to say that her first concert in San Francisco had netted her $6,855; the second, $6,985; the third, $8,980 (auction sale), which included the Captain George Green bid.[12] Bushnell's early training under the great Barnum appeared to be paying off. There was even a report that newspaper magnate Sam Brannan actually bid $5,000 for a ticket to a benefit concert at the Fireman's Charity Auction.[13]

Catherine, having completed her programme at the American Theatre, which was now booked for a series of Shakespeare plays, moved about eight blocks away to the more intimate San Francisco Hall, at Washington and Kearny Streets. For this change of venue, Catherine offered shortened versions of operas in costume called 'operas in brief'. This was unique in that no other singer had performed concert versions of operas in costume in San Francisco previously. Catherine of course had seen Anna Bishop use the concept with considerable success in New Orleans a few months previously.

This new approach did present a problem: Catherine was lacking complete opera scores. However, George Loder, an experienced first-class musician, came to the rescue. In an interesting account written five years later, Loder wrote (anonymously) a long and fascinating series of articles covering his experiences in California and Australia for the London journal, *The Musical World* . He mentioned how, fortuitously, Catherine Hayes's arrival in California coincided with his availability as musical director for her concerts. He went on to say the following:

Money now tumbled in fast upon me, for the Swan had brought no opera scores, and she wished to give operatic scenes in costume, so that I had plenty of work to do in arranging and scoring, which labour brought a liberal return upon the lady's part . . . Miss Hayes after a most triumphant reception and tour through the state [California] left for South America . . . [14]

Fortunately for Loder, another opportunity opened up some months after Catherine left, when a number of visiting prima donnas, including Anna Bishop and Bochsa, arrived, as well as the soprano Anna Thillon. In addition, an Italian opera company from Peru, armed with a strong Verdi repertoire, also came to town. This euphoria did not last too long, as the economy of the state was fast declining from the glory days of the gold rush.

During December Catherine had given eighteen concerts. In the New Year she kept up the same pace. On 6 January, Catherine rolled out her various operatic characters in condensed format, some of which were advertised with English titles, others with Italian titles, although all of the programmes featured arias sung in Italian.

The new programme started with an announcement for *Lucie de Lammermoor* [sic], but at the last minute this was changed to *The Barber of Seville*. English translations of two Donizetti works – *Elixir of Love* and *Don Pasquale* –followed the Rossini opera. Then came Donizetti's *Lucrezia Borgia*, in which the adaptable Mengis sang both the baritone and tenor roles! Donizetti was again on the programme when *Linda di Chamounix* was performed towards the end of January. These costumed performances concluded with Bellini's beautiful *La Sonnambula*.

The purpose of these truncated operatic performances had very little to do with artistic endeavour, as far as Catherine was concerned. Her motives again continued to be purely financial. Additionally, the integrity of the performances must be questioned. No matter how experienced a musician George Loder may have been, it is very doubtful that he could have reconstructed all of these musical scores to an acceptable level from memory, even though most of what was performed only involved the main arias and duets. Catherine had never sung performances of *L'elisir d'Amore*, *Don Pasquale* or *The Barber of Seville* anywhere, which raises another question.

These were strictly costumed concerts; there was no scenery involved. Some of the concerts also had additional songs, arias and piano solos as part of the programme. In general, apart from the novelty, and the financial rewards (the concerts were well attended), the entire endeavour places in question Catherine's overall artistic integrity. The day after the final concert in early February one of the local newspapers gave the following review:

> We've seldom seen in San Francisco a finer audience that were assembled in San Francisco Hall last evening to hear Miss Hayes' last concert. The house was very full, and the walls were decorated by a line of unfortunate gentlemen who could not obtain seats. Miss Hayes and Herr Mengis were in excellent voice, inspired by the full house, and perhaps desirous of leaving a pleasant impression during her absence.
>
> The opera was throughout better performed than on the previous occasion. Miss Hayes sang her part with more confidence and we did not detect any unpleasant fault. Each piece that was sung was a most meritorious performance. We were most pleased with the scena and aria [*Linda di Chamounix*] 'O luce di quest anima,' the finale 'no non e'vere,' and in *Don Pasquale*, the whole of the scene 'Signora in tanta fretta.' In the latter Herr Mengis is really excellent. We regret Miss Hayes' departure, and think it ill-advised. The musical enthusiasm of this public is at its height and she is reaping a rich harvest, which could continue, without doubt another month. It [She] is badly advised to leave at this time. At the expiration of a few weeks the weather will be more wett'ed [sic] and gold dust will be much more plenty at Sacramento.[15]

For a benefit concert for the orphans of San Francisco on January 18, Catherine went back to basics in terms of format and programme content. Ticket prices remained at $5 dollars, $3 and $1. The local newspapers acknowledged her contributions. There were two orphanage asylums in San Francisco in 1853. In January she performed in twelve concerts in all.

Before her departure for Sacramento, several leading citizens – mostly Irish names, O'Brien, Ryan, O'Farrell, Tobin, Ferguson, etc. – presented her with a large oblong gold card case. This gift was described as:

> 'massive' with designs on the face emblematic of Ireland and California. One side is engraved with the Irish Harp surrounded with a wreath of Shamrocks and with a scroll bearing the motto 'Cead mille failte, Kathleen Mavourneen,' under the harp is an Irish wolf dog in a crouching attitude. Over the harp on a scroll bedecked with flowers, is one of Miss Hayes' favorite ballads set to music with

the words 'Savourneen Deelish.' On the reverse is depicted scenes illustrative of California from its primitive days to the present; a camping scene showing miners preparing supper, after the toil of the day; a group of miners at work, excavating, pumping, etc. a view of Nevada and on a shield in the center [sic] is engraved with the inscription 'Miss Catherine Hayes from a few of her countrymen residents of San Francisco, February 5, 1853.[16]

After completing more than thirty concerts since her arrival in San Francisco in November, Catherine now moved on to Sacramento, arriving there on the riverboat *Antelope* on 6 February. She was accompanied by her mother, Josef Mengis, the concert pianist Rudolph Herold (who had arrived with her on the boat from Panama), and a clarinettist called Chenal – and of course the ever present Bushnell. Her manager's energy and skills had by now placed him in complete control of planning Catherine's schedule, her direction and in many respects her fate.

Rudolph Herold was an accomplished pianist who performed at selected Catherine Hayes concerts in San Francisco and Sacramento. He stayed on in San Francisco after Catherine left and became a prominent musician and conductor there, particularly after George Loder's departure for Australia in 1856. During Catherine's visit to Sacramento, he not only acted as a soloist but also as conductor for the group.

Her first programme in Sacramento was on Tuesday 8 February. Bushnell, taking advantage of the excitement generated by her planned visit, set up a local ticket auction, which was criticized by the local media.[17] This time he put a minimum price on the tickets, with the proviso that any unsold tickets at the time of the performance would be sold at 'regular rates', presumably $5, $3 and $2. Next day, a San Francisco newspaper ran the following article:

Last evening [in Sacramento] a large audience assembled at the Orleans [Hotel], . . . for the purpose of attending the auction sale of tickets to Miss Kate Hayes' first concert. The bidding for the first choice of seats was started at $100, and seconded instantly by a cry of $150, which brought a response from the first bidder of an additional $50; and between the two it was carried to $450, when a prominent citizen stepped into the ring, with a bid of $500!

Now be it known it was the intention of three different parties to bid $1,000; though it was kept a profound secret from the crowd.

The fever had gotten hold of the audience, and to outdo San Francisco – to show there was still some 'small change' left in our midst – and that Miss Hayes should not have occasion to regret her coming for want of public spirit was the prevalent feeling. All eyes were turned to a certain corner where, after brisk bidding $1,150 was proclaimed in a loud voice; then a voice said $1,175, and 'ere a second elapsed every one heard a full clear voice sound $1,200, and it was almost immediately knocked down, and name called for. Another long drawn breath, and the welcome, cheering sound of 'The Sutter Rifles,' was heard. Every one knew the old pioneer Capt. John A. Sutter, would be the honored recipient of the distinguished compliment, and cheer on cheer was given for many minutes for the good taste and liberal spirit shown by this well known corps. The next [ticket] was sold for $50, and then the premium went down to one dollar . . . the concert takes place this evening, and an escort was sent early to bring the gallant old captain [John Sutter] on the afternoon Marysville boat, to occupy the choice seat of the house, consisting of a sofa in front of the pews. A brilliant attendance of ladies, will welcome the cantarice on her first performance, and bestow the commendation she may by singing merit at their hands.[18]

On the day of her final concert in Sacramento, a report appeared which focused on the cost of the tickets for her concerts. The following is an extract:

A visit from Miss Kate Hayes and the honor done by the citizens of Sacramento in paying the highest price for the single ticket to her first concert ever yet known to have been offered in any country, by any people, has had the effect pleasantly to excite the public mind, and direct it into wholesome channels. A simultaneous visit by the venerable Capt. John A. Sutter, who stands pre-eminent in California estimation, heightened the *eclat* of the occasion, the bringing about of which, next to the brilliant vocal talents of Miss Hayes herself, is chiefly ascribable to the gallantry and generosity of the Sutter Rifles.[19]

Gold was first found in California in 1848 on John Sutter's land in the Sacramento area. At the time of Catherine's visit, Sutter was probably one of the most famous people in California. Because of the influx of squatters on his land once gold was found, he became embroiled in legal arguments over the title to the land, which had been given to him originally by the Mexican government for his services. The case went to the US Supreme Court and Sutter lost. He eventually had to declare himself bankrupt and the US government allocated him a modest pension of $250 a month. He never got back the title to his lands. All of this transpired a short time after he had paid $1,200 for a ticket to Catherine's concert in Sacramento!

Catherine had scheduled a second concert for the following Friday but elected not to perform because the hall was unsatisfactory and the weather oppressive. Instead, her party set off for Marysville and Grass Valley via the Feather and Bear rivers, to visit some mining camps and to take some time off and rest. As she left Sacramento, the newspapers were reporting about 'the miners doing well in the Marysville, Long Bar and Oregon Gulch areas in addition to those on the Feather River and in the Grass Valley'. During her visit to these hill-town mining camps Catherine took a fall from a horse and sustained some injuries. However, it could not have been serious, since she returned to Sacramento for a final concert on 17 February, before returning to San Francisco.

Catherine kept up her incredible performance and travel schedule, rarely taking time off to rest her body or her voice. Her mother, who was now in her mid-fifties, which was considered 'old' in Victorian times, kept pace with her all the way. In Catherine's few personal letters which have survived, there is never any mention of her mother being sick or unable to attend a performance. As it turned out Catherine's mother survived her by ten years.

After returning to San Francisco, she was scheduled for a concert on 24 February at the San Francisco Hall. The programme included scenes from *Lucrezia Borgia* and *Il Barbiere di Siviglia*; Josef Mengis was her partner, with George Loder back on the podium. There were no other participating artists. Bushnell set up the concerts on a subscription basis for the first time. Mengis got excellent reviews as he had for all of the concerts. Catherine also got good reviews, Loder was strongly criticised for changing some of the positions in the orchestra, which the reviewer felt created major problems, presumably with the sound.

By the end of the month the critics were calling for new operas, some suggesting Donizetti's *La figlia del reggimento* as an option. Instead, Catherine selected Bellini's *Norma* as her next work. The performance was in three acts. The theatre was sold out, but one critic expressed his doubts about her ability to perform *Norma*. He mentioned that he did not feel she had been successful in the aria 'Casta Diva' from the same opera, which she had performed at one of her earlier concerts. There was brief mention that she had been suffering from a slight indisposition, possibly a sore throat. At this performance, the audience liked what they heard, and applauded 'with fury'. However, the reviewer did not feel that Miss Hayes was suited to the part. There were also reservations about Mengis singing the tenor role of Pollione. A Miss Coad performed the mezzo role of Adalgisa.

The reviewer focused specifically on some of the duets and arias and had the following to say:

> 'Casta Diva,' we do not like to hear Miss Hayes sing it, nor did we like the Largretto [Cabaletta] which follows it, but the . . . '[Ah!] *Bello a mi ritorna*' [sic] was much better rendered. Miss Hayes does not succeed as well in the slow movements as in the more vivace. But in the grand trio of the second act '*Oh di qual sia tu vittima*' there was little to find fault with her denunciation of Pollione. Both voices and acting were excellent. This part was really the best of the entertainment. She seemed to feel this part and threw herself into the character with passion and energy both of voice and action that held the audience breathless. The duet in this act, '*Deh con te, con te,*' [*Mira, o Norma*] called forth considerable applause . . . the Grand Duetto '*In mia man alfin no sei!*' Miss Hayes exhibited her tragic powers to much advantage. We regretted to perceive the vibration of the notes we have before remarked, and too frequently where the energy of the priestess requires clear, full, unwavering notes, and [with] some inaccuracies which are quite excusable in a first representation.
>
> . . . Neither Miss Hayes nor Herr Mengis were well up in their parts, though for a first-time presentation the piece may be said to have gone off pretty smoothly, 'all things considered.'[20]

Despite this rather condescending review, Catherine decided to perform *Norma* for a second time on 3 March. The reviewer considered this performance was a great improvement on the last. Despite a fall-off in audience numbers, it was still considered a 'large, fashionable and intelligent assemblage'.

Her rendering of 'Casta Diva' on this occasion was praised, as well as various other solos and duets. In the third act, the critic was slightly critical of her seeming to 'hold back' to conserve herself for the final moments of the opera. In the dramatic closing minutes of the score her performance was considered 'far more beautiful', almost equal to the grand trio in the second act.

Two lighter operas were chosen for the following evenings, *Don Pasquale* and *L'elisir d'Amore*, both of which she had sung previously.

Her next venture was quite unparalleled. She announced a new musical evening called *The Musical Fanatic*, a 'Comic Operetta' with Catherine and Mengis as the principal players and George Loder conducting. Who put this together and who created the music and libretto is unknown. In any event, it turned out to be a fiasco and was poorly attended. The next performance added two acts of *Lucia di Lammermoor*. The reviewer of *The Musical Fanatic* referred to it as 'quite a stupid affair'.

Catherine then switched to a more conventional format with Donizetti's *La figlia del reggimento*, which had its first night on 15 March, with excellent reviews. She repeated it two nights later, following it up with another of Donizetti's gems, *L'elisir d'Amore*, for the second half of the evening. Her last concert was announced for Saturday 19 March. This opened with a series of songs and arias and a piano recital by Monsieur Chenal.

After this Catherine left town and went upriver again, to Sacramento and various other places. This visit to the gold country was not quite as successful as the previous one, as something went wrong with a planned charity concert for the Sacramento Fire Department. The following provides some limited details on the event, which seemed to have been caused by a miscommunication between Catherine and Bushnell or possibly between them and the Fire Department. In any event, the following appeared in the local San Francisco newspaper:

> The theme of public conversation to-day, writes our Sacramento correspondent is . . . the rupture between Miss Hayes and the Fire Department of this City [Sacramento] on account of a benefit concert of Wednesday last. Miss Hayes promised to give a concert for the firemen, it appears, and every preparation was made for a full house. But for some reason, she or her agent failed to duly notify the committee regarding the time, and it being considered by the public as a sham, they would not attend when the concert was given. There was a 'beggarly account of empty boxes' to greet her, whereat the lady was very much incensed. High words ensued between her agent [Bushnell] and the Chief of the Department, and Miss Hayes left Sacramento in something very like a miff.[21]

Catherine's break-up with the Fire Department was never resolved. She never gave any more concerts in Sacramento.

During this period, there were several articles in the San Francisco newspapers about gold in Australia. Newspapers from Melbourne and other places arrived in San Francisco regularly, albeit two months after their issue date. It's possible that Catherine and Bushnell may have seen these and decided that they might one day go to Australia.

She returned to San Francisco and gave another series of concerts there starting 13 May. During this time she and Mengis had a disagreement, possibly over a benefit concert for him as he was well received in San Francisco as a supporting artist. Bushnell would probably have been opposed to holding a benefit concert for a secondary artist. Whatever transpired, they appear to have patched up their differences, as Mengis agreed to join Catherine for a visit to Peru and Chile in South America.

Catherine and party left on the steamer *John L. Stephens* on 16 May for Panama, with connections to Lima in Peru, where she stayed for a brief time, as Biscaccianti was performing there with the Italian Opera Company.

Catherine probably did not know it then, but back in England, while she was sailing south to Peru a horse named *Catherine Hayes* won the *Oaks* Derby at Epsom Downs on Friday 27 May 1853. The horse was a famous 'bay filly' foaled in 1850, at which time it was named after Catherine, the *prima donna*. It won many races. The filly was a direct descendant of some of the greatest bloodlines in thoroughbred racing history, including *Bartlett's Childers* (1716) *Eclipse* (1764) and *Lanercost*, all of which were descendants of the most important 'Foundation' Arabian stallion, the *Darley Arabian* (1700), brought to England by Thomas Darley in 1704. At the time of the 1853 *Oaks* race, the horse was owned by a Mr. Wauchaupe, who may have been Australian.

The horse was put out to stud in 1854 and went on to give birth to a long line of colts and fillies. One colt, *Costa*, was named after Sir Michael Costa the famous conductor. A filly sired in 1863 was named *Miss Hayes*, while two others sired later were named after two great operatic stars – the *Marquise de Caux* (Adelina Patti's married name) and *Albani*, after Emma Albani, a later soprano.

In 1858, the well-known French artist Pierre Lenordez (1810–96) executed a bronze sculpture of the horse *Catherine Hayes* with one of her foals. The foal was by Irish Birdcatcher, particularly appropriate given the prima donna's origins. This was sold in 1995 by a Virginian antiques dealer for an 'undisclosed price', but estimated at around $12,000.

CATHERINE HAYES

26. Bronze circa, 1858 of the horse *Catherine Hayes* winner of the 'Oaks' at Epsom Downs, May 1853, Artist, Pierre Lenordez. (Courtesy Turner Reuter Antiques Inc., Middleburg, Virginia).

Meanwhile, in South America, Catherine decided not to stay in Lima, perhaps because of the presence of Biscaccianti. Instead she travelled on to Chile, where she spent almost three months, giving concerts at the Teatro Victoria in Valparaiso and at the Teatro Republica in Santiago.[22] Throughout the tour, she was received with great acclaim.[23] Her concerts mostly consisted of her usual repertoire, such as the aria from Meyerbeer's *Le Prophète*, Irish songs and scenes from *Lucia di Lammermoor* and *L'elisir d'Amore*, and other duets with Mengis. However, at a benefit concert for the 'Hospital de Caridad' at the *Teatro de la Victoria* in Valparaiso on 16 July she sang for the first time the Verdi aria 'Ernani, Involami' from his 1844 opera *Ernani*. She may have been studying the score of this early Verdi work during this period, having picked it up in Lima on her way south. She performed the complete opera in Lima some months later.

The following is an extract from one of her concert reviews in Chile:

All who are elegant and well bred in our capital city hurried to keep the appointment with the famous singer Catherine Hayes. All the boxes and stalls were filled, and even the corridors were overflowing. Anything we could say in praise of this eminent singer would be an inadequate assessment of the enthusiasm she evoked from the public. The applause was thunderous and the varied and beautiful flower arrangements that were prodigally, dispensed [sic] on the *Swan of Erin* were but a small thing compared to the desire that animated the crowd in outdoing itself by showing its admiration . . . Miss Hayes has more than anyone made felt the magnetic power of her divine art: in the cavatina Ah mon fils! of the *Prophete*; she transported the spectators to the world of illusion, but where the enthusiasm went wild and a feeling of inexplicable tenderness rendered the public speechless, was with the last Act of *Lucia*, 'Al fin son tuo . . . ' During those moments, which we will never forget our sensibilities were touched in such a profound way that cannot be reached without touching death . . . For the first time she made us taste the tender melody of the Irish ballad with its sweet and sad echoes as in the 'Harp of Ireland' [The Harp that Once through Tara's Halls] . . . The tender prayer 'The Last Rose of Summer' left a melancholy imprint upon hearing it from the lips of its most faithful interpreter.

. . . At the doors of the theatre, 300 youths were waiting to see Miss Hayes leave in her carriage. Many of them, and us amongst them, asked to unhitch the horses in order to pull the carriage instead [to the Hotel Aubry]. We were so carried away in the presence of genius that we were becoming animals ourselves![24]

On the personal side, a poem in Spanish was dedicated to her in the same issue of the newspaper as this review.

While in Santiago, Catherine performed with an orchestra which was conducted by Señor Pantanelli.

At the end of September Catherine left Chile, travelling north to Peru and arriving in Lima on 12 October 1853. Here she joined the Italian Opera Company where her friend from her early days in Milan, Domenico Lorini, and his wife the Boston born Virginia Whiting-Lorini, were part of a large group of opera singers performing in that city. Biscaccianti had by now returned to San Francisco.

Catherine opened her season in Lima on 25 October with *Lucia di Lammermoor* – Lorini was her Edgardo and Mengis was Enrico. This was followed by *Don Pasquale* and a series of other operas including *Maria di Rohan*, *I Puritani*, *La figlia del reggimento* and Verdi's *Ernani*. Her season concluded in February 1854 with the part of Rosina in Rossini's *Il Barbiere di Siviglia*.[25] This was by far her most ambitious opera season to date. Shortly after its conclusion, she headed back north to San Francisco, where she arrived around the middle of April.

In San Francisco, a bass called Leonardi appeared with Catherine in Bellini's *Norma*, which was not well received. Mengis performed the tenor part of Pollione, while Leonardi was Oroveso. The reviews indicated that Catherine had difficulty with the part. Anna Bishop, who was still in town, performed *Norma* six days later, receiving considerably better notices than Catherine. Mengis, meanwhile, changed loyalties and joined Bishop in various operas.

Catherine engaged George Loder with an orchestra for her first concert, on 24 May. Leonardi shared the platform, as did a baritone called Stephan G. Leach, who was the husband of Anna Thillon, an English soprano who had arrived in San Francisco the previous December. Catherine and her new partners gave a total of five concerts, in which she stuck to her usual programme, Leonardi replacing Mengis in duets from *Don Pasquale* and *L'elisir d'Amore*. Leach mostly sang Balfe arias or English songs. His wife was singing in light opera across town at another theatre. Another soprano, Clarisse Caillys, also chose to sing *Norma*, despite the presence of Bishop and Hayes.

After a final concert on 7 July 1854 in San Francisco, she attended a reception at the Hotel Oriental, where the leading male citizens presented her with a gold brooch valued at $1,100.[26] The next day, considerably richer, Catherine, her mother, Bushnell and another replacement basso, Emil Coulon (Mengis and Leonardi having elected to stay in California), set sail on the ship *Fanny Major* for Hawaii (then called the Sandwich Islands), with Australia as their ultimate destination. The *Fanny Major* was a relatively new American vessel and this was its first voyage to the South Pacific.

Catherine would never again visit America, despite the fact that she had been received with open arms everywhere she went. Financially, her visit had been more successful than she had ever dreamed. Artistically, like so many great singers who came after her, she found concerts more rewarding and less demanding than operatic performances.

Her relationship with Bushnell had grown significantly, however, it would be several more years before she would marry him. So far, he had provided everything she needed for her business and their personal relationship had grown alongside their professional one. Australia would bring them even closer together, but their arrival there was three months away. Their next stop was Honolulu, a long way from Limerick for Catherine and her mother.

CHAPTER TWELVE

Opera in Australia

AUSTRALIA, INDIA AND THE PACIFIC 1854–1856

THE SHIP *Fanny Major* reached Honolulu on Oahu in the Hawaiian Islands on 22 July 1854. In those days the Hawaiian Islands, as we know them today, were called the Sandwich Islands.

On their arrival Bushnell arranged a concert for the following Tuesday 25 July at the Court House in Honolulu, which apparently was the only place large enough to handle the demand. Catherine opened the programme with 'I know that my Redeemer liveth', perhaps respectful of the strong missionary presence in Honolulu. Emil Coulon, who was an experienced French singer, sang a different variety of arias from Josef Mengis and that must have been refreshing for Catherine. She also sang 'Kathleen Mavourneen', 'Home Sweet Home' and a bravura aria, 'Gia dalla menti involasi' (*Le Tre Nozze*), known as a vocal 'Polka' by Mantua-born operatic composer Giulio Alari (1814–91). Tickets were priced at $3 each.

After the concert, Captain James Makee and his wife invited Catherine and her party to visit their residence two days later. His home was located in the beautiful Nuuanu Valley area, about five miles north-east of Honolulu on the way to Kailua. On her arrival at her hosts' residence and a function given in her honour were reported by the local newspaper as follows:

> On Thursday last, a large party of the foreign residents of Honolulu were invited by James Makee, Esq., to meet Catherine Hayes at his beautiful residence in Nuuanu Valley, and a charming reunion it turned out to be. The day was fine, and the splendid scenery in the valley appeared in its most delightful beauty, and excited universal admiration.
>
> Miss Hayes had been the guest of Mrs. Makee during her stay in Honolulu; and the opportunity thus afforded of making her acquaintance, and of spending a few hours in her society, on the eve

240

of her departure, was a gratification to many who appreciate social excellence as well as artistic merit, and the occasion was rendered doubly agreeable by kind attentions and generous hospitality of Capt. Makee, who spared no pains to make every one feel at home. Altogether, it was a pleasant affair, and one that will long be remembered.[1]

The report of her concert which followed had an interesting perspective relative to the writer's sense of Hawaii's remoteness, saying:

Although situated in mid-ocean, two thousand miles from our nearest neighbors, recent events clearly indicate that the Sandwich Islands are not altogether without the pale of civilization, or of those influences; so abundantly enjoyed in the great world, where they have hitherto been monopolized. [sic] Commerce, religion and letters have opened the way for other influences, which are gradually stealing in upon us.

. . . But who, in his wildest dreams of progression, would have dared to predict twenty years ago, that our streets would be placarded with the name of an artist who has delighted the fastidious taste of European Courts, and the equally appreciating assemblage of the more recent Republic of America? Or that here, we should ever listen to that 'concord of sweet sounds' which has so often started the tear of sympathy from the unwilling eye of mankind by its deep pathos and soul-gushing harmony?

. . . Our eyes have seen the name Catherine Hayes, and our ears have heard her charming voice. As a whole, the concert gave entire satisfaction, and the only wish we have heard expressed on the subject is, that she might have given another . . . But the sailing of the 'Fanny Major' on Thursday, prevented another appearance, and the opportunity to hear Kate Hayes, will never again occur at the Hawaiian Islands.[2]

Catherine did not forget her brief visit to the Hawaiian Islands. Many years later in London, when editing a pamphlet outlining her career, she carefully added in her own hand the following remarks made by King Kamehameha II who attended her concert in Hawaii: 'The King . . . who declared he could listen for ever to this strange woman!'

The *Fanny Major* sailed from Honolulu for Sydney, Australia, on Thursday 27 July. Nothing is known about the voyage, other than that it took about fifty days. The vessel could possibly have stopped in Tahiti (it did not stop in Auckland, New Zealand) to pick up provisions. It arrived in Sydney on 10 September 1854.[3]

During the early 1850s Australia was booming with gold fever. Gold was discovered in 1851 near Bathurst in New South Wales, the location was about ninety miles north-west of Sydney. Later in the same year, various other nearby places also announced 'gold'. It wasn't long before all of these areas were feeling the pressure of gold fever, similar to San Francisco and Sacramento a few years earlier. All types of men and women converged on Australia, seeking their fortunes. Entertainers from the east and west coasts of America started to arrive in record numbers. Melbourne and Sydney primarily felt the benefit of the new found wealth as the diggers came to the cities to enjoy their riches, and new businesses were set up overnight to accommodate them.[4] This fever continued for a number of years and was still going strong when Catherine and Bushnell arrived in September 1854. Similar to the greater San Francisco area, Sydney, and a little later Melbourne, now found its population growing rapidly, with the arrival of new emigrants weekly.

At the time of Catherine's visit, New South Wales, which included Sydney, had an estimated population of around 240,000, while the state of Victoria, including Melbourne, had a population of 285,000.[5] Both cities had been in strong growth mode even before the gold rush. Sydney had opened its first university in 1851 and Melbourne in 1853. A steam locomotive service was also introduced around this period.

News of Catherine's arrival in Sydney spread quickly and even the people of Melbourne anxiously awaited her appearance in their city. There was considerable cultural rivalry between the two cities, which still exists today – in a slightly broader sense.

Towards evening on the first night that Catherine spent in Sydney, a group of thirty members of St. Mary's Choral Society serenaded her outside Petty's Hotel on Church Hill where she was in residence. She was perceived to be the most important European operatic star to arrive in Australia.

Within a short while of her arrival a lengthy feature article giving details of her background and accomplishments appeared in the local paper.[6] Bushnell's publicity machine was at work again. Bushnell also immediately had posters printed and circulated a brief biography outlining her achievements. Her first concert was set for Tuesday 26 September at the Royal Victoria Theatre. Louis Lavenu, whom Catherine last saw in New Orleans, had arrived in Sydney sometime earlier and was now scheduled to conduct for her again.

There was great demand for tickets to her concerts. Her programme followed earlier patterns in America, except that she included more songs than arias. The reviewer of her first concert, obviously an experienced concert-goer, began by remarking that he had last seen Catherine at the Hanover Concert Rooms in London, in 1851, then went on to praise her performance in Sydney, saying:

> We believe, Miss Hayes is the first really high-class singer with a European reputation that has appeared before a Sydney audience. Her arrival has given an impetus to the taste for music which will be felt for a long time, and her numerous auditors will henceforth possess a new standard by which to test the claims of candidates for popular favor as vocalists.[7]

The reviewer went on to say that, after her first piece (the aria from *Le Prophète*, which he thought was beautifully sung):

> Miss Hayes then sang 'Kathleen Mavourneen,' a ballad which she may be said to have made her own, as we believe, there is no other singer that can   impart to it such an amount of tenderness and sympathetic fervour. It is also admirably adapted to exhibit the great compass of Miss Hayes's voice, which is peculiarly rich in the lower tones, and even in quality. This ballad afforded the most satisfactory evidence of the power of the singer over the passions. We noticed numbers of the audience absolutely moved to tears. There can be no truer test of an artist's power . . . Miss Hayes sang, 'Coming through the Rye'. The manner of her singing this sprightly little ballad must be seen and heard to be appreciated. It brought down thunders of applause, and was vociferously encored; but the singer declined the proffered honor, and picked up several bouquets that were thrown upon the stage. Miss Hayes's performance terminated with what is called a vocal polka [Alari's polka?]. In this, astonishing flexibility and agility of her voice were very conspicuous. It would scarcely be possible for an accomplished performer on a violin to produce such a shower of sparkling notes, mingled with brilliant roulades and shakes in the same space of time. The effect of this display of vocalisation was very great, and it was warmly encored. The singer

in the most obliging manner repeated it, and retired amidst tumultuous applause, which was fairly and legitimately earned.[8]

Catherine's second and third concerts were equally well attended and she continued to receive high praise for her singing, particularly for 'Casta Diva' from *Norma*. It was reported that the third concert was filled with all the:

> most distinguished leaders of society that Sydney could produce, amongst whom we may enumerate the Chief Justice and Lady Stephens, Sir Charles Nicholson, Mr. Justice Therry and family, and indeed every person of note in this city and neighborhood, with the single exception of the governor-general, who, we regret to state, was confined to his bed by an accident . . . It is utterly out of our power to describe the scene which presented itself on Miss Hayes' entree; bouquets innumerable and offerings of every description were showered down from all parts of the house, and the most cordial and enthusiastic nature imaginable. Silence having been restored, Miss Hayes sang a very charming ballad ['On the Banks of the Guadalquiver'] from the opera of *Loretta* [London, 1846], by Mr. Lavenu, the talented conductor, which was encored, and she then substituted 'There' nae luck aboot the house' which she sang with her accustomed naïve and expressive manner, and we need hardly add drew down a perfect hurricane of applause from the audience. Her next appearance was in Tom Moore's beautiful ballad, 'The last rose of summer,' which was well received, and on its encore, Miss Hayes gave the beautiful song, 'I'll steer my bark for Erin's isle,' which was as warmly welcomed as its predecessor. She afterwards sang 'Savourneen Deelish,' which, if it be possible to criticise a performance in every way perfect, we venture to characterise as the most exquisite of the ballads which Miss Hayes has introduced to us as old friends in new garb; her rendering of this song we rank amongst her happiest efforts.
>
> Italian selections included the lovely duet from *Linda di Chamounix*, with Miss Sarah Flower . . . and the celebrated finale from *La Sonnambula* which is so well known as the 'capo d'opera' of Jenny Lind and Sontag. We need not say, that in this most elaborate and difficult rondo, Miss Catherine Hayes did not disappoint the anticipations which we have formed of her ability to measure her powers with the two distinguished songstresses who have almost

27. Sheet music cover featuring Catherine Hayes and the well known aria from *Linda di Chamounix*. London 1849. (Author's collection).

made this morceau their own exclusive property; and the audience were unmistakably of the same opinion, for, on its conclusion, they rose en masse, and amidst a scene which never found its parallel in Sydney before, demanded that Miss Hayes would give them the opportunity of listening to her again. To so spontaneous a manifestation, there could be but one response, and Miss Hayes, therefore, came forward, and in a very graceful and appropriate speech, signified her acquiescence in their wishes. The scene which the house presented at that moment verily baffles all description, and only those who have witnessed the reception of the Swedish Nightingale [Jenny Lind], during her first season in London can form any adequate idea of that which took place here. We will not conceal our gratification that the Sydney public has at length broken its apathy, and evidenced its sympathy and regard for talent and excellence so rare and so truly magnificent.

We understand that a vast number of persons were unable to obtain seats, or even entrance to the theatre on Saturday night. Miss Catherine Hayes, both on her arrival and departure was greeted in the most enthusiastic manner by the multitude assembled around the approaches to the theatre.[9]

By now, Catherine was creating a furore with each new performance in Sydney, having given about seven concerts there. However, the press also repeatedly mentioned that they expected that she would soon depart for Melbourne.

Before leaving Sydney, Catherine gave a charity concert at the Victoria Theatre on 17 October. It was for the benefit of the Destitute Children's Asylum, of Randwick, a suburb of Sydney. The total receipts for the concert were £977. After payment of the theatre expenses and some other charitable contributions to 'various other persons in distressed need', the balance of £800 was deposited in a commercial bank for credit of the Destitute Children's Asylum.[10]

This 1854 contribution by Catherine was held on deposit at the bank for many years before the asylum's Board of Governors decided what to do with it. After a whooping cough outbreak of epidemic proportions in 1867 they decided to build a hospital for the care of young children. By that time the £800 generated by Catherine's charity concert had accrued compound interest and was equal to £1,300. In 1869 additional subscriptions were solicited and the government also made a grant of

£2,000. In 1870 the Catherine Hayes Hospital for Children was formally opened.

The medical officer's of the hospital, Doctors Alleyne and Brown, making their first report stated:

> A large number of children (of the infant class), of delicate or sickly constitution, have enjoyed the benefits of judicious care and nursing, kindly carried out, amidst surroundings which approach more closely to the domestic system and the comforts of maternal home than has been hitherto practicable.[11]

Unfortunately, Catherine would not be around to see the results of her contribution to the young children of Sydney.

Catherine performed her last concert in Sydney that year in mid October and afterwards was treated to a farewell luncheon staged by Sydney's attorney-general, with Judge Therry presiding and making the farewell address.[12] There was even a new drink created for her called the 'Catherine Hayes', which was a mixture of claret, sugar and orange!

Her departure from Sydney was a public affair. Initially a steamer called the *Eagle* was reserved by a Mr. Plunkett so that all of her friends and admirers could accompany her down to the harbour. The newspapers reported on the incident as follows:

> It had been previously announced that the Eagle steamer would accompany her [Catherine] down to the harbor carrying such of her admirers as wished to pay her this parting token of respect. Accordingly, a very large number of citizens assembled at the home of Mr. Plunkett and proceeded to the Peninsular and Oriental Company's (P&O Line) Wharf on the eastern side of the Circular Quay, where she [Catherine] embarked on board the *Eagle*, leaning on the arm of Mr. Plunkett and surrounded by hundreds of enthusiastic admirers, who, in their eagerness to bid her farewell, must have put her through some inconvenience. The steamer then proceeded down the harbour, amidst the cheers of the assembled crowds, and conveyed her to the City of Sydney, steamer which was lying off Shark Island. The two steamers then proceeded to the Heads, where a hearty leave-taking was gone through, and the enchantress, who appeared deeply affected with the kindness of her friends, left us to achieve, as we hope and believe, fresh triumphs in our sister colony. We are afraid it will be some time ere our staid

28. The Catherine Hayes hospital in Sydney Australia, built in 1870, with an initial donation made by Catherine Hayes in 1854. (Courtesy Prince of Wales Hospital, Sydney, Australia).

citizens will recover that sobriety of feeling out of which they have been so charmingly bewitched.[13]

A further report on Catherine's departure appeared in Melbourne as followed:

> Miss Catherine Hayes, – A friend, at present in Sydney, writing on the 12th instant, says 'I have been enjoying a pleasure during the brief time that I have been in this city [Sydney], that is yet in store for the Melbourne community; and it has been in listening to the sweet notes of Miss Catherine Hayes's voice. You may be assured that however high your expectations may have been raised with regard to this delightful songstress that they will be fully realized [sic] when you have the opportunity of hearing her. Her success here has been most triumphant, and the public are only too sorry that she is to leave so soon; but as her stay in the colonies will be so short, she cannot spare any more time in this place, but will leave for Melbourne on the 21st instance [sic]. Too much cannot be said in praise of this talented lady, and I hope that when she honors [sic] Melbourne with a professional visit, her reception will be such as will throw Sydney entirely in the shade, and that her remembrances of the kindness of the Melbourne public will be uppermost in her thoughts when she leaves these colonies for India on the 24th proximo. In leaving Sydney for Melbourne, Miss Hayes will carry with her the most heartfelt wishes for her happiness and success in life, and to those who have had the privilege of a personal acquaintance with her, she has strongly and for ever endeared herself, by her amiability of character and lady-like deportment. To know her is to admire and esteem her, as wherever she goes, her appearance is greeted by the kind smile of welcome. I hope to be in Melbourne when Miss Hayes arrives, and join in giving her such a greeting as she will forever after remember, as no one deserves it more.'[14]

Catherine's arrival in Melbourne was announced by the leading papers of the city. Given her success in Sydney and the clamour for her appearance in Melbourne, Bushnell apparently decided to play one theatre against another in Melbourne, hoping to make a better deal. It was reported that she had decided to check out all the theatres for acoustics before she and Bushnell would settle on a location for her first concert.[15] This was probably a financial ploy by Bushnell.

Mr. Lewis, the lessee of Astley's Amphitheatre, had previously made the announcement in the form of 'a pledge' that Catherine Hayes would be appearing at his establishment. He now found himself competing with other theatres to save face, and to be the first to present the star performer. He had no option but to increase his offer in order to fulfill his promise. His final offer was £200 per night with a third of the theatre's receipts. He also agreed to cover all the expenses of operating the theatre – an exceptional offer for the time. However, Bushnell rejected it, having received a better offer from the Queen's Theatre, which had not participated in the bidding process from the beginning.

The manager of the Queen's immediately set about expanding his seating capacity by removing the orchestra area, adding new boxes, numbering every seat and issuing tickets with corresponding numbers, something Bushnell had requested. The orchestra would be located on stage, behind Catherine, rather than in the pit, which was now occupied by seating. The economics of what he had agreed to pay Bushnell required him to take this action. Her programme was also announced, with scenes from Donizetti's *Lucia di Lammermoor* and *La figlia del reggimento* to be featured along with arias from other operas.

The build-up to her first performance must have pleased Bushnell considerably. He had worked hard to maximise her debut and he was not disappointed. Catherine appreciated everything he did, particularly since he had not been too well since their arrival in Sydney.

The box office of the theatre opened at ten o'clock on the morning of 27 October and within an hour every box seat was sold out. Seating in private boxes in the theatre was then offered selectively at a 40% premium. The 'pit' [orchestra] or as it was now called the 'parquette seats' followed, with no seats being available in any part of the house by close of day. The saloon in the theatre had been fitted with every convenience for the overflowing audience.

The following day, Catherine arrived at the theatre at eleven in the morning for a rehearsal with the orchestra, or, as it was frequently called in Europe and Australia, 'the band', despite the fact that it had a sting section. Word was out that she would be attending a morning rehearsal. So many people showed up outside the theatre that the manager was compelled to direct that 'every avenue leading to the stage door should be closed'. The rehearsal, which was conducted by Louis Lavenu, went well and included 'some of the finest instrumentalists in the Australian colonies'. One of Melbourne's leading newspapers recommended to the theatre management that they consider 'in the establishment of the doors [sic] having a body of police in order to protect the visitors from the depredations of the light-fingered fraternity'.[16]

On Saturday 28 October, Catherine made her Melbourne debut at the Queen's Theatre. The whole city turned out for what was to become the event of the season. Catherine had 'unofficially' turned 36 the previous Wednesday, which she celebrated quietly with her mother and friends.

On 30 October one reviewer, dedicating a column and a half of the newspaper's space to this first concert, said:

> In the case of the Swan of Erin – truly she came saw and conquered, and this population appears now in a fair way of being added to the list of the enthralled who follow the chariot wheels of this celebrated singer. Her power seems resistless, her triumph was complete.[17]

The review went on to say the following about the audience:

> In performing before a Melbourne audience, Miss Hayes underwent a more trying ordeal than any to which she has been exposed since leaving the great cities of the Atlantic. The society of this city has for principal ingredient a class who have fresh in their recollection the merits of such artists as Jenny Lind, Grisi, and Viardot-Garcia – this is the case to a far greater extent than in Sydney, where the population is mainly composed of older colonists, who generally have not had such an opportunity instituting comparisons; but in the face of an audience capable of criticism, the Swan of Erin comes from her trial with unruffled plumage.

The physical changes that had taken place in the theatre when the contract with Catherine was signed were then described in detail:

> The lessees had certainly made the most of the little time allowed them to effect preparations suitable for the occasion. On Friday night, at twelve o'clock when the curtain fell, the appearance of the interior of the theatre was as ordinarily is the case, but by the next evening, an immense change had taken place. The marbled pillars of the proscenium had disappeared, and instead appeared on each side two private boxes, elegantly decorated with hangings of yellow silk. Over the seats of the pit, next to the stage, and on each side of the

house, an omnibus-box commanding a full view of the stage, had been erected, reserving sufficient space beneath for the occupants of the seats in the pit to see everything that passed. The house throughout has undergone a thorough cleaning.[18]

Obviously the arrival of Catherine Hayes had made a very significant impact on the community and her first night concert had turned into the major event of the season. There was also a report on the reception she received:

Miss Hayes was received with a demonstration of applause that shook the wall of the building, and its enthusiastic nature was evidently appreciated by her. The scene by her for her *debut,* and the first note, which issued from her lips was sufficient to command [and] silence the most profound. The most competent critics in the world having pronounced favorably [sic] upon the quality and capacity of her voice, we shall not, did we feel so inclined, attempt to throw a doubt upon the verdict. That Miss Hayes is a perfect mistress of her art there cannot be a doubt: the brilliant *fiorituiri* which distinguished her rendering of the lovely aria, 'Ah! bello a me ritorna,' being sufficient of itself to satisfy the most skeptical [sic] in that particular. The delicate *sotto voce* warbling was a very effective point, and her shake is made without effort, and is decided, more especially when it falls upon any of her middle notes, which are decidedly the best of her voice. Her compass is said to be most extensive, ranging indeed from A to D in alto, and her intonation is faultless. Her audience during the scene appeared spellbound, and at its conclusion gave vent to their rapture in peals of the most boisterous applause. An encore was lustily shouted, and the fair cantatrice after having left the stage returned and bowed her acknowledgement of the honor.[19]

Catherine continued with various songs and arias in between solos by a bassoonist called Winterbottem. She also sang duets with Emil Coulon, the bass-baritone. At the concert's conclusion there was an interesting description of how Catherine and Bushnell handled the continuing applause for her reappearance:

As she retired, bouquets were seen flying from all parts of the house; and seldom or never have the walls of the theatre echoed to such thunderous applause. Prior to the National Anthem being performed by the band, Mr. Bushnell, Miss Hayes's agent, stepped forward and having thanked the audience in the lady's name for the enthusiastic manner in which she had been received on her first appearance in Melbourne, announced that her second concert would take place on Tuesday. A call was raised for Miss Hayes, but it was not so general as it would no doubt have been had the audience remained in their places. Many, however being under the impression that the fair vocalist had left the house, had also retired. The call continuing, Miss Hayes came forward and silence having been obtained with some difficulty, she thanked the audience for the enthusiastic reception with which she had been met in this her first appearance in Melbourne, and added that she hoped she might still continue to meet their approbation. A little hesitation in the latter part of the sentence caused a smile, but the graceful manner in which Miss Hayes conveyed to the audience that she was at a loss for a word, secured her a round of applause that many a more proficient orator would have given his ears to obtain. An immense crowd had gathered outside the theatre to witness the departure of Miss Hayes.

We should have mentioned earlier that Miss Hayes was dressed with very great taste and splendor [sic]. The wavy masses of her beautiful sunburn [auburn] hair were entwined with a very elegant wreath of bright colored artificial flowers. Her dress was of a rich pink water silk, and both her neck and arms absolutely blazed with diamonds of great brilliancy, and evidently of considerable value. Her first appearance in Melbourne was a complete success; and we have no doubt that here as in Sydney, the enthusiasm which she creates will but increase at each of her appearances in public.[20]

Catherine and her party stayed in Melbourne performing in costumed scenes from operas in addition to regular concerts until the end of November 1854. During this time, the American photographer, Perez M. Batchelder of 57 Collins Street, announced that 'Catherine Hayes had permitted him to represent her in a daguerreotype and in costume as Marie in the beautiful opera the *Daughter of the Regiment.*'[21] It was also announced at the same time that:

a bust of the lady [Catherine Hayes], half life-size is in preparation at Huxley and Parker's, Little Collins Street. The sculpture is by Mr.

J[ames] Gilbert. The likeness is a most pleasing and faithful one. It is probable that these casts will have an extensive sale, Miss Hayes' countless admirers will find one of these busts a most agreeable souvenir of the lady's visit to Melbourne.[22]

Tasmania now wanted her to visit Hobart and give concerts there. She was offered a sum of £400 per night for concerts. Meanwhile, the town of Geelong, which is not far from Melbourne, was also interested in hearing her – she gave one concert there during the third week in November before travelling on to Adelaide.

Bushnell had now made plans for them to visit Calcutta, in India, which was one of the furthest outposts of the British Empire. Calcutta, which was dominated by the British Army, had been on the circuit for theatrical performers from Australia for several years. Catherine, her mother, Bushnell and Lavenu all boarded *SS Norna* of the P & O Line in Adelaide in early December. The captain was so impressed with having Catherine on board that Bushnell was able to persuade him to delay the sailing for a day so that she could give a concert. The captain agreed, and so Catherine added another city to her schedule.[23]

Despite its remotenesst, Calcutta had a strong social culture among the British Army personnel stationed there. There were many Irish in the ranks also. It is not known if Catherine and her party stopped anywhere on the way to India, but on 4 February 1855 a concert featuring Catherine was advertised at the Town Hall, Calcutta for Saturday 10 February as a benefit for the Patriotic Fund, which was under the patronage of the Governor-General.

Louis Lavenu was the accompanist for the programme, which included arias by Bellini. For the first time she sang the mezzo-soprano aria 'Che faro senza Euridice' from Gluck's opera *Orfeo ed Euridice*. This apparently was sung by special request, which is probably how she acquired the music for the piece. It also shows her musicality and ability to learn new pieces, even for such a remote audience. She also sang 'Regnava nel silenzio' from *Lucia di Lammermoor*, followed by 'Rule Britannia', probably also in response to another request. The concert ended with her accompanist Louis Lavenu joining her in the comic duet 'Signorina, in tanta a fretta' from *Don Pasquale* by Donizetti. The programme explained Lavenu's participation, saying that 'Mr. Lavenu most kindly offered to sing the part of Don Pasquale in order to enable Miss Hayes to appear in this celebrated role.'[24]

Louis Lavenu had come a long way and was certainly adaptable, when one considers that fourteen years earlier he had been manager and conductor for Franz Liszt's concerts in Dublin, where the very young and inexperienced, Catherine Hayes had her first exposure to Donizetti's music.

Bushnell, always in control, had insisted that all seats be numbered with a corresponding number on the ticket, even though the main seating was armchairs. He wanted no confusion or disorderly conduct from possible latecomers which might disrupt the opening of the concert.

Another concert was announced for Friday 16 February, which was billed as her last before departing for Singapore and returning to Australia. Obviously, India did not offer her the financial or cultural rewards she had been expecting, so she had elected to return to Australia. This last concert was interesting, particularly in terms of the 'cultural vacuum' of British India at that time, as expressed by one of its members. 'A Lover of Music' had written a letter to the editor of the local newspaper, which said:

> The Programme for Miss Catherine Hayes' last concert, which is to come off tomorrow evening, consisting chiefly of operatic pieces, which, however attractive in themselves, will not certainly be understood by the majority of those who will be present. The only English song is to be 'Rule Britannia' and I would suggest that Miss Hayes should give us in addition that beautiful piece composed by Mrs. Hermans – 'The Landing of the Pilgrim Fathers in New England.' Sung by Miss Hayes it will possess superior attraction, and it is to be hoped that she will, ere she departs from these shores, comply with the solution of – A Lover of Music. February 15, 1855.[25]

Catherine had no plans to change her programme to satisfy one music lover, or for that matter the rest of the audience. The programme remained as planned, all operatic except for 'Rule Britannia'. Lavenu even sang Dulcamara's buffo aria from Donizetti's *L'elisir d'Amore*. Catherine finished her programme by giving the audience 'a strong blast of the best of Italian culture' Incredible as it may seem, she performed the 'Celebrated Mad Scene' from Donizetti's *Lucia di Lammermoor*, complete and in costume! This performance lasted almost twenty minutes, featuring some of Donizetti's greatest music. She also added an orchestra to enhance the effect.[26] The 'orchestra' probably consisted of members of the local military bands, with Lavenu conducting.

It almost seemed that in some way her Irish character was roused by the stuffy British audience of the previous concert – she wanted to convey to the members of this remote colony that there was music a lot better than 'Rule Britannia', and she did it with gusto and style! As she, Bushnell and Lavenu left for Singapore, they probably had some amusing memories of their finale in Calcutta.

Historically her performance of this music was also very significant. It is almost certain that no other soprano of Catherine's experience and background had ever performed Lucia's music to an audience in Calcutta before 1855.

They arrived in Singapore on 7 March on the steamer *SS Chusan*. One of the local newspapers announced, the arrival 'from Calcutta, [of] Mrs. Hayes, Miss Catherine Hayes, Messers Bushnell and Lavenu . . .'[27] Bushnell was able to get one of the leading newspapers to publish an extensive biography of Catherine's life and career in their 15 March issue.[28]

Her concert was scheduled for Monday 19 March in the Public Rooms. The press complained about the high ticket prices compared to 'ordinary Singapore rates' but stated that, despite the high cost of admission, the concert drew a large audience. They also agreed that her singing lived up to expectations. Here, unlike Calcutta, she performed a strong mixture of Irish, Scottish and English songs. The reviewer expressed the opinion that, 'Altogether the evening was one of rare enjoyment for the community of Singapore, who will not forget the sweet notes of the Irish Nightingale.'[29]

They left Singapore on 26 March on a Dutch steamer bound for Batavia (Java), arriving there in the middle of April. A group of French singers were performing opera at the Théâtre Français de Batavia on their arrival. Catherine was invited to sing the complete opera *Lucia di Lammermoor* on 20 April. The artists who joined her in these performances included a tenor called Allard and a baritone by the name of St. Denis. The press carried an extensive biography of her achievements, similar to that published in Singapore, except that it was written in Dutch.[30] In addition, two poems dedicated to her, one in Dutch, the other in French, were published in the local press.[31] Later a poem in English was published to mark her departure from the colony. Her fame apparently had reached the Dutch East Indies ahead of her visit.

Her party stayed for about six weeks in Batavia, where she performed in *Norma*, *Don Pasquale* and *La Sonnambula*, in addition to giving several concerts. Other singers who participated in these performances were tenor M. Duchaumoni and bass M. Feraud. All of these performances were conducted by Louis Lavenu.

29. Sheet music cover for the song 'Molly Asthore' composed by Louis Lavenu for Catherine Hayes in Australia 1855. (Author's collection).

She was the guest of the Governor of the colony, enjoying many privileges not normally offered to the local society, such as being the guest of honour at a ball and other functions. She thoroughly enjoyed herself, possibly because of the warmth of Dutch hospitality when compared to the British colonies she had just left. Many years later she specifically referred to her stay in Batavia as a fond memory.

On her departure, the Governor made his private boat available to bring her out to the steamer for Australia. Coincidental with her departure the Batavia French Opera were about to mount Meyerbeer's opera *Robert le Diable* and Rossini's *Otello*, both works Catherine had learned in Europe. The press gave her a good send-off with lots of coverage and a 'Vaarwel' (Farewell) poem dedicated to her, this time in Dutch – with the hope that it might be adapted to the music of one of Thomas Moore's songs and sung by the prima donna!

At the end of June she arrived back in Melbourne. She was still irritated by her reception in Calcutta, and was publicly quite vocal about it on her return to Melbourne. The Melbourne press reported that she had 'sung in wild places to imperfectly refined audiences'.[32]

She sang in several concerts in Melbourne over the next few weeks, and also gave a charity concert for the victims of a bad storm, that had devastated a suburb of Melbourne. Late in July, she departed for Sydney for more concerts and also with the idea of setting up an opera company.

At the Prince of Wales Theatre, Sydney, in August she initiated a season of opera, complete with chorus, orchestra and various local artists. This commenced with *La Sonnambula*, then came *Norma* and after that, for the first time, Balfe's *Bohemian Girl*, which was sung in English. During the *Norma* performance, she had to stop singing due to a heavy cold, which meant that she probably should have cancelled the performance. In typically early nineteenth-century fashion, the mezzo-soprano Sara Flower (who Catherine knew from Milan, where Flower was a member of the English student community), who was singing the tenor role Pollione, took over Catherine's part and completed the opera, presumably minus a tenor! When Flower was announced as the replacement, there were hisses and boos from the audience. Later Flower also substituted for Catherine at a Philharmonic concert. Clearly Catherine had been pushing herself too much and this was taking its toll.

Feeling better in late September, she changed her plans and returned to Melbourne, where her return was celebrated with a series of concerts. It was her intention to duplicate her Sydney activities by organising an

MISS CATHERINE HAYES

Has the honor to announce that her *last* and
FAREWELL CONCERT,

In Calcutta (previous to her departure on the 20th
instant, for Singapore, *en route* to Australia,) will
take place in the
TOWN HALL,
On Friday Evening, February 16th, 1855.

On which occasion a most *choice Program* will be
given, *including the celebrated*

MAD SCENE

From Donizetti's favorite Opera of
LUCIA DE LAMMERMOOR.

Single Ticket, Reserved Seats, .. Rs. 15
Family Ticket, for 3 persons, Reserved Seats, „ 30
    „   for 5 persons, .. „ „ 40
Single Ticket, to Unreserved Seats, .. „ 6
Tickets for the Concert can be procured at the
Office, Spence's Hotel, and the Town Hall, in the
evening.

The Reserved Seats will be all arm chairs, numbered
with figures corresponding to those on the Tickets
purchased.

Doors open 8 o'clock, Concert will commence at 8½.

30. The announcement of Catherine Hayes's farewell concert, February 1855, in Calcutta,
India at which she sang 'The Mad Scene' from Lucia di Lammermoor. (Author's collection).

opera company and giving performances of her favourite roles. This time
she had a new theatre to work with and better luck. Her first opera was
Bellini's *La Sonnambula*, which she performed at the Theatre Royal on 25
October. The English press, following her activities now that she was back
in the colonies, reported through one of its representatives in Melbourne:

> Her entrance was the signal for a tumultuous burst of applause of
> cheering. She looked remarkably well, and the enthusiastic reception
> which greeted her in this first theatre of the Southern Hemisphere,
> on her first performance in real opera within its walls, appeared to
> afford her much gratification.[33]

Bellini's pastoral opera was followed by *Lucia di Lammermoor*, *Norma*
and *L'elisir d'Amore*. Then for the second time she decided to give a
performance of Balfe's *Bohemian Girl*, which she again sang in English.
The critics felt that she was out of her element in English opera, which
was probably true. However, it would have been wonderful to hear
Catherine sing Balfe's beautiful melody – perhaps the most famous ballad
in all nineteenth-century English opera – 'I dreamt I dwelt in marble halls'
that night in Melbourne in 1855. She never again sang the opera or the
ballad anywhere.

During the rest of November she repeated her earlier operas, adding
only Donizetti's *Lucrezia Borgia* to her performances. Melbourne during
this period was short of tenors. In fact, it was not uncommon, outside of
the major European cities to have a mezzo-soprano or contralto sing the
tenor part. Catherine's 'tenor' for *The Bohemian Girl* was Madame
Carandini, and for *Norma* the mezzo-soprano Sara Flower again sang the
tenor part of Pollione, while Carandini this time sang the mezzo role of
Adalgisa.

Immediately after Christmas, Catherine set off for the Bendigo gold
fields to give concerts for the 'diggers'. After returning briefly to
Melbourne in the New Year she departed for Hobart, Tasmania, arriving
there on 23 January 1856. She continued to keep up an exhausting
schedule, usually giving about four concerts weekly, in between travel
time and occasionally being ill.

She and Bushnell by this time were probably lovers. They had been
together continually for almost four years, in hotels, on boats and on
various other modes of transportation. She depended on him completely,
and he never seemed to let her down. Their relationship as lovers

Afscheidsgroete.

Indië verlatende, roep ik mijnen krijgskameraden een hartelijk vaarwel toe! Mijn trots is het te kunnen zeggen, ruim 29 jaren bij het leger te hebben gediend. Zij ontvangen dan ook de beste wenschen op hunne zoo moeijelijke, edoch schoono en eervolle loupbaan van hun aller ouden krijgskameraad.

(720) J. B. J. SUTHERLAND.

Théâtre Français de *Batavia.*

Première représentation de

Miss CATHERINE HAYES.

Avec le concours de la Compagnie Française, sous la direction de MM. *van Kinsberghe* et *Ad. Potier.*

ABONNEMENT SUSPENDU.

Vendredi, 20 Avril 1855.

Une représentation de

LUCIE DE LAMMERMOOR,

Grand opéra en 4 actes, musique de *Donizetti.*

Miss **CATHERINE HAYES** remplira le rôle de **Lucie.**

L'orchestre sera dirigé par M. **Lavenu.**

PRIX DES PLACES:

Un cavalier non-abonné *f* 10.—. Une dame *f* 6.—. Messieurs les abonnés du théâtre *f* 8.— par personne, les Dames *f* 6.—. Messieurs les officiers jusqu'au grade de capitaine inclusivement *f* 6.—. Messieurs les employes au-dessous de *f* 200.— d'appointements *f* 6.—. Les enfants au-dessous de 10 ans *f* 3.—.

On pourra retenir des places et prendre des billets à l'avance pour les représentantions de Miss *Catherine Hayes,* chez MM. *van Kinsberghe* et *Ad. Potier,* à Rijswijk, à dater de Mercredi 18 et les jours suivants, et Vendredi 20 au Théâtre, depuis 7 heures du matin jusqu'à 1 heure de relevée.

Messieurs les abonnés qui désirent conserver leurs places marquées, sont priés de le faire savoir avant le jour de la représentation au matin; passé ce delai on en disposera.

Le Spectacle commencera à 7 heures précises. (725)

---

31. Catherine Hayes performed *Lucia di Lammermoor* at the French Theatre in Batavia (Java) in April 1855. (Author's collection).

probably started when they arrived in Sydney, where they shared rooms close to each other in Petty's Hotel. Although he was still technically married and had a wife in Connecticut, whom he hadn't seen for several years, in this far off location he clearly felt closer to Catherine, who understood him intimately and emotionally.

Catherine's life had changed greatly since they first met. She was now 38 years old, sometimes feeling weary. He was only 33 and always overflowing with energy. She depended on him for everything. If she had been alone, she would never have made the daring travel plans which he had organised and executed so capably, and which had been so remunerative. She had never experienced this type of a relationship with any other man. While she had been attracted to Sims Reeves, that relationship now would have seemed frivolous and youthful compared to how she felt about William Avery Bushnell.

Catherine seemed to have achieved everything she had set out to do. She was a world famous singer, she was successful everywhere she went. She had achieved financial security, having saved a large amount of money from her earnings. She also had the warmth and security of a strong male companion, and she was able to take care of her mother, who always travelled with her and who was now 56 years old. She also financially supproted her sister Henrietta, who was unmarried and living either in England or in America.

Catherine probably wondered if some day she and Bushnell would be able to get married. How long the relationship could last, however, was very uncertain, as by this time Bushnell was beginning to suffer from the early effects of tuberculoseis, one of the dreaded incurable diseases of the nineteenth century. There is some doubt as to whether or not they even recognised it for what it was, as their hectic travel and performance schedule continued unabated, and he was virtually always at her side.

Catherine's first concert in Hobart took place on the day of her arrival, Wednesday 23 January 1856, at the Royal Victoria Theatre. Advance notices appeared in the paper. As her first number, she sang 'Casta Diva' from *Norma*, following this with her usual repertoire of Irish and Scottish songs and Bellini and Donizetti arias. John Gregg, a baritone, and a Mr. Lyall, a tenor, shared the stage with her. Strangely, Louis Lavenu did not participate; perhaps he too was sick.

Catherine received the usual rave reviews, with special praise for her rendering of 'Savourneen Deelish'. It was impossible for her to resist a requested encore, for which she sang 'Oh! Steer my bark to Erin's Isle'.[34]

32. Playbill for *The Bohemian Girl* in Melbourne Australia 1855 featuring Catherine Hayes (Courtesy of La Trobe Picture Collection, State Library of Victoria, Australia).

The next concert also took place at the Royal Victoria Theatre, attended by:

> all the Members of the Legislative Council, who mustered in full force, and added the weight of their influence to the otherwise fashionable and crowded attendance. And we might mention that even upon her arrival at the theatre the Swan of Erin was received by between two and three hundred persons, who vociferously cheered her upon alighting from her carriage.[35]

Shortly after this concert a controversy broke out regarding all of the concerts being held at the Royal Victoria Theatre, presumably because it was too small to accommodate all of the people who wanted to attend. The writer suggested that any move to change the location to the Governor's House, as had occurred in Batavia, would be inappropriate and possibly illegal.[36]

For the third concert, it appears the problem was ignored, or resolved, as there was no further mention of moving the concerts to the Governor's House. At this concert, Catherine changed her programme, performing Weber's grand scene 'Softly sighs the voice of Evening' from *Der Freischutz*, a very dramatic aria which she had not performed in a number of years. She followed this with a new Irish ballad, 'I'm sitting on a stile Mary', and with 'Qui la voce' from Bellini's *I Puritani*. After several other songs she closed the evening with the mad scene from *Lucia di Lammermoor*. This was quite a change from her usual concert programme and was certainly a most strenuous evening for any vocalist. The reviewer concluded with:

> The curtain had no sooner fallen than the theatre rang with cheers for the gifted lady who had so enchanted a crowded audience during the evening. These cheers were rendered with heartier good will after the announcement made by Mr. Bushnell, that Miss Hayes would give a fourth concert on Friday evening next. A large concourse of people assembled to witness her departure from the theatre.[37]

She had to cancel her next concert because she was ill. The same day the notice of cancellation appeared, the newspaper also featured a poem dedicated to her.[38]

For her final concert on 5 February she and her two partners, Lyall and Gregg performed a concert version of *La Sonnambula* in English which was rapturously received by all present. The newspapers report said:

Miss Hayes, who was literally besieged with bouquets throughout the operatic selections, reaped a splendid ovation at the close, and was then twice called before the curtain to receive the congratulations of a delighted audience, which filled the house with deafening cheers.[39]

Catherine gave concerts in Campbell Town and Launceston and then she and Bushnell and her mother took time off in Hobart before returning to Melbourne on 22 April. For the next three months, Catherine spent her time performing in Melbourne, including an important concert for the Melbourne Hospital which resulted in a large donation.[40] The hospital committee named one of the wards after her, since she had contributed almost £600, a significant amount of money in those days. The building was demolished in the 1950s.

She set sail for Liverpool, from Sydney on the yacht *Royal Charter* around the middle of July, giving a concert on board before her departure at which her friend Louis Lavenu officiated. Large crowds came to Circular Quay to see her off. She would never again visit Australia, and never again see Lavenu, who was now a resident of Sydney where he was to become an important musical figure. He died there in August 1859 at the age of 42 years old and is buried in Newtown cemetery.

Her visit to Australia is recorded in most books describing the early days in the colony. She was the first major European operatic star to perform in Sydney in the nineteenth century. She was also the first Manuel Garcia pupil to sing in Australia. After her came a long line of legendary names who were students of the Garcia/Marchesi school of singing, including singers such as Nellie Melba and Joan Sutherland.

CHAPTER THIRTEEN

The Hibernian Prima Donna Returns

ENGLAND AND IRELAND 1856–1860

THE *Royal Charter* arrived in Liverpool the second week in August 1856. It appears that the ship had taken the westerly route from Australia to England, which in effect meant that Catherine had circumnavigated the globe, an amazing journey in the middle of the nineteenth-century. Such an accomplishment was indicative of her character and determination.

It had been five years since Catherine had left England and much had changed in her life. Bushnell and her mother accompanied her. Newspapers in London and Dublin announced her arrival at Liverpool. In Dublin an article appeared on 14 August saying:

RETURN OF CATHERINE HAYES.

This celebrated Irish vocalist – of whom Dublin public justly feels proud, since her first triumphs were attained in our midst – has just arrived in Liverpool from Australia by the 'Royal Charter.' On 5th and 12th of May, she gave two Farewell Concerts in the Exhibition Building, Melbourne, which were most numerously attended. On the eve of her departure she was waited upon by the Committee of the Melbourne Hospital, for the purpose of presenting her with an address, engrossed on vellum, and handsomely framed, expressive of the subscribers' gratitude to this eminent vocalist for her munificent [sic] to that excellent institution.[1]

As Catherine made her way to London, she had mixed feelings about her return there. She had never felt comfortable in the London musical environment, despite the excellent reviews she had always received. She and Bushnell, who continued to have health problems, talked about going back to America, where she knew she would be very welcome.

Shortly after her arrival in London there was mention in the press that she would leave again for America at the end of the year. It was also stated that her sister was in residence in America and that Catherine planned to visit her. However, it is not in fact clear if Henrietta Hayes remained behind in New York after Catherine left for San Francisco in October 1852. We do know that she did not accompany Catherine and her party, which included their mother, to California. It's possible that she may have extended her stay with P.T. Barnum in the New York area. Henrietta's name was not on the passenger lists of ships departing for England between October and December 1852.

If in fact Henrietta Hayes spent a number of years in America while Catherine was in Australia and other places, this is the only possible connection that might support a claim by two well known American ladies of the theatre. Actress Helen Hayes and Metropolitan Opera soprano Dorothy Kirsten both claimed, in their respective biographies,[2] that Catherine Hayes was a great-grand-aunt. The evidence, however, would suggest that even if Henrietta Hayes did stay behind in America for a few years that she never married. When Catherine married in London in 1857, Henrietta signed her last name as 'Hayes' as a witness to the wedding ceremony. Therefore the claim of the two distinguished twentieth-century American artistes would appear to be more fantasy than fact, since Catherine never had any children either.

When Catherine arrived in London, she was to find that many things had changed. The Covent Garden theatre where she had made her London debut over seven years earlier had burned down the previous March.[3] It would take another two years before it was rebuilt. Public taste had changed considerably and Verdi's music was now much more popular than in previous years. His operas were playing in London and elsewhere.

Catherine knew that if she planned to resume her concert or operatic career she would need a new manager. The dominant London artists' management company was still Cramer & Beale. However, Catherine was a 'persona non grata' with them because of the 1852 New York lawsuit. Apart from Bushnell's health problems, he did not have the skills to operate in the London scene, it was far too sophisticated. As a result, she sought the advice of her long-time friend and mentor, George Osborne at the Royal Academy of Music, who recommended a well established concert agent,

J. Mitchell, of Old Bond Street. Mitchell also managed the conductor and composer Julius Benedict during this period and occasionally Jenny Lind. Early in September the London musical press announced that:

> The Hibernian Prima Donna is about to leave London for Paris and will probably return to America this winter. The artistic voyage round the world of this artiste is the most extraordinary ever undertaken by any singer.[4]

A week later there was a further announcement to the effect that Catherine had arrived in Paris, where a full season of opera was in progress at various locations, including a performance of Balfe's *Falstaff*, directed by the composer himself. There were also plans to perform Verdi's *Rigoletto* and *La Traviata*, two of the composer's most important new works.

Catherine went to Paris accompanied by George Osborne and her mother. She felt she needed some rest and Osborne had suggested Paris since he was scheduled to be there during September. She also needed to think about her relationship with Bushnell, as, if she was to be resident in London, the fact that he was still legally married could create problems. She did not want any scandals. She had to decide whether she wanted to continue to live in London, the capital of the musical world in Europe. Ireland was not an option for her if she wanted to continue her musical career, as Ireland's operatic and concert seasons were very limited, not to mention the low fees.

When Catherine arrived in Paris the 64-year-old Gioacchino Rossini was in Passy, a western suburb of the city, endeavouring to decide on a location for a new home. It was during this visit that Catherine met Rossini for the first or maybe even the second time, as he was in Italy when she was there in the 1840s. Either Osborne or Balfe introduced them or perhaps brought her to one of Rossini's 'musical afternoons'. Both Balfe and Osborne were close friends of Rossini. Catherine made only one very brief reference to having been in the great maestro's presence, but did not pass any comments on the meeting.

She stayed in Paris until the middle of October, and shortly before her thirty-eighth birthday she returned to London, having made up her mind that she would go back to full-time work. Mitchell her concert agent had in the meantime come to an arrangement with the concert organiser Louis Antoine Jullien (1812–60) for Catherine to sing on the opening night of his autumn concert series at Her Majesty's Theatre on 5 November. Jullien advertised the concert with his usual flair and extravagant manner:

CATHERINE HAYES – Wednesday, November 5 – M. Jullien has the honour to announce that with the obliging consent of the invaluable aid of J. Mitchell, Esq., he has succeeded in effecting an engagement for a few nights with the renowned cantatrice, Catherine Hayes, being her first appearance in Europe since her return from an unprecedented artistic tour in Asia, Africa, and America, Australia, Peru, Mexico, California, the Brazils, East and West Indies, United States, Canada and Russia. The burning tropics and the cold of the north have confirmed her triumphs. To her natural endowment and artistic excellence, she now arrives with a rich store of national melodies, Italian, French, Spanish, German, Dutch, Irish, English, and Scotch.[5]

Of course, Catherine's travels, however extraordinary, never included places such as Brazil, the West Indies or Russia. It is possible the ship did stop at one of the South African ports (the Suez canal had not yet been constructed) when returning from Australia, which would support M. Jullien's claim that she had visited Africa.

Jullien was a strange man. He was born in France, studied music there and after trying various occupations left France for London around 1839 where he got a job conducting concerts. He also engaged in an English-language operatic venture in the late 1840s, at Drury Lane theatre, which failed. Later, as part of a scheme to bring music to the masses, he started his 'Monster' concerts, which combined 400 instrumentalists with large choral groups, military bands and soloists. His ambitions afterwards took him to America, where he toured extensively before returning to France. His overall lack of true success apparently troubled him emotionally. Becoming insane over what he perceived to be his failures, he eventually took his own life.

Catherine's first concert, on 5 November, went very well. Her programme included much of what she had been singing for several years – the Meyerbeer *Le Prophète* aria, Alary's vocal 'Polka' from his opera *Le tre nozzi*, and Irish and Scottish songs. Jullien conducted. The programme was dominated by the orchestral pieces.

Catherine did not seem to have her heart in her performance, she was obviously having problems adjusting to her new environment. One review of the concert reflected on the level of expectation arising out of her appearance:

... the house was crammed to the ceiling, despite the fact that seats had been added to the orchestra pit to make room for the extra demand for tickets.

Two more concerts followed on 17 and 18 November. For one of these concerts she sang the grand scena from Weber's *Der Freischutz*, 'Agathe's Aria' – a ten minute musical scene that ends dramatically which she sang in English. This was followed by 'Casta Diva' from *Norma* and several songs, including one, 'The fisherman's return', specially composed for her by George Osborne for the occasion. The reviewer in the London *Times* said

> Last night Miss Hayes made her last appearance but one (to night being her 'farewell') and delighted the audience beyond measure in the highly dramatic scena of 'Agathe' from Weber's *Der Freischutz*. To this well known cosmopolitan [audience] she imparted a reading of her own, differing in a great measure from the majority of her more eminent contemporaries.[6]

Two additional concerts took place, during which she varied her programme considerably. Obviously Catherine was beginning to adjust to her London surroundings as her performance had energy and her professionalism came through. The audience were delighted:

> The applause was in every instance vociferous, and the vocalist was additionally complimented by discharges of wreaths and bouquets.[7]

After this Catherine set off on a provincial concert tour, which would take her to various parts of England and then back to Scotland and Ireland for the first time in many years. Her first stop was Brighton on the English south-east coast, after which she went to eight other English towns. She then changed her plan for travelling up to Scotland. Anxious instead to get back to Ireland, she crossed over to Belfast for her first return concert in Ireland at the Music Hall on 10 December. She went on by rail to Dublin to perform at the Antient Concert Rooms on Friday 12 December 1856.

She was accompanied by Lablache's son, Frederick, a bass-baritone, Charles Braham, tenor, a Mlle. Corelli, contralto, and the great cellist and composer Carlo Alfredo Piatti (1822–1901) now in possession of the S.J. Pigott Stradivarius (1720) violoncello – Pigott having died in 1853. Also in the group was the violinist and composer Wilhelm Ernst (1814–65).

George Osborne was the accompanist and conductor. A report on her return to Dublin said:

> Last night, at the Antient Concert Rooms, an Irish girl, whose fame has become worldwide, again stood before an Irish audience, after an eventful absence of some six years or more. It was about as much before that when Catherine Hayes left this [city], unknown almost in her own country. Her appearance is less natural, indeed, but still unfaded; her voice and singing unchanged.[8]

Following this concert in Dublin, she travelled first to Cork and then to Limerick for concerts. While in Cork she contributed to a testimonial function which recognised the work of her long-time friend Father Theobald Mathew. She then went on to Belfast, giving two concerts there on 15 and 16 December.

There was concern among the Belfast audience about the price of the tickets, according to the local press reviews. Despite this, the first concert was completely sold out. Reviews which followed clearly showed that Catherine was still in good vocal estate:

> Miss Catherine Hayes then amazed the audience with the clear, pure, mellifluent and magnificently exercised voice with which she sang the Meyerbeer aria 'Ah! mon fils,' – from Meyerbeer's *Le Prophète*. Nothing could be more eloquent than what we might call the impassioned spirit with which she inundated [sic], so to speak, the great area of her auditory. When she had come to a close, loud applause greeted her from all parts of the hall, and she had scarcely [sic] from the orchestra when she was recalled, and had the hearty applause 'of the house,' so to speak showered on her.[9]

The second and last concert in Belfast took place with equal success. Catherine ended 1856 feeling comfortable on her native terrain. Bushnell's whereabouts during this time are unknown. There was no mention of him in relation to the concert arrangements or in reviews.

In January she was active again with concerts in Dublin on 14 January with the Philharmonic Society at the Antient Concert Rooms, with the Lord Lieutenant of Ireland present; more concerts followed on 15 and 17 January, at the Rotunda. She returned to Belfast to give 'Farewell Concerts' on 26 and 30 January, when it was announced that it was 'the last time she would appear professionally in the northern [Irish] city'.[10] It was further announced in the local press that:

The public are respectfully, assured that this will be the last opportunity of hearing Miss Hayes in Belfast, as she will not again visit Ireland professionally.[11]

During the holidays, Catherine and Bushnell had made up their minds to get married in 1857. Bushnell, of course, would first have to get a divorce from his wife in Connecticut, which meant travelling to America.

While in Ireland Catherine had made an agreement with Mr. Harris, the manager of the Theatre Royal in Dublin, to perform in a series of Italian operas to be given in March. Meantime, she went to Liverpool, where she gave a concert on 24 February. Joining her were the same singers who had toured with her in Ireland, except for Frederick Lablache, who had left the group. She then went on to Manchester, where she performed three concerts at the new Free Trade Hall, the last on 28 February, and where one critic stated:

> Miss Hayes again evidenced to us, that in the ultra-expressive school she has no rival! . . . Her rendering of the fine old song 'Savourneen Deelish,' will live long in the memories of those present.[12]

After Manchester, she made a one-day stop in Bradford for a concert before returning to Liverpool to take the overnight boat to Dublin; however, before doing so, she gave another series of concerts at St. George's Hall, the last one on 13 March.

Her planned operatic season in Dublin was announced at the end of February, with six operas scheduled – all Donizetti works, with one exception. These included *Norma*, *Lucrezia Borgia*, *La figlia del reggimento*, *Don Pasquale* and *Linda di Chamounix*. While not announced initially, *Lucia di Lammermoor* subsequently became the performance for the opening night, Monday 16 March. Ticket prices were increased dramatically for these performances,[13] ranging from up to five guineas (five pounds five shillings) for a private box to one shilling in the upper gallery.[14] Her partners included some newcomers to Dublin a baritone from La Scala, Cesare Badiale (1810–65), and a tenor called Volpini. Included in the troupe was a young Italian-trained English tenor, W.J. Tennant, whom Catherine knew from her days in Milan. The programme was expanded to include Bellini's *La Sonnambula*, with the first performance of this opera scheduled for 2 April 1857.

The opening night had all the splendour of her previous visits. The Lord Lieutenant of Ireland and many members of the nobility and gentry were present. The reviews gave her high praise for the supporting cast, and stated the following about her vocal and acting performance:

> Miss Hayes realized to the full the idea of the love-lorn maiden driven to frenzy by the pressure of her intense misery. Robed in flowing white garments, her hair dishevelled, she rushes on the stage, her face wearing the vacant smile that speaks of reason fled forever. Miss Hayes's acting in this trying scena was perfect, and her singing through out [sic] a prolonged series of impassioned passages was, if we may use the expression, painfully impressive and beautiful. She was heard in deep silence by the audience, who seemed, as it were, to fear to break the saddening spell of her voice as it warbled snatches of long-remembered melodies. The effect was thrilling, as the gifted actress and vocalist sank on the stage and was born off in the arms of attendants, peels [sic] of cheering again and again greeted her success.[15]

All of her performances were highly praised during this season at the Theatre Royal. She also added an unscheduled performance of *La Sonnambula* to the list on 2 April, Handel's *Messiah* on 6 April and Rossini's *Stabat Mater* on 7 April together with selections from Haydn's *Creation*. This was an incredible schedule by any standard.

One reviewer made some interesting comments on her dramatic portrayal of *Norma*, following the 25 March performance:

> We were particularly struck with the force and truth of her acting in the chamber scene, where Norma is so stung by jealous frenzy as to contemplate the murder of her sleeping children. She was also highly effective in the concluding scenes. Her opening solo, 'Casta Diva' was finely given; but her voice seemed to soar to its highest excellence in the grand scena with Pollio[ne] in the second act. Her rendering of the passionate outburst, 'non tremare O perfido!' told with electric effect.[16]

A benefit concert in Dublin on 4 April was reported in the London musical press as follows:

> The benefit of Miss Catherine Hayes, on Saturday evening, was one of those flattering demonstrations of admiration and respect which exalted genius only has a right to expect, and which, when justly merited, the Dublin public is ever ready to concede. The house was an

overflowing bumper, in the fullest sense of the term . . . The Lord
Lieutenant arrived shortly after eight o'clock, accompanied by Lady
Fanny Howard and a brilliant suite . . . A large white banner, wreathed
with laurels and shamrocks, and inscribed with the name of the fair
vocalist, was waved from the upper gallery, and subsequently, on Miss
Hayes's appearance, and on her concluding one of the melodies, a
wreath of flowers and shamrocks, with an address appended by white
satin ribbon, was thrown at her feet. The fair cantatrice gracefully
acknowledged the compliment, amidst thunders of applause, in which
the occupants of the pit and box circles emphatically joined.[17]

At the end of her concert, she sang the quaint Bishop air, 'Home, sweet
Home', the words of which were particularly appropriate for the
sentiment of the occasion. The tradition of singing this simple Bishop
song at the close of a concert, or a career, has continued into the
twentieth century.

Linda di Chamounix followed on 28 March. *Lucrezia Borgia* was next, in
this case the critics had diverse views of her acting and interpretation of
the main role, as the following remarks reveal:

> Catherine Hayes delighted everyone by the startling earnestness,
> truth and vigour of her acting as *Lucrezia*. She evidently follows
> none of her contemporary artistes as models, but acts up to her own
> conception of the poetry of the part. This was evident in some of
> the most striking scenes in the tragedy . . . [18]

> Although the Lucrezia of Catherine Hayes lacked the power of other
> great artistes who had and have since appeared in the part, still, in
> dramatic conception, it was in every respect a study of high artistic
> merit. The change of hair, naturally light, to a very dark colour, made
> a striking alteration in Miss Hayes's appearance; her classic features and
> commanding figure lending additional effect. The tragic scenes were
> given with much force; and, indeed, the performance, as a whole,
> proved that the Irish prima-donna was equally at home in the heavier
> as in the lighter roles of the lyric drama.[19]

While her plan was to end her season early in April, she had been so
successful that she agreed to a return visit to give three additional
performances, starting on 21 April, and a concert.

During the intervening period, she visited Cork and Limerick giving operatic performances there. On arrival in Cork, for the first time in her career, she took on the Verdi role of Leonora in *Il Trovatore*, with Badiale, Volpini and Corelli singing the other leading roles. In Limerick, she sang at the first concert of the Harmonic Society where she performed the *Messiah* at the Athenaeum with Badiale, Corelli and probably also Volpini. The proceeds were donated to the purchase of an organ for the Athenaeum. As always, her hometown gave her a strong emotional welcome.

Returning to Dublin, she then gave another performance of *Il Trovatore* on 21 April with the same cast as in Cork. The assumption of the role of Leonora by Catherine shows that, as she got older, her voice got darker and more dramatic in texture. At last she was not afraid to sing Verdi's music. The first Irish performance of Verdi's *Il Trovatore* in Dublin had occurred about a year and a half earlier at the Theatre Royal, in September 1855. This was followed by another performance a year later in September 1856 with the famous Giulia Grisi, now in her declining years, in the part of Leonora and Giovanni Mario as the Manrico.

Catherine was setting herself up against one of the greatest names in opera. However, once again 'the professional' in her took over; never attempting anything she felt she couldn't execute, she entered the opera arena well rehearsed for the new role and completely confidence. The critics approved. The review of her first performance in Dublin said:

> Catherine Hayes's *Leonora* was a well studied and correct piece of acting, and her voice did the fullest justice in point of tone and modulation to the highest flights of harmony embraced in the arduous music of her part. That we have heard sweeter and richer tones in the higher passages it is impossible to deny, but we question if anything richer or softer was ever heard than her mezzo voice in this opera.[20]

Catherine then performed a repeat of *Il Trovatore*, and sang *Lucrezia Borgia* again on 25 April to conclude the series.

In between these last two operas, a Philharmonic Society concert was set for 24 April. The programme called for Catherine and the tenor Volpini to sing the famous Valentine and Raoul duet from Meyerbeer's *Les Huguenots*, another new piece for Catherine. This was to be followed by Catherine and Volpini singing excerpts from Verdi's *La Traviata*, his 1853 opera, which was now so popular.

It is difficult to say why Catherine changed from her normal programme to include Verdi material. Possibly by now the public was demanding more of Verdi's music as the operas of his middle period gained in popularity. In any event, in anticipation of the performance, the press editorial stated that: 'Verdi's music of *La Traviata* we think particularly suited to Miss Hayes's voice and exquisite vocal finish.'[21]

For some reason, on the night of the 24 April concert, the music for the Meyerbeer's *Les Huguenots* duet could not be found, and apparently Catherine did not sing at all during the first half of the concert, much to the audience's disappointment. To make up for her non-appearance, Catherine expanded her role in the second half, making the concert an all Verdi programme of solos, duets and trios!

She, Volpini and Badiale sang from *Il Trovatore*, *La Traviata* and *Rigoletto*! This was an amazing turn of events. Catherine first sang two *Trovatore* arias and then the 'Miserere' scene with Volpini. Then came the Act II 'Tutte le feste' scene from *Rigoletto*, followed by the duet, 'Piange', with Badiale. Volpini sang 'La Donna e mobile', after which the vocalists combined their talents, together with Mme Corelli, to sing the famous *Rigoletto* quartette, 'Bella figlia dell'amore'. Catherine and Volpini concluded the concert with the Brindisi 'Libiamo ne'lieti calici' from *La Traviata*.

During this entire period in Ireland, there is no mention of Bushnell, whether or not he was ill or just resting, we don't know. Catherine returned to London after this very satisfactory season in Ireland. It was the last time she would ever sing opera in Ireland.

Throughout the summer months, she and Bushnell prepared for their marriage. Catherine was not active musically during this period. Bushnell, despite his poor health, left for Connecticut in America during July. He got a divorce 'quietly' and apparently without having to advise his wife! He returned to England and the date for their wedding was set for Thursday 8 October 1857, at St. George's Church in Hanover Square, London. This was one of the most fashionable churches in London. The building of the church commenced in 1721 and was completed some years later. The church still stands today and its interior remains very much as it was when Catherine was married there. The beautiful oil painting of the Last Supper by William Kent (1648–1748) behind the main altar, is still in the same position as it was when Catherine and Bushnell were married there, as are the Flemish stained glass windows dating from 1525 which were installed in St. George's in 1840. The church survived the war years and the bombing of London in the 1940s.

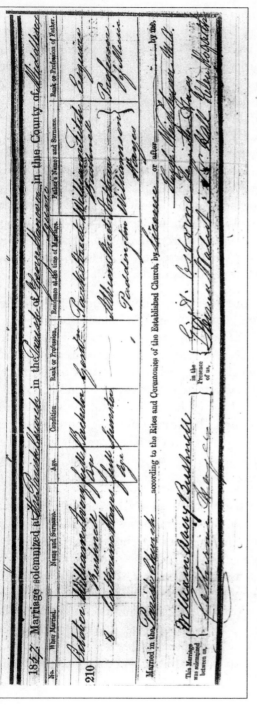

33. Marriage certificate of the wedding of Catherine Hayes and William A. Bushnell, at St. George's Church, London, October 1857. (Author's collection).

Besides Catherine's mother, her sister and George Alexander Osborne, we don't know who else may have attended the wedding ceremony. Osborne and Henrietta Hayes were the official witnesses to the event. On the marriage certificate, Catherine described her father as 'Arthur Williamson Hayes – Professor of Music', while Bushnell described his father as 'William Fitch Bushnell – Esquire'. The *London Musical Gazette* in its 31 October issue had a two-line notice to say: 'Miss Catherine Hayes is now Mrs. Bushnell, having been married to an estimable citizen of New York.'

The newly married couple went to Biarritz in France for their honeymoon. They hoped that the good coastal air might help Bushnell regain his health. On arrival, they were greeted by local English colonies and those in the town of Pau, which was not far away. By the middle of the nineteenth century the little town of Pau, had a population of around 21,000, of which approximately fifteen per cent (3,000) were from the British Isles.[22]

The London musical press again reported on the Hibernian Prima Donna in December, quoting from a correspondent in Pau:

> A delightful addition to our society has lately been made by the arrival of Mme. Catherine Hayes Bushnell and her husband. She is a most charming, unaffected person, and a favourite of every circle in which she is known. A few evenings since she gave us a soiree, at which nearly all the *Pau* world were present; it went off delightfully. Our hostess gave some Italian airs, which she sang splendidly. Many of the company, who had never heard her before, were quite enchanted; and even I, though I had heard her sing, both in Rome and in London, was really surprised at the beauty of her voice. We also had an Irish air, which was beautifully sung, and delighted the English beyond all measure. Everybody came away charmed.[23]

The year 1857 ended on a happy note for Catherine and her new husband. However, the new year began ominously for Bushnell, as his consumption worsened. They moved back to the coast, to Biarritz, desperately hoping that the sea air would help in some way. Catherine's mother came from London to visit them sometime around early spring. She must have shocked on seeing Bushnell's condition. He had less than two months to live. She stayed on to help, realising the inevitable was about to happen. William Avery Bushnell weakened, and died in his sleep on the morning of 3 July 1858. Catherine was heartbroken; they had come so far together and done so many things, and their marriage had been so short-lived.

Bushnell was buried in the English cemetery at Bayonne. He was 36 years old. The press in London and New York reported on the death of the prima donna's husband. Catherine and her mother returned to London and went into mourning. For the rest of the year she did not attend any functions or participate in social life in any way. Her close friend George Osborne had lost his wife a few years earlier and no doubt he would have comforted her during this difficult period.

In London, in April 1858, a powerful new organisation of musicians was established called the Musical Society of London. Unlike other music organisations in London, its purpose was to focus on certain aspects of the profession, to take a global view of the musical profession, its overall direction and workings and to be united as a self-supporting guild.

By 1859, the organisation had just about every noted musician of the day as a member, and, while it was created as a professional association, it also had non-professional members, both male and female. However, all members had to be musicians. Its central body, known as the 'Council', was made up of a group of eighteen particularly distinguished individuals. It included the composer and conductor Julius Benedict, the composer George A. Macferran, and Willert Beale, son of T. Frederick Beale of the music publishing house of Cramer & Beale, and a composer in his own right. The Irish members included George Alexander Osborne and William Vincent Wallace. Frank Mori, an eminent violinist and former music publisher, William Chappell of the musical instrument company of the same name and Henry Smart, the director of the Crystal Palace musical organisation, were also members. The society also had eight honorary associates – Auber, Meyerbeer, Moscheles, Spohr, Rossini, Ernst and Joachim. Conspicuous by his absence was the Irish composer Michael Balfe.

In January 1859, the society announced that it would be sponsoring four orchestral and choral concerts on Wednesday evenings starting 26 January. Probably through the influence of George Osborne, who always had a strong feeling for Catherine, she was invited to be the soloist at the first of these concerts. Obviously, after six months in mourning, the best thing for Catherine was to get back to work – this was clearly what Bushnell would have wanted her to do. George Osborne, along with her other friends, Wallace, Benedict, Smart and Macferren on the Musical Society's council, helped her get back to the thing she liked best – singing.

The first concert, which was held in St. James's Hall (where the Piccadilly Hotel was located), was considered the most prestigious affair of the new year. In addition to orchestral pieces by Mendelssohn,

Beethoven and Spontini, there were solo performances by Alfredo Piatti and Catherine. She sang as Catherine Hayes, not Hayes-Bushnell.

In a remarkable show of confidence on her part, Catherine opened with the big soprano scene from the second act of Weber's *Der Freischutz*, which lasts about ten minutes and closes with a dramatic finish. Piatti followed her, and immediately afterwards Catherine returned to perform as the soloist in Macferren's *May-Queen* Cantata, which closed the first part of the concert. In the second half, she returned to sing an aria from Rossini's 1829 masterpiece *Guillaume Tell* in Italian.

The next day one of the leading newspapers gave almost a full column to the event, which they reviewed as follows:

> The concert last night was one of the most interesting ever given in this country, and the selection was as judicious as the performance impressive. The audience numerous as it was, consisting almost exclusively of connoisseurs, might naturally have expected to be hypercritical, but proved itself enthusiastic. There was good reason, however, to be satisfied with the [following] program . . . the genial and masterly cantata of Mr. Macferren was introduced for the first time in London. Its success was complete. The execution, from first to last, was thoroughly effective . . . Madame Catherine Hayes was warmly applauded in the arduous scena from *Der Freischutz*.[24]

A representative from one of the leading musical journals who also attended praised the goals of the society and then went on to say:

> Madame Catherine Hayes, who had not appeared before a London audience for two years, was received with distinguished favour. The scena from *Der Freischutz* is one of the most difficult ever written for a soprano voice, and would tax to the utmost the powers and talents of a Lind. The performance of Madame Catherine Hayes was characterised by expression and energy. The recitative, perhaps, was somewhat elaborated, but the slow movement was well sung, and the impetuous *allegro* dashed off with spirit. The music of the 'May-Queen' in Macferren's cantata, was not so well suited to her.[25]

Catherine was back, and she could not have picked a better forum for her return than the Musical Society's first concert of the season, with the most élite audience in London in attendance. After this first event she was soon back into a frenetic schedule with two and three concert perform-ances scheduled weekly; first at St. James's Hall, then at Drury Lane, then the Crystal Palace in the suburbs and then on to Exeter Hall. She featured operatic arias, Irish songs and other pieces, including a new song especially written for her by Osborne. Mendelssohn and Handel's sacred oratorios were also performed with great frequency.

She was now almost 41-years-old and driving herself very hard, which of course had always been her custom – except that now she did not have Bushnell to guide her. Her actions were not driven by financial need, as she was significantly wealthy by this time, but there seemed to be a compulsive need to keep going.

Many new young singers were now on the scene in London, including some of opera's future greats; all were competing for the best concerts as well as operatic opportunities. While Catherine had a well-established name and reputation, she must still have felt the competitive pressures which always seemed to be a part of the musical scene in London. She continued to receive good reviews, sometimes being referred to as the 'eminent Hibernian cantatrice', other times as the 'distinguished vocalist', and sometimes with a respectful overtone that implied that she was an experienced 'ageing' prima donna, though never in a critical sense.

Catherine took September off to rest, advising her patrons and followers that she would return to London in October for the season. During this year without Bushnell, she had been living with her mother at 13 Westbourne Park in London, a property which no longer exists.

Early in October, she was back on the circuit again with the same schedule as earlier in the year – three concerts weekly, at the Crystal Palace, then Manchester and back to London. This continued virtually without any breaks up to the end of December, when a large scale orchestral, instrumental and vocal concert was announced for St. James's Hall for the New Year, featuring over 100 performers, including Catherine. The activity was incessant and exhausting.

CHAPTER FOURTEEN

The Final Years

ENGLAND AND IRELAND 1860–1861

THE YEAR 1860 opened with Catherine participating in a major concert at St. James's Hall with Sims Reeves and others. Balfe was the conductor. Immediately after this she travelled to Manchester. Here she took on a new role, in a concert performance in English of Gluck's opera *Iphigenia in Tauris*, with her friend Sims Reeves singing the role of Pylades to her Iphigenia and the young Charles Santley (1834–1932) singing Orestes. Charles Halle was the conductor. This performance was advertised in the programme as 'For the first time in England, the whole of the music of the celebrated Grand Opera'. Catherine sang in several performances of this opera, the last being in April. She was also the featured soloist at various Halle concerts. Later, when Halle brought Gluck's opera to London, Catherine was replaced by another prima donna.

The Manchester performance went off very well, with one of the leading musical publications saying:

> The performance was entirely successful, principals, band [orchestra] and chorus exerting themselves to the utmost to do it justice.[1]

Between performances of the Gluck opera she returned to London to sing at various concerts. In mid-March she appeared at Sadler's Wells Theatre for the first time, at a benefit concert, singing a Samuel Lover song, 'The Two Castles', for the first time. Towards the end of the month she sang at Crystal Palace in William Sterndale Bennett's (1816–75) *The May Queen* (a cantata with words by the critic Henry Chorley), which had its first performance in 1858. The cantata had 150 performers and was conducted by Augustus Manns (1825–1907). The baritone Charles Santley was also on the programme.

On 29 March she appeared at the newly rebuilt Covent Garden Theatre (the building that has existed up to 1997) with the Royal Italian Opera in a special concert given as a benefit for the Royal Dramatic College. She continued travelling back and forth to Manchester for Gluck's opera, and in early May she was in Liverpool performing Handel's music.

During May she also gave more concerts in and around London, sometimes singing new pieces such as 'The Forsaken One', written especially for her by Virginia Gabriel (1825–77) whose father was Irish. On another occasion she performed a trio, 'Le faccio un inchino', from the opera *Il Matrimonio Segreto* by Domenico Cimarosa (1749–1801), something she had not sung previously. For many of these concerts she shared the platform with her friend Sims Reeves. At one large affair held at the Royal Surrey Gardens for the benefit of the widow of the late Jullien, who had died the previous March, Catherine headed the list of distinguished vocalists which also included Sims Reeves.

Catherine seems to have been performing for the sake of staying busy. At a number of concerts the vocalists who shared the platform with her were artistically inferior. Clearly she was still struggling with the loss of Bushnell, who was now dead almost two years.

In June, she returned to Her Majesty's Theatre for a grand concert with many of the leading singers from the Italian Opera in London, including the great baritone Giorgio Ronconi. Sims Reeves continued to be a prominent participant in many of her concerts. In early October she sang in oratorios by Handel and Mendelssohn, and in performances of sacred music by Rossini, Mozart and Beethoven, always broadening her repertoire.

She also appeared at several Philharmonic concerts, where the standards were the very highest. One such concert took place in Exeter Hall in London, with an orchestra of 80 and a chorus of 400 during the middle of October. Catherine first sang in Mozart's Twelfth Mass, with other vocalists, then she sang an aria from *Il Trovatore* and joined in the quartette from *Rigoletto*. At another of these concerts she sang what was described as the 'beautiful finale' to Mendelssohn's unfinished opera *Die Loreley*, (earlier in the programme she had sung 'Ave Maria' from this same work), followed by two arias in French from Meyerbeer's opera *Robert le Diable*. She was continually adding new works to her repertoire.

For a November evening at Crystal Palace she included 'O luce di quest'anima' from *Linda di Chamounix* by Donizetti, and one of her regular songs, 'The Last Rose of Summer', by Moore. The reviewer said:

> Mdme. Catherine Hayes was the principal vocalist . . . displaying, her beautiful voice and her fine taste and expression.[2]

At a later concert at Crystal Palace she was joined on the platform by a tenor named Palmieri when they sang 'Parigi, o cara' from Verdi's *La Traviata*.

In the New Year, she continued her concert work in the London area. In February, she crossed over to Ireland accompanied by a Miss Lacelles, Mr. Tennant and a Mr. Burdini. The latter two had accompanied her on a previous tour. This would be the last time she would set foot on her native soil. During this visit she appears to have spent only a short time in the north of Ireland, giving a concert for the first time at the Town Hall in, Enniskillen, County Fermanagh, on 5 March. Shortly after, she went to Scotland to perform there again.

For Catherine time was running out, yet the next several months were to be taken up with more concerts. In May, in London, she announced the first a series of 'Matinee Musicales' – a popular format – at the private home of a Mrs. Rawson Reid at 25 Park Lane, a fashionable district. In mid-June she participated in a major concert at St. James's Hall with several other well-known Italian and English artists, singing among other pieces a dramatic aria from Donizetti's *Maria di Rohan*. Additional afternoon concerts were announced for the last week in June; however, these were cancelled due to illness. Early in July she was scheduled for a concert at the Hanover Square Room, London, with the tenor Italo Gardoni and Manuel Garcia's son, a baritone, Gustave Garcia (1837–1925), but it appears she was unable to keep this date either.

At the beginning of August, she visited her friends Henry and Maria Lee in Sydenham on the outskirts of London. It's quite possible that she also went there in order to see and hear the sensational 18 year old Adelina Patti, who was giving a series of concerts at Crystal Palace that first week in August 1861, as the Lees' home was just a short distance from Crystal Palace. A close friend, a Captain George J. Power, who was of Irish extraction, accompanied Catherine on this visit to the Lees.

Henry Lee was the Contractor for Public Works in the Sydenham area. He was 37 in 1861 and his wife Maria was 28. Both were close friends of Catherine's. Their large home, which was known as 'The Roccles', stood at the junction of Westwood Hill and Crystal Palace Park Road. The house survived into the twentieth century and was demolished in the 1930s.

Shortly after her arrival at the Lees' residence, Catherine felt unwell. The Lees telegraphed her doctor, a Mr. Chappel of George's Street in Hanover Square. Her mother and sister were also sent for from

CERTIFIED COPY OF AN ENTRY OF DEATH

GIVEN AT THE GENERAL REGISTER OFFICE

Application Number PAS 480641/94

REGISTRATION DISTRICT	Bromley							
DEATH in the Sub-district of	Bromley			in the County of Kent				

1	2	3	4	5	6	7	8	9
When and where died	Name and surname	Sex	Age	Occupation	Cause of death	Signature, description and residence of informant	When registered	Signature of registrar
Eleventh August 1861 Elfer Penhurst	Catherine Bushnell	Female	35 Years	Widow of William Bushnell Gentleman	Serous apoplexy 10 days Certified	M. A. McdIver present at the death Niece Elfer Penhurst	Twelfth August 1861	Charles Penrose Registrar

CERTIFIED to be a true copy of an entry in the certified copy of a Register of Deaths in the District above mentioned.

Given at the GENERAL REGISTER OFFICE, under the Seal of the said Office, the _____ 5th _____ day of _____ October _____ 19 94.

221837   See note overleaf

CAUTION:—It is an offence to falsify a certificate or to make or knowingly use a false certificate or a copy of a false certificate intending it to be accepted as genuine to the prejudice of any person or to possess a certificate knowing it to be false without lawful authority.

34. Death certificate of Catherine Hayes (Bushnell) dated 11 August 1861, showing that she died from a stroke. Her age is given as 35, when in fact she was 42. (Author's collection).

Westbourne Park. By the time they arrived it was obvious that Catherine was seriously ill, probably having suffered a minor stroke. On Thursday 8 August, it was decided that she should make a will. A Thomas Leach of Lincoln's Inn Fields arrived and prepared the two-page document. The will was signed and witnessed. Strangely, the signature to the will is not Catherine's. In fact it looks more like the handwriting of the individual who had prepared the will, Thomas Leach. There was also a subsequent need for an affidavit from Thomas Leach, as the will was signed 'Catherine Hayes', with the word 'Bushnell' added as an afterthought in the signature section. Leach in his affidavit said that he had advised Catherine that she 'had signed it incorrectly', since her legal name was 'Bushnell', and that she then added the words 'Ca. Bushnell'.

Despite the mystery of the signature on the will, Catherine, in designating her beneficiaries, seemed to have a clear mind. She left an annuity of £150 per annum to her mother, Mary Hayes, for life. Mary Hayes was now about 60 years old. She left a sum of £50 to her aunt Catherine Daly and £50 to her sister Henrietta Hayes, now 45 and still unmarried. She also left a legacy to her servant Bridget, plus back wages. To Agnes Knox, the granddaughter of the Late Bishop Knox (her mentor), in recognition of the Bishop's help, she gave a legacy of £50. To Maria Lee, her hostess, she left a diamond bracelet, which was described as having a centre which could be removed and used as a brooch. This was one of the gifts Catherine had received in Melbourne. All the residue of her estate she left to 'my dear friend George John Power, Esquire, late a Captain in the Royal Artillery, his executors and administrators'. She also appointed Power to be her executor, along with Henry Lee.

Her condition gradually worsened, and on Sunday morning, 11 August, she experienced another stroke, losing her speech in the process. There was very little the doctor could do; she was in rapid decline.[3] Her mother and sister must have been deeply affected, since Catherine had been such an important part of their lives for so long. At 6.30, that evening, never having regained consciousness, she passed away. She was just two and a half months away from her forty-third birthday.

George Power seems to be the one who took control of the funeral arrangements. On Monday, her remains we moved to her home at 13 Westbourne Park , where the funeral directors Messrs. Filmer of Berners Street prepared the remains for burial at Kensal Green Cemetery in west London. The funeral and burial did not take place until the following Saturday. The arrangement was a very solemn private affair, with a hearse and four mourning coaches carrying her immediate family and close friends. The coffin was made of plain oak with a large brass plate inscribed with her name and dates.[4]

Kensal Green Cemetery can be easily reached by underground train from anywhere in London. It is the resting-place for London's rich and famous of the nineteenth century. Catherine is buried in an above-ground sarcophagus grave, which today is in some disrepair. Its location is on the centre avenue at square 101 facing the Anglican chapel and catacombs. Not too far from where it is located rest Michael W. Balfe and William V. Wallace, Ireland's two greatest composers. Other famous names at rest in Kensal Green include writer W.M. Thackeray, who had written kind words about Catherine when she departed from Ireland as a young girl with a great many hopes and dreams, many years before. Irish composer Samuel Lover, whose songs Catherine sometimes sang, is also buried there. The famous Leigh Hunt, who reviewed so many performances for one of London's leading newspapers, is also buried there, as are many others, who knew her as she became famous in London.

Ten days after Catherine's burial, a new generation of singers was already replacing her at the Birmingham Musical Festival. Singing Mendelssohn's *Elijah* and Handel's *Israel in Egypt*, respectively, were sopranos Therese Tietjens (1831–77) and the great Adelina Patti. Singing opposite them in these sacred works were the indomitable Sims Reeves, Catherine's friend and partner on so many occasions, and Charles Santley.

When the news broke, shock waves reverberated around the English-speaking musical world in Europe, America and Australia. Even with Catherine's absence of five years from the London scene, while she was travelling she was frequently mentioned in the English press: her whereabouts, what she was singing and her successes. She was as popular as ever after her return. Her work, personal demeanour and style were greatly respected, both socially and by the press.

The London weekly, *The Musical World* (perhaps the most prestigious journal of the time covering musical events in Europe), dedicated to her passing an obituary which appeared on Saturday 17 August 1861. The following is an extract from the obituary, which covered almost two pages:

> It is with unfeigned regret we have this week to chronicle a serious loss to the Vocal Art, in the death of Catherine Hayes. The celebrated Irish songstress expired on Sunday last, at Sydenham, after a brief illness. Catherine Hayes was only forty years of age, and

in the zenith of her fame and full command of her powers. She dies universally lamented. She was a true hearted Irishwoman, and was ever ready, with her voice or purse, to assist the distressed. She was idolised by her immediate friends; and her loss will be deeply deplored by all who happen to come within the circle of her acquaintance. As a public character, she was equally respected for the strict decorum of her life, and admired for the powers and versatility of her talents. No singer, in short, ever left a fairer name behind her, or more emphatically merited the name of an 'artist'

. . . As a bravura singer, we are inclined to rate Catherine Hayes higher than a ballad singer. Indeed, her art appeared to us invariably to predominate over her natural gifts, and while that which was simple seemed to be forced, her ornamental displays were often in the highest degree satisfactory. At all events, in whatever light we may be inclined to view her, it cannot be denied that a real singer has gone from us, and as such the loss of Catherine Hayes is to be seriously lamented.

The equally prestigious *Illustrated London News* also gave editorial space, in addition to space in its musical column, to the event in its 17 August issue:

(Editorial)
The lyric drama has sustained a heavy loss in the premature death of Catherine Hayes. Well acquainted with the whole career of this lady from the earliest development of her unequaled [sic] [success] in a small provincial town in Ireland to its crowning triumphs on the boards of the Opera in London, we can safely and sincerely vouch for her honest and undeviating effort to render closely and conscientiously the works of the great masters committed to her care. No one, perhaps, encountered – especially in her native land – so many temptations to overstep this rule in favour of her own fancies – no one ever resisted that temptation more successfully. True lyric artiste! Honour to Catherine Hayes.

(Musical Column)
It is with much regret that we have to announce the untimely death of Mdme. CATHERINE HAYES. She expired at Sydenham, on Sunday last, after a few days illness. This melancholy event will be felt by the musical world as the loss of one of its brightest

35. Catherine Hayes's gravesite (1997), in *Kensal Green Cemetery*, London where she was buried in August 1861. (Author's collection).

ornaments, and will be deeply lamented by many who have known her amiable qualities and private worth. Her character as an artist is well known. Highly gifted by nature, and highly accomplished by education, she excelled in every branch of her art; while in one, – too, of the most delightful – she was unrivalled. As a singer of national songs and ballads, those especially of her native Ireland, she stood alone among all of the vocalists of the day. In music of this class, her pure and beautiful voice, not strained by the efforts of the modern Italian style, was lovely; its tones were truly 'wood notes wild,' and her simplicity and feeling had a charm which no one could resist. In her own country, as is well known, her very name was worshipped. Wherever she went she excited an enthusiasm such as no singer ever created before, and the reason was that no singer ever was so intensely Irish. Catherine Hayes, indeed, was an Irishwoman in everything – in her impulsive warmth of heart, kindliness, and generosity, as well as in her strong sense of the beautiful in music and song. Her brilliant career has been long, because it began at an early age; and she now has been cut off in the full strength and vigour of her powers, while she had still the prospect of many years of successful exertion before her. So uncertain and fleeting is human life!

The Times of London on 16 August gave almost a full column to her obituary. The following is a very brief extract:

MADAME CATHERINE HAYES

In Catherine Hayes Ireland has lost one of the greatest singers of its national airs. A daughter of the sister isle, she was thoroughly imbued with the spirit of its melody and it was in the alternately wild and tender melodies which have inspired so many poets – and foremost among them Thomas Moore, whose *'Irish Melodies,'* more than anything else that fell from his pen, proclaim his genius and perpetuate his name – that her gentle warmth of expression found its highest medium for display. As a singer of this particular class of music she was probably unsurpassed. It was here, far more than the Italian vocalisation of which she made herself an accomplished adept, that Catherine Hayes possessed the secret to charm the crowd. In her own country she had but to give a national air and hold the audience spellbound. And no wonder, for surely the best judge of what is perfect Irish-ballad singing are the Irish people themselves. When their favoured child-of-song, their Stephens and Jenny Lind in one, came forward with an Italian 'bravura' – a specimen of what she had learned in her transalpine experience – they were proud of her, as of a countrywoman who, in their estimation, could rival the practised mistress of foreign art; but it was not till the ballad came – the simple national ballad and the notes flowed with unstudied eloquence from her lips, that they were frankly enchanted. Of the first, indeed, for the most part they knew nothing, while the last touched the inner most cord of their being, and made it vibrate with delight . . .

. . . in recording the death of Catherine Hayes, at the early age of 40 years, we have not merely to console with her warm-hearted *compatriots* who saw no fault in anything she did, who applauded her foreign, and worshipped her national song, but with the British public generally, who have lost a popular favourite, and one in an eminent degree entitled to be regarded as a true and earnest artist. In private life the departed lady owned none but enthusiastic partisans, for we believe no professor of the musical art ever reflected more social honour on her calling.

In America, the *New York Freeman's Appeal* gave coverage to her passing in its 7 September issue, where her background, career and successes were outlined. The obituary ended with the brief summary: 'The deceased lady belonged to a class of vocalists whom we can ill afford to lose.' Another New York newspaper, *Frank Leslie's Illustrated*, stated in its 7 September issue, 'In the death of Catherine Hayes, the musical world will find no ordinary loss.' This was followed by an outline of her career and successes.

Dwight's Journal of Music in Boston recorded her death with an extensive review of her career extracted from the *New York Evening Post*, saying:

The latest foreign dispatches bring us the intelligence of the death of the celebrated singer Catherine Hayes . . . In 1851 Miss Hayes came to America, and after the brilliant seasons here, which most New Yorkers remember, starred with excellent acceptance through the country . . . Miss Hayes's finest operatic roles were *Lucia* and *Linda*, but her strong point was always in her own native ballads, 'Kathleen Mavourneen' and the like, where her memory must long stand unrivalled.

In Dublin the *Irish Times* of 14 August also reviewed her achievements and career highlights and had the following to say about her loss:

> The great majority of Londoners have merely a beautiful singer to regret in Catherine Hayes, but for those who knew her the sorrow felt at her death is much more poignant. Her world-wide experiences of countries and people gave an inexpressible charm to her conversation which would have been interesting and intelligent under any circumstances, while her manners always remained sweet and fascinating – quite unspoiled by the life-long adulation she had received. Her death is a personal and irremediable loss to a very large circle.

The *Limerick Chronicle* initially (14 August) picked up the *Times* of London obituary. However, an interesting extensive obituary appeared over two issues of the paper on 31 August and 4 September, provided by the paper's London correspondent, which included an explanation for the delay in getting a direct report. The following is an extract:

> Be not surprised at my not having communicated to you the sad intelligence of the death of our celebrated townswoman, Madame Catherine Hayes.
>
> On the 11th inst. [11 August], calling at her residence [13 Westbourne Park], I was informed that she had burst a blood vessel, and was dangerously ill at Sydenham, to which place I immediately proceeded, and arrived at the very instant of her death. This information so shocked me that I could not possibly write one line, though aware of the sad fact for two days before the London newspapers startled the public by this sorrowful record. But what could I do? – my pen refused to harbinger so great a sorrow – 'my right hand forgot its cunning' – my mind, confused harrowed as by some hideous dream, hardly to be realised, was utterly incapable of either thought or action; and even now, as I write my pen trembles, and the ink is mingled with tears; and though the violence of the tempest is past over and a mournful calm has ensued . . . the profound sorrow with which the death of Catherine Hayes filled the public mind was universal. Her name was long associated with those sweet, working the tenderest memories of youth and home and love, which none could portray with such vivid and thrilling effect as she did. Catherine Hayes dead! The sunlight itself looked

sorrowful, and the earth seemed robed in mourning! I can now more calmly relate some particulars of the last hours of poor dear Catherine, as she is universally called by all who knew, that is to say, by all who loved her; to me it will be a duty 'pleasing though sad to the soul,' and it will satisfy a desire you must naturally feel to know something connected with the last moments of our world-worshipped and idolised countrywoman. The last letter written by this much lamented lady, lay in her chamber unposted, addressed to your correspondent, and was handed to me at her house on the following day. It is a sorrowful [and] a precious memorial! In it there is an expression of grateful thanks for some slight services rendered by me in a communication to your journal of the 10th of July last, which contained a notice of her first and alas! that it should be so, her last concert in London. I give the extracts, which cannot fail to gratify you: – 'Thanks much for the charming notice inserted in the *Limerick Chronicle*, nothing could have been better, and I am much obliged to you.' For the sake of Limerick, and of the Limerick people I am glad that these expressions of graceful acknowledgement should have been written by her to a townsman, and on such an occasion. They evidence a trait which pre-eminently distinguished her character viz., an extreme sensibility for the least kindness rendered to her . . . But, take her for all in all, though perhaps greater singers than Catherine Hayes may exist, I must confess that I never felt so deeply moved, and so unutterably entranced, as by her whose wondrous voice seemed to thrill the soul with undefinable rapture, 'till it became, as it were, disembodied, and borne higher and higher on the wings of impassioned and rapturous song to heaven's gates, while every sense, but hearing sank absorbed in an overwhelming ecstasy of delight! . . .

I remember some years since when stating to the then Miss C. Hayes, this wonderful effect of her singing, which I and others experienced, tremulous with emotion, her eyes cast on the ground, yet filled with delight which true genius ever feels in the triumph of its power, she mildly said while the words trembled on her lips, 'that was a great triumph for an artist.' I shall ever remember the contrast between the timid gently-blushing woman I then addressed, and the glorious priestess of a divine inspiration as she stood transfigured by the light of genius, and held her audience enthralled by some entrancing spell, enshrined in her very spirit.

Catherine's will was processed through probate on 26 August 1861. The value of the estate was declared at around £16,000 or about 80,000 US dollars, at that time, truly an enormous amount of money for the period. After the legacies and the annuity for her mother, all of the remainder of her estate was left to Power of London. Power became a very rich man on Catherine's death, but what Catherine's relationship was with his is unknown. he was a bachelor at the time of her death. Born in Kent on 14 April 1824, he was also six years younger than Catherine, Power came from a well established Anglo-Irish military family.

Power's father, William G. Power, was born in Ballinderry, County Tipperary, in February 1785.[5] He married Marian Morris in London. There were six children from the marriage, five boys and one girl, who was the youngest. George was the third son born into the family. William Power had joined the Royal Artillery when he was fifteen, as a cadet, and worked his way up the ranks to initially become a 2nd Lieutenant, then a Captain, when he was assigned to the Duke of Wellington's army in the Peninsula Wars. He was mentioned for bravery in dispatches by the Duke of Wellington and eventually promoted to Colonel in 1835, when young George was about nine years old. The father ultimately achieved the rank of General in the 10th Brigade of the Royal Artillery and was later knighted. Sir William G. Power died at Shanklin on the Isle of Wight in January 1863.

Sir William's son George, the friend of Catherine Hayes, was not quite so distinguished as his father. He entered the Royal Artillery at the age of 19 (1843), first as a cadet, then was promoted to the rank of 2nd Lieutenant, on the recommendation of his father. He achieved the rank of 1st Lieutenant in January 1845 and resigned in August of that year. There is no indication on his record that he had been wounded in action during the course of his service in the army. Additionally, there was no reason given for his resignation. While he later used the rank of Captain socially, and in fact he is specifically referred to as that in Catherine's will, he never actually achieved that rank. After his departure from the army there is no known record of him or his whereabouts until he is mentioned in Catherine's will. At the time of her death he lived in Norfolk Square in central London, a respectable address.

It is difficult to say whether he was a legitimate friend of Catherine's or not. She did refer to him in her will as 'my dear friend'; however, we know nothing more. Perhaps his Irish heritage drew Catherine to him initially. She did have a large number of friends, including Irish composer William

Wallace; however, we do not have many details of most of her friends, many of whom were outside the musical profession.

How Power handled Catherine's mother and sister after her death we don't know. They were both still residents at 13 Westbourne Park, where most of Catherine's effects would have been, this may have caused some embarrassment, since legally they belonged to Power. In the months after Catherine's death there was nothing in the local London newspapers that would indicate that an auction of her effects was held, which would have been the normal way to dispose of the goods of a prominent person.

George Power did not have a happy life. He married several years later and had children. However, he was living alone in a small apartment in Melrose Terrace in Hammersmith when he developed a malignancy of the jaw, which lasted several years, eventually significantly disfiguring him. He died there in November 1887 at the age of 63. His death certificate among other things indicated that he had been a Captain in the military. He left no will or estate.

Ten years after Catherine's death, in 1871, her mother died and was buried in the same grave as Catherine. There was no record as to who handled the arrangements – presumably it was Henrietta Hayes. There is no information as to what happened to Henrietta – where she eventually lived, England or Ireland, or when she might have died.

Catherine Hayes's place in history is secure, certainly in relation to Ireland. During the nineteenth-century there were only a handful of Irish singers who made it onto the international music circuit. These were all men, except for Catherine. The first was Michael Kelly (1762–1826), a tenor who was born in Dublin, trained in Italy and who was a friend of Mozart. The next was Michael W. Balfe (1808–70), a baritone, born in Dublin, trained in England and Italy, a friend of Rossini and the first Irish person to sing at La Scala in Milan. Balfe, of course, went on to become a renowned composer of English opera. The next was Catherine Hayes (1818-61), who was the first Irish woman to sing in opera at La Scala, in Milan, Vienna, Venice, Rome, Florence, Genoa, Verona and Covent Garden in London, plus a host of other places, and always with great distinction.

Alan J. Foley (1835–99) was a bass, born in Cahir, County Tipperary, who mostly studied in Italy and later in England with Garcia. He sang all over the globe under the name of A.J. Foli. Next came Barton M'Guckin (1852–1913), a tenor born in Dublin, who studied there and in Milan and who primarily sang in England, Ireland and America. Joseph O'Mara

(1864–1927), tenor, born in Limerick, studied in Milan and sang in England, Ireland and America. John O'Sullivan (1878–1948), John McCormack (1884–1945) and Margaret Burke-Sheridan (1889–1958). The last three while born in the nineteenth century, all had careers in the following century.

Catherine Hayes's pioneering efforts were primarily driven by her desire to sing. The places she visited initially happened to be the best places for her to gain experience in her art. She was later motivated to sing in concert, after seeing Jenny Lind's financial success outside of the operatic scene.

In general Catherine Hayes appeared to be somewhat timid or withdrawn, except while on the stage singing. This shyness may have been the result of her early upbringing and related insecurity. On a one-to-one basis she was always considered very sociable and charming, a good conversationalist giving interesting and amusing accounts of her experiences.

Catherine was always generous and altruistic. She took for granted her obligation to help underprivileged children and the sick, regardless of their nationality or faith. She contributed to her mother and sister financially for years. She never sought any publicity relating to these acts.

She was incredibly honest and direct in her dealings with impresarios and business managers or agents. Her problems with the Beale concert management arrangements in New York in 1851 were created by others, who were opportunists. People liked and respected her, even the critics. Her style tended to be outside the norm for a prima donna in Italy and England.

Her correspondence with the important impresario Alessandro Lanari in Italy in the 1840s shows her frankness and her interest in being fair in her dealings. Lanari, a tough businessman who was continually plagued by borderline bankruptcy, responded in a way that shows that he liked her, always sending his affections to her mother and sister. She in turn appreciated his business advice and experience and told him so. When she was undecided about an offer from Fry, the American composer to perform in his country, Lanari took the time to give her the advice and the direction she needed to be able to make a decision, even though her contract with him had expired.

Once set on a direction, she never seemed to waver. Her experiences in England at the mid-point in her career made her very uncomfortable with all of the musical competition that descended on London after the revolutions of 1848. While she was probably better than many continental singers of similar vocal genre, she decided not to compete with them in opera. Instead, she took to the concert platform, creating a programme mixture which generated almost a cult following for years. She elected to sing Irish and other songs with style and eloquence – receiving just as much applause and response as her continental peers. It was niche marketing in its essence.

She never had a bad word to say about Jenny Lind, yet she must have continually felt in her shadow both in England and America. It's very possible the two were good friends; after all, they both had the same training around the same time. Both were of the Protestant faith and deeply committed to the sacred music of Handel, Mendelssohn and Haydn. Neither prima donna was ever associated with scandal. Lind, must have been an exceptional performer to have been such a legend in her own lifetime. As far as we can tell from reviews, Catherine's style was different, consequently, she never allowed herself to be seen as a Lind copyist, she was always Catherine Hayes, the Hibernian prima donna.

Catherine Hayes and Sims Reeves were intrinsically linked over a period of fifteen years because of their professional pursuits. It is almost certain that Reeves was Catherine's first lover, probably shortly after her arrival in England in 1849. Reeves became the most important tenor in England in the second half of the nineteenth century. Years after Catherine Hayes had died and was generally forgotten, he thought enough of their relationship to mention her with affection in his memoirs, not only in a professional sense but also as a feminine and gentle woman.

The most important man in her life, William Avery Bushnell, an American by birth, became Catherine Hayes's husband at a time when he was obviously in an advanced stage of consumption, an incurable disease in the nineteenth century. Why she married him at that point in time we don't know, perhaps she felt obligated because of their long relationship and all that they had experienced together. Catherine had needed a manager for her American tour, and Bushnell probably was the right man at the right time. He appeared to be a man of high integrity and good judgement, both of which would have appealed to Catherine. Given her character, she would have felt committed to him since becoming lovers in Australia. However, on their return to London she probably felt it would be better if he got a divorce so that they could marry. She never really seemed to get over the loss of Bushnell. Six months after his passing, when Catherine started back to work she appeared almost to have a death wish. She worked incessantly and destructively, in an attempt to counteract the effect of the great emotional loss she had suffered with Bushnell's death. She must also have been feeling the pressure of the new competition, which was everywhere in London, and the fact that she was getting older. Financially she was secure and she didn't really need to work. It was compulsive, and she was clearly at a loss as to what else to do. She continued to push herself to the limit, which in the end resulted in a stroke that was fatal.

George Power is an enigma. That Catherine left him the bulk, of her assets seems strange, particularly when she only left her mother an annuity of £150 annually, a rather modest amount, even for those days. Then there was her sister Henrietta. The two had always been close, although Henrietta elected for some reason not to go to California with Catherine. Why did Catherine only leave her the paltry sum of £50?

The will was definitely not signed by Catherine Hayes, or Catherine Bushnell. The signature clearly is that of someone else. It does not seem possible that the Lees and Power could have connived to get access to her assets. Mary Hayes, Catherine's mother was at her bedside during the final days. and she would not have permitted a falsification of the will. Additionally, when Catherine went to visit the Lees she was not anticipating having a stroke, as she had concerts lined up for later in August, therefore Lee and Power could not have had time to plan anything underhand. We must conclude that she must have had a significant personal relationship with Power, which resulted in him being her beneficiary.

Catherine Hayes literally disappeared from the music history books of Europe in the twentieth century, except for a few isolated publications. She sang more often in opera than Lind did, and for a longer period. Why Catherine's contribution is not recorded in greater detail is difficult to say. There has certainly been no new information about her activities or achievements published during the past one hundred and thirty years.

She was the foremost *Lucia di Lammermoor* in Italy in the late 1840s during Donizetti's lifetime, although the composer was then in his final years. With Jenny Lind in virtual retirement, Catherine Hayes emerged as possibly the most important female concert artist and oratorio singer in England at a time when the works of Handel, Mendelssohn and Haydn were reaching their performance zenith in the 1850s. Her concerts always had full houses and she always had good reviews.

The other prominent English speaking sopranos of the period, Anna Bishop and Clara Novello were considered second to Hayes by leading critics of the day. Catherine Hayes's prominence was such that Italian composers wrote operas for her. Racehorses, ships and hospitals were named after her. In Sydney in the 1850s, even a drink was named after her while she was performing there! Poems were written about and for her and published on three continents in various languages.

She played a significant part in the developments of the music and culture of California's gold rush frontier. Her early pioneering travels to Australia and her operatic performances there meant that she played a critical role in that country's musical growth too. She is mentioned in most books of significance relating to the early cultural history of Australia.

Last, but not least, in Ireland her position is truly monumental in a century where women had no status and no opportunity to be independent. Her tenacity and determination should be a lesson to any young person in Ireland today. She loved Ireland and never forgot her heritage. Religious differences didn't matter to her.

In Buckingham Palace, the awesome Queen Victoria, ruler of the British Empire, requested an encore at the conclusion of an Italian aria, Catherine responded by singing an Irish song. Catherine Hayes's presence in Buckingham Palace must have been an inspiration to herself and her mother – epitomising a great moment of personal achievement.

As a young Irish woman she was second to none in musical accomplishments in the nineteenth century. She earned her place in global musical history as an eminent vocalist at virtually the dawn of Italian opera and concert life as we know it today. In any century she would have stood out because of her professionalism, personal integrity and style. As one obituary writer said: 'This melancholy event will be felt by the musical world as the loss of one of its brightest ornaments, and will be deeply lamented by many who have known her amicable qualities and private worth.'

Notes

Chapter One

1 Sotheby's, Main Galleries, 34–35 Bond Street, London W1, England.
2 *Costumes, Music and Opera Memorabilia from the Collection of Dame Joan Sutherland, O.M., and Richard Bonynge, C.B.E.* Sale LN5082– 'STUPENDA'.
3 *The New Groves Dictionary of Opera 1992, Vol. 2. The Concise Oxford Dictionary of Opera 1979. Musical Biography* by David Baptie, London 1883. *Opera on the Road* by K.K. Preston, Chicago 1993.
4 Photocopy of original registry pages in possession of author.
5 Letter of confirmation from the Limerick Regional Archives office dated 27 January, 1994.
6 Ibid.
7 Letter from St. Mary's Cathedral staff dated 16 December 1994.
8 *Cambridge Historical Encyclopaedia of Great Britain and Ireland*, Cambridge University Press, England 1995.
9 *Famous Women Singers – Dorothy Kirsten*, New York 1953, by Homer Ulrich. *Dorothy Kirsten – A Time to Sing*, New York 1982, with Lanfranco Rasponi.
10 *Helen Hayes – On Reflection*, New York 1968, with Sandford Dody. *Helen Hayes – First Lady of the American Theatre*, New York 1985, by Kenneth Barrow.
11 Extract from the first issue of the *Old Limerick Journal* by J.F. Walsh. Provided by the late Kevin Hannan, Old Limerick Society.
12 *The Dictionary of National Biography*–Vol. XIV, London 1968
13 Ibid.
14 Ibid.
15 *Hector Berlioz and the Development of French Music Criticism* by Kerry Murphy, UMI Research Press, Ann Arbor, Michigan 1988.
16 *Berlioz in London*, by A.W. Ganz, London 1950.
17 *Autobiography of Charles Halle*, New York 1972.
18 Paper 'Musical Coincidences and Reminiscences' by G.A. Osborne given at the Proceedings of the Musical Association in London on 2 April 1883.
19 *Berlioz* by J.H. Elliot, London 1946.
20 *The Great Tenor Tragedy* by Nourrit, edited by Henry Pleasants, Amadeus Press Portland, OR 1995.
21 *The Times*, 10 May, 1849.
22 McCullough Pigott's music store in Suffolk Street, Dublin.
23 *Antonio Stradivari, His life and Work (1644–1737)* by W. Henry Hill, Arthur & Alfred Hill. Pages 137–9. New York (reprint) 1963
24 *Memoir of Catherine Hayes* published by Cramer & Co. London, circa 1850.

Chapter Two

1   *The History of the Theatre Royal, Dublin*, published by Edward Ponsonby, Dublin 1870.

2   Ibid.

3   *Introductory Sketch of Irish Musicality* by W.H. Gratten–Flood, London 1907.

4   *The Oxford Companion to Irish History*, edited by S.J. Connolly, Oxford 1998.

5   *Annals of the Theatre Royal, Dublin* by R.M. Levey and J. O'Rourke, Dublin 1880. Page 14.

6   Ibid. Page 17.

7   *The New Grove Dictionary of Opera*, London 1992.

8   Ibid.

9   Ibid.

10 *Opera in London – Views of the Press 1785–1830* by Theodore Fenner. Page 533. Carbondale, Illinois 1994.

11 *Opera in London – Views of the Press 1785–1830* by Theodore Fenner. Pages 533–5. Carbondale, Illinois 1994.

12 *Annals of the Theatre Royal, Dublin* by R.M. Levy and J. O'Rorke, Dublin 1880. Page 16.

13 *Harmonicon*, London 1827, Page 146, 149 and 249; London Times 23 November 1827.

14 *Harmonicon*, London 1829. Pages 119 and 145.

15 *Annals of the Theatre Royal, Dublin*, Dublin 1880. Page 78.

16 *Annals of the Theatre Royal, Dublin*, Dublin 1880. Page 81.

17 *Annals of the Theatre Royal, Dublin*, Dublin 1880. Page 83.

18 *Encyclopaedia of Dublin* by Douglas Bennett, Dublin 1994.

19 *Liszt: My Travelling Circus Life* by David Ian Allsobrook. Carbondale, Illinois 1991.

20 *Annals of the Theatre Royal, Dublin*, Dublin 1880. Page 106.

21 *The Freeman's Journal*, Dublin 3 May 1839.

22 *The Evening Packet*, Dublin 4 May 1839.

23 *The Limerick Standard*, 4 February 1840.

24 *The Evening Packet*, Dublin, 11 February 1840.

25 *The Evening Packet*, Dublin 2 May 1840.

26 *The Baltimore Sun*, 3 October 1852. Advertisement announcing Adelina Patti would sing songs of Catherine Hayes, Jenny Lind and others.

27 Ibid.

28 Pearl Gemm CD9312, *Adelina Patti, 1843–1919*.

29 *The Freeman's Journal*, Dublin, 12 January 1841.

30 A recording of Liszt's programme for this concert tour by Thomas Wakefield is available on SYMPOSIUM CD 1091.

31 The 1720 Stradivarius cello which was used by Pigott at this concert is known as the 'Piatti cello' after Alfredo Piatti who owned it in London for many years prior to his death in 1901. Today (1998) the instrument is owned and used by the celebrated Mexican violoncellist, Carlos Prieto. See *Antonio Stradivarius, His Life & Work* by W. Henry Hill; A.F. and A.E. Hill, New York 1963. Pages 137–9.

32 *Dublin University Magazine* vol. 36 1850.

33 *Liszt: My Travelling Circus Life* by David Ian Allsobrook, Carbondale, Illinois 1991.

34 *The Oxford Companion to Irish History*, edited by S.J. Connolly, Oxford 1998. Pages 45–6.

35 *Garcia the Centenarian and his Times* by M. Sterling Makinlay, New York 1908.

36 *The Limerick Chronicle*, 13 August, 1842.

37 *Memoir of Madame Jenny Lind-Goldschmidt* by Holland & Rockstro, London 1891.

38 *Memoir of Miss Catherine Hayes*, Cramer and Co. London, circa 1850.

39 *The Irish Sketch Book* by W.M. Thackeray, London 1860.

Chapter Three

1 *Garcia – The Centenarian and His Times* by M. Sterling Mackinly, reprint, New York 1976.

2 *Blue Guide to Paris*, 8th edition published by A & C Black, London 1992.

3 *Transforming Paris* by David P. Jordan, University of Chicago Press 1995.

4 *Rossini* by Herbert Weinstock, New York 1968.

5 *Verdi and His Major Contemporaries* by Thomas J. Kaufman, New York 1990.

6 *Garcia the Centenarian and his Times* by M. Sterling Mackinlay, reprint New York 1976.

7 *Maria Malibran* by Howard Bushnell, The Pennsylvania State University Press 1979.

8 *A Complete Treatise on the Art of Singing* by Manuel Garcia, Part II. Translated and edited by Donald V. Paschke, New York 1975.

9 *Marchesi and Music* by Mathilde Marchesi, New York 1898.

10 *Memoir of Madame Jenny Lind-Goldschmidt* by Holland and Rockstro, London 1891.

11 See liner notes of London CD 421 883–2, Joan Sutherland 'Tribute to Jenny Lind'.

12 *Memoir of Madame Jenny Lind-Goldschmidt* by Holland and Rockstro, London 1891.

13 *A Neighbour's Child – Signor Foli* by Dirny Reynolds, Dublin 1994.

14 *Strong on Music*, Vol. 2, by Vera Brodsky Lawrence, University of Chicago Press, Chicago 1995.

15 *The Operas of Charles Gounod* by Steven Huebner, Oxford 1992.

16 *The Autobiography of Charles Halle*, edited by Michael Kennedy, New York 1973.

17 *A Complete Treatise on the Art of Singing* by Manuel Garcia, Part I. Translated by Donald V. Paschke, New York 1984.

18 *Opera in Paris 1800–1850* by Patrick Barbier, Portland, OR. 1995.

19 *Evening Packet* newspaper, Dublin, Ireland, 31 October 1850.

20 *Groves Dictionary of Music and Musicians*, Vol. IV, T. Presser Co., Philadelphia 1916.

21 *Italy from the Revolution to Republic* by Spencer M. Di Scala, Boulder, CO. 1995.

22 *Verdi: A Biography* by Mary Jane Phillips-Matz, New York 1993.
23 *Italy from the Revolution to Republic* by Spencer M. Di Scala, Boulder, CO. 1995.
24 *Verdi: A Biography* by Mary Jane Phillips-Matz, New York 1993.
25 *Giuseppe Verdi Nelle Lettere di Emanuele Muzio ad Antonio Barezzi* by Luigi A. Garibaldi, Milan 1931.
26 Letter from the Milan Conservatory dated 20 February, 1996.
27 *Evening Packet* newspaper, Dublin, Ireland, 29 October 1850.
28 Ibid.
29 *La Fama* newspaper, Milan, 16 June 1845.

Chapter Four

 1 *Gazetta Musicale di Milano*, 13 September 1845.
 2 *The Complete Operas of Verdi* by Charles Osborne, New York. Pages 133–4.
 3 *Donizetti and the World of Opera* by Herbert Weinstock, New York 1963. Page 180.
 4 *The New Grove Dictionary of Opera*, New York 1992.
 5 *Opera on the Road 1825–60* by K.K. Preston, Chicago 1993. Pages 189–90, 321–2. *The New Grove Dictionary of Opera.*
 6 *Donizetti and the World of Opera* by Herbert Weinstock, New York 1963. Page 190.
 7 *La Fama* newspaper, Milan, November 1845.
 8 *Gazetta Musicale di Milano*, 9 November 1845.
 9 *The Musical World*, London 4 April 1846.
10 *The Musical World*, London 8 January 1846.
11 *The Musical World*, London 20 Novembe 1845.
12 See letters between Alessandro Lanari and Caterina Hayez; Biblioteca Nazionale Centrale di Firenze, 1846/7.
13 *Gazetta Musicale di Milano*, 28 December 1845.
14 *The Musical World*, London 24 January 1846.
15 *The New Grove Dictionary of Opera*, New York 1992.
16 *Memoir of Madame Jenny Lind-Goldschmidt* Vol. 1, by Holland and Rockstro, London 1891.
17 *The New Grove Dictionary of Opera*, New York 1992.
18 bid.
19 *The Musical World*, London 29 August 1846.
20 *The Musical World*, London, October 1846.
21 *Gazetta Musical di Milano*, 6 September 1846.
22 *The Verdi Companion* by William Weaver and Martin Chusid, New York 1979.
23 *Giuseppe Verdi nelle lettere di Emanuele Muzio ad Antonio Barezzi* by L.A. Garibaldi, Milan 1931.
24 *Verdi His Music, Life and Times* by George Martin, London 1965.
25 Ibid.
26 Ibid.
27 *Giuseppe Verdi nelle lettere di Emanuele Muzio ad Antonio Barezzi*, L.A. Garibaldi, Milano 1931.

28 *Letters of Giuseppe Verdi*, translated by Charles Osborne, New York 1971.
29 *Giuseppe Verdi nelle lettere di Emanuele Muzio ad Antonio Barezzi* by L.A. Garibaldi, Milano 1931.
30 *Memoir of Madame Jenny Lind-Goldschmidt*, Vol 1, by Holland and Rockstro, London 1891.
31 *The Musical World*, London 6 May 1848. Verdi's comments translate to 'she sung, but she didn't enchant'.
32 *Duecento Anni di Teatro alla Scala – Cronologia 1778–1977*, Giampiero Tintori, Bergamo 1979.
33 *The New Grove Dictionary of Opera*, New York 1992.
34 *Sims Reeves* by Charles E. Pearce, London 1924.
35 *The Musical World*, London 3 October 1846.
36 *The Musical World*, London 17 October 1846.
37 *The Musical World*, London 12 December 1846.
38 *Giuseppe Verdi nelle lettere di Emanuele Muzio ad Antonio Barezzi* by L.A. Garibaldi, Milano 1931.
39 *My Jubilee or Fifty Years of Artistic Life* by J. Sims Reeves, London.
40 *The Musical World*, London 28 November 1846.
41 *Bazar di novita and Figaro*, January 1847, quoted in *Memoir of Catherine Hayes* (London: Cramer & Co., 1849). Pages 12–13.
42 *Queens of Song* by Ellen Creathorne Clayton, 2 vols. London 1863. Page 284.
43 *The Musical World*, London 10 April 1847.
44 *Teatre Arti e Letteratura*, No. 1215, 6 May 1847, Bologna.

Chapter Five

1 *Il Teatro Donizetti, Cronologia degli spettacoli 1786–1989*, Ermanno Comuzio, Bergamo.
2 *Giornale Della Provincia di Bergamo*, 10 August 1847.
3 *The Musical World*, London, 18 September 1847.
4 *Memoir of Catherine Hayes 'The Swan of Erin'* by Cramer & Co, London 1857.
5 *Bergamo o sia Notizie Patrie, Raccolte da Carlo Facchinetti*, Bergamo 1848.
6 *The Musical World*, London 18 September 1847.
7 *The Musical World*, London 1 September 1847.
8 *The Musical World*, London 2 October 1847.
9 Contract with Alessandro Lanari dated 9 January 1847, Biblioteca Nazionale Centrale di Firenze.
10 *The New Grove Dictionary of Opera*, New York 1992.
11 Contract with Alessandro Lanari, page 1, seventh line, dated 9 January 1847, Biblioteca Nazionale Centrale di Firenze.
12 *The Musical World*, 28 February 1848.
13 Letter dated 23 October 1847 to Lanari, Biblioteca Nazionale Centrale di Firenze.
14 *Verdi: A Biography* by Mary Jane Phillips-Matz, New York 1993.
15 Letter dated 6 December 1847 to Lanari, Biblioteca Nazionale Centrale di Firenze.

16   See footnotes in a Catalogue of Verdi's operas by Martin Chusid.
17   *Teatri Arti e Letteratura*, Bologna, 8 January 1848, issue number 1248.
18   *London Morning Post* as reported by *The Musical World* on 19 February 1848.
19   *The Athenaeum*, London, 16 October 1847.
20   *The Musical World*, 19 February 1848.
21   Ibid.
22   *Marchesi and Music* by Mathilde Marchesi, New York & London 1892.
23   *Gazzetta Di Firenze*, 17 March 1848, issue number 63.
24   *Teatri Arti e Letteratura*, Bologna, 13 April 1848, issue number 1262.
25   *Revolutions of 1848* by Priscilla Robertson, Princeton 1952.
26   Ibid.
27   *Teatri Arti e Letteratura*, Bologna, 27 April 1848, issue number 1264.
28   Letter from Alessandro Lanari to Accademia degli Immobile Archive members dated 27 March 1848, contained in the Accademia della Pergola archives, Florence.
29   *Il Popolano, Firenze*, 14 April 1848.
30   *Teatri Arti e Letteratura*, Bologna, 25 May 1848, issue number 1267.
31   *Gazzetta Di Firenza*, 13 June 1848, issue number 139.
32   *Teatri Arti e Letteratura*, Bologna, 13 July 1848, issue number 1270.
33   *Teatri Arti e Letteratura*, Bologna, 11 January 1849, issue number 1280.
34   *Opera in America* by John Dizikes, Yale University 1993.
35   *Illustrated London News*, March 1849.
36   *The Musical World*, London, 31 March 1849.
37   *Dictionary of British History*, NTC Publishing Group 1997.
38   *The Romantic Age in Britain* by Bruce Ford, Cambridge 1992.

Chapter Six

1   *Memoir of Madame Jenny Lind-Goldschmidt* by Holland and Rockstro, London 1891, Vol. I.
 2   *Memoir of Madame Jenny Lind-Goldschmidt* by Holland and Rockstro, London, 1891, Vol. II.
 3   *Il Colonello*, music by Luigi and Federico Ricci; first performed in Naples, March 1845.
 4   *The Times*, London, 11 April 1849.
 5   *The Athenaeum*, London, 14 April 1849.
 6   *The Musical World*, London, 14 April 1849.
 7   *The Examiner*, London, 14 April 1849.
 8   *The Limerick Chronicle*, 14 April 1849.
 9   *Memoir of Catherine Hayes*, published by Cramer & Co., London 1850. Page 15.
10   *The Examiner*, obituary of The Hon. and Right Rev. E. Knox, Bishop of Limerick, 12 May 1849.
11   *The Times*, 10 May 1849.
12   In Italy, Hayes normally sang the original Donizetti music, 'Regnava nel silenzio', but in London she chose to follow Lind's example by interpolating the music from Donizetti's *Rosmonda d'Inghilterra*.

13   *The Times*, 27 April 1849.
14   *The Examiner*, 28 April 1849.
15   *The Musical World*, 28 April 1849.
16   See Jeremy Commons's notes, page 40, for *Opera Rara* CD recording of *Rosmonda d'Inghilterra*, 1994.
17   *The Times*, 30 April 1849.
18   *The Musical World*, 5 May 1849.
19   *The Musical World*, 19 March 1849.
20   From the *Journals of Queen Victoria*; by gracious permission of Her Majesty.
21   *Dublin University Magazine*, November 1850, vol. 36.
22   *Musical London* by Edward Lee, London 1995. Page 116.
23   *The Times*, 25 July 1849.
24   Ibid.
25   Ibid.
26   *The Musical World*, 28 July 1849.
27   *The Musical World*, 11 August 1849.
28   *The Musical World*, 18 August 1849.
29   *The Times*, 7 September 1849. (Reference Delafield bankruptcy.)
30   *The Musical World*, 18 August 1849.
31   *The Times*, 7 September 1849.

Chapter Seven

1   *The Great Irish Famine* by Cormac O Gráda, Cambridge, England 1995.
2   *The Times*, 31 March 1846.
3   *The Irish Famine*: A Documentary History by Noel Kissane, Dublin 1995. Page 20.
4   *A Dublin Anthology*, edited by Douglas Bennett, 1994; 'Morrison's Hotel' by W.H. Lawrence. Page 265.
5   *Mario and Grisi* by Elizabeth Forbes, London 1985. Page 50.
6   *Annals of the Theatre Royal, Dublin* by R.M. Levey and J. O'Rorke, Dublin 1880. Page 136.
7   *Dublin Historical Record*, vol.47, no. 2, Autumn 1994; 'Arthur Morrisson' by D. Parkinson. Page 183.
8   *The Irish Times*, 22 April 1899.
9   *Freeman's Journal*, 6 November 1949.
10   *Saunder's News Letter*, 6 November 1849.
11   *Sims Reeves, Fifty Years of Music in England* by Charles E. Pearse, London 1924. Page 144.
12   *Freeman's Journal*, 7 November 1849.
13   *Annals of the Theatre Royal, Dublin* by R.M. Levey and J. O'Rorke, Dublin 1880. Page 146.
14   *Freeman's Journal*, 8 November 1849.
15   *The Limerick Chronicle*, 14 November 1849.
16   *Caterina*, published by Blackburn, London 1887.

17 *Cork Examiner*, 16 November 1849.
18 *Edinburgh Advertiser*, 12 February 1850.
19 *Edinburgh Evening Courant*, 18 February 1850.
20 *Annals of the Theatre Royal*, Dublin, R.M. Levey and J. O'Rorke, Dublin 1880.
21 *Dublin Evening Packet*, 23 February 1850.
22 *Dublin Evening Packet*, 28 February 1850.
23 *Dublin Evening Packet*, 5 March 1850.
24 *Dublin Evening Packet*, 7 March 1850.
25 *Limerick Chronicle*, 12 March 1850.
26 *Cork Examiner*, 18 March 1850.
27 *Freeman's Journal*, 25 March 1850.

Chapter Eight

1 *The Glorious Ones* by Harold C. Schonberg, New York 1985. Pages 139–54.
2 *The Times*, 3 April 1850.
3 *Daily News*, 3 April 1850.
4 *The Times*, 19 April 1850.
5 *Dublin Evening Packet*, 20 April 1850.
6 *Dublin Evening Packet*, 20 April 1850.
7 *The Times*, 14 May 1850.
8 *The Times*, 24 May 1850.
9 *The Times*, 4 July 1850.
10 *The Times*, 10 June 1850.
11 *The Times*, 11 July 1850.
12 *Dublin Evening Packet*, 26 October 1850.
13 *Dublin Evening Packet* 5 November 1850.
14 *Dublin University Magazine*, vol.1, no. 36, November, 1850.
15 *Freeman's Journal*, 29 October 1850.
16 *Wexford Independent*, 6 November 1850.
17 *Wexford Independent* 19 October 1850.
18 *Wexford Independent*, 6 November 1850.
19 *Tipperary Free Press*, 9 November 1850.
20 Ibid.
21 *The Province of Munster*, 9 November 1850.
22 *Cork Examiner*, 11 November 1850.
23 *Dublin Evening Packet*, 26 October 1850.
24 *Limerick Chronicle*, 12 November 1850.
25 *Galway Vindicator*, 20 November 1850.
26 *Galway Vindicator* 4 December 1850.
27 *Kilkenny Moderator*, 23 November 1850.
28 *Kilkenny Journal*, 23 November 1850.

Chapter Nine

1 *Illustrated London News*, 8 February 1851.
2 *Illustrated London News*, 8 March 1851.
3 *Galignani's Messenger*, 29 March 1851.
4 *Musical World*, 25 January 1851.
5 *Strong on Music, The New York Music Scene in the Days of George Templeton Strong, Vol. 2 Reverberations 1850–1856* by Vera Brodsky-Lawrence, Chicago 1995. Page 208.
 Note: Ms. Lawrence's reference to Wardwell's first name being 'Charles' is incorrect, his first name was 'J'[James]. See letter dated 1 October 1851 from J.H. Wardwell to Catherine Hayes featured in the *New York Daily Times*, 2 October 1851. Front page.
6 Ibid. Pages 153–60.
7 *P.T. Barnum, The Legend and the Man* by A.H. Saxon, New York 1989. Page 11.
8 *The Times*, London 14 June 1852.
9 *Illustrated London News*, 24 May 1851.
10 *Illustrated London News*, 6 September 1851.
11 Ibid.
12 *Spanning the Atlantic* by F. Lawrence Babcock, New York 1931. Pages 91–101.
13 *Spirit of the Times*, 19 July 1851, quoting from Wilmer & Smith's (Liverpool) *European Times* 14 June 1851.
14 *Strong on Music, The New York Music Scene in the Days of George Templeton Strong*. Page 206.
15 Saroni's *Musical Times*, 20 September 1851.
16 *Strong on Music, The New York Music Scene in the days of George Templeton Strong*. Page 206.
17 *Democracy at the Opera: Music, Theatre and Culture in New York City, 1815–60* by Karen Ahlquist, Chicago 1997. Page 143.
18 *The Albion*, 20 September 1851.
19 *Crotchets and Quavers or, Revelations of an Opera Manager in America* by Max Maretzek, New York 1855.
20 Ibid. Pages 184–6.
21 *Strong on Music, The New York Music Scene in the Days of George Templeton Strong*. Pages 210–11.
22 *The Brooklyn Eagle*, 8 October 1851.
23 *The Musical World*, London 6 March 1852.
24 *Strong on Music, The New York Music Scene in the days of George Templeton Strong*. Pages 208–209.
25 *New York Daily Times*, 24 September 1851.
26 *The Albion*, 27 September 1851.
27 *The Irish in New Orleans 1800–1860* by Earl F. Niehaus, Baton Rouge, 1965.
28 *Boston Daily Journal*, 14 October 1851.

Chapter Ten

1 *Providence Journal*, 15 October 1851.
2 *New York Daily Times*, 17 October 1851.
3 Ibid.
4 Daniel Webster was an eminent statesman and orator. At the time of his attendance at this Catherine Hayes concert in Boston, he was U.S. Secretary of State. He died a year later almost to the day.
5 *Boston Daily Journal*, 22 October 1851.
6 Ibid.
7 *Providence Journal*, 24 October 1851.
8 *Providence Journal*, 25 October 1851.
9 *Boston Daily Journal*, 27 October 1851.
10 *New York Daily Times*, 6 November 1851.
11 *New York Daily Times*, 3 November 1851.
12 *New York Daily Times*, 10 November 1851.
13 *New York Daily Times*, 15 November 1851.
14 *Providence Journal*, 13 December 1851.
15 *North America and United States Gazette*, 10 December 1851.
16 *Baltimore Sun*, 23 December 1851.
17 *Baltimore Sun*, 20 January 1852.
18 *The Daily Picayune*, 17 February 1852.
19 *The Daily Picayune*, 19 February 1852.
20 *The Irish in New Orleans* by Earl F. Niehaus, Baton Rouge, 1965. Pages 99–104 and 123–5.
21 *The Daily Picayune*, 21 February 1852.
22 *The Daily Picayune*, 22 February 1852.
23 *Cincinnati Gazette*, 7 April 1852.
24 *Cleveland Plain Dealer*, 23 April 1852.
25 *The Republican*, Binghampton, 14 July 1852.
26 *Dwight's Journal of Music*, Boston 24 July 1852. Page 127.
27 *Struggles and Triumphs or, Forty Years' Recollections* by P.T. Barnum, Buffalo, NY 1873. Pages 367–9.
28 *Daily Alta California*, 24 October 1852.
29 *New York Daily Times*, 21 October 1852.
30 *Daily Alta California*, 21 November 1852.
31 *Strong on Music, The New York Music Scene in the Days of George Templeton Strong 1836–1875* by Vera Brodsky-Lawrence, New York 1988. Pages 461–2.
32 *Baltimore Sun*, 29 January 1852.

Chapter Eleven

1 *Verdi at the Golden Gate: Opera and San Francisco in the Gold Rush Years* by George Martin, Berkeley/Los Angeles 1993. Pages 257–8 note 2; page 92.
2 *The Man Who Built San Francisco: A Study of Ralston's Journey with Banners* by Julian Dana, New York 1936. Page 81.

3 *Verdi at the Golden Gate: Opera and San Francisco in the Gold Rush Years* by George Martin, Berkeley/Los Angeles 1993. Page 43.

4 Ibid. Page 37.

5 *Daily Alta California*, 21 November 1852. See passenger arrival list. George Martin in his book *Verdi at the Golden Gate*, page 39, is incorrect when he states that Bushnell preceded Hayes to the city.

6 *Daily Alta California*, 1 December 1852. George Martin is again incorrect in his book *Verdi at the Golden Gate*, page 42, when he state: 'at her first recital in the San Francisco Theatre the audience was small because of rain'. The reviewer, one day after the concert, clearly indicates that the hall was full.

7 *Daily Alta California*, 1 December 1852.

8 *Daily Alta California*, 3 December 1852.

9 *Daily Alta California*, 4 December 1852.

10 *Daily Alta California*, 5 December 1852.

11 *Daily Alta California*, 19 December 1851.

12 *Spirit of the Times* (New York) 22 January 1853.

13 *California: The Irish Dream* by Patrick J. Dowling, San Francisco 1989. Page 317.

14 *The Musical World*, 31 July 1858, 'Recollections of California and Australia'. Page 486.

15 *Daily Alta California*, 5 February 1853.

16 *Sacramento Union*, 8 February 1853.

17 Ibid.

18 *Daily Alta California*, 9 February 1853.

19 *Sacramento Union*, 17 February 1853.

20 *Daily Alta California*, 2 March, 1853.

21 *Daily Alta California*, 23 April 1853.

22 *Los Primeros Teatros de Valparaiso* by Roberto C. Hernandez, Valparaiso 1928. Page 204.

23 *Historia De La Musica En Chile (1850–1900)* by Eugenio Pereria Salas, Santiago 1957. Pages 19, 20 & 21.

24 *El Mensajero*, Santiago, 17 August 1853.

25 Research notes dated 11 May 1995, from Tom Kaufman (author of *Verdi and His Major Contemporaries: A Selected Chronology of Performances with Casts*, New York 1990).

26 *Verdi at the Golden Gate* by George Martin, Berkeley/Los Angeles 1993. Page 54.

Chapter Twelve

1 *The Polynesian*, 29 July 1854.

2 *The Polynesian*, 29 July 1854.

3 *The Argus*, 18 September 1854.

4 *Entertaining Australia: An illustrated history* by Katherine Brisbane (ed.), Sydney 1991.

5 *History of Australia*, CD, Webster Publishing PTY. Ltd., NSW, Australia.

6   *The Argus*, 20 September 1854, quoting from the Sydney Morning Herald.

7   *The Argus*, 3 October 1854.

8   Ibid.

9   *The Argus*, 10 October 1854.

10 *The Argus*, 28 October 1854.

11 *Randwick Asylum: A Historical Review of the Society for the Relief of Destitute Children, 1852–1815* by Joseph Coulter, published by the Board of Directors, Randwick/Sydney 1916.

12 Clyde Company papers Vol. VI, 1854–58, P.L. Brown, (ed.), Oxford University Press, London 1968. Pages 615–16

13 *The Argus*, 28 October 1854.

14 *The Argus*, 19 October 1854.

15 *The Argus*, 25 October 1854.

16 *The Argus*, 28 October 1854.

17 *The Argus*, 30 October 1854.

18 Ibid.

19 Ibid.

20 Ibid.

21 *The Argus*, 17 November 1854. Perez Batchelder and his brothers Benjamin and Nathanial were from Boston and operated daguerreotype studios in Melbourne 1852–57. Later there was a partnership with a Daniel O'Neill and the firm became known as Batchelder & O'Neill. See *The Mechanical Eye in Australia 1841–1900* by Alan Davies and Peter Stanbury, 1986.

22 *The Argus*, 17 November 1854. Little is know about James Gilbert (1830–1885) the sculptor, other than the fact that he was working on a statue of Sir Redmond Barry, a famous Victorian and founder of the State Library of Victoria, when he died.

23 *The Argus*, 5 December 1854.

24 *Bengal Harkaru & India Gazette*, 1 February 1855.

25 *Bengal Harkaru & India Gazette*, 16 February 1855.

26 *Bengal Harkaru & India Gazette*, 14 February 1855.

27 *Straits Times*, 13 March 1855.

28 *Singapore Free Press*, 15 March 1855.

29 *Singapore Free Press* 23 March 1855.

30 *Java-Bode*, 25 April 1855.

31 *Java-Bode*, 23 May 1855.

32 *The Argus*, 2 July 1855.

33 *The Musical World*, 2 February 1856.

34 *Hobart Town Courier*, 24 January 1856.

35 *Hobart Town Courier*, 26 January 1856.

36 *Hobart Town Courier*, 28 January 1856.

37 *Hobart Town Courier*, 30 January 1865.

38 *Hobart Town Courier*, 1 February 1856.

39 *Hobart Town Courier*, 6 February 1856.

40 *The Argus*, 20 May 1856.

Chapter Thirteen

1 *Dublin Evening Packet*, 14 August 1856.
2 *Helen Hayes: On Reflection*, New York 1968, with Sandy Dody. *Helen Hayes: First Lady of the American Theatre* by Kenneth Barrow, New York 1985. *Dorothy Kirsten: A Time to Sing* by Dorothy Kirsten with Lanfranco Rasponi, New York 1982. *Famous Women Singers* by Homer Ulrich, Ney York 1953.
3 *Two Centuries of Opera at Covent Garden* by Harold Rosenthal, London 1958.
4 *The Musical Gazette*, 6 September 1856.
5 *The Musical Gazette*, 1 November 1856.
6 *The London Times*, 18 November 1856.
7 *The Musical Gazette*, 22 November 1856.
8 *The Musical World*, 13 December 1856, reporting on an extract from Dublin's *Saunder's Newsletter* of the same period.
9 *The Belfast News-Letter*, 16 December 1856.
10 *The Musical World*, 31 January 1857.
11 *The Belfast News-Letter*, 10 January 1857.
12 *The Musical Gazette*, 7 March 1857.
13 *The Freeman's Journal* 27 February 1857.
14 *The Freeman's Journal*, 12 March 1857.
15 *The Freeman's Journal*, 17 March 1857.
16 *The Freeman's Journal*, 23 March 1857.
17 *The Musical Gazette*, 11 April 1857, quoting from *The Freeman's Journal*, Dublin.
18 *The Freeman's Journal*, 31 March 1857.
19 *Annals of the Theatre Royal, Dublin* by R.M. Levey and J. O'Rorke, Dublin 1880. Page 174.
20 *The Freeman's Journal*, 23 April 1857.
21 *The Freeman's Journal*, 24 April 1857.
22 *Blue Book on France*, 1995 edition.
23 *The Musical Gazette*, 26 December 1857.
24 *The Times*, 27 January 1859.
25 *The Musical World*, 29 January 1859.

Chapter Fourteen

1 *The Musical World*, 14 January 1860.
2 *The Illustrated London News*, 10 November, 1860
3 *Kentish Mercury*, 17 August 1861.
4 *Waterford News (Ireland)* 23 August 1861.
5 *Royal Artillery Muster Rolls*, Public Records Offices, Kew, England. Reference WO76/360.

Chronology of Performances/ Travels (1839–1861)

Note s = soprano; ms-mezzo, soprano, ct = contralto, t = tenor, b = baritone; bs = bass; nv = non-vocalist

Country, City/Town & Location Date, Work	(Catherine Hayes participated in all performances listed)
1839 *Ireland:* Dublin Rotunda, 3 May, Concert	A. Sapio(b)
Rotunda, 9 Dec, Concert	H. Rudersdorff (s), Mr. Rudersdorff (nv), A. Sapio(b), S.J. Pigott(nv)
Rotunda, 16 Dec, Concert (Private)	H. Rudersdorff(s), A. Sapio(b), Mr. Hodges(bs), S.J. Pigott(nv)
1840 Limerick Swinburne's, 15 Jan, Concert	A. Sapio(b), M. Castro De Gistau (nv), Wilkinson(nv)
Swinburne's, 5 Feb, Concert	A. Sapio(b), Mr. Rudersdorff(nv), S.J. Pigott(nv), Mr. H. Rogers(nv)
Swinburne's, 11 Feb, Concert	A. Sapio(b)
Belfast Anacreontic Hall, 26 Mar, Concert	A. Sapio(b), Mr. Edmonds
Dublin Rotunda, 1 May, Concert	A. Sapio(b), Mr. Hodges, Mr. M'Ghie, Mr. Rudersdorff(nv), J. Barton(nv), S.J. Pigott(nv), Mr. Wilconson(nv), Mr. Castro(nv), Mr.Conran(nv)

Country, City/Town & Location Date, Work	(Catherine Hayes participated in all performances listed)
1840 *(cont.)*	
Rotunda, 13 May, Concert	A. Sapio(b), Mrs. Wood/M.A. Paton(s), F. Robinson(nv), J. Robinson, W.S. Conran(nv)
Rotunda, 15 May, Concert	Mrs. Wood/M.A. Paton(s), A. Sapio(b), S.J. Pigott(nv), Mr. Rudersdorff(nv) R.M. Levy(nv)
5 Gardiner St., 1 Dec, Concert (Private)	Mr. Rudersdorff(nv), Miss Allen, S.J. Pigott(nv), Mr. Marsh(nv), A. Sapio(b), Mr. Sedlatzek(nv)
1841 Dublin	
Rotunda, 12 Jan, Concert	Franz Liszt(nv), Miss Steel(s), Miss L. Bassano(ms), J. Parry(t), Mr. Richardson(nv), S.J. Pigott(nv), Mr. J.P. Knight(bs)
Rotunda, 4 March, Concert	A. Sapio(b), Mr. Knight(bs), Mr. Rudersdorff(nv), S.J. Pigott(nv), Mr. Harrington(nv), Miss Rossini Collins(nv)
Rotunda, 5 Apr, Concert	Mr. Yoarkly(t), A. Sapio(b), Mr. Hudson(nv), Mr. Rudersdorff (nv), S.J. Pigott(nv)
Belfast Anacreontic Hall, 15 Apr, Concert	A. Sapio(b), S.J. Pigott(nv), Mr. Murray(nv)
Dublin Rotunda, 20 Apr, Concert	A. Sapio(b), Miss E. Collins(s), Miss V. Collins(ms), Mr. Knight(bs), Mr. Rudersdorff(nv), Mr. Pendelton(nv), Mr. Rogers (nv), S.J. Pigott(nv), Miss Rossini Collins(nv), Mr. Percival(nv), Mr. M.H. Patton(nv), Mr. Pratten(nv)

Country, City/Town & Location Date, Work	(Catherine Hayes participated in all performances listed)
1841 *(cont.)* Rotunda , 30 Apr, Concert	A. Sapio(b), Mr. J. Robinson, Mr. Frazer(bs), Mr. T. Yoakly(t), Miss Smith, Mr. Rudersdorff(n.v), Mr. J. Barton(n.v.), Mr. M. Levey(n.v.), S.J. Pigott(n.v.), Mr. Patton(n.v.)
Rotunda, 13 May, Concert	A. Sapio(b), Mr. King, Mr. Pearsall, Miss M.B. Hawes,
Rotunda, 17 May, Concert	Miss M.B. Hawes, A. Sapio(b), Mr. King, Mr. Pearsall, S.J. Pigott(nv), Miss Rossini Collins(nv), Mr. Rudersdorff(nv)
Morrison's Hotel, 5 Sep, Audition	Catherine Hayes auditions for Luigi Lablache, accompanied on the piano by Julius Benedict
1842 Dublin Rotunda, 19 Jan, Concert	Miss Birch(s), Sig. Guglielmi(t), A. Sapio(b), Mr. Yoakly(t), S.J. Pigott(nv)
Rotunda, 15 Feb, Concert	A. Sapio(b)
Rotunda, 8 Mar, Concert	A. Sapio(b), Mr. Knight(bs), Mr. Yoakly(t), Mr. Geary, Mr. H. Lidel(nv), S.J. Pigott(nv), Mr. Percival(nv), Mr. Harrington (nv), Mr. Conran(nv)
Rotunda, 28 Apr, Concert Belfast, April Concert	A. Sapio(b), Mr. Knight(bs), S.J. Pigott(nv)
Limerick 22 July, Concert	A. Sapio(b)
14 August, Concert	A. Sapio(b)
Dublin Private Home, Sept, Concert	Lady de Gray's home?

Country, City/Town & Location Date, Work	(Catherine Hayes participated in all performances listed)
1842 *(cont.)* *France:* Paris Square d'Orleans, 12 October, Study	Study with Manuel Garcia Jr. commences
1843 Paris Square d'Orleans, Jan–Dec, Study	Study with M. Garcia
1844 Paris Square d'Orléans, Jan–Mar, Study	Completes study with M. Garcia
Italy: Milan Ronconi' s Studio, Apr, Study	Commences coaching with Felice Ronconi
1845 Milan, Jan-May, Study	Coaching with Ronconi continues
Ronconi's Studio?, Feb, Concert	
France: Marseilles Teatro Grand, 10 May, I Puritani (Debut)	A. Castellan(t), O. Ventura(b), A. Alizard(bs), A. Alba(bs)
Teatro Grand, May–Jul, Lucia di Lammermoor	A. Castellan(t), O.Ventura (b), A. Alizard(bs)
Teatro Grand, May–Jul, Mose	A. Castellan(t), A. Alizard(bs)
Italy: Milan G. Ricordi' s Home, 6 Sep, Concert	D. Lorini(t), A.Bosio(s), D. Coletti(b)
La Scala, 4 Nov, Linda di Chamounix (debut)	G. Sinico(t), E. Angri(ms), A. De Bassini(b), G.F. Beneventano(bs)
La Scala, 26 Dec, Otello	G. Sinico(t), G.F. Beneventano(bs), S.L. Bouche(bs), Perelli(t)

Country, City/Town & Location Date, Work	(Catherine Hayes participated in all performances listed)
1846 Milan	
La Scala, 20 Jan, Anna Bolena	E. Scotta (s), S.L. Bouche(bs), E. Music(t)
La Scala, 21 Feb, Estella (Premiere)	G.F. Beneventano(bs), A. De Bassini(b), G. Sinico(t)
La Scala, 11 Mar, Il Bravo	R. Basso-Borio(s), G.F. Beneventano (bs), Masset(t), Labocetta(t)
Austria: Vienna Kärntnertortheter, 23 Apr, Lucia di Lammermoor	G. Fraschini(t), F. Coletti(b), A.Rodas(bs), G.Soldi(t)
Kärntnertortheter, 10 Jun Il Giuramento	F. Coletti(b), E. Angri(ms), G. Fraschini(t)
Italy: Milan La Scala, 1 Sep, Mose	I. Marini(bs), R. Porchini(t), L. Mei(t), S. De Breuil(b), N. Marconi(bs), A. Janich(s)
La Scala, 13 Oct, Ricciardo e Zoraide	E. Calzolari(t), E. Angri(ms), Masset(t), S.L. Bouche(bs)
La Scala, 31 Oct, Lucia di Lammermoor	S. Reeves(t), Bozzani(b), G. Lodi(bs)
Venice La Fenice , 26 Dec, Albergio da Romano (Premiere)	L. Ferretti(t), G. Lodi(bs), E. Crivelli(b)
1847 Venice La Fenice, 23 Jan, Lucia di Lammermoor	L. Flavio(t), C. Badiale(b), G. Lodi(bs)
La Fenice, 24 Feb, Linda di Chamounix	L. Flavio(t), C. Badiale(b), G. Lodi(bs)
La Fenice, 13 March, Griselda (Premiere)	L. Ferretti(t), C. Badiale(b), E. Crivelli(b), M. Zambelli(s)

Country, City/Town & Location Date, Work	(Catherine Hayes participated in all performances listed)
1847 *(cont.)* *Austria:* Vienna Kärntnertortheter, 10 Apr, Lucia di Lammermoor	N. Ivanoff(t), F. Varesi(b), G. Catalano(bs), G. Bottegisi(t)
Kärntnertortheter, 23 Apr, Estella	R. Mirate(t), F. Collini(b), A. Rodas(bs)
Kärntnertortheter, 18 Jun, Olivo e Pasquale	E. Calzolari(t), G. Soldi(t), F. Collini(b), C. Soares(bs)
Italy: Bergamo Teatro Riccardi, 9 Aug, Maria di Rohan	E. Calzolari(t), G. B. Bencich(b), G. Locatelli(bs)
Teatro Riccardi, Aug, Banquet	Hayes and G.B. Rubini(t) sing from Lucia d Lammermoor
Teatro Riccardi, 28 Aug, Concert	Benefit concert for Hayes
Milan Verdi/Muzio Milan Residence, Aug/Sep, I Masnadieri	Hayes studies Verdi's new opera with E. Muzio, Verdi's assistant
La Scala, 18 Sep, Linda di Chamounix	A. Poppi(ms), E. Musich(t), G. Corsi(b), P. Derivis(bs)
La Scala, 25 Oct, Mortedo	P. Derivis(bs), G. Corsi(b), G. Gruitz(ms)
Verona Teatro Filarmonica, 26 Dec, I Masnadieri (Premiere-Italy)	F. Borioni(t), A.. De Bassini(b), G. Romanelli(bs), F. Dell'Asta(bs)
1848 Verona Teatro Filarmonica, 17? Jan , Lucia di Lammermoor	F. Borioni(t), A. De Bassini(b), F. Rossi(t), G. Romanelli(bs)

Country, City/Town & Location Date, Work	(Catherine Hayes participated in all performances listed)
1848 (*cont.*) Milan City, Mar	All Milan in revolt against the Austrians
Florence Teatro della Pergola, 13 Mar, I Masnadieri (Local premiere)	F. Borioni(t), A. De Bassini(b), N. Benedetti(bs)
Teatro della Pergola, 5 Apr, Gennaro Arnese (Premiere)	A. Brunacci(t), A. De Bassini(b), N. Benedetti(bs), F. Rossi(t),
Bergamo, 8 Apr, Gaetano Donizetti	Composer Donizetti dies in his home town of Bergamo
Reggio Emilia Teatro Comunale, 6 May, Lucia di Lammermoor	L. Graziani(t), A. De Bassini(b), N. Benedetti(bs)
Teatro Comunale, 24 May, Gennaro Arnese	E. Pancani(t), A. De Bassini(b), N. Bemedetti(bs)
Florence Real Teatro degli Intrepidi, 13 Jun, Lucia di Lammermoor	L. Graziani(t), A De Bassini(b), N. Benedetti(bs)
Genoa Teatro Carlo Felice, 26 Dec, Lucia di Lammermoor	R. Mirate(t), F. Monari(bs), L.Vita(b),
1849 Genoa Teatro Carlo Felice, 25 Jan, I Masnadieri	R. Mirate(t), F. Monari(bs), L. Vita(b), F. Galberini(t)
Teatro Carlo Felice, 14 Feb, I Puritani	R. Mirati(t), F. Monari(bs), L. Vita(b), T. Barattini(bs)
England: London Covent Garden, 10 Apr, Linda di Chamounix (debut)	L. Salvi(t), A. Tamburini(b), de Meric(ms), Polonini(bs)

Country, City/Town & Location Date, Work	(Catherine Hayes participated in all performances listed)
1849 *(cont.)*	
Covent Garden, 26 Apr, Lucia di Lammermoor	G. Mario(t), A. Tamburini(b), A. Polonini(bs)
Covent Garden, 28 Apr, Lucia di Lammermoor	Hayes performs at Covent Garden
Her Majesty's, 28 Apr, Lucia di Lammermoor	Lind performs same opera, same night, at Her Majesty's
Her Majesty's, 8 May, Concert	G. Mario(t), G. Grisi(s), A. Tamburini(b), G. Ronconi(b)
Covent Garden, 12 May, Robert le Diable	Hayes, scheduled to sing, cancels due to bad cold
Covent Garden, 29 May, Lucia di Lammermoor	G. Mario(t), A. Tamburini(b), A. Polonini(bs)
Her Majesty's, 30 May, Concert	G. Mario(t), S. Reeves(t), A. Tamburini(b), G. Grisi(s), F. Taccinardi-Persiani(s), J. Dorus-Gras(s), E. Angri(ms)
Buckingham Palace, 2 Jun, Concert	G. Mario(t), G. Grisi(s), I. Gardoni(t), F. Coletti(b), M. Alboni(ms), L. Lablache(bs)
London Exeter Hall, 4 Jun, The Creation	Miss Byers(ct), Mr Lockey(t), Mr Lawler(bs)
Exeter Hall, 6 Jun, Concert	L. Pine(s), E. Poole(ms), Miss E. Lyons(s)
Covent Garden, 13 Jun, Concert	G. Grisi(s), F. Taccinardi-Persiani(s), G. Mario(t)
Hanover Square, 14 Jun, Concert	G.Grisi(s), F. Taccinardi-Persiani(s), S. Reeves(t), A. Tamburini(b), L.Salvi(t)
Hanover Square, 20 Jun, The Messiah	S. Reeves(t), Miss Dolby(ct), H. Phillips(bs), Sir H. Bishop(nv)

Country, City/Town & Location Date, Work	(Catherine Hayes participated in all performances listed)
1849 (*cont.*) Her Majesty's , 22 Jun, Concert	M. Alboni(ms), T. Parodi(s), M. Giuliani(s), I. Gardoni(t), S. Reeves(t), E. Calzalori(t), F. Coletti(b), G. Belletti(b), L. Lablache(bs), F. Lablache(b)
Covent Garden, 6 Jul, Concert	G. Grisi(s), F. Tassinardi-Persiani(s), J. Dorus-Gras(s), E. Angri(ms), G. Mario(t), L. Salvi(t), A. Tamburini(b), S. Reeves(t), I. Marini(bs)
Covent Garden, 11 Jul, Concert	G. Mario(t), T. Parodi(s), A. Tamburini(b)
Hanover Square, 18 Jul, Concert	G. Grisi(s), M. Alboni(ms), T. Parodi(s), G. Mario(t), A. Tamburini(b), L. Lablache(bs), H. Phillips(bs)
Covent Garden, 21 Jul, Lucia di Lammermoor	At the close of the opera La Donna del Lago featuring Giulia Grisi in the title role, Hayes sings an act from Lucia di Lammermoor with L. Salvi(t), A. Tamburini(b), E. Polonini(bs), M. Costa(nv)
Covent Garden, 24 Jul, Le Prophète (London/premiere)	G. Mario(t), P. Viardot-Garcia(ms), J. Taliafico(bs), E. Polonini(bs), I. Marini(bs)
Drury Lane, 15 Aug, Concert	G. Grisi(s), P. Viardot-Garcia(ms), J. Dorus-Gras(s), E. Angri(ms), G. Mario(t), I. Marini(bs), J. Taliafico(bs), E. Polonini(bs), Paglieri(t), H. Mengis(b), L. Lavenu (nv)
Covent Garden, 23 Aug, Le Prophète (acts 2 & 3)	After acts 2 & 3 of Les Huguenots, Hayes sings in acts 2 & 3 of Le Prophète with P. Viardot-Garcia(ms), G. Mario(t), and I. Marini(bs)

Country, City/Town & Location Date, Work	(Catherine Hayes participated in all performances listed)
1849 (*cont.*) Liverpool	
New Concert Hall, 27 Aug, Concert	M. Alboini(ms), G. Grisi(s), G. Mario(t), S. Reeves(t)
New Concert Hall, 28 Aug , Elijah	S. Reeves(t)
New Concert Hall, 29 Aug, Concert	P. Viardot-Garcia(ms), G. Mario(t), S. Reeves(t)
New Concert Hall, 30 Aug, Messiah	S. Reeves(t)
Birmingham Town Hall, 4–7 Sep, Concerts	H. Sontag(s), M. Alboni(ms), E. De Meric(ms), G. Mario(t), S. Reeves(t), E.Calzolari(t), L. Lablache(bs)
Town Hall, 6 Sep , Messiah	S. Reeves(t)
Liverpool Concert Hall, 23 Oct, Concert	Burdini(b), Damke(t), Briccaldi(?), E. Poole(ms)
Concert Hall, 30 Oct, Concert	Burdini(b), Damke(t), E. Poole(ms), J. Benedict(nv)
Sheffield, 31 Oct, Concert	Burdini(b), Damke(t), E. Poole(ms), J. Benedict(nv)
Newcastle, 1 Nov, Concert	Burdini(b), Damke(t), E. Poole(ms), J. Benedict(nv)
Leeds, 2 Nov, Concert	Burdini(b), Damke(t), E. Poole(ms), J. Benedict(nv)
Manchester, 3 Nov, Concert	Burdini(b), Damke(t), E. Poole(ms), J. Benedict(nv)
Ireland: Dublin, 4 Nov, Return to Ireland	Stays at Morrison's Hotel, Dublin

Country, City/Town & Location Date, Work	(Catherine Hayes participated in all performances listed)
1849 (*cont.*) Concert Hall, 5 Nov, Philharmonic Concert	Burdini(t), Damke(t), E. Poole(ms), J. Benedict(nv)
Theatre Royal, 6 Nov, Lucia di Lammermoor (Debut)	Paglieri(t), Damke(t), S. Reeves(t), Burdini(b), J.Benedict(nv), L. Lavenu(nv)
Theatre Royal, 7 Nov, Norma	E. Poole(ms), Damke(t), Burdini(b), J. Benedict(nv)
Theatre Royal, 10 Nov, Concert	Hayes gives a benefit Concert
Limerick Theatre Royal, 12 Nov, Concert	Damke(t), Burdini(b), E. Poole(ms), J. Benedict(nv)
Theatre Royal, 13 Nov, Concert	Damke(t), Burdini(b), E. Poole(ms), J. Benedict(nv)
Cork Theatre Royal, 14 Nov, Concert	Damke(t), Burdini(b), E. Poole(ms), J. Benedict(nv)
Waterford, 15 Nov, Concert	Damke(t), Burdini(b), E. Poole(ms), J. Benedict(nv)
1850 *England:* London Beaumont Institution, 7 Jan, Concert	E. Poole(ms), Miss Birch(s), Mr. Allen(t),
Exeter Hall, 14 Jan, Concert	Miss Birch(s), Huddart(?), E. Poole(ms), L. Lablache(bs) W. Harrison(t), H. Phillips(bs), Thalberg(nv), J. Benedict(nv)
Exeter Hall, 26 Jan, St. Paul	Miss Dolby(ct), Mr. Lockey(t), Herr Formes(bs), M. Costa(nv)
Scotland: Edinburgh, 1 Feb	Hayes arrives in Edinburgh

Country, City/Town & Location Date, Work	(Catherine Hayes participated in all performances listed)
1850 (*cont.*) Edinburgh Music Hall, 13 Feb, Reid Concert	E. Poole(ms), Mr. Travers(t), J. Mengis(b), E. Polonini(bs) Sig. Vera(nv)
Music Hall, 15 Feb, Concert	E. Poole(ms), Mr. Travers(t), J. Mengis(b), E. Polonini(bs) Sig. Vera(nv)
Ireland: Belfast, 19 Feb, Concert	E. Poole(ms), Mr. Travers(t), J. Mengis(b), E. Polonini(bs)
Dublin Theatre Royal, 21 Feb, Linda di Chamounix	E. Poole(ms), Mr. Travers(t), J. Mengis(b), E. Polonini(bs) Sig. Vera(nv)
Theatre Royal, 25 Feb, Norma	E. Poole(ms), Mr. Travers(t), E. Polonini(bs), Mr Houghton(t) Sig. Vera(nv)
Theatre Royal, 26 Feb, La Sonnambula	Mr. Travers(t), E. Polonini(bs), Sig. Vera(nv)
Theatre Royal, 2 Mar, Lucia di Lammermoor	Mr. Travers(t), J. Mengis(b), E. Polonini(bs), Sig. Vera(nv)
Theatre Royal, 9 Mar, La Sonnambula	Benefit performance for Hayes
Limerick Theatre Royal, 11 Mar, La Sonnambula	Mr. Travers(t), E. Polonini(bs), E. Poole(ms), Sig. Vera(nv)
Theatre Royal, 12 Mar, Norma	Mr. Travers(t), E. Poole(ms), E. Polonini(bs), Sig. Vera(nv)
Cork Theatre Royal, 14 Mar, La Sonnambula	Mr. Travers(t), E. Poole(ms), E. Polonini(bs). Sig. Vera(nv)

Country, City/Town & Location Date, Work	(Catherine Hayes participated in all performances listed)
1850 (*cont.*) Cork	
Theatre Royal, 15 Mar, Norma	Mr. Travers(t), E. Poole(ms), E. Polonini(bs), Sig. Vera(nv)
Theatre Royal, 16 Mar, Linda di Chamounix	Mr. Travers(t), E. Poole(ms), J. Mengis(b), E. Polonini(bs)
Theatre Royal, 18 Mar, Concert	Selections from La Sonnambula
Dublin	
Theatre Royal, 21 Mar, La Sonnambula	Mr. Travers(t), E. Poole(ms), E. Polonini(bs), Sig. Vera(nv)
Concert Rooms, 22 Mar, Concert	Mr. Travers(t), J. Mengis(b), E. Polonini(bs), E. Poole(ms)
Theatre Royal, 23 Mar, Linda di Chamounix	Mr. Travers(t), J. Mengis(b), E. Polonini(bs), E. Poole(ms) Sig. Vera(nv)
Theatre Royal, ? Mar, Lucia di Lammermoor	Mr. Travers(t), J. Mengis(b), E.Polonini(bs), Sig. Vera(nv)
Theatre Royal, ? Mar, Linda di Chamounix	Mr. Travers(t), J. Mengis(b), E. Polonini(bs), E. Pool(ms)
England: London	
Her Majesty's, 2 Apr, Lucia di Lammermoor	S. Reeves(t), G. Belletti(b), F. Lablache(bs)
Exeter Hall, 12 Apr, Elijah	Miss Dolby(ct), Mr. Lockey(t), Herr Formes(bs)
Hanover Square, 16 Apr, Concert	Miss Birch(s), E. Poole(ms), F. Lablache(b), S. Reeves(t), J. Benedict(nv), M. Ernst(nv), Briccialdi(nv), B. Richards(nv)
Her Majesty's, 18 Apr, Le Nozze di Figaro	H. Sontag(s), F. Coletti(b), G. Belletti(b), F. Lablache(b), E. Calzalori(t), T.Parodi(s) (Hayes sang Cherubino)

Country, City/Town & Location Date, Work	(Catherine Hayes participated in all performances listed)
1850 (*cont.*) London	
Hanover Square, 24 Apr, Concert	Miss C. Birch(s), L. Pyne(s), L. Bassano(ct), S. Reeves(t), Miss Dolby(ct), H. Phillips(bs), F. Lablache(b), M. Costa(nv)
Exeter Hall, 6 May, The Creation	Mr. Lockey(t), Mrs. Temple(ms)
Hanover Square, 8 May, The Messiah	Miss Dolby(ct), L. Bassano(ct), Mr. Lockey(t), H. Phillips(bs), M. Costa(nv)
Beethoven Rooms, 11 May, Concert	S. Reeves(t), L. Bassano(ct), A. Gadded(nv),
Her Majesty's, 13May, Concert	H. Sontag(s), S. Reeves(t), E. Calzolari(t), G. Belletti(b), F. Coletti(b), T. Parodi(s), Baucade(t), F. Lablache(b), L. Lablache(bs), M. Balfe(nv)
Hanover Square, 14 May, Concert	Miss Dolby(ct), Miss C. Birch(s), J. Benedict(nv), L. Lavenu(nv)
Hanover Square, 15 May, Concert	Miss C. Birch(s), Miss E. Birch(s), F. Lablache(b), Mr. Lockey(t), H. Phillips(bs)
Her Majesty's, 16 May, Concert	H. Sontag(s), Baucade(t), S. Reeves(t), F. Coletti(b), G. Belletti(b), F. Lablache(b), L. Lablache(bs), E. Calzolari(t), M. Taglione(nv)
Sussex Hall, 20 May, Concert	Sig. Marchesi(b), Herr Ernst(nv),
Her Majesty's, 27 May, Concert	H. Sontag(s), T. Parodi(s), I. Gardoni(t), E. Frezzolini(s), S. Reeves(t), E. Calzolari(t), Baucade(t), F. Coletti(b), G. Belletti(b), L. Lablache(bs)
Her Majesty's, 30 May, Concert	H. Sontag(s), E. Frezzolini(s), S. Reeves(t), E. Calzolari(t), Baucade(t), G. Belletti(b), F. Lablache(b), L. Lablache(bs), T. Parodi(s), M. Balfe(nv)

Country, City/Town & Location Date, Work	(Catherine Hayes participated in all performances listed)
1850 *(cont.)* London Exeter Hall, 31 May, The Creation	Miss Kent(ct), Mr. Lockey(t), Mr. Lawler(bs)
Highbury, 3 Jun, Concert	E. Angri(ms), W. Harrison(t), F. Smith(bs)
Her Majesty's, 4 Jun, Lucia di Lammermoor	Hayes ill, does not sing at the last minute; E. Frezzolini substitutes for Hayes
Her Majesty's, 8 Jun, La Tempesta	Hayes, scheduled for this Halevy opera premiere, was ill.
St. James's Hall, 12 Jun, Concert	Mme. Sainton-Dolby(ct), C. Santley(b), Miss Lacelles(s)
St. James's Hall, 14 Jun, Concert	E. Parepa(s), C. Santley(b), A. Goddard(nv),
St. James's Hall, 15 Jun, Concert	E. Parepa(s), G. Belletti(b), C. Santley(b), S. Reeves(t), C. Halle(nv)
Her Majesty's, 21 Jun, Concert	H. Sontag(s), E. Frezzolini(s), I. Gardoni(t, E. Calzolari(t), T. Parodi(s), F. Lablache(b), L. Lablache(bs), Baucade(t), G. Belletti(b), M. Balfe(nv)
St. James's Hall, 28 Jun, Concert	S. Reeves(t), Mme. Borghi-Mamo (ms), L. Pyne(s), Mrs. S. Reeves(s), G. Belletti(b), J. Benedict(nv)
St. James's Hall, 29 Jun, Concert	Mme. Sainton-Dolby(ct), W. Ganz(nv),
Her Majesty's, 10 Jul, Concert	H. Sontag(s), E. Frezzolini(s), F. Coletti(b), F. Lablache(b), L. Lablache(bs) E. Calzolari(t), I. Gardoni(t), G. Belletti(b) (Hayes & Reeves did not show-up)

Country, City/Town & Location Date, Work	(Catherine Hayes participated in all performances listed)
1850 *(cont.)* *Scotland:* Edinburgh Music Hall, 12 Oct, Concert	Macfarren(ms), Formes(bs), Rainforth(ms), Bordas(t), L. Lavenu(nv)
Music Hall, 14 Oct, Concert	Bordas(t), MacFarren(ms), Formes(bs), L. Lavenu(nv)
Ireland: Dublin Theatre Royal, 21 Oct, La Sonnambula	Bordas(t), Galli(b), Paltoni(bc), Macfarren(ms), L. Lavenu(nv)
Theatre Royal, 22 Oct, Linda di Chamounix	Bordas(t), Macfarren(ms), Paltoni(bs), J. Mengis(b), L. Lavenu(nv)
Theatre Royal, 24 Oct, Lucrezia Borgia	Bordas(t), Macfarren(ms), J. Mengis(b), Paltoni(bs), L. Lavenu(nv)
Theatre Royal, 25 Oct, Concert for Poor	Bordas(t), J. Mengis(b), Macfarren(ms), Paltoni(bs), L. Lavenu(nv)
Theatre Royal, 26 Oct, Lucia di Lammermoor	Bordas(t), J. Mengis(b), Paltoni(bs), L. Lavenu(nv)
Theatre Royal, 28 Oct, Lucrezia Borgia	Bordas(t), J. Mengis(b), Paltoni(bs), Macfarren(ms). L. Lavenu(nv)
Theatre Royal, 29 Oct, Norma	Bordas(t), Macfarren(ms), Paltoni(bs), L. Lavenu(nv)
Theatre Royal, 30 Oct, La Sonnambula	Bordas(t), Macfarren(ms), J. Mengis(b), L. Lavenu(nv)
Theatre Royal, 1 Nov, Linda di Chamounix	Bordas(t), Paltoni(bs), Macfarren(ms), J. Mengis(b), L. Lavenu(nv)

Country, City/Town & Location Date, Work	(Catherine Hayes participated in all performances listed)
1850 *(cont.)*	
Theatre Royal, 2 Nov, Lucrezia Borgia	Bordas(t), Macfarren(ms), Paltoni(bs), J. Mengis(b), L. Lavenu(nv)
Wexford Theatre Royal, 4 Nov, Concert	Bordas(t), J. Mengis(b), Macfarren(ms), Paltoni(bs), L. Lavenu(nv)
Waterford Town Hall, 5 Nov, Concert	Bordas(t), Macfarren(ms), Paltoni(bs), J. Mengis(b), L. Lavenu(nv)
Clonmel Mechanics' Institute, 6 Nov, Concert	Bordas(t), Macfarren(ms), Paltoni(bs), J.Mengis(b), L. Lavenu(nv)
Cork Theatre Royal, 8 Nov, La Sonnambula	Bordas(t), Macfarren(ms), J. Mengis(b), L. Lavenu(nv)
Theatre Royal, 9 Nov, Lucrezia Borgia	Bordas(t), Macfarren(ms), J. Mengis(b), Paltoni(bs), L. Lanenu(nv)
Theatre Royal, 11 Nov, Lucia di Lammermoor	Bordas(t), J. Mengis(b), Paltoni(bs), L. Lavenu(nv)
Theatre Royal, 12 Nov, Don Pasquale	Bordas(ill?), J. Mengis(b), Paltoni(bs), L. Lavenu(nv)
Limerick, 13 Nov, Concert	Bordas(t), Macfarren(ms), J. Mengis(b), Paltoni(bs), L. Lavenu(nv)
14 Nov, Concert	Bordas(t), Macfarren(ms), J. Mengis(b), Paltoni(bs), L. Lavenu(nv)
15 Nov, Harmonic Society,	Hayes admitted into the Limerick Harmonic Society 2

Country, City/Town & Location Date, Work	(Catherine Hayes participated in all performances listed)
1850 *(cont.)* Galway Theatre Royal, 16 Nov, Concert	Bordas(t), Macfarren(ms), J. Mengis(b), Paltoni(bs), L. Lavenu(nv)
Kilkenny Court House, 19 Nov, Concert	Bordas(t), J. Mengis(b), Macfarren(ms), L. Lavenu(nv)
Dublin Theatre Royal, 20 Nov, Lucia di Lammermoor	Bordas(t), J. Mengis(b), Salabert(bs), L. Lavenu(nv)
Theatre Royal, 21 Nov, La Sonnambula	Bordas(t), J. Mengis(b)
Belfast Music Hall, 22 Nov, Concert Anacreontic	Society Hayes and L. Lavenu(nv)
Dublin Theatre Royal, 23 Nov, La Sonnambula	Bordas(t), J. Mengis(b), Macfarren(ms), L. Lavenu(nv)
Italy: Rome Teatro Apollo, 20 Dec	Hayes arrives in Rome for the opera season at the Teatro Apollo
Teatro Apollo, 26 Dec, I Puritani	E. Naudin (t), A. Ottavani (b). Opening night of the Carnivale season
1851 Rome, 13 Jan, Lucia di Lammermoor	E. Naudin(t), A. Ottavani(b)
Jan?, I Puritani	E. Naudin(t), A. Ottavani(b)
3 Feb, Maria di Rohan	E. Naudin(t), R. Ferlotti(b), Z. Sbrica, Liverani
13 Mar, Concert	?

Country, City/Town & Location Date, Work	(Catherine Hayes participated in all performances listed)
1851 *(cont.)* Rome, 15 Mar,	Accademia di Santa Cecilia; Hayes awarded a Diploma
England: London, 2 May, Elijah	S. Reeves(t), E. Birch(s), Formes(bs),
16 May, Elijah	S. Reeves(t), E. Birch(s), Formes(bs)
Hanover Square, 19 May, Concert (morning)	Hayes and L. Lavenu(nv)
Exeter Hall, 19 May, Concert (evening)	Hayes and H. Phillips(bs)
Exeter Hall, 23 May, The Messiah	E. Birch(s), Dolby(ct), S. Reeves(t), M. Costa(nv)
Liverpool, 27 May, Concert	Replaces L. Pyne(s) at a Philharmonic Society Concert
London, 30 May, The Messiah	S. Reeves(t)
6 Jun, Elijah	S. Reeves(t), Formes(bs)
13 Jun, Concert	S. Reeves(t), Formes(bs), E. Poole(ms), A. Braham(t)
Exeter Hall, 27 Jun, Elijah	S. Reeves(t), Formes(bs)
France: Trouville, Jul/Aug	Catherine Hayes takes a rest in France
England: Manchester Free Trade Hall, 28 Aug, Concert (Farewell)	A. Braham(t), J. Mengis(b), L. Lavenu(nv)
Free Trade Hall, 29 Aug, Concert	A.Braham(t), J. Mengis(b), L. Lavenu(nv)
Free Trade Hall,30 Aug, Concert	A. Braham(t), J. Mengis(b), L. Lavenu(nv)

Country, City/Town & Location Date, Work	(Catherine Hayes participated in all performances listed)
1851 (*cont.*) Liverpool Theatre Royal, 1 Sep, Concert	A. Braham(t), J. Mengis(b), L. Lavenu(nv)
SS Pacific, 3 Sep, Concert	Hayes and party give a concert on board the SS Pacific prior to departing for New York City

America:
During this period in America, Hayes shared the concert platform with A. Braham (t), J. Mengis (b) and L. Lavenu (nv). When other artists joined the group, or Hayes participated in other activity, it will be indicated.

America: New York City Tripler Hall, 23 Sep, Concert	
Brooklyn, 6 Oct	Hayes sings to children at the orphanage in east Brooklyn, NY
8 Oct, Concert	
Boston, 14 Oct, Concert	
Providence, RI, 15 Oct, Concert	
Boston, 20 Oct, Concert	
Providence, RI, 22 Oct, Concert	
Boston, 23 Oct, Concert	Handel & Haydn Society
Springfield, MA, 26 Oct, Concert	
New Haven, CT, 30 Oct, Concert	Brewster Hall
Hartford, CT, 31 Oct, Concert	Charity concert for the children in the Deaf and Dumb Asylum
1 Nov, Concert	Charity concert at the Retreat for the Insane

Country, City/Town & Location Date, Work	(Catherine Hayes participated in all performances listed)
1851 (*cont.*) New York City Tripler Hall, 3 Nov, Concert	
4 Nov, Concert	
5 Nov, Concert	Charity concert for Father T. Mathew
8 Nov, Concert	
Albany, NY, 17 Nov, Concert	
Albany, 24 Nov, Concert	
Utica, NY, 25? Nov, Concert	
Syracuse, NY, 27 Nov, Concert	
Providence, RI, 4 Dec, Concert	
Philadelphia, 6 Dec, Concert	Musical Fund Society. Concert cancelled due to Hayes's illness
9 Dec, Concert	Musical Fund Society
Baltimore, MD, 17 Dec, Concert	
19 Dec, Concert	
New York City Union Place Hotel, 23 Dec	Hayes and Party check in for holidays. Jenny Lind, L. Salvi, G. Belletti also check in on same date
Metropolitan Hall, 25 Dec, Concert (formerly Tripler Hall)	
29 Dec, Concert	
30 Dec	(Concert by Jenny Lind cancelled due to her mother's death)
31 Dec, Concert	

Country, City/Town & Location Date, Work	(Catherine Hayes participated in all performances listed)

1852
New York City
Metropolitan Hall, 8 Jan, Concert

Metropolitan Hall, 10 Jan, Concert | Charity concert for the children of Public Schools, City of New York (A. Braham stays in New York. Only Mengis and Lavenu continue on the tour)

Washington DC, 17 Jan, Concert | U.S. President Millard Fillmore and his family attend the concert

19 Jan, Concert

20 Jan, Concert

Richmond, 24 Jan, Concert

25 Jan, Concert

Wilmington, SC, 27 Jan, Concert

Charleston, SC, 28 Jan, Concert

29 Jan, Concert

Savannah, GA, 31 Jan, Concert

Augusta, GA, 2 Feb, Concert

Montgomery, AL, 4 Feb, Concert

Mobile, AL, 6 Feb, Concert

New Orleans, LA, Feb-Mar, Concerts | Hayes gives an extended series of concerts in New Orleans

Baton Rouge, LA, 6 Mar, Concert

Natchez, MS, 8 Mar, Concert

Jackson, MS, 9 Mar, Concerts | Hayes gives several concerts while on the Mississippi river boats

Country, City/Town & Location Date, Work	(Catherine Hayes participated in all performances listed)

1852 *(cont.)*
Memphis, TN, 12? Mar, Concert

Nashville, TN, 26 Mar, Concert

   27 Mar, Concert

Louisville, KY, 1 Apr, Concert

   3 Apr, Concert

Cincinnati, OH, 5 Apr, Concert

   7 Apr, Concert

   10 Apr, Concert

   12 Apr, Concert

Wheeling, WV, 15 Apr, Concert

   16 Apr, Concert

Pittsburgh, PA, 17 Apr, Concert

   19 Apr, Concert

Cleveland, OH, 21 Apr, Concert

   22 Apr, Concert

   24 Apr, Concert

   26 Apr, Concert

Buffalo, NY, 27 Apr, Concert

   8 May, Concert

Utica, NY, ? May, Concert

Canada:
Montreal, PQ, 21 May, Concert

Country, City/Town & Location Date, Work	(Catherine Hayes participated in all performances listed)
1852 (*cont.*) Toronto, OT, 24 May, Concert	
Kingston, OT, Jun, Concert	
America: Detroit, MI, 18 Jun, Concert	
19 Jun, Concert	
Chicago, IL, 21 Jun, Concert	
23 Jun, Concert	
Racine, WI, 25 Jun, Concert	
26 Jun, Concert	
Milwaukee, WI, 28 Jun, Concert	
29 Jun, Concert	
St. Louis, MO, Jul, Concerts	
Binghampton, NY, 12 Jul, Concert	
Boston, MA, 9 Oct	Hayes goes to Boston to purchase a wardrobe for travel to California
Bridgeport CT, 11 Oct	Hayes, her mother and sister stay in the home of P.T. Barnum for a week
15 Oct, Concert	Charity concert at Barnum's request: Mountain Grove Cemetery
Oct	Hayes attends the wedding of P.T. Barnum's daughter
New York, 20 Oct	Hayes and party depart for San Francisco via Panama
Panama, 2 Nov,	Arrival Panama

Country, City/Town & Location Date, Work	(Catherine Hayes participated in all performances listed)
1852 *(cont.)* San Francisco, CA, 20 Nov,	Arrival San Francisco
30 Nov, Concert	George Loder conducts first in a series of Hayes concerts in San Francisco
1853	
	During this period, J. Mengis shared the concert platform with Hayes; Lavenu accompanied them
San Francisco, Jan–Feb, Concerts	Hayes first appears in a series of costumed performances of operas
18 Jan, Concerts	Benefit concert for the orphans of San Francisco
Sacramento, CA, 8 Feb, Concerts	
Marysville, CA, 11–15 Feb, Concerts	
Sacramento, 16 Feb, Concerts	
18 Feb, Concert	
San Francisco, Feb-May, Concerts	Hayes gives an extended series of concerts into May
17 May	Hayes and party depart for Lima, Peru
(England), 28 May,	A horse called Catherine Hayes wins the 'Oaks' at Epsom Downs, England
Peru: Lima, 16 Jun	Hayes arrives for a brief stay before going on to Chile
Chile: Valparaiso Teatro Victoria, 7 Jul–Sep, Concerts	Extensive concerts include scenes from Lucia di Lammermoor

Country, City/Town & Location Date, Work	(Catherine Hayes participated in all performances listed)
1853 (*cont.*) Santiago Teatro de La Republica, 4 Aug-Sep, Concerts	Extensive concerts
Peru: Lima, 25 Oct, Lucia di Lammermoor	D. Lorini(t), J. Mengis(b), A. Dupuy(bs), C. Lietti(nv)
29 Oct, Norma	J. Mengis(b), F. Leonardo(bs)
4 Nov, Don Pasquale	D. Lorini(t), J. Mengis(b), F. Leonardo(bs), C. Lietti(nv)
14 Nov, Linda di Chamounix	D. Lorini(t), J. Mengis(b), F. Leonardo(bs), C. Lietti(nv)
22 Nov, La Sonnambula	D. Lorini(t), J. Mengis(b) C. Lietti(nv)
26 Nov, Maria di Rohan	D. Lorini(t), J. Mengis(b), C. Lietti(nv)
29 Nov, Concert	
2 Dec, Lucrezia Borgia	
6 Dec, La figlia del reggimento	D. Lorini(t), J. Mengis(b), C. Lietti(nv)
16 Dec, Norma	J. Mengis(b), F. Leonardo(bs)
30 Dec, Lucrezia Borgia	
1854 *Peru:* Lima, Jan, Operas/Concerts	
Feb, Ernani	D. Lorini(t), J. Mengis(b), F. Leonardo(bs), C. Lietti(nv)
Mar, Operas/Concerts	

Country, City/Town & Location Date, Work	(Catherine Hayes participated in all performances listed)
1854 *(cont.)* *America:* San Francisco, CA, 16 May, Concerts	
8 Jul	Hayes departs for Australia via Honolulu with E. Coulon(bs)
Hawaii: Honolulu, HA, 22 Jul,	Arrival at Honolulu
25 Jul, Concert	E. Coulon(bs)
Australia: Sydney, 14 Sep	Hayes and party arrive in Australia
Sep–Oct, Concerts	E. Coulon(bs), L. Lavenu(nv)
Melbourne, Oct–Nov, Concerts	E. Coulon(bs), L. Lavenu(nv)
Geelong, ? Nov, Concert	E. Coulon
Adelaide, 5 Dec, Concerts	L. Lavenu(nv)
1855 *India:* Calcutta, Town Hall, 10 Feb, Concert	L. Lavenu(nv/b), concert in aid of the Patriot Fund
Town Hall, 16 Feb, Concert	L. Lavenu(nv/b)
Singapore: Public Rooms, 19 Mar, Concert	L. Lavenu(nv)
Public Rooms, 26 Mar	Hayes and party depart for Java
Java: Batavia, 11 Apr, Concert	L. Lavenu(nv)
Théâtre Français, 20 Apr, Lucia di Lammermoor	Allard(t), St. Denis(bs)
Théâtre Français, 18 May, Concert	

Country, City/Town & Location Date, Work	(Catherine Hayes participated in all performances listed)
1855 (*cont.*) Théâtre Français, 21 May, La Sonnambula (Last Act) Théâtre Français, 21 May, Norma (Last Act)	Allard(t), St. Denis(bs), Bathilde(ms), L. Lavenu(nv) Duchaumont(t), Ferand(bs), Lagardere(ms), L. Lavenu(nv)
Théâtre Français, 25 May, Don Pasquale	
Australia: Melbourne, Jun	Hayes and party return to Australia
7 Jul, Concert	
9 Jul, Concert	Charity concert in aid of storm victims at Collingswood
Sydney, 16 Aug, Concert	
18 Aug, Concert	
27 Aug, La Sonnambula	
31 Aug	
Melbourne, 27 Sep, Concert	
25 ?Oct, La Sonnambula	Carandini(s) in tenor role, J. Gregg(bs), L. Lavenu(nv)
30 Oct, Concert	Benefit concert
2 Nov, Lucia di Lammermoor	Carandini(s) in tenor role, J. Gregg(b), L. Lavenu(nv)
9 Nov, Norma	S. Flower(ms/tenor role), Carandini(ms), J. Gregg(bs)
12 Nov	
14 Nov, The Bohemian Girl	Carandini(ms/tenor role), J. Gregg(bs)

Country, City/Town & Location Date, Work	(Catherine Hayes participated in all performances listed)
1855 *(cont.)*	
27 Nov, Concert	Benefit concert for L. Lavenu
28 Nov, Lucia di Lammermoor	
8 Dec, Lucrezia Borgia	
18 Dec, Concert	Benefit concert for Mme. Carandini
26 Dec, Concert	
1856 Bendigo, 11 Jan, Concert	
12 Jan, Concert	
14 Jan, Concert	
Tasmania Hobart Royal Victoria, 23 Jan, Concert	C. Lyall(t), J. Gregg(bs), Hodson(b)
Royal Victoria, 25 Jan, Concert	C. Lyall(t), J. Gregg(bs), Hodson(b)
Royal Victoria, 29 Jan, Concert	C. Lyall(t), J. Gregg(bs), Hodson(b)
Royal Victoria, 5 Feb, Concert	C. Lyall(t), J. Gregg(bs), Hodson(b)
Campbell Town, 11 Feb, Concert	
Launceston, 14 Feb, Concert	
28 Feb, Concert	
Melbourne, 26 Apr, Concert	Benefit concert for Melbourne Hospital
28 Apr, Concert	
30 Apr, Concert	

Country, City/Town & Location Date, Work	**(Catherine Hayes participated in all performances listed)**
1856 (*cont.*)	
3 May, Concert	
6 May, Concert	
13 May, Concert	
Sydney, 11 Jul, Concert	Hayes gives a concert on departure for England on the ship Royal Charter
England: Liverpool, 12 Aug	Hayes arrives back in England after a five-year absence
France: Paris, 21 Sep	Hayes visits Paris for a rest
England:	Hayes was the primary vocalist at these M. Jullien concerts
London, 5 Nov, Concert	
6 Nov, Concert	
7 Nov, Concert	
17 Nov, Concert	
18 Nov, Concert	
Brighton Pavilion, 20 Nov, Concert	C. Braham(t), L. Corelli(ct), G. Osborne(nv)
St. Leonard's, 21 Nov, Concert	C. Braham(t), L. Corelli(ct), G. Osborne(nv)
Brighton, 22 Nov, Concert	C. Braham(t), L. Corelli(ct), G. Osborne(nv)
Clifden, 24 Nov, Concert	C. Braham(t), L. Corelli(ct), G. Osborne(nv)

Country, City/Town & Location Date, Work	(Catherine Hayes participated in all performances listed)
1856 (*cont.*) Exeter, 25 Nov, Concert	C. Braham(t), L. Corelli(ct), G. Osborne(nv)
Plymouth, 26 Nov, Concert	C. Braham(t), L. Corelli(ct), G. Osborne(nv)
Oxford, 27 Nov, Concert	C. Braham(t), L. Corelli(ct), G. Osborne(nv)
Cheltenham, 28 Nov, Concert	C. Braham(t), L. Corelli(ct), G. Osborne(nv)
29 Nov, Concert	C. Braham(t), L. Corelli(ct), G. Osborne(nv)
Worcester Music Hall, 1 Dec, Concert	C. Braham(t), L. Corelli(ct), G. Osborne(nv)
Ireland: Belfast Music Hall, 10 Dec, Concert	L. Corelli(ms), C. Braham(t), F. Lablache(b), G. Osborne(nv)
Dublin Antient Concert Rooms 12 Dec, Concert	L. Corelli(ct), Weiss(b), C. Braham(t)
Limerick Athenaeum, Dec, Concert	L. Corelli(ct), C. Braham(t), F. Lablache(b), G. Osborne(nv)
Cork, Dec, Concert	L. Corelli(ct), C. Braham(t), F. Lablache(b), G. Osborne(nv)
Belfast Music Hall, 15 Dec, Concert	C. Braham(t), L. Corelli(ct), G. Osborne(nv), Piatti(nv)
Music Hall, 16 Dec, Concert	C. Braham(t), L. Corelli(ct), G. Osborne(nv), Piatti(nv)

Country, City/Town & Location Date, Work	(Catherine Hayes participated in all performances listed)
1857	
Dublin Philharmonic Society, 14 Jan, Concert	L. Corelli(ct), Millardi(t), F. Lablache(b)
Rotunda, 15 Jan, Concert	L. Corelli(ct), Millardi(t), F. Lablache(b), G. A. Osborne(nv)
17 Jan, Concert	
Belfast Music Hall, 20 Jan, Concert	Formes(bs), W. Tennant(t), Rainsford(ms)
26 Jan, Concert	L. Corelli(ct), Millardi(t), F. Lablache(b), G. Osborne(nv)
30 Jan, Concert	L. Corelli(ct), Millardi(t), F. Lablache(b), G. Osborne(nv)
England: Liverpool Philharmonic Society, 24 Feb, Concert	C. Braham(t), A. Irving(b), L. Corelli(ct), G. Osborne(nv)
Manchester Free Trade Hall, 25 Feb, Concert	C. Braham(t), L. Corelli(ct), G. Osborne(nv)
27 Feb, Concert	C. Braham(t), L. Corelli(ct), G. Osborne(nv)
28 Feb, Concert	C. Braham(t), L. Corelli(ct), G. Osborne(nv)
Bradford, 5 Mar, Concert	
Liverpool St. George's Hall, 13 Mar, Concert	L. Corelli(ct), C. Braham(t), G. Osborne(nv)

Country, City/Town & Location Date, Work	(Catherine Hayes participated in all performances listed)
1857 *(cont.)*	
Ireland:	
Dublin	
Theatre Royal, 16 Mar, Lucia di Lammermoor	Badiale(b), Volpini(t), Pierini(bs), Mariani(t), Anzchuz(nv)
19 Mar , Don Pasquale	W. Tennant(t), Badiale(b), Maggiorotti(bs)
21 Mar, Norma	J. Cruise(ms), Volpini(t), Mariani(t), Maggioratti(bs), Anchuez(nv)
23 Mar, Linda di Chamounix	W. Tennant(t), Corelli(ct), Badiali(b), Mariani(t), Pierini(bs)
25 Mar, Norma	Volpini(t), J. Cruise(ms), Mariani(t), Maggiorotti(bs)
28 Mar, Linda di Chamounix	W. Tennant(t), Corelli(ct), Badiale(b), Mariani(t), Pierini(bs)
30 Mar, Lucrezia Borgia	Volpini(t), Badiale(b), Corelli(ct), Maggiorotti(bs), Pierini(bs)
2 Apr, La Sonnambula	F. Cruise(ms), Volpini(t), Badiale(b)
4 Apr, Lucia di Lammermoor/ Don Pasquale (2 acts each opera)	Badiale(b), Volpini(t), Pierini(bs), Mariani(t)
6 Apr, The Messiah	W. Tennant(t), F. Cruise(s), J. Cruise(ms),
7 Apr, Stabat Mater (Rossini) The Creation (selections)	Volpini(t), Badiale(b), Pierini(bs), Corelli(ct), W. Tennant(t), F. Cruise(s), J. Cruise(ms),
Limerick	
Theatre Royal, 8 Apr, La Sonnambula	Volpini(t), Badiale(b)
Athenaeum, 29 Apr, The Messiah	L. Corelli(ct), C. Badiale(b), W. Tennant(t) R.M. Levey(nv)

Country, City/Town & Location Date, Work	(Catherine Hayes participated in all performances listed)
1857 *(cont.)* Cork Theatre Royal, 17 Apr, Il Trovatore	Volpini(t), Badiale(b), Corelli(ct), Pierini(bs)
Dublin, 21 Apr, Il Trovatore	Volpini(t), Badiale(b), Corelli(ct), Pierini(bs)
23 Apr, Il Trovatore	Volpini(t), Badiale(b), Corelli(ct), Pierini(bs)
24 Apr, All Verdi Concert	Volpini(t), Badiale(b), Mariani(t), Maggiorotti(bs), Corelli(ct)
25 Apr, Lucrezia Borgia	Volpini(t), Badiale(b), Corelli(ct), Maggiorotti(bs)
Wales: Bangor Ferry, 21 May	Resting and recovering from a sore throat!
England: London, 8 Oct St. George's	Hayes and W.A. Bushnell are married
France: Biarritz, 15 Nov	Hayes takes Bushnell to Biarritz for his health
Pau, Dec, Concert	Hayes gives concert for English residents
1858 Biarritz, 3 Jul	Bushnell dies from consumption and is buried in the English Cemetery at Bayonne, France
England: London, Jul–Dec	Hayes in mourning for the death of her husband

Country, City/Town & Location Date, Work	(Catherine Hayes participated in all performances listed)
1859 London St. James's Hall, 26 Jan, Concert	A. Mellon(nv)
St. James's Hall, 10 Feb, Concert	L. Pyne(s), Castellan(s), S. Reeves(t), G. Belletti(b), Weiss(b)
Drury Lane, 16 Feb, Concert	Vaneri(s), Faure(s), Dolby(ct), E. Poole(ms), H. Braham(t), Weiss(b),
Crystal Palace, 19 Feb, Concert	
Exeter Hall, 25 Feb, Solomon (Handel)	Dolby(ct), Weiss(b), M. Smith(t?)
St. James's Hall, 2 Mar, Concert	C. Santley(b), Lacelles(ms), J. Benedict(nv)
Manchester, 16 Mar, Concert	C. Halle(nv)
London St. James's Hall, 23 Mar, Concert	C. Santley(b), L. Vining(ct), G. Perrin(t?)
25 Mar, Season's (Haydn)	S. Reeves(t), Weiss(b)
30 Mar, Concert	A. Goddard(nv), A. Mellon(nv)
6 Apr, Concert	W. Tennant(t), A. Bishop(s), Dolby(ms)
Exeter Hall, 13 Apr, The Messiah	S. Reeves(t), G. Belletti(b), Dolby(ms), M. Costa(nv)
St. James's Hall, 6 May, The Messiah	S. Reeves(t), Dolby(ms), Lacelles(ct), W. Cooper(b)
9 May, Concert	
14 May, Concert	L. Vining(ct, G. Belletti(b), A. Irving(t?), C. Halle(nv)
4 Jul, Concert	R. Csillag(s), V. Balfe(s), L. Graziani(t), C. Badiale(b)

Country, City/Town & Location Date, Work	(Catherine Hayes participated in all performances listed)
1859	
Crystal Palace, 1 Oct, Concert	
8 Oct, Concert	Oliva(t), A. Manns(nv)
? Nov, Concert	
Manchester	
Free Trade Hall, 9 Nov, Concert	Piatti(nv), C. Halle(nv)
31 Dec, Concert	S. Reeves(t), C. Santley(b), L. Vining(ct)
1860	
London	
St. James's Hall, 9 Jan, Concert	S. Reeves(t), L. Vining(s), E. Poole(ms), M. Balfe(nv)
Manchester	
Free Trade Hall, 11 Jan, Iphigenia in Tauris (Gluck)	S. Reeves(t), C. Santley(b), C. Halle(nv)
8 Feb, Iphigenia in Tauris	S. Reeves(t), C. Santley(b), C. Halle(nv)
22 Feb, Concert	S. Reeves(t), G. Belletti(b), C. Halle(nv)
London	
St. James's Hall, 10 Feb, Concert	S. Reeves(t), A. Bishop(s), Caradori(s), Castellan(s), G. Belletti(b) Formes(bs),
Salder's Wells, 19 Mar, Concert	S. Reeves(t), G. Perren(s), E. Parpea(s), Piatti(nv), L. Baxter(ms)
St. Martin's Hall, 28 Mar, Concert	Lacelles(ms), Pauer(bs?), Chisholm(t?)
Covent Garden, 29 Mar, Concert (Benefit)	L. Pyne(s), W. Harrison(t)

Country, City/Town & Location Date, Work	(Catherine Hayes participated in all performances listed)

1860 *(cont.)*
Crystal Palace, 31 Mar,   C. Santley(b), W. Cooper(t?)
Cantata May Queen

Manchester
Free Trade Hall, 11 Apr, Iphigenia   S. Reeves(t), C. Santley(b),
in Tauris   C. Halle(nv)

    27 Apr, Concert (Private),   E. Garcia(s), G. Belletti(b)

Liverpool, 2 May?, Acis and Galatea   Huddart(ms), Perren(t), Weiss(b)
(Handel)

London
St. James's Hall, 15 May, Concert   L. Baxter(ms), S. Reeves(t),
    A. Irving(b), W. Weiss(bs)

St. Martin's Hall, 25 May, Concert   L. Vining(s), W. Cooper(t?),
    C. Santley(b)

Hanover Square, 29 May, Concert   E. Poole(ms), W. Cooper(t?),
    W. Weiss(b)

Grosvenor Square, 31 May, Concert   L. Baxter(ms), A. Irving(b),

St. James's Hall, 12 Jun, Concert   Dolby(ms), Olivia(t), C. Santley(b),
    W. Cooper(t), Piatti(nv)

    13 Jun, Concert   Rudersdorff(s), Piatti(nv)

Campden House, 14 Jun, Concert   E. Parepa(s), Dolby(ms),
    W. Cooper(t?), C. Santley(b)

    15 Jun, Concert   E. Parepa(s), S. Reeves(t),
    G. Belletti(b), L. Sloper(nv)

    16 Jun, Concert   E. Parepa(s), Dolby(ms),
    G. Belletti(b), C. Santley(b),

Her Majesty's , 18 Jun, Morning Concert   G. Ronconi(b), Mongini(t),
    E. Parepa(s), M. Alboin(ms)

    19 Jun, Morning Concert   Private concert at 19 Grosvenor
    Street

Country, City/Town & Location Date, Work	(Catherine Hayes participated in all performances listed)
1860 *(cont.)*	
Hanover Square, 19 Jun, Evening Concert	S. Reeves(t), W. Cooper(t), C. Santley(b)
St. James's Hall, 23 Jun, Concert	S. Reeves(t), E. Parepa(s), Dolby(ms), G. Belletti(b)
28 Jun, Concert	G. Belletti(b), Dolby(ms), L. Pyne(s), Faure(s)
29 Jun, Morning Concert	Dolby(ms), S. Reeves(t), W. Cooper(t), C. Santley(b)
29 Jun, Concert	C. Santley(b), C. Halle(nv)
30 Jun, Concert	E. Parepa(s), L. Vining(ms),
2 Jul, Concert	Olivia(t), Del Sadie(b)
6 Jul, Concert	M. Wieck(?)
Campden House, 12 Jul, Afternoon Concert	L. Baxter(ms), Oliva(t), Delle Sadie(b), E. Parepa(s)
St. James's Hall, 12 Jul, Concert	E. Parepa(s), Lacelles(ms), Olivia(t), Delle Sadie(b)
13 Jul, Concert	Lacelles(ms, Delle Sadie(b)
20 Jul, Concert	L. Vining(s), L. Baster(ms), W. Harrison(t), C. Santley(b)
25 Jul, Concert (Benefit)	S. Reeves(t), C. Santely(b), C. Halle(nv)
Surrey Gardens, 31 Jul, Concert	S. Reeves(t), Gassier(s), L. Vining(s), W. Weiss(b)
Exeter Hall, 11 Oct, Concert	
17 Oct, The Messiah	L. Baxter(ms), W. Cooper(t), W. Weiss(b)

Country, City/Town & Location Date, Work	(Catherine Hayes participated in all performances listed)
1860 *(cont.)*	
18 Oct, Concert	
20 Oct, Mozart's Twelfth Mass	L. Baxter(ms), W.Cooper(t), W. Weiss(b)
21 Oct, Elijah	L. Baxter(ms), W. Cooper(t), W. Weiss(b)
Brighton, 22 Oct, Concert	W. Cooper(t), W. Weiss(b), L. Baxter(ms)
Exeter Hall, 24 Oct, The Messiah	L. Baxter(ms), W. Cooper(t), W. Weiss(b)
25 Oct, Concert	W. Weiss(b), W. Cooper(t)
26 Oct, The Messiah	
27 Oct, Concert (Rossini Night)	W. Cooper(t), L. Baxter(ms), W Weiss(b),
Crystal Palace, 3 Nov, Concert	
8 Nov, Concert	Palmieri(t) (Hayes sings a La Traviata duet with Palmieri)
1861	
London, 9 Jan, Concert	S. Reeves(t), L. Baxter(ms), E. Poole(ms), L. Vining(s)
Covent Garden, 4 Feb, Concert	L. Pyne(s), W. Harrison(t), S. Reeves(t)
Ireland: Belfast, Mar, Concerts	
Enniskillen Town Hall, 5 Mar, Concert	Lacelles(ms), W. Tennant(t), Burdini(bs)

Country, City/Town & Location Date, Work	(Catherine Hayes participated in all performances listed)
1861 *(cont.)* *Scotland:* Edinburgh, 15 Mar, Concert	
England: London St. James's Hall, 11 Apr, Concert	
6 May, Concert	
Exeter Hall, 20 May, Concert	W. Tennant(t), L. Vining(ms), Ferrari(b), M. Alboni(ms)
St. James's Hall, 30 May, Concert	E. Parepa(s), C. Santley(b), S. Reeves(t), Lascelles(ms)
5 Jun, Morning Concert	Gassier(s?), S. Reeves(t), E. Parepa(s), G. Perren(t)
18 Jun, Concert	
20 Jun, Concert	E. Parepa(s), G. Belletti(b), W. Tennant(t), Gassier(s?)
21 Jun, Concert	E. Parepa(s), Dolby(ms), I. Gardoni(t), S. Reeves(t), G. Belletti(b)
22 Jun, Concert	E. Parepa(s), S. Reeves(t), C. Santley(b), I. Gardoni(t)
25 Jun, Concert	W. Tennant(t), Dolby(ms), Delle Sedie(b), Formes(bs)
27 Jun, Concert	Caradori(s), Dolby(ms), W. Tennant(t)
28 Jun, Concert	
Hanover Square, 1 Jul, Concert	G. Garcia(b), I. Gardoni(t) (Hayes was advertised for this concert, but it is doubtful that she sang)

Country, City/Town & Location Date, Work	(Catherine Hayes participated in all performances listed)
1861 *(cont.)* Sydenham, Kent, 5 Aug	Hayes ill at H. Lee's home in London suburb of Sydenham
9 Aug	Hayes suffers a stroke
11 August 1861	Hayes, aged 42, dies in the home of Henry Lee, at Sydenham
Kensal Green, 16 Aug	Hayes buried at Kensal Green Cemetery
1871	Mary Hayes buried with Catherine at Kensal Green

Selected Female Vocal Contemporaries

Performer (Birthplace/Year)	1800	1810	1820	1830	1840	1850	1860	1870	1880	1890	1900
Alboni, Marietta (Italy)			1822————————————————————————							1894	
Biscaccianti, Eliza (America)			1824————————————————————————								1896
Bishop, Anna (England)		1810————————————————————————							1884		
Bosio, Angelina (Italy)				1830————————1859							
Dorus-Gras, Julie (France)	1805————————————————————————										1896
Frezzolini, Erminia (Italy)		1818————————————————————————							1884		
Garcia-Viardot, Pauline (France)		1821————————————————————————									1910
Grisi, Giulia (Italy)		1811————————————————————————					1869				
Hayes, Catherine (Ireland)		**1818————————————————————**					**1861**				
Lind, Jenny (Sweden)			1820————————————————————————						1887		
Novello, Clara (England)		1818————————————————————————									1908
Parodi, Teresa (Italy)			1827————————————————————————							1892?	
Parepa, Euphrosyne (Scotland)				1836————————————————				1874			
Patti, Adelina* (Spain)					1843———————————————————						1919
Piccolomini, Marietta (Italy)				1834————————————————————————						1899	
Sontag, Henrietta (Germany)	1808————————————————					1854					
Strepponi, Giuseppina (Italy)		1815————————————————————————								1897	
Tacchinardi-Persiani, Fanny (Italy	1812————————————————————————						1867				
Tadolini, Eugenia (Italy)	1809————————————————————————							1872			
Tietjens, Therese (Germany)				1831————————————————————				1877			

*Note: Adelina Patti sang in concerts in America from the age of eight.

Repertoire and Roles

Composer	Opera/Other	Hayes's First Performance	Place	Role
Balfe	The Bohemian Girl	November 1855	Sydney	Arlene
Bellini	I Puritani	May 1845	Marseilles	Elvira
	Norma	November 1849	Dublin	Norma
	La Sonnambula	February 1850	Dublin	Amina
Bennett W. S.	May Queen/ Cantata	March 1860	London	
Capecelatro	Mortedo	November 1847	Milan	Elmira
Donizetti	Linda di Chamounix	November 1845	Milan	Linda
	Lucia di Lammermoor	May 1845	Marseilles	Lucia
	Don Pasquale	November 1853	Lima	Norina
	L'elisir d'Amore	February 1853	San Francisco	Adina
	Lucrezia Borgia	October 1850	Dublin	Lucrezia
	Maria di Rohan	August 1847	Bergamo	Maria
	Anna Bolena	January 1846	Milan	Smeton
	Olivo e Pasquale	June 1847	Vienna	Isabella
	La figlia del reggimento	December 1853	Lima	Maria
Gluck,	Iphigenia in Tauride	January 1860,	Manchester	Iphigenia
Halevy	La Tempesta	June 1850[1] (P)	London	Spirit of the Air[2]
Handel	Acis and Galatea	May 1860	Liverpool	
	The Messiah	May 1850	London	
	Israel in Egypt	May 1850		
	Samson	May 1850		
Haydn	The Creation	May 1850	London	
	The Seasons	March 1859	London	

Composer	Opera/Other	Hayes's First Performance	Place	Role
Malespino	Albergo da Rommano	December 1846[3] (P)	Venice	
Mendelssohn	St. Paul	May 1850	London	
	Elijah	May 1851	London	
Mozart	Nozze di Figaro	April 1850	London	Cherubino
	Twelfth Mass	October 1860	London	
Mercadante	Il Giuramento	June 1846	Vienna	Elaisa
	Il Bravo	March 1846	Milan	Violetta
Meyerbeer	Le Prophète	July 1849[4] (P)	London	Berta
	Robert il Diabolo	May 1849[5]	London	Alice
Ricci (F.)	Estella	February 1846[6]	London	Estella
	Griselda	March 1847[7]	Venice	Griselda
Rossini	Mose	June 1845	Marseilles	Anaide
	Otello	November 1845	Milan	Desdemona
	Il barbiere di Siviglia	February 1854	Lima	Rosina
	Ricciardo e Zoraide	October 1846	Milan	Zoraide
	Stabat Mater	April 1857	Dublin	
Sanelli	Gennaro Annese	March 1848[8]	Florence	Adele
Verdi,	I Masnadieri	December 1847[9]	Verona	Amalia
	Il Trovatore	April 1847[10]	Cork	Leonora
	Ernani	February 1854	Lima	Elvira
	La Traviata[11]	April 1857	Dublin	Violetta
	Rigoletto[12]	April 1857	Dublin	Gilda

1 Hayes was sick and did not perform at this premiere
2 Hayes did not sing due to indisposition
3 Opera premiere
4 London premiere
5 Hayes became ill the afternoon of first performance and did not sing
6 Opera première
7 Opera première
8 Opera première
9 Italian opera première
10 Cork city première
11 Hayes only sang excerpts not the complete opera
12 Hayes only sang excerpts, not the complete opera

Selected Bibliography

BOOKS, PERIODICALS, JOURNALS,
NEWSPAPERS & LETTERS)

Author/Editor, Book/Article/Periodicals, Published

Ahlquist, Karen, Democracy at the Opera – New York, 1815–60, Illinois, 1997
Allsobrook, David I., Liszt: My Travelling Circus Life, Illinois, 1971
Arditi, Luigi, My Reminiscences, London, 1895

Babcock, F. Lawrence, Spanning the Atlantic, New York, 1931
Baptie, David, A Handbook of Musical Biography, London, 1883
Barbier, Patrick, Opera in Paris – 1800–1850, Oregon, 1995
Barnum, P. T., Struggles and Triumphs or Forty Years of Recollections, New York, 1873
Barrett, William A, Balfe, His Life & Works, London, 1882
Barrow, Keith, Helen Hayes, First Lady of the American Theatre, New York, 1985
Becker, Heinz , Giacomo Meyerbeer: A Life & Letters, Oregon, 1989
Bennett, Douglas, Encyclopedia of Dublin, Dublin, 1994
Bennett, Douglas, A Dublin Anthology, Dublin, 1994
Biddlecombe, George, English Opera from 1834–1864 with particular reference to the works of Michael Balfe, New York, 1994
Brisbane, Katherine, Entertaining Australia, Sydney, 1991
Brown, P. L. (ed.), Clyde Company Papers 1854–58 Vol. 6, London, 1968
Brownstein, Rachel M., Tragic Muse – Rachel of the Comédie Française, New York, 1993
Budden, Julian, The Operas of Verdi – Vol. 1 Oberto to Rigoletto, London 1973
Bulman, Joan, Jenny Lind, London, 1956
Bushnell, Howard, Maria Malibran, Pennsylvania 1979

Cargher, John, Two Hundred Years of Opera in Australia, Melbourne, 1988
Cavanah, Frances, Jenny Lind's America, New York, 1969
Chambers, Anne, La Sheridan, Adorable Diva, Dublin, 1989
Cheke, Dudley, Josephine and Emilie, Oxford, 1993
Christiansen, Rupert, Prima Donna, A History, England 1986
Chorley, Henry F., Thirty Years' Musical Recollection, New York 1972

Clayton, Elizabeth C., Queens of Song (2 Vols.), London, 1863
Conati, Marcello, Encounters with Verdi, New York, 1984
Cone, John F., Adelina Patti Queen of Hearts, Oregon, 1993
Connolly, S. J., The Oxford Companion to Irish History, New York, 1998
Coulter, Joseph, Randwick Asylum – A Historical Review 1852–1915, Sydney, 1916
Cox, Rev. E, Musical Recollections of the Last Half Century (2 Vols.), London, 1872
Cramer & Co, Memoirs of Catherine Hayes, London, 1850

Dana, Julian, The Man Who Built San Francisco, New York, 1936
Davidson, James (ed.), The Musical World – 1845–1863, London
Davis, Richard, Anna Bishop, The Adventures of an Intrepid Prima Donna, Sydney, 1997
De Merlin, Countess, Memoirs of Madame Malibran, London, 1844
Dictionary of Biography, Dictionary of National Biography, London, 1968
Di Scala, Spencer M., Italy, from the Revolution to the Republic, Colorado, 1995
Dizikes, John, Opera in America, New Haven, 1993
Dowling, Partick J., California, The Irish Dream, San Francisco 1989
Dublin University, Dublin University Magazine (Nov.), Dublin, 1850

Ehrlich, Cyril, First Philharmonic, New York, 1995
Ellis, Katherine, Music Criticism in Nineteenth-century France, England, 1995
Elliot, J. H., Berlioz, London, 1946

Fenner, Thomas, Leigh Hunt and Opera Criticism, Kansas, 1972
Fenner, Thomas, Opera in London – Views of the Press 1785–1830, Illinois, 1994
Ferguson, Niall, The House of Rothschild, New York 1998
Fitzlyon, April, Maria Malibran, Diva of the Romantic Age, London, 1987
Flood, W. H. Gratten, Introductory Sketches of Irish Musicality, London, 1907
Forbes, Elizabeth, Mario and Grisi a Biography, London, 1985
Ford, Boris, Cambridge Cultural History – The Romantic Age in Britain, England 1992

Garibaldi, Luigi A., Giuseppe Verdi, nelle Lettere di Emanuele Muzio, ad Antonio Barezzi, Milano, 1931
Ganz, A. W., Berlioz in London, London, 1950
Garcia, Manuel P., A Complete Treatise on the Art of Singing (2 Vols.) – Reprint, New York, 1984
Gatti, Carlo, Verdi, The Man and His Music, New York, 1955
Girdham, Jane, English Opera In Late 18th Century London, New York, 1997
Grieve, Averil Mackenzie, Clara Novello – 1818–1908, London, 1955
Gyger, Alison, Opera for the Antipodes, Sydney, 1990

Halle, Charles, Autobiography (Reprint), New York, 1973
Hayes, Helen, On Reflection, New York, 1968

Heintze, James R., American Musical Life in Context and Practice To 1865, New York, 1994

Hernandez, Roberto C., Los primeros Teatros de Valparaiso, Valparaiso 1928

Hill, W. Henry, Antonio Stradivari his Life & Work (Reprint), New York, 1963

Holland, Henry S. & Rockstro, W. S., Memoir of Madame Jenny Lind-Goldschmidt, London, 1891

Hyde, Derek, New Found Voices – women in nineteenth-century English music, England 1998

Jackson, Kenneth T. (ed.), The Encyclopedia of New York City, New Haven, 1995

Jacobs, Arthur, Arthur Sullivan – A Victorian Musician, Oregon, 1992

Jordan, David P., Transforming Paris, Chicago, 1995

Kaufman, Thomas G., Verdi and His Major Contemporaries, New York, 1990

Kemmy, Jim, The Limerick Anthology, Dublin, 1996

Kennedy, Michael (ed.), The Oxford Dictionary of Music, Oxford 1998

Kenny, Charles L., A Memoir of Michael William Balfe (Reprint), New York, 1978

Kirsten, Dorothy, A Time to Sing, , New York, 1982

Kissanne, Noel, The Irish Famine, A Documentary History, Dublin, 1995

Kutsch, K. J. & Riemens, L, Grosse Sangerlexikon (3 Vols.), Bern, 1987

Lawrence, Vera Brodsky-, Strong on Music Vol. I, New York, 1988

Lawrence, Vera Brodsky-, Strong on Music Vol. II, Chicago, 1995

Ledbetter, Gordon T., The Great Irish Tenor – John McCormack, London, 1977

Lee, Edward, Musical London, London, 1995

Levey, R. M. & O'Rorke, J., Annals of the Theatre Royal Dublin, Dublin, 1880

Loesser, Arthur, Men, Women and Pianos – a Social History, New York, 1990

Love, Harold, The Golden Age of Australian Opera, Sydney, 1981

Lucchetti (ed.), It Teatro Donizetti – Cronologia degli spettacoli 1786–1989, Bergamo, 1989

Lumley, Benjamin, Reminiscences of the Opera, London, 1864

MacLoughlin, Adrian, Guide To Historic Dublin, Dublin, 1979

Makinlay, M. Sterling, Garcia the Centenarian and His Times, New York, 1908

Major, Norma, Joan Sutherland – Biography, New York, 1987

Mapleson, J. H., The Mapleson Memoirs 1848–1888 (2 Vols.), London,1888

Marchesi, Mathilde, Marchesi and Music, New York, 1898

Maretzek, Max, Crochets and Quavers, New York, 1855

Martin, George, Verdi His Music, Life and Times, London, 1965

Martin, George, Verdi at the Golden Gate, Berkeley, 1993

Maude, Mrs. Raymond, The Life of Jenny Lind, New York, 1977

McCall, Edith, Biography of a River – the Living Mississippi, New York, 1990

Miller, Kerby A., Emigrants and Exiles, New York, 1988

Moffat, James, Florence Austral, Sydney, 1995

Murphy, Kerry, Hector Berlioz and the Development of French Music, Michigan, 1988

Musgrave, Michael, The Musical Life at The Crystal Palace, England, 1995

Newman, Ernst, Memoirs of Hector Berlioz 1803–1865, New York, 1960
Niehaus, Earl F., The Irish in New Orleans, Baton Rouge 1965

O'Garda, Cormac, The Great Irish Famine, England, 1995
Osborne, Charles, Letters of Giuseppe Verdi, New York, 1972.
Osborne, George A, Musical Coincidences and Reminiscences (Paper), London, 1883

Pearce, Charles E., Sims Reeves – Fifty Years of Music in England, London, 1924
Pearce, Mrs. Godfrey, The Romance of a Great Singer – A Memoir of Mario, London, 1910
Phelan, Robert, William Vincent Wallace, A Vagabond Composer, Waterford, 1994
Phillips-Matz, Mary Jane, Verdi, a biography, New York, 1993
Pistone, Daniele, Nineteenth-century Italian Opera, Oregon, 1995
Pleasants, Henry, The Great Singers, London, 1977
Pleasants, Henry (ed.), The Great Tenor Tragedy by Nourrit, Oregon, 1995
Ponsonby, Edward (pub.), The History of the Theatre Royal Dublin, Dublin, 1870
Preston, Katherine K, Opera on the Road – Traveling Troupes in the US. 1825–60, Chicago, 1993

Reid, Charles, The Music Monster – A Biography of James Davison, London, 1984
Reeves, Sims, My Jubilee; or Fifty Years of Singing, London, 1889
Reynolds, Dirny, A Neighbour's Child – Signor Foli 1835–1899, Dublin, 1994
Robertson, Priscella, Revolutions of 1848, Princeton, 1971
Roselli, John, Singers of Italian Opera, New York, 1992
Roselli, John, Music & Musicians in Nineteenth-century Italy, Oregon, 1991
Rosentahl, Harold, Two Centuries of opera at Covent Garden, London, 1958
Rosenthal, Harold & Warrack, John (eds.), The Concise Dictionary of Opera, London, 1979

Sadie, Stanley (ed.), The New Grove Dictionary of Opera (4 Vols.), New York, 1992
Salas, Eugenio P., Historia Del La Musica En Chile – 1850–1900, Santiago, 1957
Santley, Charles, Student and Singer, New York, 1892
Sander, Peter Southwell-, Verdi his life and times, London, 1978
Saxon, A. H., P. T. Barnum, The Legend and the Man, New York, 1989
Schonburg, Harold, The Glorous Ones, New York, 1985
Sevadio, Gaia, The Real Traviata, the Life of Giuseppina Strepponi, London, 1994
Seymour, Bruce, Lola Montez, A Life, New Haven, 1995
Stendahl, Life of Rossini (Reprint), London, 1985
Smith, Gus, Irish Stars of the Opera, Dublin, 1994

Sonneck Society, American Music – Vol 10, Number 2, Illinois 1992
Steane, J. B., The Grand Tradition, New York, 1974
Sutherland, Joan, The Autobiography of Joan Sutherland, Washington, 1997

Thackeray, William M., The Irish Sketch-Book, London, 1860
Tintori, Giampiero, Duecento anni di Teatro alla Scala – Cronologia – 1778–1977, Bergamo, 1979
Toye, Francis, Rossini, London, 1954

Ulrich, Homer, Famous Women Singers, New York, 1982

Walker, Alan, Franz Liszt – The Virtuoso Years 1811–1847, New York, 1988
Walker, Frank, The Man Verdi, Chicago, 1982
Wallace, Phillip Hope-, A Picture History of Opera, London, 1959
Walsh, T. J., Opera in Dublin 1705–1797, Dublin, 1973
Walsh, T.J., Opera in Dublin 1798–1820, New York, 1993
Warrack, John & West, Ewan (eds.), The Oxford Dictionary of Opera, New York, 1992
Weaver, William, The Golden Century of Italian Opera, New York, 1980
Weaver, William & Chusid, Martin, The Verdi Companion, New York, 1979
Weinstock, Herbert, Donizetti and the World of Opera, New York, 1963
Weinstock, Herbert, Rossini, A Biography, New York, 1968
Weinstock, Herbert, Vincenzo Bellini, His Life and His Operas, New York, 1971
Wheatcroft, Andrew, The Habsburgs, London, 1995
Williams, William H. A., 'Twas Only an Irishman's Dream, Illinois, 1996
Wyndham, H. S., The Annals of Covent Garden – 1732–1897, London, 1906

Periodicals/Journals/Newspapers & Letters of the Period

Albion, New York,
Argus, Melbourne
Athenaeum, London
Baltimore Sun
Bazar di Novito, Venice
Belfast News-Letter, Ireland
Bengal Harkrau & India Gazette, Calcutta
Boston Daily Journal
Brooklyn Eagle, New York
Cincinnati Gazette
Cleveland Plain Dealer
Cork Examiner
Daily Alta California, San Francisco
Daily News, London
Daily Picayune, New Orleans
Dublin Historical Record (1994)
Dublin University Magazine
Dwight's Journal of Music, Boston
Edinburgh Advertiser
El Mensajero, Santiago, Chile
Evening Packet, Dublin
Examiner, London
Figaro, Venice
Frank Leslie's Illustrated, New York
Freeman's Journal, Dublin
Galigano's Messenger, Rome
Galway Vindicator
Gazetta Musicale di Milano
Gazetta di Firenze
Giornale Della Provincia di Bologna
Harmonicon, London
Hobart Town Courier, Tasmania
Irish Times, Dublin

I Populano, Firenze
Illustrated London News
Illustrated Sydney News
Impartial Reporter, Fermanagh, Ireland
Java Bode, Batavia
Journals of Queen Victoria, Windsor
Kentish Mercury, Sydenham
Kilkenny Moderator, Ireland
Kilkenny Journal, Ireland
La Fama, Milano
Lanari, A., Correspondence/Biblioteca
    Nationale, Firenze
Limerick Chronicle
Limerick Leader
Limerick Standard
Memoirs of Catherine Hayes 'The Swan
    of Erin,' London
Morning Post, London
Milan Conservatory Correspondence (1996)

Musical World, London
Musical Gazette, London
New York Daily Times
Old Limerick Journal
Opera Quarterly
Polynesian, Honolulu
Providence Journal, Rhode Island
Province of Munster, Ireland
Sacramento Union
Saroni's Musical Times, New York
Saunder's Newsletter, Dublin
Singapore Free Press
Spirit of the Times, New York
Teatre Arti e Letteratura, Bologna
The Republican, Binghampton NY
Times, London
Tipperary Free Press
Verona Gazette
Wexford Independent

Index